Extending Microsoft Dynamics 365 Finance and Supply Chain Management Cookbook
Second Edition

Create and extend secure and scalable ERP solutions to improve business processes

Simon Buxton

BIRMINGHAM - MUMBAI

Extending Microsoft Dynamics 365 Finance and Supply Chain Management Cookbook
Second Edition

Commissioning Editor: Kunal Chaudhari
Acquisition Editor: Ashitosh Gupta
Content Development Editor: Divya Vijayan
Senior Editor: Mohammed Yusuf Imaratwale
Technical Editor: Shubham Sharma
Copy Editor: Safis Editing
Project Coordinator: Kinjal Bari
Proofreader: Safis Editing
Indexer: Pratik Shirodkar
Production Designer: Nilesh Mohite

First published: May 2017
Second edition: March 2020

Production reference: 1270320

Published by Packt Publishing Ltd.
Livery Place
35 Livery Street
Birmingham
B3 2PB, UK.

ISBN 978-1-83864-381-2

www.packt.com

I would like to thank my colleagues at Binary for their continued support throughout the writing process. I would also like to thank all those who helped review this book, Glyn Wilson in particular, who put in a lot of effort into reviewing each recipe. A lot of the insight included in this book was only possible by being part of the Dynamics 365 Finance and Supply Chain Management community technical preview program and by working with Microsoft's R&D team, which is a true privilege.

Finally, I am told that I have to thank my partner, Evi, for her patience and support as I disappeared for hours each night and weekend working on "yet another book?". Of course, no bio could be complete without mentioning my children, Tyler and Isabella, who continue to be not that impressed.

- Simon Buxton

Packt.com

Subscribe to our online digital library for full access to over 7,000 books and videos, as well as industry leading tools to help you plan your personal development and advance your career. For more information, please visit our website.

Why subscribe?

- Spend less time learning and more time coding with practical eBooks and Videos from over 4,000 industry professionals

- Improve your learning with Skill Plans built especially for you

- Get a free eBook or video every month

- Fully searchable for easy access to vital information

- Copy and paste, print, and bookmark content

Did you know that Packt offers eBook versions of every book published, with PDF and ePub files available? You can upgrade to the eBook version at www.packt.com and as a print book customer, you are entitled to a discount on the eBook copy. Get in touch with us at customercare@packtpub.com for more details.

At www.packt.com, you can also read a collection of free technical articles, sign up for a range of free newsletters, and receive exclusive discounts and offers on Packt books and eBooks.

Contributors

About the author

Simon Buxton has worked with Dynamics 365 Finance and Supply Chain Management since its earliest incarnations, starting with the product in early 1999 when Dynamics 365 Finance and Supply Chain Management was known as Damgaard Axapta 1.5.

Simon has been the technical lead on many highly challenging technical projects in countries all around the world. These projects included complex integrations with on-premises and external systems, ISV solutions, and many technically challenging customer solutions.

Now working with Binary, he was part of a team that implemented the first Dynamics 365 Finance and Supply Chain Management implementation as part of the **Community Technical Preview** (**CTP**) program, which led to the close working relationship with Microsoft that made this book possible.

About the reviewers

Glyn Wilson is a computer science graduate based in the UK with 27 years of development experience and 12 years of experience with Dynamics 365 Finance and Supply Chain Management and its previous iterations in AX. He has worked in AX development for a customer in the printing industry, Pamarco, that has multiple entities in the USA and the UK. Starting with AX 4 in 2008, he has gone through the upgrade process to AX 2009 and then onto their current platform, AX 2012.

In embarking on an upgrade project to Dynamics 365 Finance and Supply Chain Management, Glyn has worked with the author of this book on various projects. Reviewing this book provided Glyn with a great introduction to the techniques needed for developing in Dynamics 365 Finance and Supply Chain Management. He hopes that readers will get as much benefit from this book as he did.

Deepak Agarwal is a **Microsoft Certified Solution Expert** (**MCSE**) and has been working professionally on Dynamics AX since 2011. He has had a wide range of development, consulting, and leading roles, while always maintaining a significant role as a business application developer.

He has been recognized as a Microsoft **Most Valuable Professional** (**MVP**) for business solutions six times in a row; he has held this title since 2013.

Packt is searching for authors like you

If you're interested in becoming an author for Packt, please visit `authors.packtpub.com` and apply today. We have worked with thousands of developers and tech professionals, just like you, to help them share their insight with the global tech community. You can make a general application, apply for a specific hot topic that we are recruiting an author for, or submit your own idea.

Table of Contents

Preface

Microsoft Dynamics 365 Finance and Supply Chain Management form an ERP solution for complex single-site, multi-site, and multi-language global enterprises. This flexible and agile solution provides advanced functionality for manufacturing, retail, public sector, and service sector industries. Not only does this solution provide a strong set of built-in functionality, but it also provides an industry-leading integrated development environment, allowing an organization to provide even higher levels of fit. This book should be in the tool belt of any software engineer who works with or is about to embark on a career with Microsoft Dynamics 365 Finance and Supply Chain Management.

This book provides software engineers and those involved in developing solutions within Dynamics 365 Finance and Supply Chain Management with a toolkit of practical recipes for common development tasks, with important background information to provide deep insight to allow the recipes to be adapted and extended for your own use. Even for experienced software engineers, this book will provide a good source of reference for efficient software development.

For those moving from Microsoft Dynamics AX 2012, we cover critical changes in how software is adapted, how to use the new extensibility features of Microsoft Dynamics 365 Finance and Supply Chain Management, and tips on how to use them practically. We also cover the fundamental changes in the physical structure of the application metadata, the application development life cycle, and how everything fits in with the new cloud-first development paradigm with Lifecycle Services and Visual Studio Team Services. The integration will be a concern for AX developers, and we cover this in detail with working examples of code that can be adapted to your own needs.

The book follows the development of a solution as a means to explain the design and development of tables, classes, forms, BI, menu structures, workflow, and security. We begin at the start of the development process by setting up an Azure DevOps project, integrating Lifecycle Services, and explaining new concepts such as Packages, Models, Projects, and what happened to layers. The book progresses with chapters focused on creating the solution in a practical order, but it is written in such a way that each recipe can be used in isolation as a pattern to follow.

The sample solution was designed and developed as the book was written and is available for download. There are sample projects covering the development of new features, extending standard functionality, writing test cases, and integration with external services and from C# projects back into Finance and Supply Chain Management.

With this comprehensive collection of recipes, you will be armed with the knowledge and insight that you will need to develop well-designed solutions will help your organization to get the most value from this comprehensive solution for both the current and the upcoming releases of Microsoft Dynamics 365 Finance and Supply Chain Management.

What this book covers

Chapter 1, *Starting a New Project*, covers setting up a new Azure DevOps project, integrating with Lifecycle Services, and creating a Microsoft Dynamics 365 Finance and Supply Chain Management package and model.

Chapter 2, *Data Structures*, contains common recipes for creating data structure elements such as tables, enumerated data types, and extended data types. The recipes are written to patterns, guiding you through the steps you would take when creating the types of table used in Microsoft Dynamics 365 Finance and Supply Chain Management application development.

Chapter 3, *Creating the User Interface*, explains how to create user interface elements such as menus, forms, form parts, tiles, and workspaces. This chapter includes recipes for each of the main types of user interfaces used when creating or extending Dynamics 365 Finance and Supply Chain Management user interfaces with practical guidance and tips on how to do this efficiently.

Chapter 4, *Working with Form Logic and Frameworks*, helps us step into writing the business logic to handle table and form events. It then explains how to create and hook up a number sequence to a form and how to use it in a record to create dialog. It finishes with a recipe on how to update form controls at runtime.

Chapter 5, *Application Extensibility*, looks at extensibility, which can be said to be one of the biggest changes in Dynamics 365 Finance and Supply Chain Management. This chapter pays special attention to the key aspects of how to use extend the standard application while avoiding regression as Microsoft release updates to the base application.

Chapter 6, *Writing for Extensibility*, moves from using extensibility features to writing extensible code. This is done through practical examples of the use of delegates, interfaces, extension attributes, facades, and how to avoid hardcoding business rules by the use of metadata. This also covers the most important features of the SysOperation framework.

Chapter 7, *Advanced Data Handling*, covers more advanced data model features such as table inheritance, date-time effectiveness, and views with computed columns.

Chapter 8, *Business Events*, shows you how to write, implement, and process business events, an exciting new feature in Microsoft Dynamics 365 Finance and Supply Chain Management. The recipes in this chapter follow a real-world example from initial event development, Azure Service Bus setup, and configuration in Microsoft Dynamics 365 Finance and Supply Chain Management in a way to augment the standard documentation.

Chapter 9, *Security*, explains the security model design in Microsoft Dynamics 365 for Operations and provides recipes for the creation of the elements used in security. The recipes augment the standard documentation to provide real-world examples of how to create and model Microsoft Dynamics 365 Finance and Supply Chain Management security.

Chapter 10, *Data Management, OData, and Office*, focuses on data integrations that an organization can use to leverage their data stored in Microsoft Dynamics 365 Finance and Supply Chain Management. This covers writing Edit in Excel experiences, using the data import/export framework with extended data entities, and reading and writing data in Microsoft Dynamics 365 Finance and Supply Chain Management through OData.

Chapter 11, *Consuming and Exposing Services*, provides recipes for creating services from within Dynamics 365 Finance and Supply Chain Management, consuming external services, and also on consuming Dynamics 365 Finance and Supply Chain Management services in C# using SOAP and JSON. All this is covered using practical examples that should easily translate into your specific requirements.

Chapter 12, *Unit Testing*, provides recipes to show you how to create unit tests and how they are used with the application life cycle. This chapter covers an insight into test-driven development, automated unit testing on the build server, and how to write and use the new acceptance test library (atl).

Chapter 13, *Automated Build Management*, helps us move more into application life cycle management, providing recipes for setting up and using a build server.

Chapter 14, *Workflow*, covers the development of workflow approvals and tasks in Dynamics 365 Finance and Supply Chain Management. The recipes are given context by continuing to work with the sample application that is worked on through the course of this book, effectively explaining state management, which is easily misunderstood.

Chapter 15, *State Machines*, covers state machines, which is another new feature in Dynamics 365 Finance and Supply Chain Management. This chapter covers all key areas of this feature, explaining when and how to use this feature appropriately.

Who this book is for

If you are a software developer new to Dynamics 365 Finance and Supply Chain Management programming or an experienced software engineer migrating from its predecessor, Dynamics AX, this book is an ideal tutorial to help you avoid the common pitfalls and make the most of this advanced technology. This book is also useful if you are a solution architect or technical consultant, as it provides a deeper insight into the technology behind the solution.

In order to gain access to Microsoft Dynamics 365 for Operations, you need to be either a Microsoft partner or a Microsoft customer. To sign up for access as a partner, you can refer to *Lifecycle Services (LCS) for Finance and Operations apps partners* at `https://docs.microsoft.com/en-us/dynamics365/operations/dev-itpro/lifecycle-services/getting-started-lcs`.

To sign up for a subscription as a customer, refer to *Lifecycle Services (LCS) for Finance and Operations apps customers* at `https://docs.microsoft.com/en-us/dynamics365/fin-ops-core/dev-itpro/lifecycle-services/lcs-works-lcs`.

You will need to download or deploy a Dynamics 365 Finance and Supply Chain Management development **virtual machine** (**VM**) in Azure. To run the VM locally, you will need at least 100 GB free space available and a minimum of 12 GB free memory, ideally 24 GB. It can run on as little as 8 GB of assigned memory, but the performance would suffer as a result.

The official system requirements are as follows:

- System requirements (`https://docs.microsoft.com/en-us/dynamics365/operations/dev-itpro/get-started/system-requirements`)
- Development system requirements (`https://docs.microsoft.com/en-us/dynamics365/operations/dev-itpro/dev-tools/development-system-requirements`)

If you are using the digital version of this book, we advise you to type the code yourself or access the code via the GitHub repository (link available in the next section). Doing so will help you avoid any potential errors related to the copying and pasting of code.

Download the example code files

You can download the example code files for this book from your account at `www.packt.com`. If you purchased this book elsewhere, you can visit `www.packtpub.com/support` and register to have the files emailed directly to you.

You can download the code files by following these steps:

1. Log in or register at www.packt.com.
2. Select the **Support** tab.
3. Click on **Code Downloads**.
4. Enter the name of the book in the **Search** box and follow the onscreen instructions.

Once the file is downloaded, please make sure that you unzip or extract the folder using the latest version of:

- WinRAR/7-Zip for Windows
- Zipeg/iZip/UnRarX for Mac
- 7-Zip/PeaZip for Linux

The code bundle for the book is also hosted on GitHub at https://github.com/PacktPublishing/Extending-Microsoft-Dynamics-365-Finance-and-Supply-Chain-Management-Cookbook-Second-Edition. In case there's an update to the code, it will be updated on the existing GitHub repository.

We also have other code bundles from our rich catalog of books and videos available at https://github.com/PacktPublishing/. Check them out!

Conventions used

There are a number of text conventions used throughout this book.

CodeInText: Indicates code words in text, database table names, folder names, filenames, file extensions, pathnames, dummy URLs, user input, and Twitter handles. Here is an example: "If we wanted to create an extension of the WHSLoadTable table, it would call the WHSLoadTable.extension object by default."

A block of code is set as follows:

```
public Name StandardCarrierName()
{
    return 'Ziriqi';
}
```

When we wish to draw your attention to a particular part of a code block, the relevant lines or items are set in bold:

```
public static ConVMSVehicleTable Find(ConVMSVehicleId _vehicleId, boolean
_forUpdate = false)
{
    ConVMSVehicleTable vehicle;
    vehicle.selectForUdate(_forUpdate);
    select firstonly * from vehicle where vehicle.VehicleId == _vehicleId;
    return vehicle;
}
```

Bold: Indicates a new term, an important word, or words that you see onscreen. For example, words in menus or dialog boxes appear in the text like this. Here is an example: "Right-click on **59** in the **Solution Explorer** and choose **Properties**."

 Warnings or important notes appear like this.

 Tips and tricks appear like this.

Sections

In this book, you will find several headings that appear frequently (*Getting ready*, *How to do it...*, *How it works...*, *There's more...*, and *See also*).

To give clear instructions on how to complete a recipe, use these sections as follows:

Getting ready

This section tells you what to expect in the recipe and describes how to set up any software or any preliminary settings required for the recipe.

How to do it...

This section contains the steps required to follow the recipe.

How it works...

This section usually consists of a detailed explanation of what happened in the previous section.

There's more...

This section consists of additional information about the recipe in order to make you more knowledgeable about the recipe.

See also

This section provides helpful links to other useful information for the recipe.

Get in touch

Feedback from our readers is always welcome.

General feedback: If you have questions about any aspect of this book, mention the book title in the subject of your message and email us at customercare@packtpub.com.

Errata: Although we have taken every care to ensure the accuracy of our content, mistakes do happen. If you have found a mistake in this book, we would be grateful if you would report this to us. Please visit www.packtpub.com/support/errata, selecting your book, clicking on the Errata Submission Form link, and entering the details.

Piracy: If you come across any illegal copies of our works in any form on the Internet, we would be grateful if you would provide us with the location address or website name. Please contact us at copyright@packt.com with a link to the material.

If you are interested in becoming an author: If there is a topic that you have expertise in and you are interested in either writing or contributing to a book, please visit authors.packtpub.com.

Reviews

Please leave a review. Once you have read and used this book, why not leave a review on the site that you purchased it from? Potential readers can then see and use your unbiased opinion to make purchase decisions, we at Packt can understand what you think about our products, and our authors can see your feedback on their book. Thank you!

For more information about Packt, please visit `packt.com`.

Starting a New Project **1**

Microsoft Dynamics AX 2012 underwent a name change in what would have been version 7. The product has been split, in terms of licensing, into Microsoft Dynamics 365 Finance and Microsoft Dynamics 365 Supply Chain Management. This is a further evolution from the previous name of Microsoft Dynamics 365 for Finance and Operations.

Even though it appears to be a component of Microsoft Dynamics 365, it is a separate product, so we can't abbreviate the name to Dynamics 365. We will refer to the product as either its full name or the SCM abbreviation that is used by Microsoft internally. You may see references to Unified operations in some Microsoft documentation.

 A large change was made to the way in which updates are applied in the first two quarters of 2019. For more information, please read the following article at `https://docs.microsoft.com/en-us/dynamics365/unified-operations/fin-and-ops/get-started/one-version`.

The concept here is to make it easy to stay current and to avoid having customers on many different versions (such as 7.1, 7.2, 7.3, 8.1, and 8.1.2), hence the name One-Version. The associated challenges are mitigated through strong extensibility features that should allow partners and **Independent Software Vendors (ISVs)** to write code that is much easier to maintain and should not be impacted by updates.

For some time, we have had the platform updates being deployed in this way, so this is just a further evolution that brings some great benefits.

There are many references to the platform and application that we come across. Let's explain the difference between them, as follows:

- **Platform**: This can be considered the core kernel. This contains X++ language features, communication with SQL Server, integration services, and so on.
- **Application**: This is what the users actually use.

ISVs can get very excited about platform updates as they often contain new extensibility features and improvements for the language. The impact on users can be performance improvements and the way the controls look and feel.

All development work is carried out in conjunction with Azure DevOps, which was previously named Visual Studio Team Services. The application life cycle largely depends on this association. A simplified flow of this process is as follows:

1. A new task or bug is logged in Azure DevOps.
2. This task is then added to a sprint and allocated to a developer.
3. A new feature or fix for an existing feature is developed in Visual Studio and checked into Azure DevOps. Here, it is marked as resolving the task or bug.
4. The build server will build the new feature and automatically run test projects. The physical build server is being removed, but this step will still be performed, just not by a dedicated server.
5. The resulting build package will be uploaded to **Life Cycle Services** (**LCS**) as a deployable package in the Asset library. Again, this will be an automated step as the build pipelines evolve.
6. The package can then be deployed to the Sandbox environment for testing.
7. Once tested, the package can be deployed to the production/live environment.

Please see the following links for further reading on Microsoft Dynamics 365 for Finance and Supply Chain Management:

- Development and administration for Finance and Supply Chain Management can be found at `https://docs.microsoft.com/en-us/dynamics365/unified-operations/dev-itpro/`.
- An overview of Microsoft Dynamics 365 for Finance and Supply Chain Management for Developers is available at `https://docs.microsoft.com/en-us/dynamics365/unified-operations/dev-itpro/dev-tools/developer-home-page`.
- To obtain an evaluation copy of Microsoft Dynamics 365 for Operations, please go to `https://docs.microsoft.com/en-us/dynamics365/operations/dev-itpro/dev-tools/get-evaluation-copy`.

All development work in SCM is either performed on a development **Virtual Machine (VM)** hosted in Azure or a local VM. Each developer will use their own VM. Azure-hosted VMs are deployed through LCS under your own Azure subscription and can be used for development, learning, and demonstration. When a customer buys a cloud-hosted subscription through their cloud service provider (partner), they are provided with two environments as part of that subscription, namely Sandbox and production. This is hosted on Microsoft's subscription and is managed by Microsoft as the service provider. The build server that was provided prior to the One-Version (or version 10) release is no longer required as there are new pipelines that can build, test, and deploy directly to LCS.

The Sandbox server is a full environment, with multiple servers using a separate Azure SQL Server. The production environment is the environment that you (as a customer) will go live with. All the code first be deployed to the Sandbox before it can go live, which is enforced by LCS – no more "quick fixes" directly into live and no access to SQL server for the production environment.

The on-premises version is still managed through LCS, and the development process is the same as it would be for the cloud version.

For local development, VMs are often the cheapest option, and we will download the VM from the LCS Asset library. This is a website that's used for many programs at Microsoft, and access is provided to partners and customers.

In this chapter, we will cover the following recipes:

- Creating the Azure DevOps project
- Connecting Visual Studio to Azure DevOps
- Creating a new package and model
- Configuring project and build options
- Creating a Label file

Technical requirements

You can find the code files for this chapter on GitHub at `https://github.com/PacktPublishing/Extending-Microsoft-Dynamics-365-Finance-and-Supply-Chain-Management-Cookbook-Second-Edition/blob/master/Chapter1.axpp`.

Creating the Azure DevOps project

The project is normally created under the end user's Azure DevOps site unless the work is being written as an ISV solution (or a personal development or learning project). The reason we use the client's Azure DevOps system is that LCS is associated with the Azure DevOps site, and support calls that are created through cloud-powered support are generated within the associated Azure DevOps. Cloud-powered support is an online support solution within LCS that is exposed to the SCM client, allowing users to log support issues with their internal support team.

Azure DevOps is free for up to five users, and the customer can create many accounts with limited access without charge. These accounts are called stakeholder accounts and allow the user to access work items. This account type also allows users to log support calls from within SCM. Accounts with an MSDN subscription do not consume free user accounts, which means that the free account total is only used by accounts that do not have an MSDN subscription.

This process is normally performed as part of LCS project creation. If this were an implementation project type, the project would be created when the customer signs up for SCM. The customer would then invite their cloud solution provider (referred to as their CSP or partner) to the project. If this were an internal development project, such as a new vertical solution by an ISV, a **Migrate, create solutions, and learn Dynamics 365 for Operations** project type would be used.

In either case, we will have an LCS project, which will usually have an Azure VM deployed that acts as a build server.

For simplicity, and to keep the focus on software development, a project of the **Migrate, create solutions, and learn Dynamics 365 for Operations** was created for the purposes of writing the code for this book.

Getting ready

Before we get started, we will need an LCS project and an Azure DevOps site. An Azure DevOps site can be created at `https://www.visualstudio.com/en-us/products/visual-studio-team-services-vs.aspx`.

Once we have created the site, we can create our project.

How to do it...

To create the project, follow these steps:

1. Navigate to your Azure DevOps site; for example, `https://<yourdomain>.visualstudio.com/`.
2. On the top right of the home page, click on **Create project....**
3. Complete the form as shown as follow. Do **not** press **Create**:

Project name	A unique name. Be careful to name the projects for easy recognition and how they are ordered. This is more important for ISVs who may have many projects.
Description	Short description of the project.

4. Click **Advanced** and fill in the following two fields like so:

Work item process	Agile
Version control	Team Foundation Version Control

5. Press **Create**.
6. Once complete, you can then navigate to your project and work with Azure DevOps in order to plan your project.
7. To authenticate with LCS, we will need to generate a personal access token; from within Azure DevOps, click on your user's account name and select **Security** from the drop-down options.
8. The personal access tokens option is selected by default; on the right-hand pane, click on **New token**.
9. On the **Create a personal access token** form, enter a short description; for example, the LCS project's name. Set the **Expires** field based on how long you would like it to last for.
10. Set the **Scopes** to **Full access**. Then, press **Create token**.
11. Finally, copy the personal access code into a safe place; we will need it when we link Azure DevOps to LCS. If we don't, we will have to create a new access token as we won't be able to see it after this point.

Next, we will need to link the project to our LCS project. If an LCS project is not currently linked to an Azure DevOps project, we get the following message on the left-hand side:

Action center

Visual Studio Team Services has not been configured correctly for this project. Click on the Setup Visual Studio Team Services button below to configure a site for this project.

Privacy statement

Setup Visual Studio Team Services

To configure Azure DevOps for the LCS project, follow these steps:

1. Click on the **Setup Visual Studio Team Services** button in the **Action center** dialog box.
2. On the **Enter the site** page, enter the URL of our Azure DevOps site into the Azure DevOps site URL field; for example, `https://<mysite>.visualstudio.com/`.
3. Enter the personal access token we generated earlier into the **Personal access token** field.
4. Press **Continue**.
5. On the **Select the Visual Studio Team Service project** page, select the project from the **Visual Studio Team Service** list.

> You will sometimes see Azure DevOps referred to as its former name of **Visual Studio Team Services** (**VSTS**). This will change over time, and all areas will eventually use the name Azure DevOps.

6. Press **Continue**.
7. On the final **Review and save** page, press **Save**.

> If you use a **Microsoft account** in Azure DevOps, you will need to add the account you use in LCS to your project security so that it has access.

To complete the setup, we need to create some folders in the project's repository. To do this, follow these steps:

1. Open your Azure DevOps site and select the project we created earlier.
2. You will see a list on the left for each area of Azure DevOps. Select the **Repos** section and then click **Files**.
3. On the right, you will see a folder named **BuildProcessTemplates**. We need a sibling folder called Trunk. Against the root node (this will be in the format of $/<ProjectName>), click the ellipses (**...**) and select **New | Folder**.
4. In the **Check-in** dialog, enter Trunk and press **Check-In**.
5. Click the ellipses icon (**...**) on the new Trunk folder, click **New | Folder**, and create a folder named Main. This will be the main development branch containing metadata (the actual source code) and projects.
6. Click the ellipses on the new Main folder and create two sibling subfolders named Metadata and Projects. The final structure should be as follows:

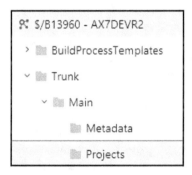

How it works...

The steps in this recipe resulted in a new folder structure that will contain code that is ready for deployment to the Sandbox and then production. Based on experience, in development, having a two-branch **Application Lifecycle Management** (**ALM**) strategy works best in most scenarios. The concept is that all development is to be done in Dev, and when the work passes testing, the Dev branch is merged into Main and Main is deployed to the Sandbox for final testing and then moved to production. Once the code has been moved to production, the Dev branch is reset from Main. We will create the Dev branch from within Visual Studio in the next recipe.

SCM uses Azure DevOps for its source control, work, and build management. The personal access token provides the security context in which LCS can interact with Azure DevOps. This means that when issues are logged by users, they will appear as issues in Azure DevOps. This is done using an area called **LcsGeneratedIssues**, which you can then use as a triage list in order to plan a resolution to the reported issue. These issues can then be submitted to Microsoft for support assistance directly from within LCS.

The structure of the repository is the way it is so that we can use branch management strategies that keep source code and project files together, even though they are stored in different locations on the development workstations.

See also

For more information on Azure DevOps and LCS, please check out the following links:

- **Lifecycle Services (LCS)** for Finance and Supply Chain Management, at `https://docs.microsoft.com/en-us/dynamics365/unified-operations/dev-itpro/lifecycle-services/lcs/`.
- LCS for Microsoft Dynamics 365 for Operations customers, at `https://docs.microsoft.com/en-us/dynamics365/unified-operations/dev-itpro/lifecycle-services/lcs-works-lcs/`.
- For more information on LCS, please go to `https://lcs.dynamics.com/Logon/Index`.
- The following link doesn't quite match the current state of Azure DevOps but provides some great background information on version control, metadata search, and navigation, at `https://docs.microsoft.com/en-us/dynamics365/unified-operations/dev-itpro/dev-tools/version-control-metadata-navigation`.
- The following link contains some useful background knowledge, but a lot of this based on when using an implementation LCS project, at `https://docs.microsoft.com/en-us/dynamics365/unified-operations/dev-itpro/lifecycle-services/cloud-powered-support-lcs/`.

This link is for when we have a customer implementation project and we want to demonstrate some of the synergies of leveraging Azure DevOps and LCS with SCM.

Connecting Visual Studio to Azure DevOps

Each developer has their own development **virtual machine** (**VM**), hosted either in Azure or locally. This is by design and is part of the application life cycle process. Connecting to Azure DevOps allows our code to be checked into source control and allows the team to work together on the same code base. Each developer would get the latest code from the source control and then check in their changes according to their organization's development methodology. As part of this check-in process, they can associate the check-ins to work items that were created in Azure DevOps (tasks, bugs, user stories), which allows us to easily determine what work is being deployed in a build. This process also allows test projects to be automatically executed when the build is generated.

We will be working with a two-branch strategy, which means starting with the Main branch and creating a Dev branch from that.

Getting ready

Once the VM has started, ensure that it has internet access and that you have used the admin user provisioning tool to associate your O365 account with the administrator account of SCM.

When working with multiple developers, one often overlooked task is renaming the VM. This has gotten easier with each update, and the steps we take at the current release are as follows:

1. Use computer management to rename the machine. I use a project reference, version, and initials, such as `CON-V10-PU24-SB`. `CON` could be the reference to a vertical solution or the customer's initials if you're developing their specific requirements. **CON** (short for **Contoso**) in this case, which is a fictitious partner organization.
2. Restart the VM.
3. Use the SQL Server Reporting Services configuration utility so that it references the correct server name.

How to do it...

1. When we are linking up the first workstation, we would use that to set up the branching strategy. This means creating two sets. We start with the Main branch, so create folders that match the following structures:

   - `C:\Trunk\Main\Projects`
   - `C:\Trunk\Dev\Projects`

2. Start Visual Studio.
3. You will be presented with the licensing page. Use the page to log in to the account you used to create the project within Azure DevOps, which could be either your Microsoft account or Work (O365) account.
4. On the top toolbar, select **Team** and then **Manage Connections**.
5. The **Team Explorer** will open, under default layout, on the right-hand side. On this pane, select **Manage Connections** | **Connect to Team Project**:

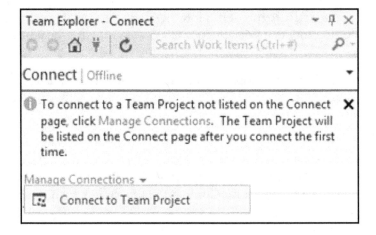

6. This will open the **Connect to Team Foundation Server** dialog. From the **Select a Team Foundation Server** drop-down list, select your Azure DevOps site.
7. Select your project in the lower portion of the dialog, as shown in the following screenshot:

Connect to Team Foundation Server

Select a Team Foundation Server:

<YourAzureDevOpsSite>.visualstudio.com

Team Project Collections:	Team Projects:
⚎ <YourAzureDevOpsSite>	◼ (Select All)
	☑ B13960 - AX7DEVR2

8. After pressing **Connect**, Visual Studio will be connected to your project.

9. We have one final step to complete before we continue; we have to configure our workspace so that Visual Studio knows which folders are under source control and how they map to Azure DevOps. On **Team Explorer**, click on **Configure workspace** under the **Project** section. This will show the **Configure Workspace** section at the top of the **Team Explorer**.

10. Don't press **Map & Get**.

11. Press **Advanced...**.

12. Alter the mappings so that you have two lines that follow the format shown in the following screenshot:

Working folders:		
Status	Source Control Folder ▲	Local Folder
Active	$/B13960 - AX7DEVR2/Trunk/Main	C:\Trunk\Main
Active	$/B13960 - AX7DEVR2/Trunk/Main/Metadata	C:\AOSService\PackagesLocalDirectory
	Click here to enter a new working folder	

13. Press **OK**.

14. On the **Workspace Modified** dialog, press **Yes** to get the files from Azure DevOps.

15. On the right-hand side, under the **Team Explorer**, click on the **Source Control Explorer** tile.

16. You will see all the sites available to you in an explorer view. On the Source Control Explorer's left pane, expand your project. Do the same for the Trunk folder so that you can see the Main folder. Right-click on this folder, choose **Branching and Merging | Convert to Branch...**, and click **Convert** when the appropriate dialog is displayed.

17. Next, we need to create our Dev branch. Right-click on the Main branch and choose **Branching and Merging | Branch…**.

18. In the Branch from the Main dialog, change the name from Main-branch to Dev. It must sit under `$/<project name>/Trunk/`.

19. Finally, we need to change our mapping so that it links to the Dev branch. Click the home button on the Team Explorer pane on the right-hand side and click **Manage Workspaces…**, as shown in the following screenshot:

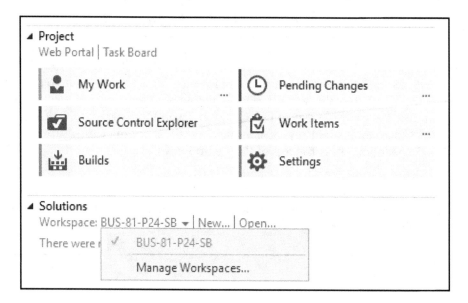

20. Click **Edit** and rename all the references from `Main` to `Dev`, as shown in the following screenshot:

Status	Source Control Folder ▲	Local Folder
Active	$/B13960 - AX7DEVR2/Trunk/Dev	C:\Trunk\Dev
Active	$/B13960 - AX7DEVR2/Trunk/Dev/Metadata	C:\AOSService\PackagesLocalDirectory
	Click here to enter a new working folder	

Working folders:

21. Press **OK**, and then **Yes**.

How it works...

Source control in SCM has come a long way in this release, mainly because our development tool is now Visual Studio and the source files are now actual files in the filesystem. SCM no longer needs special code to integrate with a Team Foundation Server.

The reason we have two folders is that our projects don't actually contain the files we create when writing code. When we create a file, such as a new class, it is created within the local packages folder and referenced within the project. This also means that we can't just zip up a project and email it to a co-worker. This is done by connecting to the same Azure DevOps project or using the project export feature.

See also

The following links provide further relevant information for when we're setting up new VMs with Azure DevOps:

- Renaming a VM, at `https://docs.microsoft.com/en-us/dynamics365/fin-ops-core/dev-itpro/migration-upgrade/vso-machine-renaming`
- Continuous delivery home page, at `https://docs.microsoft.com/en-us/dynamics365/fin-ops-core/dev-itpro/dev-tools/continuous-delivery-home-page`

Creating a new package and model

When creating a new project, we usually create a new package and a new model. This keeps things simple, and there is usually no benefit in separating them. You may wish to create a test project in a different model in the same solution, but you may not wish to deploy the test projects to live.

There are two types of projects:

- An extension project
- An over-layer project

Over-layering means modifying the source code of SCM and requires a code upgrade for each application hotfix. Extension projects work on delta changes to the standard object or use delegates to affect code execution. Extension projects are less likely to require a code upgrade when application hotfixes are applied. Avoiding over-layering cannot be overstated because, at the time of writing, all Microsoft supplier packages are locked. The ability to write good code through extension has been improved with each release, and now that over-layering is only available to ISV solutions, the development paradigm has had to shift significantly from the AX2012 development days.

In this recipe, we will use extension projects exclusively in order to avoid conflicts with future upgrades. They make it possible for us to service the environment without having to deploy a new build of the custom solution. This is very exciting for ISV solutions, but also very important for partners/**Value-Added Resellers** (**VAR**) and end-user customers.

See *There's more...* section for information on the relationship between packages, models, and projects.

Getting ready

Start Visual Studio and ensure that we are correctly connected to Azure DevOps. With the current release, you must start Visual Studio as an administrator.

How to do it...

1. Under the **Dynamics 365** menu, choose **Model Management** | **Create model....**
2. The model name is named as it would be in AX 2012, and should be named like a new type, such as `<prefix><ShortName>`.
3. Complete the first page as follows:

   - **Model name**: In our case, our company is called Contoso, so our prefix will be Con, and we are writing a vehicle management solution. Therefore, we have named it `ConVehicleManagement`. You should use your own prefix and prefixes, as well as a unique name, which is explained further in the *There's more...* section.
   - **Model publisher**: Your organization's name.
   - **Layer**: ISV or vertical solution. Here, choose ISV. For partner projects choose VAR. Customers can use CUS or USR.
   - **Version**: Leave as 1.0.0.0.

- **Model description**: A full description of the model for other developers to read.
- **Model display name**: This should be something like **Contoso – vehicle management** in our case.

The custom layers were traditionally used to segregate a customer's global solution layer from the requirements of each country's implementation. The layer technology is processed very differently for the extension projects and has lost some significance in this release.

4. Press **Next**.
5. On the **Select package** page, choose **Create new package**.

If you choose **Select existing package**, it will mean that your model will be placed under the package and is intended to over-layer the elements in that package. You cannot over-layer elements in extension projects, but unless we absolutely must over-layer, always choose **Create new package**.

6. Press **Next**.
7. We are now offered a list of packages that we can reference, listed as package names and the models that each package contains. Leave **ApplicationPlatform** checked. Additionally, check **ApplicationFoundation**, **ApplicationCommon**, and **ApplicationSuite** and then press **Next**.

Most of the elements in SCM are in **ApplicationSuite**; so, unless our package doesn't need any standard type, this will always be selected. The others would be selected based on the elements we know we will use. We can add more package references later, but if we know which elements we will use, it saves us some time.

8. The **Create new project** and **Make this my default model for new projects** checkboxes should both be checked.
9. Press **Finish**.
10. This opens the **New Project dialog**. The project name is usually the same as the package and model name. Now, enter the package name in the **Name** field.
11. The **Location** field must be changed; it will be created in the default project folder. Here, we linked `C:\Trunk\Dev` to source control. The project must be created under this folder. So, in my case, **Location** must be `C:\Trunk\Dev\Projects`.
12. The **Solution** name field should be left as the project name.

13. Ensure that both **Create directory** for the solution and **Add to source control** are checked.
14. Press **OK**.

How it works...

To see what we just did, we can simply look at the results. Use Windows Explorer to navigate to the local packages folder, which is usually `C:\AOSService\PackagesLocalDirectory`. There, you will see the following structure for our example package, that is, `ConVehicleManagement`:

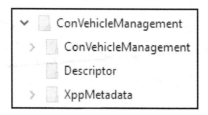

The root folder is the Package and contains a subfolder for the model, which has the same name. All of the code is under the model folder in a separate folder for each type. The descriptor folder contains an XML definition file. `XppMetaData` is a system-managed folder for the Xpp metadata for all the models in the package. This holds compiler metadata information about each element, not the actual source code. This includes the methods in a class, the type of method, and the parameters.

We would never normally change anything here, but there are exceptions:

- If two developers create a different package at the same time, they can both get the same model ID, in which case conflicts will occur when they check in. The solution is to check out the model's descriptor XML file in the **Source Control Explorer** and manually change the ID to the next number.
- You may decide that a standard package should be deleted, such as the tutorial or the sample fleet management solution. You can do this by simply deleting the package folder. Should you want to remove a standard model, you can delete the model folder, but you must also delete the relevant model descriptor file from the package's `Descriptor` folder. Obvious care needs to be taken, as you can't get it back!

The former point can be prevented by nominating a person to create packages and models.

If you look in the Source Control Explorer in Visual Studio, you will only see that the projects folder has been added. This is correct. The folders under the Metadata folder will only appear when we create new elements.

There's more...

When a solution is designed, it will be done by breaking the solution into packages of functionality. This is a normal design paradigm that has now been implemented (and, to an extent, enforced) within SCM. This means that our solution design will now define the various packages and their dependencies. In the case of SCM, a Package is a deployable unit.

We can make a hotfix to a package and, technically, deploy it separately to other packages in the solution. Although this is possible, we would normally create a release of packages as a deployable package. A deployable package is a collection of one or more packages that contain both the built code and the routine required to install them. This process is simplified using a build server that performs the build process for us, executes any tests, and creates deployable packages that we can then apply to our test environment.

There is a further level within SCM, which is a model. A model is a subset of elements, such as classes, within a package and can be used to move code from one development system to another, for example. A model can only belong to one package, and a Package can contain one or more models. Each package becomes (effectively) a **Dynamic Link Library (DLL)**, which has to have references added in order to see elements in order packages. Because of this, we should use a limited number of packages. As a guide, we tend to have one package for mainstream development. To simplify the management of development tasks, we tend to have a project per **Specification/Technical Design Document (TDD)**, all within the main package, simplifying multi-developer projects. Just like working on complex C# projects, we can perform code merges, branching, and shelving within Azure DevOps. This means having a label file per project; otherwise, we will have a conflict each time we check in a change to the label file.

Layers have been a core part of prior releases from its first release but are no longer that significant. As a partner, we still use the VAR layer and recommend the same guidelines as before to customers, but since we avoid over-layering, this feature will not be covered in this book.

 The dependencies are defined against the package, not the model. When we create a project, the project is associated with a model. It is typical, and desirable, to keep this structure simple and only have one model for each package and to give both entities the same name.

The following diagram shows a typical **Package**, **Model**, and **Project structure**:

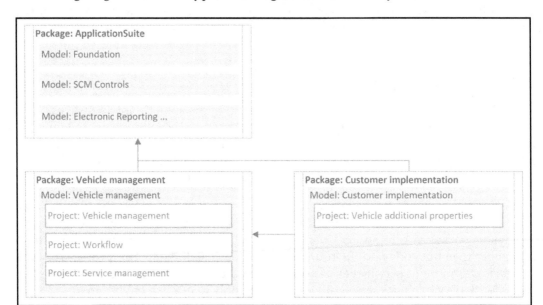

The **ApplicationSuite** package is a standard package that we normally always reference as it contains the majority of the types that we usually need. The arrows in the preceding diagram indicate the reference direction, showing that it is not possible for the Vehicle management package to see the elements that were created in the Vehicle management reporting package.

Prefixes and naming conventions

SCM does not use namespaces. Neither packages nor models equate to a namespace. A model simply implies a scope, but all types must be globally unique, even in different models and packages. A namespace would allow a class to have the same name as another class in a different namespace.

Therefore, every element must be globally unique by type; this includes models, packages, and every element in the application metadata. So, we will still need prefixes. Even if we create an extension of an element, such as a form, we must change the name so that it is guaranteed to be globally unique.

For example, if we wanted to create an extension of the `WHSLoadTable` table, it will call the `WHSLoadTable.extension` object by default. As our customer might want an add-on that also adds fields to this table, we need to ensure that the element is unique.

The best way to do this would be to use our prefix, which is `Con` in our case. To make it obvious where the element is used, we use the package name as the suffix; for example, `WHSLoadTable.ConVehicleManagement`. There is no official best practice available for this, but remember that all the elements of a type must be globally unique – and extensions are no exception.

This naming also applies to extensions to classes and event handler classes. We always start with the type name being extended, followed by the project name and then the type of extension. The following examples show this in a project named `ConVehicleManagement`:

Type	Reason	Type being extended	Example name of the extension type
Table	Data event	`CustTable`	`CustTable_ConVehicleManagement_DataHandler`
Class	Delegate or pre-post	`InventMovement`	`InventMovement_ConVehicleManagement_EventHandler`
Class	Extension	`InventMovement`	`InventMovement_ConVehicleManagement_Extension`
Form code	Code extension	`CustTable`	`CustTable_ConVehicleManagement_FormHandler`
Form	Form extension	`CustTable`	`CustTable.ConVehicleManagement`

This is what works for us, as we can easily see all the areas that a standard type is augmented in or has events handled and know which project (and roughly the reason for the change) at a glance. The key here is to be consistent at all times.

Configuring project and build options

Before we start developing code for the first time in a new VM, we should set up some parameters in Visual Studio. Many of the settings that are described here are good for all projects, but you may wish to change some, depending on the scenario. This recipe explains how to configure the required parameters.

Getting ready

This follows the previous recipe but can apply equally to any SCM project. Just load up Visual Studio and the project you wish to configure.

How to do it...

This recipe will be split into two parts, that is, Finance and Supply Chain Management are generic options for all projects and project-specific parameters.

Before we do either, we should always have the **Application Explorer** open, which is hidden by default. This is the **Application Object Tree** (**AOT**) of prior versions, and it can be opened from the **View** menu.

Dynamics 365 for Finance and Supply Chain Management' options

To configure the generic options for all projects, follow these steps:

1. Select **Options** from the **Dynamics 365** menu.

 The form is actually the Visual Studio options dialog, but it takes you to the section specific to SCM.

2. The default option in the left-hand tree view is Debugging; the options here are usually fine. The Load symbols for items in this solution option affect debugging and should be left checked for the performance of the debugger. We would uncheck this if we wanted to trace code that calls code outside of the current package.
3. Select the **Projects** option on the left and **Organize projects by element type**. When adding new elements to the project, it will automatically create a subfolder in the project for the element type. This makes the organization much easier to maintain.
4. The other two options should be left blank. Although the **Synchronize database on build for newly created projects** option can be useful, this database synchronization takes time, and it is usually preferable to do this as required.
5. The **Best practices** node lets you choose which best practice checks you wish to be executed on the build. This detail is beyond the scope of this book as the checks that are required are case-specific.

The project-specific parameters

The project-specific parameters are usually fine as they are for development. Some changes are required when we want to debug using the sample data that comes with the VM. Primarily, it needs to know the entry point to debug and the company data that the session should start with.

To set up the common parameters, follow these steps:

1. Right-click on **59** in the **Solution Explorer** and choose **Properties**.
2. To save time while debugging, select which object you wish to start with. To start with the form `SalesTable`, set the **Startup Object Type** option to **Form** and **Startup Object** to `SalesTable`.
3. Set **Company** to `USMF` or any other company you wish to start with when debugging.
4. Leave **Partition** as initial. These are now only supported for certain unit test scenarios.
5. If you wish to always synchronize the database on the build, you can set **Synchronize Database on Build**. My advice is to do this manually as required after the build completes.

 You may notice that we can change the Model in the project's parameters. Our advice is, don't do it. Changing the project's Model also means that the folders have to be moved in the local packages folder.

Creating a Label file

Most projects have some kind of user interface, so we need to display text to the user, as well as the field names. The best practice way to do this is to use a label file. The label file contains a language-specific dictionary of label IDs and their translation.

Standard elements tend to have the legacy label IDs of an @ symbol, followed by a three-digit label ID and a number. This format has worked well for the past 15 years, but the prefix was potentially limiting, especially for aiding ISVs. Labels are no longer restricted to three digits, which helps Microsoft attain one of its goals of making ISV add-ons easier to write, maintain, and adopt.

The choice of how many and which packages need a label file depends on the solution design.

We tend to create a label file for each project as this ensures that the developer of the project can correct and change labels without worrying about regression in other projects in the same package.

Getting ready

To get started, open Visual Studio and the project in question. In my case, I will continue with the `ConVehicleManagent` project.

How to do it...

1. Right-click on the project and select **Add** | **New item...** or use the *Ctrl + Shift + A* keyboard shortcut.
2. Choose **Labels and Resources** from the **Dynamics 365 items** list.
3. From the list on the left, select **Label File**.
4. In the **Name** field, enter a short but unique label name. In my case, this is `ConVMS`. I want it to be as short as possible but still be completely sure it will be globally unique, regardless of any future add-on we may choose to install.
5. Press **Add**.
6. In the **Label file wizard**, leave the Label file ID as its default.

 It seems that we can specify a different name in this step, but we only called this wizard with a suggested file name. The Label file ID is both the ID and the filename that will be created.

7. Press **Next**.
8. In the language selection, move the languages from the left-hand list into the right-hand list using the buttons. Only leave languages selected that you will maintain. This involves creating a label in each language file.
9. Press **Next**.
10. Check that the **Summary** page is correct and press **Finish**.

How it works...

The creation process is straightforward. The process creates a text file on the disk that contains a tab-separated list of label IDs and the translation.

When a label is selected against a control, it will be given a label file ID that ensures it is unique. In our example, the label file ID was `ConVMS`. When we create a label, we will state the ID as a short identifier name as this makes the label easier to read in code and in property sheets. `@ConVMS:L001` is not very memorable, but `@ConVMS:ItemNotExists` is far easier to understand.

This also applies to language with subtle differences, such as English and Spanish. Even though the label will often be the same, we still need to manually maintain each language file. Currently, this also means we have to be careful that we give them the correct ID.

There's more...

Currently, the maintenance of labels can be time-consuming in that we don't have a translation list per label ID as we did in Dynamics AX 2012. Instead, we have a separate file per language. This has been done as an improvement and may change by release. The concept, however, will remain the same.

When writing labels for variants of the same or similar languages, we can copy and paste the labels between files. To do so, we can expand the label file to the lowest node to the file with a `.txt` extension, right-click on it to select **Open With...**, and choose **Source Code (Text) Editor** from the list.

Each label will have two lines – one for the label and another for the comment – as shown in the following extract from an `en-gb` label file:

```
VehicleType=Vehicle type
 ;
VehicleTypeHT=The type of vehicle
 ;
VehTransComplete=Complete inspection
 ;
VehTransCompleteHT=Complete, and finalise the vehicle inspection
 ;
```

You can then translate to the desired language and paste it into the target label file, again by opening the text file in the source code editor. You must do this from within Visual Studio (and not in a separate editor outside of Visual Studio); otherwise, the file may not be checked out from source control. Be careful when editing in this way as the source code editor will not validate that there aren't duplicates or file formatting errors.

If you intend to write add-ons, you should always maintain the en-us language file. You will get compilation warnings that the label ID does not exist if you do not. If you are to release the software to a region with a variant of a language (en-au, en-gb, en-ie, en-us, and so on), please use the correct translation. Not only will it make your add-on more professional and global, but some terms across even English-speaking countries have completely different meanings. For example, stock means inventory in en-gb, but means financial shareholdings in en-us.

2
Data Structures

In this chapter, we will cover the tasks required to write the data dictionary elements commonly used within **Supply Chain Management (SCM)** development.

Data structures in SCM are not just tables and views—they also include the ability to define a data dictionary. This is now called the data model in SCM. The data model hasn't changed much in structure since AX 2012, but is much more refined, with many more features to aid development and minimize the footprint when extending standard tables and types.

 This chapter does not cover creating extensions of standard types, but it does cover how to create types that allow your structures to be extensible. Extensibility is covered in Chapter 5, *Application Extensibility*.

Most development in SCM is based on patterns, even if we are not aware of it. This classically means code patterns, but SCM unifies the code, data model, and user interface design. So we have patterns to follow when creating the data model. For example, the vendor and customer lists are very similar and are called main tables. Purchase orders and sales orders are also very similar, which are worksheet tables; in this case, order headers and lines.

Tables in SCM have a property that defines the type of table, and each type is associated with a particular style of form for the user interface. We could, therefore, consider these types as patterns. If we think of them as patterns, it is far easier to apply the recipes to our own development.

The following list is of the common table types, listed with the usual form design and the typical usage:

Table group	Form design pattern	Usage
Miscellaneous	None	This is essentially "undefined" and shouldn't be used, other than for temporary tables.
Parameter	Table of contents	This is used for single-record parameter forms.
Group	Simple list Simple list and details-ListGrid	This is used for the backing table for drop-down lists. The Simple list design pattern is suitable for when only a few fields are required; otherwise, the Simple list and Details patterns should be used so the fields are presented in a useful way to the user.
Main	Details Master	This is used for main tables, such as customers, suppliers, and items.
Transaction header Transaction Line	Simple List and Details with standard tabs	This is used for datasets, such as the invoice journal form, which contain posted transactional data with a header and lines.
Transaction	Simple List and Details w/ standard tabs	This is used for tables, such as the inventory transaction form, which contain posted transactional data but at a single level.
Worksheet header Worksheet line	Details transaction	This is used for data entry datasets, such as the purchase order, where the dataset is made up of header and line tables. The pattern has two views, a list view of header records, and a detail view where the focus is the lines.
Worksheet	Details Master	This is a single-level data entry dataset, which is rarely used in SCM.

In this chapter, we will create types and tables for the common types of table, but we will complete the patterns when we cover the user interface in Chapter 3, *Creating the User Interface*.

In this chapter, we will cover the following recipes:

- Creating enumerated types
- Creating extended data types
- Creating setup tables
- Creating a parameter table
- Creating main data tables
- Creating order header tables
- Creating order line tables

Technical requirements

You can find the code files for this chapter on GitHub at `https://github.com/
PacktPublishing/Extending-Microsoft-Dynamics-365-Finance-and-Supply-Chain-
Management-Cookbook-Second-Edition/blob/master/Chapter%202.axpp`.

Creating enumerated types

Enumerated types are called **base enums** in SCM, which are similar to enumerated types in
C#. They are commonly referred to as enums. An enum is an integer referenced as a
symbol, which can be used in code to control logic. It can also be used as a field in a table
that provides a fixed drop-down list to the user. When used as a field, it has the ability to
provide user-friendly labels for each symbol.

 Base enums are usually only used as a drop-down list if we need to
understand, in code, what each value means. They should contain a small
number of options, and when used as a field, the list cannot be searched
or extended by the user.

All enums have to be defined in the data model before we use them and can't be defined
within a class or method.

 Base enums are given the ability to be extensible in this release; the
mechanics of this are covered in more detail in the *There's more...* section.

Getting ready

The following tasks continue the vehicle management project, `ConVehicleManagement`,
which was created in `Chapter 1`, *Starting a New Project*, although this is not a prerequisite.
We just need an SCM project that was created as an extension project.

How to do it...

In order to create a new Enum, follow these steps:

1. Either right-click on the project (or any sub folder in the project) and choose **Add New item...**.

 Always try to use keyboard shortcuts, which are displayed next to the option. In this case, try *Ctrl + Shift + A*.

2. This will open the **Add New Item** window. From the left-hand list, select **Data Types**, which is under the **Dynamics 365 Items** node.

3. This will filter the available options in the right-hand list. From this list, choose **Base Enum**.

4. Enter a name, prefixed appropriately. In this example, we are creating an enum to store the type of vehicle; so, we will enter ConVMSVehicleType as **Name** and click **Add**.

 This should have created a folder called Base Enums or added the new Enum to the folder if it already existed. This is regardless of the folder we selected when the Enum was created. If this did not happen, the **Organize projects by element type** setting in **Dynamics 365 | Options** was not checked. You can remove the base enum and add it back from **Application Explorer** after the setting is checked.

5. We will now have a new tab open with our empty enum. Before we continue, we must create labels for the **Label** and **Help** properties. Double-click on the label file so we can add a new label.

 This was created in Chapter 1, *Starting a New Project*; if you don't have a label file, one must be created before we continue. We should always maintain the en-us label file, as this drives the labels displayed on the designers in Visual Studio (for example, the form designer). Since we develop in English, we would maintain en-gb, en-ie, and en-gb as standard, as it is usually just a copy and paste with minor changes for en-us.

6. This will add an empty line for us. On this empty line, click on **Label ID** and enter a short name, in the style of an identifier, such as VehicleType.

7. Enter `Vehicle type` in the **Label** column. You can add a comment in order to provide context for other developers, in case it is reused.

8. Press **New** and repeat for the next label. Use `VehicleTypeHT` for the **Label ID** and enter the text: `Defines the basic type of vehicle, used to govern static vehicle type specific properties` for the **Label** property. It would be tempting to just write *The type of vehicle*, but this provides nothing to the user in addition to what the field name suggests. The result should be shown as follows:

Label ID	Label
NewLabel0	Label files created on 03/02/2019 13:29:01 for label file Id ConVMS and language en-GB
VehicleType	Vehicle type
VehicleTypeHT	Defines the basic type of vehicle, used to govern static vehicle type specific properties

We could repeat this for each label file language we created, but this is more efficiently done in bulk. We could also use a translator to assist after project completion in order to avoid translation errors. Most online translation tools aren't appropriate for this task as they won't have the necessary context or industry knowledge.

9. Without left-clicking first, right-click on **Label ID** for `VehicleType`, and choose **Copy**. Left-clicking first might select the text in the field, which is undesirable. We should end up with `@ConVMS:VehicleType` in the paste buffer.

10. Reselect the editor tab for the **Enum**, and look for the property sheet. If this isn't visible - it's usually at the lower right of the screen - right-click on the **Enum** inside the tab and select **Properties**.

11. In the property sheet, click in the **Value** field for the **Label** property and choose paste (or press *Ctrl + V*).

You could instead type in `Vehicle type` in the **Label** field, click on the ellipsis (...), and search for the label. This is OK when trying to use standard labels, but when we are creating labels, copy and paste is much faster.

12. Since we just added `HT` to the label for the help text label, select the **Repeat this process** for the **Help** property and paste again. Then, click on the property's value control and add `HT` to the end of the label; remember that **Label ID** is case-sensitive.

These properties do not have to be populated, but it will cause a best practice deviation warning when the project is built if these properties are left empty. The time spent here is of great value to a user, reducing mistakes and subsequent support calls.

13. This enum is used to define the type, and if we want the end-user customer (or other partners if we are an ISV), we should make this an extensible enum. Locate the **Is Extensible** property and set it to true. See the *There's more...* section for more information on this.

14. We will no longer be able to set the **Use Enum Value** property, so we will now add the elements to the Enum. The options we will add should be created as follows:

Name (symbol)	Label
NotSelected	Not selected
Bike	Motorbike
Car	Car
Truck	Truck

The **Label** column in the preceding table shows the literal to use; the actual value will be the label ID, such as @ConVMS:Motorbike.

15. To add each symbol, or element as it is referred to in the editor, right-click on the **Enum** and choose **New Element**.

16. Complete the property sheet as per the table, and repeat for each required element.

For non-extensible enums, we can control the ranking, which is done by setting the **Enum value** property. For readability, we would alter the order in the designer with the *Alt + up* and *Alt + down* keys. This property is not visible in our case as we set the **Is Extensible** property.

17. Press the **Save** or **Save all** buttons in the toolbar.

How it works...

Enums are stored as integers in the database, and we can assign an integer value to a field based on an enum.

When the values of the enum are shown to the user, SCM will look this up using the enum's definition from the field in the user's language. If a label is not defined for the user's language, the label ID (`@Con:MyLabelId`) is shown to the user. If a label was not defined in the `enum` element, the symbol (`MyEnum:Value`) is shown.

For standard, non-extensible enums, the following lines of code are effectively the same:

```
InventTable.ABCRevenue = 1;
InventTable.ABCRevenue = ABC::B;
```

Of course, we would never write the first option—we use enumerated types specifically to avoid having to remember what each number means. If the enum was created as extensible, the values associated with the symbol are not assigned at design time, they are installation-specific. Extensible enums are implemented as a class, and we, therefore, have a slight performance hit as we are no longer dealing with numbers.

We use enums for many purposes, ranging from table inheritance (different fields are relevant to a type of vehicle) to providing an option list to a user, and even controlling which type of class is created to handle logic specific to the vehicle type.

There's more...

Base enums are therefore a great way to provide a link between logic and the user interface. However, there are limitations; the options are defined in code and the user cannot add to the list. The problem with making the options user-definable is that we can't use the values in code, unless we want to add the options to a parameter form, which is not very extendable.

What we can do is use the code pattern exemplified in the item model group form. Here, we have a user-definable list, with an Enum that determines the inventory model that the items will use.

Using enums for comparison and status

It is very common to use an enum to define the status of a record, and we will cover state machines in `Chapter 15`, *State Machines*. When defining an enum for status, we order the elements so that we can compare them in code.

Given that standard enums are essentially a symbol representing an integer, we can use relative comparisons. These are commonly used in status fields. Let's look at the following vehicle status:

Symbol	Value
Created	0
Review	1
Active	2
Removed	3

If we want all vehicles not removed from service, we could write the following:

```
select * from vehicles where vehicles.VehicleStatus <
VehicleStatus::Removed;
```

If we want a list of vehicles that have ever been active (for example, every status on or after `Active`), we could write the following:

```
select * from vehicles where vehicles.VehicleStatus >=
VehicleStatus::Active;
```

If we want all vehicles not yet active, we could write the following:

```
select * from vehicles where vehicles.VehicleStatus <
VehicleStatus::Active;
```

We could also use query ranges to create lists so that users can see pertinent lists of vehicles using the same concept.

Extensibility in base enums

There are two notable limitations when an enum is created as extensible.

One is that we can't use it in conjunction with the mandatory property on fields in order to force a user to select a value. The first element is probably zero (which is not valid for mandatory fields), and will usually work—we can't guarantee this behavior and must not use this technique.

The other limitation when using comparisons on enums is using relative comparisons, such as *greater than*. For example, the options for the `SalesStatus` base enum are as follows:

- None
- Backorder
- Delivered
- Invoiced
- Canceled

This enum was changed from a standard to an extensible enum in an early application update. Prior to the update, the following code would normally return a list of the `SalesTable` records that are not yet invoiced with `SalesId` and `SalesName` populated:

```
select SalesId, SalesName from salesTable where salesTable.SalesStatus <
SalesStatus::Invoiced;
```

This will now fail with a compilation error. Extensible enums are designed to be extended by third parties, who may add their own options to the type. This means that there is no ranking in extensible enums, which means that we can't use *greater than* or *less than* expressions. We must, therefore, write code such as the following:

```
select SalesId, SalesName
    from salesTable
    where salesTable.SalesStatus == SalesStatus::Backorder
        || salesTable.SalesStatus == SalesStatus::Delivered;
```

The code upgrade tool in the **Life Cycle Service** (**LCS**) would look for this and assist the developer in correcting the code so that it is built correctly.

The actual values of the `SalesStatus` enum are stored in tables in SQL, where the values are set when the database is synchronized. The values will not change after this, but new elements that are subsequently added will be appended to this table. Since the development, OneBox VMs come with SQL Server Management Studio; you can open this, and use the following Transact-SQL against the database AxDB in order to see the way in which this data is stored:

```
SELECT   E.[NAME], V.NAME AS SYMBOL, V.ENUMVALUE AS VALUE
  FROM ENUMIDTABLE E
  JOIN ENUMVALUETABLE V ON V.ENUMID = E.ID
  WHERE E.[NAME] = 'SalesStatus'
```

This will show the following result if this enum has not been extended:

NAME	SYMBOL	VALUE
SalesStatus	None	0
SalesStatus	Backorder	1
SalesStatus	Delivered	2
SalesStatus	Invoiced	3
SalesStatus	Canceled	4

This can occasionally be useful during development and testing when extensible enums are used.

The lesson here is that we are free to use comparisons on the enums that we control, but we can't assume that a third party (ISV or Microsoft) will not change a standard enum to be extensible. This also means when referencing enum values in query ranges, we must use the SalesStatus::Backorder format and not 1. Even if the enum is not extensible, we should still use this format.

Creating extended data types

Extended data types are commonly referred to as **EDTs**. They extend base types, such as Strings and Integers by adding properties that affect the appearance, behavior, data (size), and table reference/relationships. This means that we can have types like CustAccount that have a label, size, table relation information, and other properties that provide consistency and greater understanding within the data model.

Another example of an EDT is Name. Should we change the StringSize property of this field, all fields based on this EDT will be adjusted; and if we reduce the size, it will truncate the values to the new size.

All fields should be based on an EDT or an enum, but they are not just used to enforce consistency in the data model but are used as types when writing code.

The EDT in this example will be a primary key field for a table that we will use later in the chapter.

Getting ready

We just need to have an SCM project open in Visual Studio. To look at standard examples, ensure that **Application Explorer** is open by selecting **View** | **Application Explorer**.

How to do it...

We will create an EDT for a vehicle number. A vehicle table is of a similar pattern to customers and vendors, and we will extend the Num EDT for this type.

 The Num EDT is used (at some level in the type hierarchy) for fields that will use a number sequence.

To create the EDT, follow these steps:

1. Creating an EDT starts in the same way as all new Dynamics 365 items: by pressing *Ctrl + Shift + A* or right-clicking on a folder in the Solution Explorer and choosing **Add** | **New Item**.
2. Select **Data Types** from the left-hand list, and then select **EDT String**.
3. In the **Name** field, enter ConVMSVehicleId and click **Add**.
4. Next, we need to complete the property sheet; the main properties are covered in the following table:

Property	Value	Description
Label	Vehicle ID	This is the label that will be presented to the user on the user interface when added as a field to a table.
Help Text	A unique reference for the vehicle record	This is the help text shown to the user when this field is selected or the mouse hovers over the controls based on this EDT.
Extends	Num	This should be completed for all EDTs, as we are usually following a pattern, such as ID, name, and grouping fields. This is explained in the *There's more...* section.
Size		This will be read-only, as we have based this EDT on another EDT. Although this is under the **Appearance** section, it controls the physical size of the associated fields in the database.

Reference Table		For types used as a primary key field on a table, this property should be populated. Along with the table references, it can be used to create a foreign key relation on child tables.

As always, remember to create labels for the **Label** and **Help Text** properties for each of your supported languages.

5. If this EDT is to be used as a primary key field, we will need to populate the **Table References** node.

We will complete this later in the chapter, but you can see a good example by looking at the standard `AssetId` EDT. Navigate through the **Application Explorer** to **AOT** | **Data Types** | **Extended Data Types**, right-click on **AssetId** and select **Open designer**.

6. Press **Save** (*Ctrl + S*) or **Save all** (*Ctrl + Shift + S*) in the toolbar to save the changes.

How it works...

There is a back and forth element to EDT creation when we are creating a primary key field. We can't create the field without the EDT, yet we can't complete the EDT when the field is on the table.

EDTs are types. Therefore, they must be globally unique among all other types, such as tables, views, data entities, enums, classes, and other EDTs. The EDT properties aren't just defaults, but they control behavior too. Should we add an unbound control to a form based on an EDT, the EDT can use the **Table Reference** property to provide a drop-down list, and the contents will be taken from a field group on the table.

There's more...

EDTs can also extend other EDTs; although, child EDTs can only affect appearance properties. This is useful when we want to enforce the physical storage attributes of a range of types, but have a different label depending on the context. If we change the size of a base EDT, all the EDTs that extend it will be affected and, consequently, all of the fields that are based on them.

We often extend specific EDTs when creating an EDT for certain types of fields.

The typical EDTs we use for this are shown in the following table:

EDT	Base type	Size	Reason
SysGroup	String	10	This is used for the primary key fields for group tables. Group tables are those used for backing tables for drop-down lists. They may provide further definition to a record, or just be used for reporting. Examples include the following: • Item group • Customer group • Item model group
Num	String	20	This is used for primary keys on worksheet tables, such as the sales order table (`SalesTable`). These fields are usually numbered based on a number sequence, which must have a string size of 20 characters. Examples include the following: • Sales order number • Purchase order number
AccountNum	String	20	This is used for primary key fields for main tables, such as the customer table. These tables are also, usually, based on a number sequence. Examples include the following: • Customer account • Vendor account
Name	String	60	All name fields should be based on this EDT, such as vehicle name, customer name, and so on. This EDT can be used as is, unless we wish to specify a label and help text.
Description	String	60	This is used as the description field on group tables. This EDT is usually used as is, and isn't usually extended.
AmountMST	Real		All monetary value EDTs that store the amount in local currency should be based on this EDT. MST stands for Monetary Standard.
AmountCur	Real		All monetary value EDTs that store the amount in the transaction currency should be based on this EDT.
Qty	Real		All fields that store a quantity should be based on this EDT.

There are many more. Rather than listing them all here, a good practice is to locate a pattern used in standard SCM and follow the same pattern.

Creating setup tables

In this section, we will create a group table. A group table is used as a foreign key on main tables, such as the customer group on the customer table and the vendor group on the vendor table; the customer and vendor tables are examples of main tables. Group tables have at least two fields, an ID and a description field, but can contain more if required.

In this case, to aid the flow, we will create the group table first.

Getting ready

We just need our SCM project open in Visual Studio.

How to do it...

We will create a vehicle group table. We don't have much choice about the name in this as it has to start with our prefix, and end with `Group`; therefore, it will be `ConVMSVehicleGroup`. To create the table, follow these steps:

1. Using the recipe for creating EDTs, create a vehicle group EDT using the following parameters:

Property	Value
Name	ConVMSVehicleGroupId
Label	Vehicle group
Help Text	Used to group vehicles for sorting, filtering, and reporting
Extends	SysGroup

2. Save the EDT, but don't close the designer.
3. From within the project, choose to create a new item.
4. Choose **Data Model** from the left-hand list, and select **Table** from the right.
5. Enter `ConVMSVehicleGroup` in the **Name** field and click **Add**.

6. This opens the table designer in a new tab. From the project, drag the `ConVMSVehicleGroupId` EDT on top of the **Fields** node in the table, as shown in the following screenshot:

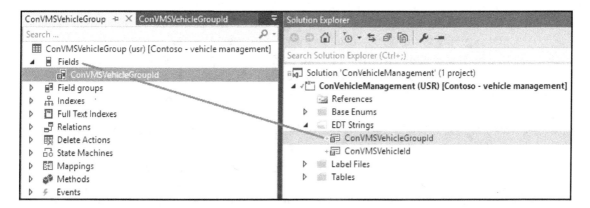

7. This creates the field with the same name as the EDT. As this is our table, we should remove the prefix and name it `VehicleGroupId`.

8. Click **Save**.

9. We can now complete our EDT, open the `ConVMSVehicleGroupId` EDT (or select the tab if it is still open), and enter `ConVMSVehicleGroup` in the **Reference Table** property.

10. Right-click on the **Table References** node, and select **New | Table Reference**.

11. In the property sheet, select the **Related Field** property, and then select **VehicleGroupId** from the drop-down list.

 If the drop-down list is blank, it means that the table is not saved or the **Reference Table** was typed incorrectly.

12. Check that the result is shown as follows:

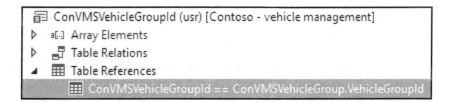

13. Save the EDT, and close its designer. This should make the active tab the `ConVMSVehicleGroup` table designer; if not, reselect it.

14. From **Application Explorer**, which is opened from the **View** menu, expand **Data Types,** and then expand **Extended Data Types**.

15. Locate the **Name** field, and drag it onto the **Fields** node of our table. You can also just type the **Name** field directly into the property value.

16. We will now need to add an index; even though this table will only have a few records, we need to ensure that the **ID** field is unique. Right-click on the **Indexes** node, and choose **New Index**.

17. With the new index highlighted, press the *F2* function key and rename it to `GroupIdx`. Change the **Alternate Key** property to **Yes**. All unique indexes that will be the primary key must have this set to **Yes**.

18. Drag the `VehicleGroupId` field on top of this index, adding it to the index.

 The default for indexes is to create a unique index, so they are correct in this case. Indexes will be discussed later in this chapter.

19. Open the `VehicleGroupId` field properties, and set the **Mandatory** property to **Yes**, **AllowEdit** to **No**, and leave **AllowEditOnCreate** as **Yes**.

 Since we will leave **AllowEditOnCreate** as **Yes**, we can enter the ID, but not change it after the record is saved; this helps enforce referential integrity. The **Mandatory**, **AllowEdit**, and **AllowEditOnCreate** field properties only affect data manipulated through a form. These restrictions aren't enforced when updating data through code.

20. We can now complete the table properties select the table node in the table design (the table name), and complete the property sheet as follows:

Property	Value	Comment
Label	Vehicle groups	This is the plural name that appears to the user. `VehicleGroupTable` is a good label ID for this, as it gives context to others that might want to reuse this label.
Title Field 1	VehicleGroupId	These two fields appear in automatic titles generated when this table is used as a title data source.
Title Field 2	Name	

Cache Lookup	Found	This is linked to the table type, and warnings will be generated should an inappropriate cache level be selected. **None**: no caching is fetched from the DB every time. **NotInTTS**: Fetched once per transaction. **Found**: Cached once found, not looked up again. **EntireTable**: The entire table is loaded into memory. The cache is only invalidated when records are updated or flushed.
Clustered Index	`GroupIdx`	This index is created as a clustered index. Clustered indexes are useful as they include the entire record in the index, avoiding a bookmark lookup. This makes them efficient, but the key should always increment, such as a sales order ID; otherwise, it will need to reorganize the index when records are inserted. This table is small, so it won't cause a performance issue. It will also sort the table in Vehicle Group order.
Primary Index	`GroupIdx`	This defines the primary index and is used when creating foreign key joins for this table.
Table Group	`Group`	This should always be `Group` for a group table. Please refer to the table of table groups in the `Introduction` section.
Created By Created Date Time Modified By Modified Date Time	Yes	This creates and maintains the Created by tracking fields and is useful if we want to know who created and changed the record, and when.
Developer Documentation	The `ConVMSVehicleGroup` table contains definitions of vehicle groups.	This is required for best practice and should contain information that other developers should understand about the table.
FormRef	`ConVMSVehicleGroup`	This is a reference to the display menu item that references the form that is used to view the data in this table. When you choose **View** details in the user interface, it is this property that is used to determine which form should be opened. It is fine to fill this in now for speed, but the build will fail unless we have created the form and menu items.

21. All visible fields should be placed in a field group. Since this is a group table with two fields, we only need an **Overview** field group. Right-click on the **Field groups** node, and choose **New Group**.

22. Press *F2* to rename the group to **Overview** and enter **Overview** in the label property before clicking the ellipsis button in the value. This opens the **Label Lookup** form.

23. Select **Match exactly**, and click search (the magnifying glass icon). Scroll down to find the first **@SYS** label with no description or one that exactly matches our intent, as shown in the following screenshot:

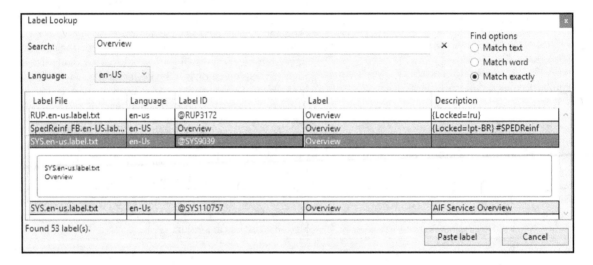

24. Select the **@SYS9039** label and click **Paste label**.

There are some labels provided by the system for purposes like this, and it is useful to remember them. Two common ones are **@SYS9039** for **Overview** field groups and **@SYS318405** for **Details** field groups (with the **Description [group]Details**).

25. Drag the two fields onto the group, and order them so that `VehicleId` is first in the list.

26. In order for any automatic lookups to this table to show both the **ID** and **Description** fields, add both fields to the **AutoLookup** field group.

27. We can skip to the **Methods** node, where best practice dictates we need to provide the `Find` and `Exist` methods.

28. Right-click on the **Methods** node, and choose **New Method**.

29. This will open the code editor, which now contains all methods, and will create a simple method stub, as shown in the following block:

```
/// <summary>
///
/// </summary>
private void Method1()
{
}
```

30. Remove the XML documentation comment section and the method declaration, and then create the `Find` method as follows:

```
public static ConVMSVehicleGroup Find(ConVMSVehicleGroupId
_groupId, boolean _forUpdate = false)
{
    ConVMSVehicleGroup vehGroup;
    if (_groupId != '')
    {
        vehGroup.selectForUpdate(_forUpdate);
        select firstonly * from vehGroup
            where vehGroup.VehicleGroupId == _groupId;
    }
    return vehGroup;
}
```

31. Create a blank line above the method declaration and type three slashes (`///`), which causes SCM to create the XML documentation based on the method declaration. Fill in this documentation as follows:

```
/// <summary>
/// Returns a record in <c>ConVMSVehicleGroup</c>based on the
_groupId
/// parameter
/// </summary>
/// <param name = "_groupId">The Vehicle group ID to find</param>
/// <param name = "_forUpdate">True if the record should be
selected for
/// update</param>
/// <returns>The <c>ConVMSVehicleGroup</c> record</returns>
```

 Should the supplied vehicle group not be found, it will return an empty buffer (where the system `RecId` field is zero). The `_forUpdate` parameter is explained in the *There's more...* section.

32. Now, to create the `Exist` method, go to the end of our `Find` method and create a new line after the method's end brace and just before the final brace for the table, and type as follows:

```
/// <summary>
/// Checks if a record exists in <c>ConVMSVehicleGroup</c>
/// </summary>
/// <param name = "_groupId">
/// The Vehicle group ID to find
/// </param>
/// <returns>
/// True if found
/// </returns>
public static boolean Exist(ConVMSVehicleGroupId _groupId)
{
    ConVMSVehicleGroup vehGroup;
    if (_groupId != '')
    {
        select firstonly RecId
            from vehGroup
            where vehGroup.VehicleGroupId == _groupId;
    }
    return (vehGroup.RecId != 0);
}
```

33. We will have two tabs open, the code editor and the table designer. Close the code editor and save the changes. Then close and save the table designer.

How it works...

Creating a table creates a definition that SCM will use to produce the physical table in the SQL server. Tables are also types that contain a lot of metadata at the application level.

When creating the fields, we don't specify the label, size, or type. This comes from the EDT. We can change the label and give it a specific context, but the size and type cannot be changed.

The relations we created are used at the application level and not within SQL. They are used to generate drop-down lists and handle orphan records. Within the client, you can navigate to the main table. It determines the table via the relation, and uses the **FormRef** property on the table to work out which form to use.

The `Find` and `Exist` methods are a best practice rule, and should always be written and used. For example, although `Select * from PurchLine where PurchLine.InventTransId == _id` may appear to be correct as `InventTransId` is a unique key, it would be wrong as there is now a field on `PurchLine` to flag whether it is marked as deleted. Using `PurchLine::findInventTransId` would only find a record if it was not marked as deleted.

There are also many methods that we can override to provide special handling. When overriding a method, it creates a method that simply calls the `super()` method. The `super()` method calls the base class's (`Common`) method, which for `update`, `insert`, and `delete` is a special method that starts with `do`. The `do` methods cannot be overridden but can be called directly. The `do` method is a method on a base class called `xRecord` that performs the database operation.

The methods for validation, such as `validateField`, `validateWrite`, and `validateDelete`, are only called from events on a form data source; this is covered in `Chapter 3`, *Creating the User Interface*.

There's more...

If you are following this chapter step by step, the following steps will cause a compilation error as we have not yet created the `ConVMSVehicleGroup` display method as specified in the **FormRef** property of the `ConVMSVehicleGroup` table. You can remove this property value for now and complete it when the menu item is created.

It may seem odd to do add this property at this stage, but this is because of the way the recipes have been split in order to aid readability. When creating a table, we would normally create the table, form, menu item, and security privileges all at the same time.

This process has not created the physical table, which is done by the database synchronization tool. The database synchronization is performed against the metadata created when the package is built.

To perform a full database synchronization, we would follow these steps:

1. From the menu, select **Dynamics 365** and then **Build models...**.
2. Check **ConVehicleManagement [Contoso - vehicle management]** and click **Build**.
3. This will take a few minutes to complete, depending on the speed of the VM and the size of the package. When it finishes, you can click **Close**. Any errors will be reported in the **Error list** pane in Visual Studio.

4. Then select **Synchronize database...** from the same menu. This can easily take 20 minutes to complete.

For incremental changes, we can save a lot of time after the first build by taking these steps as we want to test our progress as we develop our solution:

1. Right-click on the project in the **Solution Explorer** and choose **Build**. Monitor the **Output** pane to see when it is complete. Again, any errors are shown in the **Error list** pane.
2. Next, right-click on the project again and choose **Synchronize ConVehicleManagement (USR) [Contoso – vehicle management] with database**.

This process should only take a few minutes to complete.

A note on best practices

You may notice several warnings that state a best practice deviation. Some are to help follow good code standards, such as method header documentation, and others are warnings that could mean a possible error.

There are always two messages that are safe to ignore:

- Assembly "Microsoft.Xbox.Experimentation.Contracts, Version=1.0.0.0, Culture=neutral, PublicKeyToken=d91bba2b903dc20f" failed to load because it was not found.
- Assembly "System.Xml, Version=2.0.5.0, Culture=neutral, PublicKeyToken=7cec85d7bea7798e" failed to load because it was not found.

All best practices aside from the above should be dealt with. Some typical code that BP will highlight is shown in the following sections.

The warnings are generated depending on what is enabled in the **Dynamics 365 | Options | Best Practices** list. You can navigate to this to see the rules that the compiler will check. When suppressing a warning, which should only happen because the rule is a false positive (and not simply to make it go away), you add the following attribute to the method:

```
[SuppressBPWarning('BPErrorSelectUsingFirstOnly', 'A list is required as
the result is processed using next')]
```

In this case, we are suppressing a warning where we have written the following code:

```
private CustTable GetCustomers(CustGroupId _custGroupId)
{
    CustTable custTable;
    select * from custTable where custTable.CustGroupId == _custGroupId;
    return custTable;
}
public void ProcessCustGroup(CustGroupId _custGroupId)
{
    CustTable custTable = this.GetCustomers(_custGroupId);
    while (custTable.RecId != 0)
    {
        // do stuff
        next custTable;
    }
}
```

We would add the declaration just above the method declaration for `GetCustomers`.

Other errors include the following:

- **Updating parameter values directly**: If this is needed, copy the parameter to a local variable instead; this tells the compiler it was deliberate.
- **Assigning an extensible enum to an int**: This should never be done, as the integer value is environment-specific and can vary.
- **Adding a field list to a select call and using select custTable**: This is treated as `select * from custTable`. The compiler is telling us to check whether we really need all of the fields from `custTable`.

There are hundreds of checks like this, and when they refer to any element we have written, we should always take action.

Creating a parameter table

A parameter table only contains one record per company. The table contains a list of fields, which can be defaults or company-specific options used in code to determine what should happen. The parameter table is usually created first, and the various fields that act as parameters are added as we create the solution.

This follows on directly from the *Creating setup tables* recipe.

How to do it...

To create the parameter table, follow these steps:

1. Create a new table called ConVMSPararameters; again, the prefix and suffix are based on best practice. Usually, the name will only be <Prefix>+<Area – if required to scope table>+Parameters.

2. Set the table parameters as follows:

Property	Value
Label	Vehicle management parameters
Title Field 1	
Title Field 2	
Cache Lookup	EntireTable
Table Group	Parameter
Created By, Created Date Time Modified By, Modified Date Time	Yes
Developer Documentation	The ConVMSParameters table contains settings used within the vehicle management solution.

3. Drag the ConVMSVehicleGroupId EDT onto the **Fields** node and rename it to DefaultVehicleGroupId.

4. Drag the ParametersKey EDT from the **Application Explorer** to our **Fields** node.

5. Rename it to Key and change the **Visible** property to No.

This is only used as a constraint to limit the table to only having one record. All visible fields need to be in a field group.

6. Create a field group named Defaults and set the **Label** property. Use the label lookup (the ellipsis button) to locate a suitable label. Note that @SYS334126 is suitable in this case. As always, check the description of the label to understand its usage.

7. Drag the DefaultVehicleGroupId field to the new **Defaults** field group.

We will use this on the parameter form so that it has the heading as `Defaults`. This is why we don't need to change the field's label to specify the context.

8. Right-click on the **Relations** node, and select **New | Foreign Key Relation**. Rename the relation to `ConVMSVehicleGroup`.
9. Complete the parameters as follows; if not specified, leave them as the default:

Property	Value	Description
Related Table	`ConVMSVehicleGroup`	The table to which our foreign key relates.
Cardinality	`ZereOne`	There will be either one or no parameter record relating to the vehicle group record. A one-to-many relationship would use **ZeroMore** or **OneMore**.
Related Table Cardinality	`ZeroOne`	The value is not mandatory, so we can therefore relate to zero vehicle group records, or one.
Relationship Type	`Association`	The parameter record is associated with a vehicle record. Composition would be used in header/lines datasets, where deleting the header should delete the lines records.
On Delete	`Restricted`	This will prevent a vehicle group record from being deleted, if it is specified on this table. See the *There's more* section for more information on delete actions.
Role		This is the role of the relation, and it must be unique within this table. We will need to specify this if we have two foreign key relations to the same table. For example, on the `SalesTable` table, this has two relations to `CustTable` as there are two fields that relate to this table. In that case, the `Role` will need to be populated in order to differentiate them.

10. Right-click on the `ConVMSVehicleGroup` relation and choose **New | Normal**.
11. In the **Field** property, specify the foreign key (the field in this table): `DefaultVehicleGroupId`.
12. In the **Related Field** property, specify the key in the parent table: `VehicleGroupId`.
13. Create a new index called `KeyIdx` and add the `Key` field to it. It is unique by default, so it acts as a constraint index.

14. We can now create the `Find` and `Exist` methods. There is a difference for parameter tables, in that the `Find` method creates a record in a particular way. Create the `Find` method as shown in the following piece of code:

```
public static ConVMSParameters Find(boolean _forUpdate = false)
{
    ConVMSParameters parm;
    parm.selectForUpdate(_forUpdate);
    select firstonly parm where parm.Key == 0;
    if (!parm && !parm.istmp())
    {
        Company::createParameter(parm);
    }
    return parm;
}
```

15. We will use a slightly different `select` statement where we can write the `select` statement inline, which means that we don't have to declare the type as a variable; write the `Exist` method as follows:

```
public static boolean Exist()
{
    return (select firstonly RecId from ConVMSParameters).RecId !=
0;
}
```

16. We want to ensure that the record cannot be deleted. So, we will override the `Delete` method. Press **Return** at the start of the `Find` method to create a blank line at the top. Right-click on this blank line and choose **Insert Override Method | validateDelete**. Change the method so that it reads as follows:

```
public boolean validateDelete()
{
    return checkFailed("@SYS23721"); //Cannot delete transaction
}
```

 This is called to check whether the record can be deleted when the user tries to delete the record in the UI. We could also override the `delete` method should we wish to prevent the record from being deleted in the code. This is done by either commenting out the `super()` call or replacing it with `throw error("@SYS23721")`.

17. We set the **Table Cache** property to `EntireTable`. Whenever this table is updated, we will need to flush the cache so that the system uses the updated values. Override the `update` method as follows:

```
public void update()
{
    super();
    flush ConVMSParameters;
}
```

This tells SCM to write the record buffer with the `super()` call and then flush the cache in order to force the system to read it from the database when it is next read.

There's more...

The build operation will validate and compile the package into a **Dynamic Link Library** (**DLL**). This must be done before we synchronize the database. This can fail, and at this stage, it is normally due to missing references. Within the **Application Explorer**, each element shows the package to which it belongs. We must ensure that our model references all types that we use within our project. If we don't, we will get build errors like this:

Description	Project	File	Line
Path: [AxEdtString/ConVMSVehicleGroupId/Extends]:Extended data type 'SysGroup' does not exist.	ConVehicleManagement (USR) [Contoso - vehicle management]	ConVMSVehicleGroupId.xml	0

To add the required references, we can follow these steps:

1. Locate the type with the error in **Application Explorer**.
2. Note the package it is in, which is in square brackets.
3. Navigate to **Dynamics 365 | Model Management | Update model parameters....**
4. Select the **ConVehicleManagement** model.
5. Click on **Next**.
6. Check if the required package is checked, and then press **Next**.

 We normally reference the `ApplicationPlatform`, `ApplicationFoundation`, and `ApplicationSuite` packages, as we often use elements from these packages.

7. Press **Finish**.
8. Navigate to **Dynamics 365 | Model Management** and select **Refresh models**.
9. Try the build operation again; you may need to repeat this as one error can mask another.

Capitalization of method names

You may notice that the `Find` method started with a capital letter, yet the overridden methods did not. When SCM was first released as AX 7, new methods were created in the same way as with C# and started with a capital letter. Existing methods were then refactored. There is no direct advice as yet as to whether to capitalize the first letter of a method, although it is my preference as it helps to more easily differentiate between methods and public variables when using IntelliSense. So the reason I choose to do this is for readability and because new methods in SCM were created with the first letter capitalized.

Whichever route you take, it is important to be consistent. When overriding methods or implementing a method from an interface, it is critical. In this case, if you implement a method from an interface and change the casing, this will build without error, but will fail at runtime. You may find strange behavior even when overriding methods if the case is different. This is not just the first letter, of course, so using IntelliSense is a much safer way to override methods.

Copying and pasting methods to save time

Be careful when copying the `Find` and `Exist` methods to other tables as a template. As they are static, the methods can technically be on any class or table—that is, check the return type. This can cause some confusion when they behave strangely. As EDTs can be used interchangeably, we won't get a type error unless the base type of the EDT is different. This means that you could pass a variable of the `ConVMSVehicleGroupId` type to `InventItemGroup::Find()` and it would simply return a record (or empty buffer) of the `InventItemGroup` type. So, if we copied the `Find` method from `InventItemGroup` to our table, the following scenarios would be possible:

Code	Result
`ConVMSVehicleGroup group = CustGroup::find(_VehGroupId);`	This would cause a compilation error, as you can't assign an object of the `CustGroup` type to the `ConVMSVehicleGroup` type.

`return` `CustGroup::find(_vehGroupId).Name;`	This would compile without error as the compiler only checks that the base type is correct. `ConVMSVehicleGroupId` and `CustGroupId` are both strings. It will just not behave as expected and will return an empty string as the customer group record will not be found: records are never null.

Optimistic concurrency and selectForUpdate

There are several system fields that are always created on all tables. One of which is `RecVersion`, which is used by **Optimistic Concurrency (OCC)**. Optimistic concurrency is enabled by default on new tables. We select a record "for update" by adding a `forUpdate` clause to a select or while select statement, or by using the `selectForUpdate(true)` method that exists on all tables.

When we select a record for update, a physical lock is **not** placed on the record, and it is therefore possible for two different processes to select the same record for update.

As the record or records are read, they are read from the database into an internal record buffer. When the record is written back, it will check that the value of the `RecVersion` field in the physical table is the same as when the record was fetched into the internal buffer.

If `RecVersion` is different, an exception will be thrown. If this is thrown whilst editing data, the user is given a message that the record has changed and is asked to refresh the data. If the error is thrown within code, we will get an update conflict exception that can be caught. Should the update succeed, the `RecVersion` field will be changed to a different number.

If we are using OCC, we can make the call to `selectForUpdate()` even after the record has been fetched from the database. This is because it does not lock the selected records but states intent that we wish to do so.

See also

The following is some further reading on properties used when creating elements such EDTs and tables:

- Application Explorer properties: `https://docs.microsoft.com/en-us/dynamics365/unified-operations/dev-itpro/dev-ref/application-explorer-aot-properties`

Creating main data tables

In this section, we will create a main table, similar to the customer table. The steps are similar to the vehicle group, and we will abbreviate some of the steps we have already done. The pattern described in this recipe can be applied to any main table using your own data types.

The table in this example will be to store vehicle details. The table design will be as follows:

Field	Type	Size	EDT (: indicates extends)
VehicleId	String	20	*ConVMSVehicleId : Num
VehicleGroupId	String	10	ConVMSVehicleGroupId
RegNum	String	10	* ConVMSRegNum
AcquiredDate	Date		*ConVMSAcquiredDate : TransDate

Note that (*) means we will create the marked EDTs later in this section.

Getting ready

In order to follow these steps, the elements created earlier in this chapter must have been created.

If you haven't created the ConVMSVehicleId EDT, follow the *Creating extended data types* recipe before starting this recipe.

How to do it...

We will first create the required new EDTs, which is done by taking the following steps:

1. Create the ConVMSVehRegNum string EDT with the following properties:

Property	Value
Name	ConVMSVehRegNum
Size	10
Label	Registration—add a comment that this is a vehicle registration number
Help Text	The vehicle registration number

2. We now need the date acquired EDT, so create a date EDT named
   `ConVMSAcquiredDate` with the following properties:

Property	Value
Name	`ConVMSAcquiredDate`
Extends	`TransDate`
Label	Date acquired
Help Text	The date that the vehicle was acquired

 Although we created this EDT as a date, this is mainly for the way it appears. It is created in the database as a date time, and compiles to a **Common Language Runtime** (**CLR**) date time type.

 When creating labels, create the help text label with the same name as the main label, but suffixed with `HT`. You can use copy on the main label (putting, for example, `@ConVMS:DateAcquired` in the paste buffer) and paste it in the **Label** property as usual, but we can simply paste our label into the **Help** property and add `HT` on the end by clicking on the value, pressing *Ctrl + V*, **End**, and typing `HT`. Note that label IDs are case-sensitive!

3. Create a new table and name it `ConVMSVehicleTable`. The convention for main and worksheet header tables is that they starts with a prefix, followed by the entity name as a singular noun, and suffixed with `Table`. Remember tables are types and can't have the same name as other types, such as classes and data types.

4. Drag the following EDTs on to the Fields node in this order:

   - `ConVMSVehicleId`
   - `Name`
   - `ConVMSVehicleGroupId`
   - `ConVMSVehicleType`
   - `ConVMSVehRegNum`
   - `ConVMSAcquiredDate`

 The reason for the order is specifically for the ID, description, and group fields. These are usually placed as the first three fields, and the ID field is usually first.

5. Remove the `ConVMS` prefix from the fields as they are on a table that is in our package. An efficient way is to use the following technique:

   1. Click on the field.
   2. Press *F2*.
   3. Left-click just after `ConVMS`.
   4. Press *Shift + Home*.
   5. Press *Backspace*.
   6. Click on the next field, and repeat from the *F2* step (step 2) for each field.

6. On the `VehRegNum` field, change the **AliasFor** property to `VehicleId`.

 The **AliasFor** property allows the user to enter a registration number in the `VehicleId` field in foreign tables, causing SCM to look up a vehicle and replace the entry with `VehicleId`. This concept is common on most main tables.

7. Make the `VehicleGroupId` field mandatory.

8. Save the table, and open the `ConVMSVehicleId` EDT. Complete the **Reference Table** property as `ConVMSVehicleTable`, right-click on the **Table References** node, select **New Table Reference,** and complete the **Related Fields** property as `VehicleId` from the drop-down list. If the drop-down list does not show the field, we have either not entered the correct table in the **Reference Table** property or we forgot to save the table.

9. Close the designer table for the EDT and navigate back to the table designer.

10. Change the `VehicleId` field properties as an ID field like so:

Property	Value
AllowEdit	No
AllowEditOnCreate	Yes
Mandatory	Yes

 The preceding properties only affect the way the field behaves on a form.

11. A main table `GroupId` field usually has an impact on logic, and is usually mandatory. Even if it does not, we should still make the `VehicleGroupId` field mandatory.

 Careful consideration must be taken when deciding on whether the field is mandatory or when it can be edited. In some cases, the decision on whether it can be changed is based on data in other fields or tables. This can be accomplished in the `validateField` event methods.

12. Do not make the `VehicleType` field mandatory.

 Enums start at zero and increment by one each time. SCM validates this using the integer value, which would make the first option invalid. Since enums always default to the first option, the only way to force a selection from the list would be to make the first element, called `NotSet`, for example, with a blank label. Note that extensible enums cannot be used this way as we can't be certain what the numeric value of the first element is.

13. Create a unique index called `VehicleIdx` with the `VehicleId` field.

14. Group fields are often used for aggregation or search queries; create an index called `VehicleGroupIdx` and add the `VehicleGroupId` field to it. The index must not be unique, which is the default setting for this property.

15. Complete the table's properties as follows:

Property	Value
Label	The vehicles label ID should be `VehicleTable`
Title Field 1	`VehicleId`
Title Field 2	`Name`
Cache lookup	`Found`
Clustered Index	`VehicleIdx`
Primary Index	`VehicleIdx`
Table Group	`Main`
Created By Created Date Time Modified By Modified Date Time	`Yes`
Developer documentation	`ConVMSVehicleTable` contains vehicle records. If there is anything special about this table, it should be added here.
Form Ref	Leave this blank until we have created the form.

16. Create a field group named `Overview`, labeled appropriately (for example, **@SYS9039**), and drag in the fields you wish to show on the main list grid on the form: for example, `VehicleId`, `Name`, `VehicleGroup`, and `VehicleType`. This is to give the user enough information to select a vehicle before choosing to view the details of it; if we add too many fields, it becomes confusing as there is too much information to easily digest.

17. Create a field group, `Details`, and find an appropriate label. Drag in the fields that should show on the header of the form when viewing the details of the vehicle. This should repeat the information from the overview group, as these field groups are not visible to the user at the same point; **Overview** is for the list of records, and **Details** is placed at the top of the details form, where the user would want to review the full details of a vehicle.

18. Main tables are usually referenced in worksheet tables, and SCM will create a lookup for us based on the relation on the foreign table. To control the fields in the automatic lookup, drag the fields you wish to see into the **AutoLookup** field group, and ensure that `VehicleId` is first.

19. Create a foreign key relation for the `VehicleGroupId` field using the following properties:

Parameter	Value
Name	ConVMSVehicleGroup
Related Table	ConVMSVehicleGroup
Cardinality	OneMore: The field is mandatory
Related Table Cardinality	ZeroOne
Relationship Type	Association
On Delete	Restricted

20. Add a normal field relation to the relation, connecting the `VehicleGroupId` fields.

21. It is common to initialize main tables from defaults, held in parameters. The `initValue` method is called when the user creates a new record. Right-click on the **Methods** node and select **Override | initValue**.

22. In the code editor, adjust the code so that it reads as follows:

```
public void initValue()
{
    super();
    ConVMSParameters parm = ConVMSParameters::Find();
    this.VehicleGroupId = parm.DefaultVehicleGroupId;
}
```

There is another method, using the `defaultField` method, which is shown in the *There's more...* section.

23. Next, add the `Find` and `Exist` methods using the table's primary key field as usual.
24. Finally, we will add a field validation method to ensure that the acquisition date is not before today. Override the `validateField` method and add the following code between the `ret = super();` line and `return ret;`:

```
switch (_fieldToCheck)
{
    case fieldNum(ConVMSVehicleTable, AcquiredDate):
        Timezone clientTimeZone =
         DateTimeUtil::getClientMachineTimeZone();
        TransDate today =
         DateTimeUtil::getSystemDate(clientTimeZone);
        if(this.AcquiredDate < today)
        {
            // The acquisition date must be today or later
            ret = checkFailed("@ConVMS:AcqDateMustBeTodayOrLater");
        }
    break;
}
```

25. Create a label for the error message returned by `checkFailed` and replace the literal with the label ID.
26. Once complete, save and close the table code editor and designer tab pages.
27. Should we try to build, we may get the following error:

```
A reference to 'Dynamics.AX.Directory, Version=0.0.0.0,
Culture=neutral, PublicKeyToken=null' is required to compile this
module.
```

28. The error might also read similar to `The identifier Name does not represent a known type`. This means that our package does not reference the `Directory` package. Use **Dynamics 365 | Model Management | Update model parameters**. Select our package, and then add the missing package on the next page. Then choose **Refresh models** from **Dynamics 365 | Model Management**.

How it works...

We have introduced a couple of new concepts and statements in this recipe.

The switch statement should always be used on the `validateField` method, even if we only ever intend to handle one case. An `if` statement might seem easier, but it will make the code less maintainable. This goes for any check like this, where the cases have the possibility to increase.

The next new concept is that we can now declare variables as we need them. This helps with scope, but shouldn't be overused. The `initValue` and `validateField` methods are good examples of explaining where the code should be declared.

The AX 2012 `systemGetDate()` function is deprecated in this release. `DateTimeUtil` provides better handling for time zones. The date can be different across time zones, and can differ between the client's machine (the browser) and the server where SCM is hosted. With SCM the user is completely unaware of where the server is, and could be working anywhere in the world.

In the `validateField` method, we will allow the standard code to run first; the standard call will validate the following:

- That the value is valid for the type, such as a valid date in a date field.
- If the field is a foreign key, check the value exists in the parent table.
- If the field is mandatory, check that it is filled in or that it is not zero for numeric and enum fields.

There's more...

Every element (table, table field, class, form, and so on) has an ID. Tables and fields are commonly referenced by their ID and not by their name. The `validateField` method, for example, uses the field ID as the parameter and not the field name. As we can't know the ID, SCM provides intrinsic functions, such as `tableNum` and `fieldNum` to assist us. The peculiar nature of these functions is that they do not accept a string; they want the type name.

Other intrinsic functions, such as `tableStr`, `fieldStr`, and `classStr`, simply return the type as a string. The reason is that these functions will cause a compilation error should the type be typed incorrectly. If we don't use them, not only do we fail a best practice check, but we make any future refactoring unnecessarily difficult.

Using the defaultField and initValue methods for setting field defaults

When the user presses **New** on a form, the form's data source will create a new empty record buffer for the user to populate prior to saving. A number of events are fired when this occurs and eventually results in a call to `initValue` on the table. This is traditionally where all defaulting logic is placed, and when trying to determine what defaults are set, this is the first place to look.

There seems to be another way in which developers can accomplish this defaulting logic, which is to override the `defaultField` method. This is called as a result of a call to `defaultRow`. The `defaultRow` method is called when a data entity creates a record, and is not called as part of X++ nor the form engine (the events that fire as part of creating a new record on a form's data source). Data entities are used in the office add-in (to enable editing records in Excel, for example) or when importing and exporting data.

We do not use `defaultField` to initialize fields as part of data entry in a form.

Sample code to default the vehicle group field is as follows:

```
public void defaultField(FieldId _fieldId)
{
    super(_fieldId);
    switch (_fieldId)
    {
        case fieldNum(ConVMSVehicleTable, VehicleGroupId):
            this.VehicleGroupId =
             ConVMSParameters::Find().DefaultVehicleGroupId;
            break;
    }
}
```

We would usually create a method called `defaultVehicleGroup` to allow code reuse.

To default field values on new records, we would use `initValue`. The `defaultField` option is described here as it is sometimes used in standard code, such as `PurchReqTable`. It is unusual to look for this method, and can, therefore, cause confusion when fields magically get a default value.

For more information on this, refer to the following:

- Validations, default values, and unmapped fields: https://docs.microsoft.com/en-us/dynamics365/unified-operations/dev-itpro/data-entities/validations-defaults-unmapped-fields

More on indexes

Table indexes are a physical structure that are used to improve read performance, ensure the uniqueness of records, and for the ordering of data in the table. When records are inserted, updated, or deleted, the index is also updated. We must therefore be careful when adding indexes, as they can carry a performance hit when writing data back to the table.

A typical index is an ordered collection of keys and a bookmark reference to the actual data. Finding a record matching a given key involves going to the appropriate location in the index where that key is stored. Then, you will have to follow the pointer to the location of the actual data. This, of course, requires two SCM: an index seek and a lookup to get the actual data.

When we search for a record, SQL Server is able to determine the best index, or indexes, to use for that particular query. If we realize that we often require the same set of fields from a specific query, we can create an index that contains the keys we wish to search on, and the fields we wish to fetch. This improves performance considerably, as SQL will use that index and can then simply return the values that already exist in the index.

We can improve this further by marking the fields we simply wish to return as `IncludedColumn` (a property of the fields in an SCM index). So, in our case, we may wish to select the description from the vehicle table where the vehicle group is `Artic`, for example. Therefore, a solution can be to add the `Name` field to our `VehicleGroupIdx` index and mark it as `IncludedColumn`. However, there is a better solution in this case, which is to use **clustered indexes**.

A clustered index is similar to indexes with included columns, but the clustered index will contain the entire record, avoiding a lookup in the data for any field in the table. Clustered indexes are sorted by their keys; as the index contains the entire record, it can add a significant load to the SQL Server if records are inserted, as opposed to being appended at the end of the table.

For setup tables, where the number of records is small and changes infrequently, this isn't a problem, and the read benefit far outweighs any drawback. For transaction tables, we must be careful. We should always have a clustered index, but the key must be sequential and the records must be added at the end of the table.

An example of this is the sales order table, which has a clustered index based on `SalesId`. This is a great choice as we will often use this key to locate a sales order record, and the field is also controlled by a number sequence; records should always be appended at the end. However, should we change the number sequence so that records are inserted "mid-table," we will experience a delay in inserting records, and we will be adding unnecessary load to the SQL Server.

See also

The following links provide further reading on the topics covered in this recipe:

- X++ compile-time functions (also referred to as **Intrinsic** functions): `https://docs.microsoft.com/en-us/dynamics365/unified-operations/dev-itpro/dev-ref/xpp-compile-time-functions`
- X++ variables and data types: `https://docs.microsoft.com/en-us/dynamics365/unified-operations/dev-itpro/dev-ref/xpp-variables-data-types`

The following link focuses on modeling aggregate data for business intelligence applications, but also contains useful information on **Non-Clustered Column store Indexes** (**NCCI**), which are in-memory indexes used for analyzing aggregate data:

- Model aggregate data: `https://docs.microsoft.com/en-us/dynamics365/unified-operations/dev-itpro/analytics/model-aggregate-data`

Creating order header tables

Order and line tables are used whenever we need a worksheet to enter data that is later acted upon. Once they have been processed, they should no longer be required. Reports should act upon the transactions that the order created, such as inventory transactions, sales ledger transactions, invoices, and more.

Getting ready

Although we will be using the tables created earlier, this pattern can be followed with your own solution.

How to do it...

We will first create the worksheet header table, which will be a vehicle service order table:

1. Create a new table named `ConVMSVehicleServiceTable`.
2. Create a primary key EDT, `ConVMSVehicleServiceId`; this time, extend `Num`. Complete the **Label** and **Help Text** properties with appropriate labels.

3. Drag the EDT from **Solution Explorer** to the **Fields** node of our table and rename it `ServiceId`.

4. Complete the `ServiceId` field as an ID field: **Mandatory** = Yes, **Allow Edit** = No, and **Allow Edit On Create** = Yes.

5. Complete the relation information on the `ConVMSVehicleServiceId` EDT.

6. Create the primary key index as `ServiceIdx` with `ServiceId` as the only field.

7. Set the **Clustered Index** and **Primary Index** properties as `ServiceIdx`.

8. Drag the `ConVMSVehicleId` EDT to our table and rename it `VehicleId`.

9. Make the `VehicleId` field mandatory set **Ignore EDT relation** to Yes.

 The decision to make the field editable depends on the associated logic (referential integrity) and the business requirements. Ignoring the EDT relation is the best practice method, and forces us to create a relation on the table.

10. Create a foreign key relation for `ConVMSVehicleId` to `ConVMSVehicleTable.VehicleId`. Dragging the table on to the **Relations** node can save some time, but this creates a normal relation and not a foreign key relation.

 The cardinality should be `OneMore` as it is mandatory. **On Delete** should be `Restricted` on foreign key relations to main tables.

11. Drag the `Name` EDT onto our table from **Application Explorer**.

12. Create a new `Base Enum` for the service status, as defined here:

Property	Value
Name	ConVMSVehicleServiceStatus
Label	Status (for example, @SYS36398 will suffice)
Help	The service order status
Is Extensible	True: remember we cannot use this for the ranking of relative comparisons (> or <) with this set

13. Add the following elements:

Element	Label
None	No label so that it appears empty in the UI
Confirmed	Confirmed
Complete	Complete
Cancelled	Cancelled

14. Save and drag the new `ConVMSVehicleServiceStatus` enum to our table and rename it `ServiceStatus`.
15. Make the `ServiceStatus` field read only. **Allow Edit** and **Allow Edit On Create** should be **No**. This is because **Status** fields should be controlled through business logic.
16. Create the date EDTs `ConVMSVehicleServiceDateReq` "Requested service date" and `ConVMSVehicleServiceDateConfirmed` "Confirmed service date." The dates should extend `TransDate`. Label them appropriately and drag them to the new table.
17. Rename the fields to `ServiceDateRequested` and `ServiceDateConfirmed`.
18. Complete the table properties as shown here, which are common for all tables of this type:

Property	Value
Label	Vehicle service orders
Title Field 1	`ServiceId`
Title Field 2	`Name`
Cache lookup	Found
Clustered Index	`ServiceIdx`
Primary Index	`ServiceIdx`
Table Group	WorksheetHeader
Created By Created Date Time Modified By Modified Date Time	Yes
Developer Documentation	`ConVMSVehicleServiceTable` contains vehicle service order records
Form Ref	Blank until we have created the form

19. Create the fields groups as follows:

Group name	Label	Fields
Overview	Overview (@SYS9039)	• ServiceId • VehicleId • Name • ServiceStatus
Details	Details (@SYS318405) You could also create a more helpful label of service details	• ServiceId • VehicleId • Name • ServiceStatus
ServiceDates	Service dates	• ServiceDateRequested • ServiceDateConfirmed

20. Create the now usual `Find` and `Exist` methods using `ServiceId` as the key.

21. You can also create your own validation on the service dates, using `validateField`. For example, check that the service dates can't be before today.

22. We can also validate that the record itself can be saved. This introduces the `validateWrite` method. This is to enforce the requirement that only service orders at status confirmed or less can be changed; the method should be written as follows:

```
public boolean validateWrite()
{
    boolean ret;
    ret = super();
    ret = ret && this.CheckCanEdit();
    return ret;
}
public boolean CheckCanEdit()
{
    if (!this.CanEdit())
    {
        //Service order cannot be changed.
        return checkFailed("@ConVMS:ServiceOrderCannotBeChanged");
    }
    return true;
}
public boolean CanEdit()
{
    switch (this.ServiceStatus)
    {
        case ConVMSVehicleServiceStatus::None:
        case ConVMSVehicleServiceStatus::Confirmed:
```

```
        return true;
    }
    return false;
}
```

23. Finally, we will write a method that initializes the defaults from the main table record, that is, `vehicle`, when it is selected. Write the following two methods:

```
public void InitFromVehicleTable(ConVMSVehicleTable _vehicle)
{
    this.Name = _vehicle.Name;
}
public void modifiedField(FieldId _fieldId)
{
    super(_fieldId);
    switch(_fieldId)
    {
        case fieldNum(ConVMSVehicleServiceTable, VehicleId):

    this.InitFromVehicleTable(ConVMSVehicleTable::Find(this.VehicleId))
;
            break;
    }
}
```

24. Save the table and close the editor tabs.

How it works...

There are few new concepts here. I'll start with the code structure at the end of the step list.

The most important part of this code is that we didn't write `this.ServiceStatus <= ConVMSVehicleServiceStatus::Confirmed`. This is an extensible enum, and we can't be sure of the numeric value that the symbols have.

The other part is that we have split what may seem to be a simple `if` statement in `validateWrite` into three methods. The reason is reusability. It is nicer to make a record read-only in the form than it is to throw an error when the user tries to save. So, we can use `CanEdit` to control whether the record is editable on the form, making all controls greyed out.

Check methods are written to simplify the creation and maintenance of validation methods, and also to make the checks reusable, ergo consistent. Check methods are expected to return a silent true if the check passes, or to display an error should the check fail. The error is sent to the user using the `checkFailed` method, which does not throw an exception.

The next method is the `InitFrom` style method. This is a very common technique and should always be used to initialize data from foreign tables. It may seem odd that we don't check that it exists first.

This is deliberate. Records in SCM initialize so that all the fields are empty or zero (depending on the field type). So, if the record is not found, the values that are initialized will be made to be empty, which is desirable. Also, `modifiedField` occurs after the field is validated. So, the method won't be triggered should the user enter an invalid vehicle ID. If the vehicle is not mandatory, we may find the vehicle ID is empty; however, again, this is fine.

There's more...

The **On Delete** property for table relations is similar to the functionality controlled by the **Delete Actions** node on the table. The difference is that the **Delete Action** is placed on the parent table. This is a problem if the parent table is a standard table, as this is now locked for customization (over-layering). Using the **On Delete** property is therefore controlled in a much better location, even if the result is the same. Because of this, we should always use the same place for this, which should be the relation.

We have the following options for both **Delete Actions** and the **On Delete** property:

- None
- Restricted
- Cascade
- Cascade + Restricted

None has no effect, and effectively disables the delete action; this is useful if you want to specifically state "Do nothing" so someone else doesn't try to correct what seems to be an omission.

Restricted will prevent the record from being deleted, if there are records in the related table that match the selected relation. This occurs within the `validateDelete` table event, which is called by the `validateDelete` form a data source event.

Cascade will delete the record in the related table based on the relation; it is no use having a sales order line without a sales order. This is an extension to the delete table event.

Cascade + Restricted is a little special. In a two-table scenario, it is the same as Restricted; it will stop the record from being deleted if a related record exists. However, if the record is being deleted as part of a cascade from a table related to it, which records will be deleted.

Creating order line tables

This recipe continues from the *Creating order header tables* recipe. The example in this recipe is that we will have service order lines that reflect the work required on the vehicle. The concepts in this recipe can be applied to any order line table; to follow along exactly, the previous recipes should be completed first.

How to do it...

To create the order line table, follow these steps:

1. Create a new table named ConVMSVehicleServiceLine.
2. Drag the following EDTs onto the table:

   - ConVMSVehicleServiceId (set **Ignore EDT** relation to **Yes**)
   - LineNum
   - ItemId (set **Ignore EDT** relation to **Yes**)
   - ItemName
   - ConVMSVehicleServiceStatus

3. Remove the ConVMSVehicle prefixes.
4. The ServiceId and LineNum fields are usually controlled from code, so make them read-only and mandatory (this ensures that the code that sets them has run before the user saves the line).

 The LineNum field is usually used to order the lines, and can be made not visible if it isn't to be displayed in the user interface. All visible (non-system) fields should either be in a field group or made not visible.

5. Make ItemId mandatory and only allow it to be edited on creation.

6. Create a unique index called `ServiceLineIdx`, and add the `ServiceId` and `LineNum` fields. We will use this as a clustered index as it will naturally sort the lines on the form.

7. Add a relation to `ConVMSVehicleServiceTable`, but service lines are contained within a service order record, so complete it as follows:

Property	Value
Name	ConVMSVehicleServiceTable
Related Table	ConVMSVehicleServiceTable
Cardinality	ZeroMore
Related Table Cardinality	ZeroOne
Relationship Type	Association
On Delete	Cascade

8. Ensure that this relates to `ServiceId`, and then add a relation to `InventTable` on `ItemId`, using the following properties:

Property	Value
Name	InventTable
Related Table	InventTable
Cardinality	OneMore
Related Table Cardinality	ExactlyOne
Relationship Type	Association
On Delete	Restricted

9. Create an `Overview` group to control what appears on the lines and add all fields. In our case, this is sufficient. We would usually have many more fields on a line, and we would organize the fields into logical groups that are used in the form design. We wouldn't usually add the foreign key or line number; these would be in a group called `Identification` (`@SYS5711`).

10. Update the table properties as follows:

Property	Value
Label	Vehicle service order lines
Title Field 1	ItemId
Title Field 2	ItemName
Cache lookup	Found
Clustered Index	ServiceLineIdx
Primary Index	SurrogateKey (default)
Table Group	WorksheetLine

Created By Created Date TimeModified By Modified Date Time	Yes
Developer documentation	`ConVMSVehicleServiceLine` contains vehicle service order line records

11. The `Find` and `Exist` methods will need two keys in this case, `ServiceId` and `LineNum`. The `select` statement clause should be written as follows:

```
select firstonly *
    from line
    where line.ServiceId == _id
        && line.LineNum == _lineNum;
```

12. Finally, we need to initialize the `ItemName` field, and the user selects an item; write the following two methods:

```
public void InitFromInventTable(InventTable _inventTable)
{
    this.ItemName = _inventTable.itemName();
}
public void modifiedField(FieldId _fieldId)
{
    super (_fieldId);
    switch (_fieldId)
    {
        case fieldNum(ConVMSVehicleServiceLine, ItemId):
          this.initFromInventTable(
          InventTable::find(this.ItemId));
            break;
    }
}
```

13. Once complete, save and close the code editor and designer tabs.

How it works...

The first new concept is the use of the clustered index to control the order in which the records are displayed in grid controls. This is simply using the fact that SQL will return records in the order of the clustered index. Composite keys are fine for this purpose, but we just wouldn't usually use them as a primary key. See the *There's more...* section on surrogate keys.

One point to be highlighted here is to look at the `initFromInventTable` method. The pattern is straightforward, but the call to `inventTable.itemName()` is a method, hence the parentheses. The declaration for the method is as follows:

```
public ItemName Display itemName([Common]).
```

As all tables derive from `Common`; we can pass in any table, which is as true as it is pointless. If we look at the method, it can actually only handle `InventDim`. The reason isn't obvious, but it could be used to handle a different table through the extension of a pre-post handler method. Reading through the methods is always a good investment, taking time to understand the reason why the code was written that particular way.

There's more...

Surrogate keys have some history, which is important to understand. These were introduced in AX 2012 as a performance aid and allowed features like the ledger account lookup when entering general ledger journals. The problem is that they are hardwired to be `RecId`. So, when we added foreign key relations, the field created contained an unhelpful 64-bit integer. To solve this, an alternate key was added, which is a property on the index definition. This allows a more meaningful relation to be used for a foreign key. The primary key could only be unique indexes that have the **Alternate Key** property set.

The other type of key introduced was the replacement key. The replacement key is a way to show a meaningful key, other than the numeric `RecId` based `SurrogateKey`.

What `SurrogateKey` still allows us to do is to use `RecId` as the foreign key, but shows meaningful information from a field group on the parent table. An example is that we could add a foreign key relation to `ConVMSServiceOrderLine`, which should use `SurrogateKey`. When we add the foreign key, containing the meaningless number, we add a `ReferenceGroup` control that can display fields from a field group on the `ConVMSServiceOrderLine` table; the user is oblivious to the magical replacement that is going on behind the scenes.

Performance is no longer a reason to use surrogate keys, and they should be seldom used. The following are the main drawbacks of surrogate keys:

- Tables that don't have a natural index as a primary key cannot be used in a data entity (unless they are manually crafted).
- It will not be possible to use the table using the *Open in Excel* experience.
- Transferring data between systems is more complicated.
- Reporting and business intelligence is made more complex.

In the case of our service line table, a new natural key would be needed if we wanted to use it with data entities or to edit the data in Excel.

See also

For more information on the history surrogate keys from AX 2012, please read:

- Table Keys: Surrogate, Alternate, Replacement, Primary, and Foreign: `https:// docs.microsoft.com/en-us/dynamicsax-2012/developer/table-keys- surrogate-alternate-replacement-primary-and-foreign`

3
Creating the User Interface

In this chapter, we will perform many of the tasks required while creating a user interface. This chapter continues from Chapter 2, *Data Structures*. As we discussed in that chapter, we usually create tables and forms as part of the same process. So, the recipes in this chapter will involve completing a few properties in the data model.

When creating forms, we must provide consistency to the users, and to aid with this, we will use form design patterns. The form design pattern is determined by the table group, as stated in Chapter 2, *Data Structures*. There are special cases when we can have variations but, for the main part, we should stick to the patterns suggested in this chapter.

The process of creating data structures, forms, and menu items has been split into discrete steps in order to make the recipes easier to read and digest. This also allows for more advanced concepts to be introduced as we progress. The actual workflow when creating a data entry form would be as follows:

1. Create new items for the table, form, and menu items using copy and paste so that they all have the same name (such as ConVMSVehicleTable).
2. Create a label and help text and object reference properties for the menu item.
3. Populate the table labels, the form design caption property, and menu item labels.
4. Complete the table as per the recipe in Chapter 2, *Data Structures*.
5. Complete the form design as described in this chapter.
6. Complete any business logic as described in Chapter 4, *Working with Form Logic and Frameworks*.
7. Create security keys (at least privileges and duties) as per Chapter 10, *Data Management, OData, and Office*.

In this chapter, we will cover the following recipes:

- Creating the menu structure
- Creating a parameter form
- Creating menu items
- Creating setup forms
- Creating details master (main table) forms
- Creating a details transaction (order entry) form
- Creating form parts
- Create tiles with counters for the workspace
- Creating a workspace
- Adding a filter to a workspace

Technical requirements

You can find the code files for this chapter on GitHub at `https://github.com/PacktPublishing/Extending-Microsoft-Dynamics-365-Finance-and-Supply-Chain-Management-Cookbook-Second-Edition/blob/master/Chapter%203.axpp`.

Creating the menu structure

The menu structure is carried over from the user interface concepts in AX 2012. In **Supply Change Management** (**SCM**), the menus have the same structure, but are opened from the *burger* menu button, just below **Finance and Operations** on the top left of the page, as shown in the following screenshot:

Each menu appears under the **Modules** option, as shown in the following screenshot:

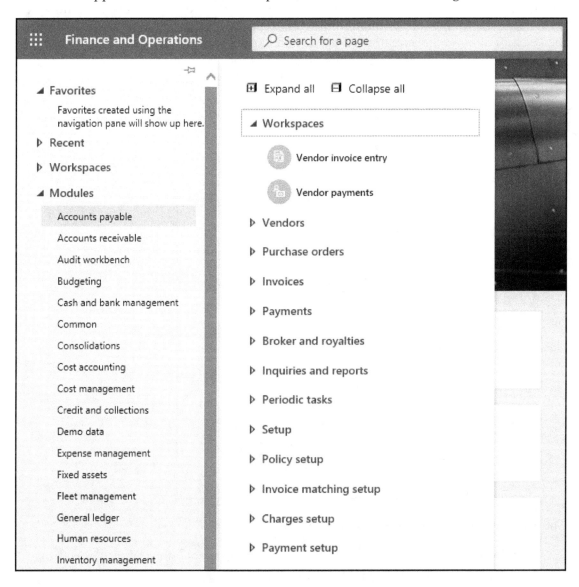

All the menu items for forms, reports, and processes must be placed in the menu structure, even if we create a workspace later.

The menu structure may seem to have been relaxed slightly from the rigid structure recommended in Dynamics AX 2012. In Dynamics AX 2012, we always have the following main headings in a menu: **Common**, **Inquiries**, **Reports**, **Periodic**, and **Setup**. If we look at the `AccountsPayable` menu in the **Application Explorer**, we will see that the old structure has been flattened, as shown in the following screenshot:

The actual structure is now organized as follows:

- **Workspaces**: `VendInvoiceWorkspace, VendPaymentWorkspaceTile`
- **Details Master (Main) tables**: `Vendors`
- **Details Transaction (Worksheets)**: `PurchaseOrders, VendorInvoices`
- **Journals**: `Payments`
- **Inquiries and Reports**: `VendPackingSlipJournal, VendTransList, VendAccountStatementInt`

- **Periodic tasks**: `PeriodicTasks`
- **Set up and configuration**: `Setup`, `PolicySetup`, and so on

The menu still needs a common structure in order to make it easier for users to find the options more easily, but we aren't constrained to a rigid structure. You may argue that the menu does not have a workspace node. This is because this was added through a menu extension, as shown in the following screenshot:

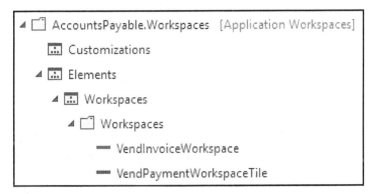

There is a drawback to Microsoft using extensions on their own elements: we cannot hide elements that have been added through extensions.

Getting ready

We are continuing from `Chapter 2`, *Data Structures*, so we should have the project from that chapter open.

How to do it...

To create the menu structure, follow these steps:

1. Add a new item to the project (select a folder node and press *Ctrl + Shift + A*).
2. Select **User Interface** from the left-hand list and then **Menu** from the right.
3. Type `ConVMSVehicleManagement` into the **Name** field and press **OK**.
4. In the designer, create a label for **Vehicle management** and enter this as the menu's **Label** property.

5. Right-click on **New Menu** in the designer and choose **New | Submenu**.
6. Add the following labels for the submenus:

Name	Label
Workspaces	Workspaces
Vehicles	Vehicles
ServiceOrders	Service orders
PeriodicTasks	@SYS76406
InquiriesAndReports	@SYS3850
Setup	@SYS333869

7. We can add more submenus to help organize the structure, should this be required.
8. Save and close the menu designer.
9. Now, we need to extend the main menu so that we can navigate to our menu.
10. In the **Application Explorer**, navigate to **AOT | User Interface | Menus**.
11. Right-click on **MainMenu** and choose **Create extension**.

 This creates an extension to the **MainMenu** menu, but does not customize (over-layer) it, allowing our change to sit nicely alongside the other extension of the same element without having to do a code merge, should a colleague also change the same element in a different project. In that case, they would suffix their extension with the project name (for example).

12. Rename the new item in our project from `MainMenu.ConVehicleManagement` to `MainMenu.ConVMSVehicleManagement`.

 A recent change in the development tools caused the naming extensions of tables, forms, and menus to be suffixed with the package name. This was `ConVehicleManagement` in our case. This isn't much different from the package name, but in most cases, it will be very different. For example, we must have a package named `ConContractManagementSystem` and the project could be `ConCMSPurchOrderEntry` – we want to know the change was for the purchase order entry change at a glance.

13. Open `MainMenu.ConVMSVehicleManagement`.
14. Right-click on the root node and choose **New | Menu reference**.
15. Set the **Name** and **Menu Name** properties to `ConVMSVehicleManagement`.
16. Save and close the designer.

How it works...

This is a structure that we can add various menu items to. This structure is present when the user opens the menu from the left-hand **Menu** button from within the client-user interface.

This will become more apparent as we complete the user interface.

Creating a parameter form

Parameter forms show settings grouped into field groups and tabs using a table of contents-style form. They are also used to show the number of sequences that have been set up for that module. Number sequences will be covered in Chapter 4, *Working with Form Logic and Frameworks*. We will be following our vehicle management sample solution in this recipe, but this pattern can be applied to any parameter table.

How to do it...

To create a parameter form, follow these steps:

1. Select a group in the project and press *Ctrl + Shift + A* or choose **New | Item** from the right-click context menu.
2. Select **User Interface** from the left-hand pane and **Form** from the right-hand pane. Use ConVMSParameters as the **Name**.

 It is the convention to give the form and table the same name for most forms that are used to edit or maintain data.

3. This will open the form designer. Drag the ConVMSParameters table from the project onto the **Data Sources** node in the top-left pane of the form designer.

4. Data sources provide additional options for how this table should behave on this form. We don't want the user to be able to delete and create records, so change the following properties to **No**:

- **Allow Create**
- **Allow Delete**
- **Insert At End**
- **Insert If Empty**

5. The form designer is broken into three areas: the **Form** pane, the **Design** pane, and the **Preview/Pattern** conformance pane, as shown in the following screenshot:

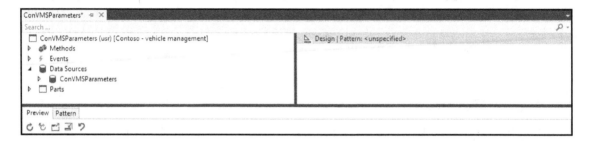

6. Let's apply some basic properties for the form, which are held against the **Design** node, as shown here:

Property	Value	Comment
Caption	Vehicle management parameters	This is shown in the title of the form and is usually the table's label.
Data Source	ConVMSParameters	Child nodes in the form will use this as the default Data Source property.
Title Data Source	ConVMSParameters	This form will use the title field properties from the table and display them on the form.

7. The **Design** node states that a pattern is unspecified, which we must specify. To apply the main form pattern, right-click on the **Design** node and choose **Apply Pattern | Table of Contents**.

8. The lower pane changes to the **Pattern** tab and shows the pattern's required structure, as shown in the following screenshot:

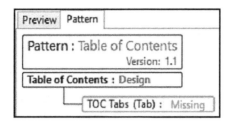

9. This allows us to add a Tab control, so right-click on the **Design** node and choose **New I Tab**.

10. The error is removed from the **Pattern** pane but shows that we have no tab pages within the **TOC Tabs (Tab)** pattern element.

11. First, rename the new control to `ParameterTab`, and then add a new **Tab Page** by right-clicking on it in the **Design** pane and selecting **New Tab Page**.

12. The first tab is usually a general settings tab, so name this new control `GeneralTabPage`.

13. Find a suitable label for **General** and enter that into the **Caption** property.

14. As we alter the design, the designer will continually check that we are conforming to the pattern. It has found the following issues with the tab page control:

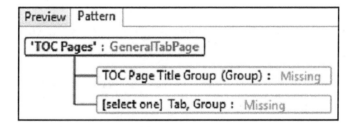

15. Here, we must add two **Group** controls: one for title fields that will provide help to the user and another for the fields we wish to show on this page.

16. Right-click on the `GeneralTabPage` control and select **New I Group**.

Once this is done, reselect the `GeneralTabPage` control and note that the pattern conformance pane has changed from a red error to a yellow warning. This means that the controls below this level have pattern conformance errors.

17. Rename the new group control `GeneralTitleGroup`.

All controls must be unique and named in a way that helps us navigate to the control easily, should we get a build error later on.

18. The pattern conformance pane shows we must have a `StaticText` control for the main title, and 0 or 1 `StaticText` controls for a secondary title. Right-click on `GeneralTitleGroup` and choose **New | Static Text**.

19. Rename the new `StaticText` control `GeneralTitleText`.

20. Create a new label for the text **General** parameters and enter the ID into the **Text** property.

21. Reselect the `GeneralTitleGroup` control and check if the pattern errors are gone.

22. Reselect `GeneralTabPage`, as we now have one pattern error for a missing group, and add a new **Group** control.

23. The new **Group** control knows that it must also have a pattern applied to it, as indicated by the **Pattern: <unspecified>** text after the control's name. Right-click on the control and choose **Apply Pattern | Fields and Field Groups**.

24. Rename the **control** `GeneralFields`.

25. On the form pane, expand **Data Sources**, `ConVMSParameters`, and then **Field Groups**.

26. Drag **Field group** and **Defaults** onto the `GeneralFields` control in the design pane, as shown in the following screenshot:

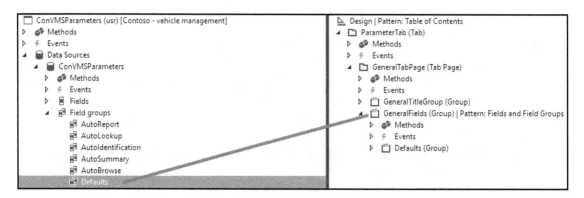

We can manually create groups and then add the appropriate fields. However, when using a field group, any new fields that are added to the group will be automatically added to the form, and the **Label** property will be set based on the field group's label.

27. Check each node for pattern conformance errors.

28. Finally, we have a special task for parameter forms: to ensure that at least one record exists. For this, click on the form's **Methods** node and choose **Override | init**.

29. Create a blank line before the call to super() and enter the following line of code:

```
ConVMSParameters::Find();
```

> We don't care about the return value in this case. We are using the fact that the Find method for parameter tables will automatically create a record if the table is empty.

30. Save and close the code editor and form designer tabs.

How it works...

When we specify the form design's main pattern, we are then guided regarding what controls we should add and where. This helps us ensure that the forms we design follow a best-practice user interface design, which in turn makes our forms easier to use, quicker to train, and less prone to user error.

We can still opt out of the pattern using the Custom pattern; this allows us to add any control in any order. This should be avoided, and the form's design should be redesigned so that it uses standard patterns.

There's more...

The form is based on the FormRun class. We can see this by opening (double-clicking) classDeclaration for the ConVMSParameters form:

```
public class ConVMSParameters extends FormRun
```

This differs from AX 2012, where the declaration was public class FormRun extends ObjectRun, which was probably a little more honest as the form is not a type; this is why it can have the same name as a table.

This is actually a definition file that FormRun instantiates in order to build and execute the form.

Once the system has built the form design using SysSetupFormRun, it will perform the initialization tasks and run the form. The key methods in this are Init and Run. These can be overridden on the form in order to perform additional initialization tasks.
One of FormRun's Init method's key tasks is to construct the form's data sources; these aren't table references but FormDataSource objects constructed from the tables listed under the Data Sources node.

In the case of the ConVMSParameters form, the system creates the following objects from the ConVMSParameters data source for us:

- ConVMSParameters as ConVMSParameters (table)
- ConVMSParameters_DS as FormDataSource
- ConVMSParameters_Q as Query
- ConVMSParameters_QR as QueryRun

We aren't normally concerned with the Query and QueryRun objects as we can access them through the FormDataSource object anyway.

The data sources are declared as global variables to the form and provide a layer of functionality between the form and the table. This allows us to control the interaction between the bound form controls and the table.

Let's override the init method on the data source, and then override the modifiedField event (which is triggered from a form's data source events); the code editor will present the change as follows:

```
[Form]
public class ConVMSParameters extends FormRun
{
    public void init()
    {
        ConVMSParameters::Find();
        super();
    }
    [DataSource]
    class ConVMSParameters
    {
        public void init()
        {
```

```
        super();
    }
    [DataField]
    class DefaultVehicleGroupId
    {
        public void modified()
        {
            super();
        }
    }
    }
}
```

It adds the data source as a class within the form's class declaration, and then adds the field as a class within the data source class. This is the only place in SCM where this occurs. If the data source class were a class, it would have to extend `FormDataSource`. The `Form`, `DataSource`, and `DataField` attributes are a clue as to what's going on here. As all executable code compiles to .NET types, the compiler uses these attributes in order to create the actual types. The structure is written as such for our convenience in order to present the code.

Let's take the `modifiedField` method. This is an event that occurs after the `validateField` event returns true. The call to `super()` calls the table's `modifiedField` method. We may wonder why the call to `super()` has no parameter. This happens behind the scenes, and it is useful that this is handled for us.

This pattern is followed for the following methods:

DataSource method	Calls table method
validateWrite	validateWrite
write	write (in turn, insert or update)
initValue	initValue
validateDelete	validateDelete
delete	delete
DataField.validateField	validateField(FieldId)
DataField.modifiedField	modifiedField(FieldId)

The table's `initValue`, `validateField`, `modifiedField`, `validateWrite`, and `validateDelete` methods are only called from form events; the `write` method does not call `validateWrite`.

From this, we have a choice as to where we place our code, and this decision is very important. The rule to follow here is to make changes as high as possible: table, data source, and form control.

It is important that the code on a form is only written to control the user interface. It should not contain validation or business logic.

We can go further with this and write form interaction classes that allow user interface control logic that can be shared across forms; for instance, controlling which buttons are available to a list page and the associated detail form.

See also

For further reading on what was covered in this recipe, please check out the following links:

- General form guidelines: `https://docs.microsoft.com/en-us/dynamics365/unified-operations/dev-itpro/user-interface/general-form-guidelines`
- Form styles and patterns: `https://docs.microsoft.com/en-us/dynamics365/unified-operations/dev-itpro/user-interface/form-styles-patterns`

Creating menu items

Menu items are references to an object that we wish to add to a menu. We have three types of menu items: `Display`, `Output`, and `Action`. `Display` is used to add forms, `Output` is used for reports, and `Action` is used for classes.

Menu items are also added as privileges to the security system. Users that aren't administrators will not be able to see the menu items unless they are assigned a role, duty, or privilege that gives them access to the menu item's required access level.

Getting ready

We will just need a form, report, or class to create a menu item.

How to do it...

To create a new menu item, follow these steps:

1. Choose to add a new item to the project.
2. Select **User Interface** from the left-hand pane and **Display menu item** from the right-hand pane.
3. Give the menu item the same name as the form; in this case, ConVMSParameters.
4. Use the label from the table (vehicle management parameters). It is also OK to use the label @SYS7764 as the **Label** property, but having a label enhances the search experience when users try to find your form through the search feature.
5. Create a help text label for maintaining the vehicle management settings and number sequences. Assign the ID to the **HelpText** property.
6. Enter ConVMSParameters for the **Object** property.
7. The ObjectType property is a **Form** by default, so this is correct.
8. Save the menu item and open the ConVMSParameters table, and then enter ConVMSParameters into the **Form Ref** property.
9. Finally, open the ConVMSVehicleManagement menu and drag the ConVMSParameters menu item on top of the **Setup** node.
10. Save and close the open tabs.

How it works...

Although this recipe is listed in isolation, this should always be done.

For example, the process of creating a parameter table involves four main steps:

1. Create the table.
2. Create the form.
3. Create the menu item.
4. Add the menu item to the menu.

Nearly all of the tables that we create in SCM will have a form that is used to maintain it. So, the last part of the table's design is to tell the table design which form is used for that purpose. This is how the **View details** option works in the client. The foreign key is used to determine the table, while the table's **Form Ref** property is used to determine the form to be used. The foreign key's details are then used to filter the form. All this happens automatically based on the metadata.

Menu items for forms and reports trigger the system to build and execute the form or report definition. The form is rendered in the browser using some very clever JavaScript that interfaces with the server and reports are essentially rendered using SSRS. Classes must have a static entry point method in order to be called. This will be covered in Chapter 4, *Working with Form Logic and Frameworks*.

Creating setup forms

This follows a similar pattern to the parameter form. Using the table in Chapter 2, *Data Structures*, we know that we should use **Simple list** or **Simple list and Details - List Grid** patterns. Our table has two fields, so we will use the **Simple list** form design pattern here. This follows the pattern of creating a table of the **Group** type.

How to do it...

To create a form, follow these steps:

1. Choose to add a new item to the project.
2. Select **User Interface** from the left-hand pane and **Form** from the right-hand pane.
3. Name the form as per the table's name; in this case, ConVMSVehicleGroup.
4. Drag the ConVMSVehicleGroup table from the project onto the **Data Sources** node of the form designer.
5. Use the same label that you used for the table for the **Caption** property of the **Design** node.
6. Set the **Title Data Source** and **Data Sources** properties to the table name, that is, ConVMSVehicleGroup.
7. Apply the **Simple List** pattern to **Design** (right-click and choose **Apply Pattern | Simple List**).

We will use the pattern's conformation errors as our to-do list. If we don't conform to the pattern, the project will not build. However, just conforming to the pattern may not be enough; the build will also spot some errors in properties, which are stated as being mandatory by the pattern.

8. Add an **ActionPane** control; rename this `FormActionPaneControl` as there will only be one on this form.

We don't need to specify the **Data Source** property as this will default from the **Design** node.

9. Reselect the **Design** node. The pattern highlights that we need a **Custom Filter Group**, which is a Group control. So, add a new control of the **Group** type.
10. Rename the control `CustomFilterGroup` for ease of reference.

Apart from navigating form build errors, this becomes more important for complicated patterns as we will be able to see if the pattern is using the correct control. The name is how the pattern knows which controls map to the pattern's structure.

11. We can see that the new group control needs a pattern; assign **Custom and Quick Filters**.
12. Now, we need to go even further. The pattern highlights that we must have one **QuickFilterControl**. Right-click on the `CustomFilterGroup` control and choose **New | QuickFilterControl**.

We will need to link this to a **Grid** control, so we will complete this control a little later.

13. Right-click on the **Design** node and select **New | Grid**.
14. We can rename the control `FormGridControl` as there will only be one grid control with this pattern.
15. The **Data Source** property does not inherit from the parent node. We must specify this as `ConVMSVehicleGroup`.
16. We created an `Overview` field group for this table, so set the **Data Group** property to `Overview`.

Rename the container controls before adding fields to them or setting the **Data Group** property as the fields will be prefixed with the container control's name.

17. Go back to the **QuickFilter** control and set **Target Control** to the grid control's name and **Default Column** to the desired default control of the target control.
18. Double-check the pattern pane for errors and save the form.
19. Next, create a menu item using the same name as the form and the same label that we used in the **Caption** property.
20. Fill in the table's **Form Ref** property with the menu item name.
21. Finally, add the menu item to the setup menu so that it lies under the **Parameters** menu item.

How it works...

The steps for this recipe were similar to the steps for the parameter form, although there were just a few more to complete. We can see that the pattern is actually a to-do list, although pattern errors will prevent the project from being built.

There's more...

If you want to actually test the form, you can do so by following these steps:

1. Build the package using **Dynamics 365 | Build Models**; select the package from the list.
2. If we added tables or fields since the last database synchronization, synchronize the databases by right-clicking on the project and choosing **Synchronize <your project name> with database**.
3. Open the project's properties.
4. Set the **Startup Object Type** option to `MenuItemDisplay`.
5. Set the **Startup Object** option to the menu item to open, for example, `ConVMSVehicleGroup`.
6. Specify **Initial Company**; `USMF` is a useful company for when we are using the developer VMs that use Microsoft's demo data.
7. Close the property form and press *F5*.

This is a typical method of how to debug code, and should a breakpoint be encountered, Visual Studio will move to the fore and allow us to debug the code.

Creating details master (main table) forms

For those of you who are used to Dynamics AX 2012, this style of form replaces the List page and separates the Details form that's used for main tables, such as Products and Customers. List pages are effectively deprecated for this purpose. This may seem a little confusing at first, as we are developing two views of a form at the same time. However, once we have done this a few times, we will get used to the process.

The pattern pane will be our guide in this recipe as it will help us simplify the process and remind us when we have forgotten a key step. We will be continuing with the form design for the main table, that is, ConVMSVehicleTable. However, this recipe can be used as a pattern for any main table.

How to do it...

To create the details master form, follow these steps:

1. Choose to add a new item to the project.
2. Select **User Interface** from the left-hand pane and **Form** from the right-hand pane.
3. Name the form as per the table's name; in this case, ConVMSVehicleTable.
4. Drag the ConVMSVehicleTable table from the project onto the **Data Sources** node of the form designer.
5. Select the ConVMSVehicleTable data source and set the **Insert If Empty** and **Insert At End** properties to **No**.

 Insert If Empty will create a new record if there are no records, which is undesirable for the main table and order header tables. The **Insert At End** property can also be undesirable; if the user presses the down arrow key on the last record, a new empty record will be created.

6. Use the same label as the table for the **Caption** property of the **Design** node.
7. Set the **Title Data Source** and **Data Sources** properties to the table name, that is, ConVMSVehicleTable.

8. Apply the **Details Master** pattern to the **Design**.

9. As required by the pattern, add an **Action Pane** control named `FormActionPane`.

10. Add a **Group** control called `NavigationListGroup`. This section is used in the details view so that the user can change records without going back to the list view.

 The tasks for `NavigationListGroup` are similar to the **Simple List** pattern, so the steps will be summarized here.

11. Under the `NavigationListGroup` control, create a **Quick Filter** control and name it `NavgationQuickFilter`.

12. Then, create a **Grid** control named `NavigationGrid`.

 The tasks for `NavigationListGroup` are similar to the **Simple List** pattern, so the steps will be summarized here.

13. Set the **Data Source** property of the grid control to `ConVMSVehicleTable` and add the **VehicleId** and **Name** fields by dragging them from the **Fields** node of the data source.

 We can add whichever fields we like here, but keep the number of fields to just a few as this information is presented in cards on the left-hand side of the form. It is intended to allow the user to select a record without them having to navigate back to the main list view of the form.

14. Complete the quick filter control with **Target Control** as the **Grid** control and **Default Column** as desired.

15. Checking the nodes on and under the **Design** node, we need to create a **Tab** control for the **Panel** Tab. Create a new **Tab** control named `PanelTab`.

 Here, you can see that we have a tab page for the details panel and the list panel. The system controls the pages that are visible for us.

16. Add a tab page named `DetailsPanelTabPage` first, and then `ListPanelTabPage`.

> The pattern seems to make a mistake as we add `DetailsPanelTabPage` and it thinks that we are adding the list panel. It corrects itself once we have created the second tab page control.

17. Let's complete the `ListPanelTabPage` control first. As required by the pattern, under this control, add a **Group** control named `ListQuickFilterGroup` and a **Grid** control named `ListGrid`.

18. Complete the **Grid** control's **Data Source** property and use the Overview field group for the **Data Group** property.

19. We will complete `ListQuickFilterGroup` in the same way as we did for the Simple List pattern. Apply the **Custom** and **Quick Filters** patterns to the control. Then, add a **Quick Filter** control and name it `ListQuickFilter`. Complete the control by referencing it to the **Grid** control we named `ListGrid`.

20. The `ListPanelTabPage` pattern now states that we will need **Main Grid Default Action**, which is a Command Button control. Add a **Command Button** to `ListPanelTabPage` named `ListGridDefaultActionButton`.

21. On the `ListGrid` control, enter `ListGridDefaultActionButton` for the **Default Action** property, which is in the **Behavior** group toward the top of the property sheet.

22. Moving on to the **Details Panel** pattern element, reselect the `DetailsPanelTabPage` control and add a Group control named `DetailsTitleGroup`.

23. Add a **String** control named `DetailsHeaderTitle` for the heading title. Set the **Data Source** property to `ConVMSVehicleTable` and the **Data Method** property to `titleFields`.

> The `titleFields` method is a system-provided data method that uses the title field properties from the table. We can write our own, should we wish to.

24. Checking our progress against the pattern pane, we will see that we need to add the **Details Tab (Tab)** pattern element. Add a new **Tab** control to the `DetailPanelTabPage` tab page control named `DetailsTab`.

25. Add a new tab page named `DetailsTabGeneral` and apply the **Fields and Field Groups** pattern. The first tab page is usually named this and shows key information about the record. Create a label for **General vehicle details** and use the label as the **Caption** property.

26. In this case, we can simply drag the **Details** field group from the `ConVMSVehicleTable` data source, but feel free to reorganize the fields into more appropriate groups as desired.

 Should new field groups (or fields) be added, you can refresh the data source by right-clicking on the data source and choosing **Restore.**

27. We will need to create the display menu item using the same label as the table's, but we will need to default **Form View Option** to **Grid** so that we can get the list view when the form is opened.

28. Next, complete the **Form Ref** property of the `ConVMSVehicleTable` table.

29. Finally, add the menu item to our menu under the **Vehicles** section.

How it works...

The concept is the same as for any form – we just have more features. The peculiar part of this form is that we have two views – one for the list view and the other for editing or viewing the details of the form.

This is done by showing and hiding the detail and list tabs. It knows which control to show or hide because we followed the pattern, which means that pattern conformation errors must result in a compilation error.

To test this on the development virtual machine provided by Microsoft, build the project and use the following URL:
`https://usnconeboxax1aos.cloud.onebox.dynamics.com/?cmp=usmf&mi=ConVMSVehicleTable`.

You can use this pattern to open any display menu item.

There's more...

Since we aren't using a special create form to create new vehicles, SCM will just add a record using the current form view. If the form is in the **Grid** view, it will just add a new line to the grid. This isn't great as it won't usually have all the required fields when creating a new record. So, we should tell the form to change to the details view when a record is created.

To do this, right-click on the **method** for the main table (ConVMSVehicleTable, in this case) and choose **Override** | **Create**.

Write the following code:

```
public void create(boolean _append = false)
{
    element.viewOptionHelper().setViewOption(FormViewOption::Details);
    super(_append);
}
```

This should always be done when we are not using a specialized form to create new records.

Creating a details transaction (order entry) form

These worksheet forms are the most complicated in terms of the steps required as we now have three states to design: list, header, and lines views. To familiarize yourself with the end result, open and use the **All purchase orders** form from **Accounts Payable** | **Purchase orders** | **All purchase orders**.

The first part of the pattern is very similar to the **Details Master** pattern, so we will summarize the details slightly. We will continue with the vehicle service order table, but again, this recipe has been written so that it can be applied to any worksheet table.

How to do it...

To create the details transaction form, follow these steps:

1. Choose to add a new item to the project.
2. Select **User Interface** from the left-hand pane and **Form** from the right-hand pane.
3. Name the form as per the table's name; in this case, `ConVMSVehicleServiceTable`.
4. Drag the `ConVMSVehicleServiceTable` table from the project onto the **Data Sources** node of the form designer.
5. Select the `ConVMSVehicleServiceTable` data source and set the **Insert If Empty** and **Insert At End** properties to **No**.
6. Drag the `ConVMSVehicleServiceLine` table to the **Data Sources** node and set **Insert If Empty** to **No**.
7. Select the `ConVMSVehicleServiceLine` data source and set the **Join Source** property to `ConVMSVehicleServiceTable`.

 We don't specify any join information beyond the name as it will use the foreign key relation defined in the child table.

8. Override the `initValue` method on `ConVMSVehicleServiceLine` so that we can set the `ServiceId` field as this is not set for us. Use the following code to do so:

```
public void initValue()
{
    super();
    ConVMSVehicleServiceLine.ServiceId =
ConVMSVehicleServiceTable.ServiceId;
}
// Whilst here, add the form view change code so that the form
changes to the details form
// when new is pressed1
public void create(boolean _append = false)
{
element.viewOptionHelper().setViewOption(FormViewOption::Details);
    super(_append);
}
```

9. Close the code editor and go back to the form-designed tab.
10. Set the properties as follows:

Property	Value
Caption	It is usually fine to use the label from the table. You can also create a label such as `Service order details` as this caption shows when the details view of the form is shown.
Data Source	`ConVMSServiceTable`.
Title Data Source	This can be `ConVMSServiceTable`. If you wish the title bar to use the title fields from the line table, use this instead.

11. Apply the **Details Transaction** pattern to the **Design** node.
12. Add an Action Pane control named `HeaderActionPane` and then a **Group** control called `NavigationListGroup` under the **Design** node.

We will have two Action Panes: one for the header and one for the lines.

13. Add a **Quick Filter** control to the `NavigationListGroup` control named `NavgationQuickFilter`.
14. Then, create a **Grid** control named `NavigationGrid`.
15. Set the **Data Source** property of the **Grid** control to `ConVMSVehicleServiceTable` and add the `ServiceId` and `Name` fields from the `ConVMSVehicleServiceTable` data source.
16. Fill in the Quick Filter control with **Target Control** as the **Grid** control and **Default Column** as desired.
17. Under the **Design** node, create a **Tab** control for **Main Tab**. Create a new **Tab** control and name it `MainTab`.
18. Add a tab page named `DetailsPanelTabPage` first, and then `GridPanelTabPage`.

The names differ from the **Details Master** pattern. We will name our controls after the text control descriptions in the **Pattern** pane.

19. We will complete the `GridPanelTabPage` control first. Under this control, add a **Group** control named `GridPanelQuickFilterGroup` and a **Grid** control named `MainGrid`.

20. Complete the **Grid** control's **Data Source** property and use the `Overview` field group for the **Data Group** property.

21. For `GridPanelQuickFilterGroup`, apply the **Quick Filters** pattern to the control. Then, add a **Quick Filter** control and name it `GridPanelQuickFilter`. Complete the control by referencing it to the grid control we named `MainGrid`.

22. The pattern now states we need **Main Grid Default Action**, which is a Command Button control. Add a **Command Button** to `GridPanelTabPage` called `MainGridDefaultAction`.

23. On the `MainGrid` control, enter `MainGridDefaultAction` for the **Default Action** property.

> After platform 21, this feature will be deprecated and removed in future versions. This will be replaced with sticky actions, as described at `https:/ /docs.microsoft.com/en-gb/business-applications-release-notes/ October18/dynamics365-finance-operations/sticky-default-action`.

24. To complete the **Details Panel (TabPage)** pattern element, reselect the `DetailsPanelTabPage` control and add a **Group** control named `DetailsPanelTitleGroup`.

25. Add a String control named `DetailsPanelHeaderTitle`, setting **Data source** to `ConVMSVehicleServiceLine` and the **Data Method** property to `titleFields`.

> To have more control, we can add fields manually to a group. To do this, create a group under the `DetailsPanelTitleGroup` control called `DetailsPanelStatusGroup`, and then drag the `ServiceStatus` field from the `ConVMSVehicleServiceTable` table. Rename the field control to `DetailsPanelTitle_ServiceStatus`.

26. Now, we need to complete the **Header and Line Panels (Tab)** pattern element. Add a new **Tab** control to `DetailPanelTabPage` named `HeaderAndLinePanelTab`.

27. Add a new tab page for the **Lines Panel** pattern element named `LinesPanelTabPage`.

28. Add a second tab page for the Header panel named `HeaderPanelTabPage`.

29. Add a new **Tab** control to the `LinePanelTabPage` control named `LineViewTab`.

30. We will now add three tab pages to this control.

31. Add the **Line View Header Details (TabPage)** pattern element named `LineViewHeader` and apply the **Field and Fields Groups** pattern. Set the **Label** property to `Vehicle service order details`.

32. Drag the `Details` and `ServiceDates` field groups from the `ConVMSVehicleServiceTable` data source to the `LineViewHeader` tab page.

33. Add the **Line View Lines (TabPage)** pattern element named `LineViewLinesPage` and set the **Caption** property to a label such as `Service order lines`.

34. Add the **Line View Line Details (TabPage)** pattern element named `LineViewLineDetailsTabPage` with the **Label** property set to `Service order line details`.

35. Set the **Data Source** properties for `LineViewLineDetailsTabPage` and `LineViewLinesPage` to `ConVMSVehicleServiceLine`.

36. Add an **Action Pane** control to the `LineViewLinesPage` tab page control named `LinesActionPane`, and under that, a **Button group** control named `LineActionRecordActions`. Do not set the **Data Source** property as this will inherit from the parent tab page control.

> For this action pane, we will need to add buttons to add and remove lines. These are only added automatically in the main header Action Pane control.

37. Under the `LineActionRecordActionsGroup` button group, add a **Command** button named `LineActionAddLine`.

38. This is to allow the user to add and remove lines to and from the lines grid. Set the properties of the command control as follows:

Property	Value	Description
Normal Image	AddLine	This adds a plus symbol (+).
Text	@SYS319116	Adds a line.
Command	New	This triggers the new record task for the data source.

> See the *See also* section of this recipe for the link to the Symbol Fonts home page, where you can find the current list of symbols that can be used.

39. Then, add a second **Command** button named `LineActionRemove` and set the properties as follows:

Property	Value	Description
Normal Image	`Delete`	This adds a waste bin symbol.
Text	`@SYS135131`	Removes a line.
Command	`DeleteRecord`	This triggers the delete record task for the data source.

Since the Action Pane control takes its data source from the parent tab control, the Action Pane is generic and can be copied to other forms that need add and delete controls, which is where the **Toolbar and List pattern** is used.

40. Add a new **Grid** control to the `LineViewLinesPage` tab page control named `LinesGrid`. Set the **Data Source** to `ConVMSVehicleServiceLine` and the **Data Group** to `Overview`. Even though the data source is set on the parent control, this is not used by **Grid** controls, which means it must be set explicitly on the control.

As we usually have many more fields that can realistically fit in the grid, we have a tab control that allows the user to see these fields grouped in a logical order using tab pages.

41. Create a **Tab** control under `LineViewLineDetailsTabPage` named `LineViewDetailsTab`.

42. We would usually add one or more tab pages here, but for our case, we will only need one.

43. Add a **Tab Page** control named `LineViewDetailsTabDetails` using the **Fields and Field Groups** pattern. Then, create a label and use it to set the **Caption** property.

44. Drag `AutoIdentification` and `Details` from the `ConVMSVehicleServiceLines` data source.

45. Now, we need to complete the header view of the form, which is governed by the **Header Panel** pattern element. Right-click `HeaderPanelTabPage`, choose **New | Tab**, and set the **Data Source** property to `ConVMSVehicleServiceTable`.

46. We usually have many field groups to add but, in this case, we just need one. Create a new **Tab Page** control named `HeaderDetailsTabDetails`, apply the **Fields and Field Groups** pattern, and set the **Caption** property to `@ConVMS:Details` (a generic label that's created for `Details`).

47. Drag the `Details` and `ServiceDates` field groups from the `ConVMSVehicleServiceTable` data source, but rename them with a prefix of `HeaderDetailsTabDetails`.

48. We will need to create the menu item using the same label as the table's, but we will need to default **Form View Option** to **Grid** so that we can get the list view when the form is opened.

49. Then, complete the **Form Ref** property of the `ConVMSVehicleServiceTable` table.

50. Finally, add the menu item to our menu.

How it works...

This process, albeit extended, is the same as it is for the **Details Master** pattern. There are some additional properties to set in this case to help with the form's behavior. There are a lot of steps to follow here, and it is easy to get lost and potentially set the wrong property. This is why we name the controls after the pattern element.

This form pattern was deliberately as simple as it can be. Once we are comfortable with this process, it should become more straightforward to expand it to more complicated data structures.

See also

It is always very important to keep track of new features, as well as those that have been deprecated. Deprecated features are those that will be removed in future updates and will show a build warning when they are used. For further reading regarding this and what was covered in this recipe, check out the following links:

- What's new or changed: `https://docs.microsoft.com/en-us/dynamics365/unified-operations/fin-and-ops/get-started/whats-new-changed`
- Deprecated features: `https://docs.microsoft.com/en-us/dynamics365/unified-operations/dev-itpro/migration-upgrade/deprecated-features`
- Symbol fonts page: `https://mbs.microsoft.com/customersource/Global/AX/downloads/hot-fixes/AXSymbolFont`

Creating form parts

Form parts are used for two purposes. One is to provide a pop-up form as you hover over a foreign key, such as the popup when you hover over the product number when entering sales or purchase orders. This is great for users as it means they don't necessarily have to navigate away from the task they are performing.

Their other purpose is to create a reused form part that we can place within other forms. We could have a form part that contains product information, which we could add to the product and sales order forms. We can specify a link when we add the form part, making them easy to implement.

The example that we're going to use in this recipe is used so that we can add a list of service orders to a workspace form.

Getting ready

In this recipe, we will create a simple form part, which is a list of vehicle service orders, so we will only need to create a table that the data will be displayed on.

How to do it...

To create a form part for open vehicle service orders, follow these steps:

1. Create a new form called `ConVMSVehicleServiceOpenPart`.
2. Drag the `ConVMSVehicleServiceTable` table to the **Data Sources** node.
3. Set the properties of the data source as follows:

Property	Value
Allow Edit	No
Allow Create	No
Allow Delete	No
Insert If Empty	No
Insert At End	No

4. Set the properties of the Design node as follows:

Property	Value
Data Source	ConVMSVehicleServiceTable
Show Delete Button	No (although the data source properties should hide the Edit, Delete, and New buttons)
Show New Button	No

5. Apply the **Form Part Section List** pattern as we intend to add this to a workspace as a subform. The other options for usage scenarios are as follows:

Pattern	Usage scenario
Form Part Section List	Typically used in the section list area of a workspace form.
Form Part Section List Double	Not commonly used. This is so that you can have two grids on the form part.
Form Part Factbox Card	Added to the Parts node of a form to show key information related to the current record in a card view.
Form Part Factbox Grid	Added to the Parts node of a form to show key information in a grid view.

6. Add a new group control named HeaderGroup and apply the **Filters and Toolbar - inline** pattern.
7. Add a group to this called FilterGroup and add a **Quick Filter** control to this.
8. Reselect the HeaderGroup control and add an **Action Pane** control called ToolbarActionPane.
9. Add a **Button Group** control named ToolbarButtonGroup.
10. Drag the ConVMSVehicleServiceTable **Display menu item** onto the button group and set the properties as follows:

Property	Value
Name	ActionNew
Text	@SYS2055 (New)
Normal Image	New
Form View Option	Details
Open Mode	New
Data Source	ConVMSVehicleServiceTable

11. Drag the menu item a second time, this time to edit the currently selected service record. To do this, set the following properties:

Property	Value
Name	ActionEdit
Text	@SYS453 (Edit)
Normal Image	Details
Form View Option	Details
Open Mode	Edit
Data Source	ConVMSVehicleServiceTable

12. Create a new grid control under the **Design** node named ContentGrid.

13. Set the **Data Source** property to ConVMSVehicleServiceTable and drag the fields, as desired, from the data source to the grid. The list should be as small as possible, but should provide enough information to the user so that they can decide on the appropriate action to take.

 A field group is a good choice, but ensure that the group name provides enough context regarding its purpose so that it can be used to guide other developers in the team.

14. Set the **Default Action** property of the grid to ActionEdit.

15. Create a menu item using the same name as the form part, that is, ConVMSVehicleServiceOpenPart. Set the **Object** and **Label** properties as usual.

How it works...

Form parts are just forms, but the pattern forces us to design them in accordance with how the form part will be used. This is why there are four types of form part patterns.

We will use what we've learned in this recipe when we create the workspace form later. **Form Part FactBox Card** is also very useful and easy to create. Just use the pattern to create the form part, create a menu item from it, and complete the table's **Preview Part Ref** property.

Later, we will use queries and composite subqueries to apply filters to forms. We can use the technique of specifying a query, or one of the query's composite queries, to a menu item. This means that we can have one form part, but the menu item can be used to apply a filter to the form.

Creating tiles with counters for the workspace

Tiles are used as entry points to a form while also having the ability to show information about the data at hand. They can act as prompts for actions and are presented on the tile section of a workspace, as shown in the following screenshot:

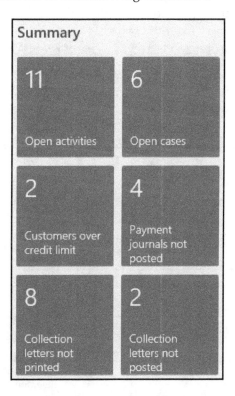

The page that opens when you first sign into SCM is also a list of tiles, and each opens a workspace. The workspace will have an image resource that we can design. A key guideline is that all the graphics are minimalistic. All solutions should look and feel as if they are part of the standard solution.

Getting ready

This recipe can be used to create a tile for any form and is usually done for **Details Master** and **Details Transaction** to show all the records and commonly used subsets of data.

In this case, we will create a tile for all vehicles, and then a tile for a type of vehicle. The most efficient method of creating tiles is to create a query (or composite query), then a tile, and then a menu item. The tile and query usually have the same name.

How to do it...

To create tiles, follow these steps:

1. First, we will create a query that the tile will use. Create a new Dynamics 365 item and select **Query** from the **Data Model** artifacts.
2. Set **Name** to `ConVMSVehicleTableAll` and press **Add**.
3. Drag the `ConVMSVehicleTable` table to the **Data Sources** node.
4. Change the **Dynamics Fields** property to **Yes** as we need all the fields to be available when queries are used with a form. Any fields that aren't selected are initialized with empty values, not null.
5. Choose to add a new **Dynamics 365 item** and select **Tile** from the **User Interface** node.
6. Change **Name** to `ConVMSVehiclesAllTile` and press **Add**.
7. Set the following properties:

Property	Value	Description
Query	ConVMSVehicleTableAll	The query the tile is based on and to be passed to the target menu item.
Label	All vehicles	Create a label just for this purpose.
Menu Item Name	ConVMSVehicleTable	The target menu item that's opened when the tile is clicked.
Normal Image	GenericDocument	The icon. This should be blank if the tile needs a counter. Not all tiles have counts as the number acts as a call to an action.
Copy Caller Query	**Yes**	Copies the query from the caller to this element and can be passed onto the target menu item.

Now, we will create a tile for bikes, which uses a composite query. These are used to add filters to a base query.

8. Create a new artifact and choose **Composite Query** from the **Data Model** node.
9. Set **Name** to `ConVMSVehicleTableBikes` and press **Add**.
10. In the **Query** property, enter `ConVMSVehicleTableAll`.
11. Right-click on the **Ranges** node and select **New Composite Query Range**.
12. In the **Data Source** property, select `ConVMSVehicleTable`.
13. Set the **Field** property to `VehicleType`.
14. We will enter the criteria by entering the enum's symbol in the **Value** property. So, enter `Bike` in the **Value** property.
15. Create a new tile called `ConVMSVehicleBikesTile`.
16. The tile will adjust the count correctly, but the resulting list of vehicles may not be filtered – even with **Copy Caller Query** set. We should create a new menu item named `ConVMSVehicleTableBikes` and set the **Query** property to `ConVMSVehicleTableBikes`.
17. Complete the properties of the tile as follows:

Property	Value	Description
Query	ConVMSVehicleTableBikes	The query the tile is based on. It controls the count value on the tile.
Label	Bikes	Create a label just for this purpose.
Menu Item Name	ConVMSVehicleTableBikes	The target menu item that's opened when the tile is clicked.
Normal Image	Blank	The icon. This should be blank if the tile has a counter. Not all tiles have counts as the number acts as a call to an action.
Copy Caller Query	**Yes**	Copies the query from the caller to this element and can be passed onto the target menu item.
Type	Count	Changes the type of the tile so that it shows a count of the records in the query.

18. This process would need to be followed for each vehicle type. Once you're done, save and close all the designer tabs.

How it works...

Tiles have two basic properties: the source query and the target form's menu item. When the tile is clicked, the query is applied to the target form, filtering the data. The **Copy Query Caller** property is important here, and if the filter doesn't appear to work, it is nearly always because this property wasn't set. This technique of applying queries can also be applied to menu items, and we can create menu items that will open the vehicle table filter based on the query. This is done by specifying the **Query** and **Copy Caller Query** properties on a duplicate of the menu items.

When experimenting with filters, don't filter based on data that the user can change; a tile for a particular vehicle group would be a bad idea or an anti-pattern. Tiles are static metadata, and vehicle groups are end-user controlled. If a vehicle group is to be used to control business logic, it must be related via a parameter or enumerated type.

There's more...

A good tile is a tile that takes you to service orders due tomorrow, so we will need to filter based on a function.

In the query range's **Value** property, we can also enter query functions. The standard functions are defined in the `SysQueryRangeUtil` class. So, to filter on today's orders, you will enter `(currentDate())` in the query range's **Value** property.

We used to modify this class to add new functions in Dynamics AX 2012, but since overlayering is no longer possible against standard elements, we have to look at other methods.

Create a new class and call it `ConVMSQueryRangeUtil`. The name is not important. To create a method that returns a date a number of days away from today, use the following code:

```
[QueryRangeFunction]
public static date RelativeDate(int relativeDays = 0)
{
    utcdatetime currentDateTime;
    currentDateTime = DateTimeUtil::applyTimeZoneOffset(
        DateTimeUtil::getSystemDateTime(),
        DateTimeUtil::getUserPreferredTimeZone());

    return
DateTimeUtil::date(DateTimeUtil::addDays(currentDateTime, relativeDays));
}
```

To use the preceding function to return tomorrow's date, add a new range for the required date field and enter `(ConVMSQueryRangeUtil::RelativeDate(1))` in the **Value** property. To filter records on or before tomorrow, use `..(ConVMSQueryRangeUtil::RelativeDate(1))`.

Creating a workspace

The workspace is an area where everything a user will need for a task or group of tasks will be held. The workspace should be able to display all of the key information without scrolling, and is structured as a horizontal space with the following sections:

- Tiles
- Tabbed lists of key data
- Charts (optional)
- Power BI (optional)
- Related information; for example, links to key forms

The dashboard is normally created once we have completed most of the solution; otherwise, we will have nothing to add. The pattern can be easily transposed to your own requirements.

How to do it...

To create the workspace, follow these steps:

1. Create a new form and name it `ConVMSVehicleWorkspace`.
2. Apply the **Workspace Operational** pattern to the **Design** node.

 You can also use the Workspace, which provides a simpler design where we will only show tiles and links

3. Complete the **Caption** property for the **Vehicle management** workspace.
4. Add a **Tab** control and call it `PanoramaTab`, following the idea that we will name controls along the lines of the pattern element we are creating.

5. Create the `PanoramaSectionTiles`, `PanoramaSectionTabbedList`, and `PanoramaSectionRelatedLinks` tab pages. Apply the form pattern. You should only have one choice here. It should be related to the name of the page we created. This only happens if we create it in the order listed.

6. Complete `PanageSectionTiles` by setting the **Caption** property to Summary (which means we need to create a label for Summary).

7. Right-click on `PanageSectionTiles` and choose **New | Tile Button**.

8. Set the name to `ConVMSVehiclesAllTile` and enter this as the **Tile** property. Set the **Copy Caller Query** property to **Yes**.

9. Repeat this for the remaining tiles.

10. Select the `PanoramaSectionTabbedList` control and set the **Caption**; for example, `Service orders`.

11. Add a new **Tab** control named `TabbedListTab`.

12. Add a page named `TabbedListPageOrders`. Set the **Caption** property to `Service orders`.

13. On this tab page, add a new **Form Part** control, setting the **Name** and **MenuItemName** properties to `ConVMSVehicleServiceOpenPart`. Set the **Run Mode** property to `Local`.

14. Select the `PanoramaSectionRelatedLinks` tab page control and set the **Caption** property to `Related information`.

15. Add a new Group control to the page named `LinksSetupGroup`. Create a label named `Setup` and use it as the **Caption** property.

16. Drag the `ConVMSParameters` and `ConVMSVehicleGroup` menu items to this group.

17. Save and close the designer tabs.

18. Create a menu item for the form using the label we used in the **Caption** property.

19. We will need a tile for the main navigation workspace. Create the tile as follows:

Property	Value
Name	ConVMSVehicleWorkspaceTile
Menu Item Name	ConVMSVehicleWorkspace
Normal Image	Workspace_PurchaseReceiptAndFollowup (this is a cheat way of doing things; more on resources later)
Size	Wide
Tile Display	BackgroundImage

20. Locate the `navpanemenu` menu in **Application Explorer**, right-click on it, and choose **Create extension**.

21. Rename it `navpanemenu.ConVMS`.

22. Open the menu extension. Right-click on the root node and choose **New** | **Submenu**.

23. Rename the new submenu `ConVMSMenu`.

24. Right-click on the submenu and choose **New** | **Menu Element Tile**.

25. Set the **Tile** property to `ConVMSVehicleWorkspaceTile`.

26. Copy the **Menu Element Tile** control and paste it under the `Workspace` node of our menu, that is, `ConVMSVehicleManagement`.

27. Save and close all the windows and perform a build.

How it works...

The form design here is just like the other forms, and much simpler than the Details Master and Transaction patterns. The clever part of this is that we are thinking in the form of the task at hand. We are creating a workspace based on what the user does. The traditional form design from Dynamics AX 2012 provided all the features that the user could want, which resulted in a lot of features that most users never used. With workspaces, the concept is that most of the workspace is used regularly. The user shouldn't have to change workspaces to locate a form for that task. It is also OK for a user to use more than one workspace. We want to provide everything the user needs, but without clutter.

Adding a filter to a workspace

It can be useful to focus the task being worked on in the workspace to a dataset, such as a specific vehicle group. Workspaces have the ability to implement an interface that automatically filters the data presented on the workspace. This recipe follows on from the previous recipe.

How to do it...

To add filters, follow these steps:

1. On the Design node, right-click on **Design** and choose **New** | **Group**.

2. Move it to the top (*Alt* + *Arrow* is useful) and apply the **Workspace Page Filter Group** pattern. Name it `WorkspacePageFilterGroup`.

3. Add a new **String** control and name it `VehicleGroupFilter`. Change the **Extended Data Type** property to `ConVMSVehicleGroupId` and set **Auto Declaration** to **Yes**.

4. Expand **Methods** and double-click on `ClassDeclaration`.

5. We need to tell the form engine that this workspace now implements the `SysIFilterProvider` interface. Change the declaration so that it reads as follows:

```
public class ConVMSVehicleWorkspace extends FormRun implements
SysIFilterProvider
```

6. We need to declare a change event handler on the form that is used by the form engine. Add the following line as a form global variable (the first line after the brace, after the class declaration):

```
SysFilterChangeEvent changeEvent;
```

7. Next, we need to initialize the `changeEvent` variable, and also restore the value of the filter from the user's last session. Add the following method, which overrides the `FormRun init` method:

```
public void init()
{
    super();
    // restore the value of the filter from the user's saved data
    SysFilterLastValueHelper::getLastValue(VehicleGroupFilter);
    // initialise the changeEvent variable
    changeEvent =
     SysFilterChangeEvent::newFromFormControl(VehicleGroupFilter);
}
    // override close so that it saves the last value used in the
    // filter control
public void close()
{
    super();
    // save the last filter option chosen by the user for next time
    // the form is opened
    SysFilterLastValueHelper::saveLastValue(VehicleGroupFilter);
}
```

8. Add the following methods, as required by the interface:

```
public SysFilterChangeEvent parmChangeEvent()
{
    return changeEvent;
}
public SysIFilter parmFilter()
{
    SysIFilter filter = SysFilterFactory::createEmptyFilter();
    SysFilterValueResolutionMethod filterValueResolutionMethod =
      SysFilterValueResolutionMethod::All;

    ConVMSVehicleGroup vehGroup =
     ConVMSVehicleGroup::Find(VehicleGroupFilter.text());
    SysIFilterValue filterValue =
            SysFilterValueFactory::createFilterValueForString(
                vehGroup.VehicleGroupId,
                extendedTypeNum(ConVMSVehicleGroupId));
    if (vehGroup)
    {
        filterValueResolutionMethod =
         SysFilterValueResolutionMethod::None;
    }
    filter.addItem(filterValue, SysFilterOperator::Equal,
     filterValueResolutionMethod);
    return filter;
}
```

9. Save and close the designers. Then, build the model to test our work.

How it works...

The form engine tests if the form implements the `SysIFilterProvider` interface. It then uses the `parmFilter` method to know what it has to filter. It does this based on metadata and relies on the fact that the EDT used in the call to `createFilterValueToString` exists on the tables in the tile and section lists in the workspace.

This is why this adjusts the tile count as the filter is changed, but doesn't filter the service orders list.

You may also be surprised that the form engine knows how to build a lookup when all we have specified is the data type. This is determined by looking at the EDT reference table and the `autoLookup` field group on the table.

When applying this filter pattern, you may need to adjust the **Copy Caller Query** property and ensure that the queries have a join that the filter can use. If the menu item that the tile calls does not have this value set, the filter will not apply to the form that it opens.

There's more...

Sometimes, it isn't possible to filter the target form, which means we must write some code on the target form to handle this.

The issue for the form is that we don't want to write a switch statement for each caller. A solution would be to write an interface that forms a code contract between the caller and the form.

After doing this, we can create an interface with the following code:

```
interface ConVMSVehicleGroupFilterableI
{
    public ConVMSVehicleGroupId VehicleGroupId () {}
}
```

On the workspace, change the class declaration to the following:

```
public class ConVMSVehicleWorkspace
    extends FormRun
    implements SysIFilterProvider, ConVMSVehicleGroupFilterableI
```

Then, add the following method:

```
public ConVMSVehicleGroupId VehicleGroupId()
{
    return VehicleGroupFilter.text();
}
```

Save and close the designers and then open the code for the `ConVMSVehicleTable` form. Override the `init` method, as follows:

```
public void init()
{
    super();
    // we don't care what the type of the calling element is, only if it is
    // (or implements) our interface
    if (element.args().caller() is ConVMSVehicleGroupFilterableI)
    {
        ConVMSVehicleGroupFilterableI filterable = element.args().caller();
        if (filterable.VehicleGroupId() != '')
        {
```

```
                     // get the instance of the query data source
                     // builder so we can get a query range to filter on
                     QueryBuildDataSource qbds =
                      ConVMSVehicleTable_Ds.queryBuildDataSource();
                     // Use SysQuery to find or create a range on the
                     // VehicleGroupId field
                     QueryBuildRange vehGroupRange = SysQuery::findOrCreateRange(
                         qbds, fieldNum(ConVMSVehicleTable, VehicleGroupId));
                     vehGroupRange.value(filterable.VehicleGroupId());
                 }
             }
         }
```

Save all the designers and editor tabs, and build the solution in order to test this. This is a simple example but shows how we can access the state of the caller without coupling the forms by using a switch statement based on the form's name. Even then, we would need to use the object class to call the method. This is because forms are not types that we can access in the same way as classes or tables – they are definitions.

Working with Form Logic and Frameworks

4

In this chapter, we will get straight into writing code. The recipes chosen for this chapter are common tasks that will be used on many development projects.

As we progress through this chapter, references to code placement will be made. Code placement is critical to a maintainable and extendable solution. We will see that code can be written on the form, in a class, or in a table. The rule of thumb here is that we must place code as low in the stack as possible. If we write code on a form, that code is only available to that form and cannot be reused. This is fine when we are hiding a button, but data (validation and other data-specific code) logic usually belongs to a table. As the code on the form or table gets more complicated, the code should be moved to a class.

The SalesTable form and table is an example. In this case, table events are handled by the SalesTableType and SalesLineType classes and form logic is handled by the SalesTableForm class. The reason here is that there can be different types of sales orders, and the best solution is to have a base class for the base code and a specialized class to handle the different requirements of each order type.

The first three recipes in this chapter are typical of order entry style forms (details-transaction), where we would have a number sequence to handle the ID field, a create form to place key information that the header record requires, and a form handler class to help make the code easier to read, maintain, and extend. The order is important and we will perform these tasks as part of the same process, as the elements can't be fully completed in isolation.

In this chapter, we will cover the following recipes:

- Creating a table handler class
- Creating a form handler class
- Hooking up a number sequence
- Creating a create dialog for details transaction forms
- Updating form controls at runtime

Technical requirement

You can find the code files for this chapter on GitHub at `https://github.com/ PacktPublishing/Extending-Microsoft-Dynamics-365-Finance-and-Supply-Chain- Management-Cookbook-Second-Edition/blob/master/Chapter%204.axpp`.

Creating a table handler class

Although we can write code directly onto the table, this can limit the extendability of the code, should its complexity increase. In later chapters, we will refactor this class so that it uses the `SysExtension` pattern. This is where the actual class is constructed in a factory method based on metadata. This would be very difficult should the code be on the table, as we need to change all of the code that calls the methods on the table.

We will, therefore, create a table handler class and move the existing instance methods to this class.

How to do it...

To create the table handler class, follow these steps:

1. Create a new class named `ConVMSVehicleServiceTableType`.

2. We will construct the instance from `ConVMSVehicleServiceTable` and will, therefore, store this as a global variable on the class. Add this as follows:

```
class ConVMSVehicleServiceTableType
{
    ConVMSVehicleServiceTable serviceTable;
}
```

3. In order to construct the class, we will need to be able to set the value of serviceTable using an accessor method (a way to get and set internal variables), which is called a Parm method in SCM:

```
public ConVMSVehicleServiceTable ParmConVMSVehicleServiceTable(
        ConVMSVehicleServiceTable _serviceTable = serviceTable)
{
    serviceTable = _serviceTable;
    return serviceTable;
}
```

4. Override the new method so that it reads as follows:

```
protected void new()
{
}
```

5. Then, create the public constructor by writing the following method:

```
public static ConVMSVehicleServiceTableType Construct(
    ConVMSVehicleServiceTable _serviceTable)
{
    ConVMSVehicleServiceTableType tableHandler;
    tableHandler = new ConVMSVehicleServiceTableType();
    tableHandler.ParmConVMSVehicleServiceTable(_serviceTable);
    return tableHandler;
}
```

6. Now, we need to create a method on the table that returns the preceding class; the method is always called type. Open the code editor for the ConVMSVehicleServiceTable table and create the following method:

```
public ConVMSVehicleServiceTableType Type()
{
    return ConVMSVehicleServiceTableType::Construct(this);
}
```

7. The standard pattern for table handler classes is that all table event methods (and any other methods that we might want to specialize or allow to be specialized through extensibility) are moved to the class. Ensure that all of the following table events are overridden on the ConVMSVehicleServiceTable table:

- insert
- update

- delete
- validateField
- validateDelete
- validateWrite

8. To handle the insert and update methods, we can write two methods that are called either side of the `super()` call. Create placeholder methods for `Insert`, `Delete`, and `Update` in our table type class using the following pattern:

```
public void Inserting()
{
}
public void Inserted()
{
}
```

9. On the table's overridden methods for `Insert`, `Delete`, and `Update`, write methods that follow this pattern:

```
public void insert()
{
    this.Type().Inserting();
    super();
    this.Type().Inserted();
}
```

10. For the rest, the quickest way is to copy all the table event methods to the class and refactor them, as shown in the following piece of code:

```
public boolean ValidateWrite()
{
    boolean ret = true;
    ret = ret && this.CheckCanEdit();
    // more checks can be added using the same pattern return ret;
    return ret;
}
public void ModifiedField(FieldId _fieldId)
{
    switch (_fieldId)
    {
        case fieldNum(ConVMSVehicleServiceTable, VehicleId):
            serviceTable.InitFromConVMSVehicleTable(
                ConVMSVehicleTable::Find(serviceTable.VehicleId));
            break;
    }
}
```

```
public boolean ValidateField(FieldId _fieldId)
{
    return true;
}
public boolean ValidateDelete()
{
    return true;
}
public boolean CheckCanEdit()
{
    if (!this.CanEdit())
    {
        //Service order cannot be changed.
        return checkFailed("@ConVMSServiceOrderCannotBeChanged");
    }
    return true;
}
public boolean CanEdit()
{
    switch (serviceTable.ServiceStatus)
    {
        case ConVMSVehicleServiceStatus::None:
        case ConVMSVehicleServiceStatus::Confirmed:
            return true;
    }
    return false;
}
```

 Do not be tempted to call `serviceTable.validateWrite()` in the `Insert` or `Update` methods, or `validateDelete()` in the `Delete` method. The form's `FormDataSource` object must do this.

We will now complete the changes required to `ConVMSVehicleServiceTable`.

11. Remove the `CheckCanEdit` and `CanEdit` methods from the table; the `Can` or `May` methods should always be on the handler class if one exists.
    The `InitFrom<Table>` methods must always remain on the table, but they can call methods on the `type` class.

12. Alter the table's event methods so that they use the handler class instead; to `insert`, `update`, and `delete`, use the following pattern:

```
public void insert()
{
    this.Type().Inserting();
    super()
    this.Type().Inserted();
}
```

When overriding `insert`, `delete`, or `update`, consider performance, as this will force the operations to be done one at a time, and not as a set. So the `delete_from`, `update_recordset`, and `insert_recordset` commands will no longer be a set-based operation, significantly affecting performance. Also, if you remove `super()` from the call, the table event delegates will not be called. Order tables, where records are updated, are usually fine as they are usually updated one record at a time by user interaction. Other tables, such as transactions, need more thought regarding the benefits.

13. For the table's `validate` and `modified` methods, use the following piece of code:

```
public boolean validateField(FieldId _fieldIdToCheck)
{
    boolean ret = super(_fieldIdToCheck);
    if(ret)
    {
        ret = this.type().ValidateField(_fieldIdToCheck);
    }
    return ret;
}
public boolean validateWrite()
{
    boolean ret = super();
    if(ret)
    {
        ret = this.type().ValidateWrite();
    }
    return ret;
}
public boolean validateDelete()
{
    boolean ret = super();
    if(ret)
    {
```

```
            ret = this.type().ValidateDelete();
        }
        return ret;
    }
    public void modifiedField(FieldId _fieldId)
    {
        super(_fieldId);
        this.type().ModifiedField(_fieldId);
    }
}
```

How it works...

This may seem like a lot of effort, and since we only have one actual useful method on the handler class, it seems excessive. If we were to use a building metaphor, *We can add windows, change decor, partition the floors differently later, but we can't add a basement garage;* the data structures and associated structure of the business logic are akin to the foundations of a building. If we write it in a flexible, albeit quicker-to-write, manner in the beginning, our solution is naturally less flexible later. By writing the code in this way, we lay the groundwork, should a change to the underlying business logic be required later. When we hear the phrase "The customer will never ... " to justify coding business rules in code or to get the code out quickly, it usually turns out not to be incorrect later; an aggregate takes a bit more time to write code in an extendable manner but saves a lot of time later.

The first part of this recipe was to create the table handler class. Since the class's purpose is to handle events on the ConVMSVehicleServiceTable table, the class is constructed from a ConVMSVehicleServiceTable record, which is stored as an internal class state variable. This is done in *steps 1* through *5*. We override the New method to make it private in order to prevent the class from being instantiated without a ConVMSVehicleServiceTable record.

We added the Type method to ConVMSVehicleServuceTable in order to ease access to the table handler class. You will see the same usage pattern on SalesLine and PurchLine.

Once the basics were done, we then wrote code to handle the common table events, which were as follows:

- insert
- update
- delete
- validateField
- validateDelete
- validateWrite

In prior versions, the method in the table handler would be the same name and the standard call to `super()` on the table, and the method would be removed. This has the effect of disabling table events, so this is no longer done. The new pattern is to create a pre and post method in the style of `inserting` and `inserted` to state that the method is to be called pre or post `super()`.

The final wiring of the table handler class is to override the relevant methods using the pattern:

```
this.Type().Inserting();
super();
this.Type().Inserted();
```

`modifedField` and `validateField` require a parameter, so the pattern is changed to accommodate this. When dealing with methods that return a value, such as `validateField` and `validateWrite`, the code was written so that we don't change the standard return value unless we deliberately need to. This is nearly always to return `false` if a further validation check that we wrote fails.

We will see how this initial effort is rewarded later in this chapter, and how it really comes into its own when we extend the solution to construct it through the attribute-based extension framework.

Creating a form handler class

Technically, form handler classes are not required as all code can be added directly to a form. The problem with this is that, as form logic gets more logic, it becomes harder to read as the purpose of each method becomes less obvious and less easy to maintain as the amount of code increases. Code placed directly on a form is usually much harder to use by third parties and the code is not reusable.

For this reason, we would usually create a form handler class to handle user interface logic on order entry style forms. These forms usually need a create form in order to make order creation easier. The form handler will act as a way to pass data between the main order entry form and the create form.

Form handlers were used to handle number sequences, but the pattern has changed now as number sequence handling is more logically handled on the form, or on a table handler class. This means that a form handler has two main functions:

- To control the user interface in terms of visibility, allowing edits, and adjusting labels
- To act as a mechanism that allows communication from the create form and the main entry form

The purpose of our form handler class will be to control whether the data can be edited on our `ConVMSVehicleServiceTable` form based on the service order status. We will not place any business logic on this class, only form handling code. The rules of whether we can edit or not will be written onto the table, which again could be a table handler class, should this be required.

Getting ready

To do this, we will need a form based on the `Details Transaction` form pattern. This example follows the `ConVMSVehicleServiceTable` form we created in `Chapter 3`, *Creating the User Interface*, and builds on the code in the previous recipe, *Creating a table handler class*.

How to do it...

To create the form handler class, follow these steps:

1. First, we should add all the business logic that relates to data in the table code or table handler class (should the complexity require it). Open the `ConVMSVehicleServiceTableType` class's code and add the following two methods:

```
public boolean CanEditStatus()
{
    // we want to test this on the service status that the record
    // currently is, not the status that we might be changing it to
    ConVMSVehicleServiceStatus localServiceStatus =
     serviceTable.ServiceStatus;
    if (serviceTable.orig().RecId != 0)
    {
        ConVMSVehicleServiceTable origServiceTable =
         serviceTable.orig();
        localServiceStatus = origServiceTable.ServiceStatus;
```

```
        }
        switch (localServiceStatus)
        {
            case ConVMSVehicleServiceStatus::None:
            case ConVMSVehicleServiceStatus::Confirmed:
                return true;
        }
        return false;
    }
    public boolean CheckCanEditStatus()
    {
        if (!this.CanEditStatus())
        {
            // Label reads: Service order %1 cannot be edited at status
            // %2 strFmt will replace %1 with the current record's
            // service Id and %2 with status checkFailed returns false
            // and shows an warning message to the user.
            return checkFailed(
                strFmt("@ConVMS:ServiceCannotBeEdited",
                serviceTable.ServiceId, serviceTable.ServiceStatus));
        }
        return true;
    }
```

These methods resemble the CanEdit and CheckCanEdit methods we created in Chapter 2, *Data Structures*. While these sufficed in explaining the idea, the message wasn't that useful as to why the record can't be edited – effectively, *Computer says no*. We are changing the code to make it more user-friendly and to add some granularity.

2. Change the CanEdit and CheckCanEdit methods so that they read as follows:

```
public boolean CanEdit()
{
    Boolean ok = true;
    ok = ok && this.CanEditStatus();
    // add a line for each CanEdit method as ok = ok &&
    return ok;
}
public boolean CheckCanEdit()
{
    boolean ok = true;
    ok = ok && this.CheckCanEditStatus();
    return ok;
}
```

The `CheckCanEdit` method is still used in the `validateWrite` method, and this must provide a warning to the user. We will use the `CanEdit ()` method to make the data source read-only if this returns `false`; we, therefore, don't want this to show a warning message.

3. Next, we can write our form handler class. Add a new class to our project named `ConVMSVehicleServiceTableForm`.

4. The first task is to override the new method so that the class can't be constructed incorrectly. This is done by changing the accessibility from `public` to `protected` or `private`. `Protected` is the standard pattern, any classes that extend it can construct using the new method. The method should read as follows:

```
protected void new()
{
}
```

5. Add a global variable for the form's element instance, `FormRun`, and also a `FormDataSource` instance variable, as follows:

```
FormRun thisFormRun;
FormDataSource ConVMSVehicleServiceTable_ds;
```

6. We will construct the class from a `FormRun` instance, but to save writing code in the constructor, an `InitFromFormRun` method is more appropriate. Write the following method:

```
protected void InitFromFormRun(FormRun _formRun)
{
    thisFormRun = _formRun;
    conVMSVehicleServiceTable_ds =
     thisFormRun.dataHelper().FindDataSource(
        formDataSourceStr(ConVMSVehicleServiceTable,
         ConVMSVehicleServiceTable));
}
```

 The `dataHelper` function is provided so that we can easily gain access to the form's data sources. `formDataSourceStr` is a compile-time function that ensures that the data source name actually exists on the form; it will not compile if it doesn't.

7. The actual `public` constructor will be a static method and is as follows:

```
public static ConVMSVehicleServiceTableForm NewFromForm(FormRun
_element)
{
    ConVMSVehicleServiceTableForm form;
    form = new ConVMSVehicleServiceTableForm();
    form.InitFromFormRun(_element);
    return form;
}
```

8. To complete this initial part of the form handler, we will write a method that will make the data source editable or not based on the return value of the current service order's `CanEdit()` method. To get the current record, we use the `cursor()` method of `FormDataSource`, as shown here:

```
public void ServiceTable_Active()
{
    ConVMSVehicleServiceTable currentService;
    currentService = conVMSVehicleServiceTable_ds.cursor();

    boolean allowEdit = currentService.Type().CanEdit();
    conVMSVehicleServiceTable_ds.allowDelete(allowEdit);
    conVMSVehicleServiceTable_ds.allowEdit(allowEdit);
}
```

9. Now, we need to hook this up to the form. Open the `ConVMSVehicleServiceTable` form and double-click on `ClassDeclaration` to open the code editor.

10. In the declaration portion (above the methods), and after the opening brace, type the following:

```
ConVMSVehicleServiceTableForm formhandler;
```

11. We need to instantiate the variable, which we will do by overriding the `init` method of the form:

```
public void init()
{
    super();
    formHandler =
     ConVMSVehicleServiceTableForm::NewFromForm(element);
}
```

12. Next, we will override the `Active` method of the
`ConVMSVehicleServiceTable` data source. This is done by expanding
the `ConVMSVehicleServiceTable` node, right-clicking on the **Methods** node,
and choosing **Override** | **Active**. Change the method that opens in the code
editor so that it reads as follows:

```
public int active()
{
    int ret;
    ret = super();
    formHandler.ServiceTable_Active();
    return ret;
}
```

 The method was named `ServiceTable_Active` because it was intended
to be used specifically in the ConVMSVehicleServiceTable's `active`
method.

13. Save and close all the tabs, and then build the solution so that we can test our
progress.

How it works...

This was a relatively simple example to show how to create a class to handle the form user
interface, this time just to make a record editable or not. This wouldn't usually necessitate a
class for this purpose, but it is much easier to refactor the code when this is already in a
class. For example, we could decide to have a subclass for each service status or vehicle
type in order to better encapsulate the type-specific logic. This is relatively simple when the
user interface logic is handled in a class.

When a form opens, the first usable call is to `init`. This `init` method builds the form
controls and instantiates the data sources' objects. We override the `init` method to
initialize the internal state variables and to perform any initialization from the caller, such
as filtering the current form based on the calling form.

Code should always be placed after the `super()` call, with one exception: when we want
the form to abort. This is only done when the form is a dialog that relies on a specific caller
or state. To abort the form from loading (and giving a suitable warning to the user), the
`throw error("Error message");` command is used.

The next method is `Run`. This is when the form is actually presented to the user. We can place code here if the code requires the form to be in a running state. This is not usually required.

The other methods that are used are on the data sources. We overrode the active method. This method is called whenever a record is made the active record, and is ideal for our scenario of making the record editable or not.

Hooking up a number sequence

The number sequence framework is used on most `Details Master (Main tables)` and `Details Transaction (Worksheet tables)` forms; for example, the sales order number is generated through a number sequence. These used to be hooked up to the form directly, or in the form handler class, which made sense previously as user interface events (new record, delete record, abandon a new record, and so on) would need to be handled. The problem with this is that if we have two forms that handle the same table, we may need to write the code twice.

The new pattern is that it is handled on the table or table handler, but called from the form or form handler class. First, we will create a class that defines our number sequences, and then we'll write the code to handle them.

Getting ready

To do this, we should have a table and form complete, ideally using the handler classes for the table and form.

How to do it...

To create the number sequence definition class, follow these steps:

1. First, we will need to add an element to the `NumberSeqModule` base enum. To do so, locate this enum, right-click on it, and choose **Create extension**.
2. Rename the new base enum extension `NumberSeqModule.ConVMS`.
3. Open it in the designer and add a new element. Set the **Name** property to `ConVMSVehicleManagement` and the **Label** property to `Vehicle management`.
4. Save and close the designer and create a new class named `NumberSeqModule_ConVMS`.

5. Change the declaration so that it extends `NumberSeqApplicationModule` and overrides the following methods so that they read as follows:

```
public NumberSeqModule numberSeqModule()
{
    return NumberSeqModule::ConVMSVehicleManagement;
}
/// <summary>
/// Appends the current class to the map that links
/// modules to number sequence data type generators.
/// </summary>
[SubscribesTo(classstr(NumberSeqGlobal),
    delegatestr(NumberSeqGlobal, buildModulesMapDelegate))]
static void buildModulesMapSubscriber(Map numberSeqModuleNameMap)
{
    NumberSeqGlobal::addModuleToMap(
        classnum(NumberSeqModule_ConVMS), numberSeqModuleNameMap);
}
protected void loadModule()
{
}
```

Those migrating from Dynamics AX 2012 may remember the manual job that must be run to initialize the number sequence. This is now done automatically by subscribing to `NumberSeqGlobal.buildModulesMapDelegate`.

6. To complete the `loadModule` method, we will define each number sequence from the EDT. This is done in blocks of code. The following code defines sequences for `ConVMSVehicleId` and `ConVMSVehicleServiceId`:

```
protected void loadModule()
{
    NumberSeqDatatype datatype;
    datatype = NumberSeqDatatype::construct();
    // Vehicle number
    datatype.parmDatatypeId(extendedTypeNum(ConVMSVehicleId));
    // Unique key for the identification of vehicles.
    // The key is used when creating new vehicles
    datatype.parmReferenceHelp(literalstr("<label id>"));
    datatype.parmWizardIsContinuous(false);
    datatype.parmWizardIsManual(NoYes::No);
    datatype.parmWizardIsChangeDownAllowed(NoYes::No);
    datatype.parmWizardIsChangeUpAllowed(NoYes::No);
    datatype.parmWizardHighest(999999);
    datatype.parmSortField(1);
    datatype.addParameterType(NumberSeqParameterType::DataArea,
```

```
        true, false);
    this.create(datatype);
    // Vehicle service order
datatype.parmDatatypeId(extendedTypeNum(ConVMSVehicleServiceId));
    // Unique key for the identification of service orders.
    // The key is used when creating new services orders
    datatype.parmReferenceHelp(literalstr("<Label Id>"));
    datatype.parmWizardIsContinuous(false);
    datatype.parmWizardIsManual(NoYes::No);
    datatype.parmWizardIsChangeDownAllowed(NoYes::No);
    datatype.parmWizardIsChangeUpAllowed(NoYes::No);
    datatype.parmWizardHighest(999999);
    datatype.parmSortField(2);
    datatype.addParameterType(NumberSeqParameterType::DataArea,
     true, false);
    this.create(datatype);
}
```

For the `parmReferenceHelp` methods, you should create a label and use its label ID in place of **<Label Id>**. Remember that the label ID is case-sensitive, so copying and pasting it is preferred.

The next part is to update the parameters form so that we can maintain the new number sequence:

1. We can save time here with some copying and pasting. Open the design for our `ConVMSVehicleParameters` form and then the designer for the `InventParameters` form from the Application Explorer.

2. In the form design for `InventParameters`, expand **Data Sources**.

3. Right-click on the `NumberSequenceReference` data source and choose **Copy**.

4. Change tabs to our `ConVMSVehicleParameters` form designer, right-click on the **Data Sources** node, and select **Paste**.

5. We will need to refactor the code that was brought, but we will need to set up the number sequence handling code. Double-click on the `classDeclaration` node of the **Methods** node on the form.

6. Just after the first brace, enter the following lines:

```
boolean runExecuteDirect;
NumberSeqReference   numberSeqReference;
NumberSeqScope scope;
NumberSeqModule_ConVMS numberSeqApplicationModule;
TmpIdRef  tmpIdRef;
container numberSequenceModules;
```

7. Now, we need to create code to initialize the number sequence class, which is done by the following method:

```
private void numberSeqPreInit()
{
    runExecuteDirect    = false;
    numberSequenceModules =
     [NumberSeqModule::ConVMSVehicleManagement];
    numberSeqApplicationModule = new NumberSeqModule_ConVMS();
    scope = NumberSeqScopeFactory::createDataAreaScope();
NumberSeqApplicationModule::createReferencesMulti(numberSequenceMod
ules, scope);
tmpIdRef.setTmpData(NumberSequenceReference::configurationKeyTableM
ulti(numberSequenceModules));
}
```

8. We require a second method that performs some further initialization, but needs the data source to be set up. This must, therefore, run after the super() call in the init method. Write the post init initialization code as follows:

```
private void numberSeqPostInit()
{
    boolean sameAsActive =
     numberSeqApplicationModule.sameAsActive();
    numberSequenceReference_ds.object(
     fieldNum(NumberSequenceReference,
       AllowSameAs)).visible(sameAsActive);
}
```

9. The preceding two methods should be placed above and below the super() call in the init method, as demonstrated in the following piece of code:

```
public void init()
{
    ConVMSVehicleParameters::Find();
    NumberSeqApplicationModule::loadAll();
    this.numberSeqPreInit();
    super();
    this.numberSeqPostInit();
}
```

10. When we copy a data source, it will bring over the code as well. Any code that is implementation-specific should be removed or refactored.

11. Let's cheat again and copy the tab page from InventParameters. Select (or open) the form designer for InventParameters.

Normally, I prefer creating everything manually, but adding the number sequence elements to a form saves a lot of time and is relatively risk-free from copy-and-paste errors or omissions.

12. Expand the `Tab` control, right-click on the `NumberSeq` tab page control, and choose **Copy**.
13. Next, go back to our form's designer, right-click on the `ParameterTab` control, and choose **Paste**.
14. Expand the `NumberSeq` and `NumberSeqBody` controls.
15. Within the `NumberSeq` tab page, expand the Header group control.
16. Change the **Text** property of the `StaticText10` control to `Set up number sequences for vehicle management documents`.
17. For consistency, and to avoid potential naming conflicts, rename the following controls:

Original control name	Correct control name
Header	NumberSeqHeader
StaticText10	NumberSeqHeaderText
GridContainer	NumberSeqGridContainer
Grid	NumberSeqGrid

18. We don't need the toolbar, so remove the `ActionPane` control from the tab page.
19. Save and close all designers and code editors.
20. Open the code editor for the `ConVMSVehicleParameters` table.
21. Add a new method that will return the number sequence reference, as shown in the following method:

```
public static NumberSequenceReference NumRefServiceId()
{
    return
NumberSeqReference::findReference(extendedTypeNum(ConVMSVehicleServ
iceId));
}
```

It is the convention to place a static method per sequence on the parameters table, and other developers will expect to find these helper functions there.

22. Build the project, look out for compilation errors, and correct them as required.

The final stage is to integrate the service order form with the number sequence framework:

1. Open the code editor for the `ConVMSVehicleServiceTableType` handler class.

2. At the top of our class, declare a variable global of the `NumberSeqFormHandler` type, as shown here:

```
NumberSeqFormHandler numberSeqFormHandler;
```

3. Next, create a method to construct an instance, if it is not already instantiated, as per the following code:

```
protected NumberSeqFormHandler numberSeqFormHandler(
    FormRun _formRun, FormDataSource _serviceTableDS)
{
    if (!numberSeqFormHandler)
    {
        RefRecId localNumSeqId;
        RefFieldId serviceIdField;
        localNumSeqId =
         ConVMSParameters::NumRefServiceId().NumberSequenceId;
        serviceIdField = fieldNum(ConVMSVehicleServiceTable,
         ServiceId);
        numberSeqFormHandler = NumberSeqFormHandler::newForm(
            localNumSeqId,
            _formRun,
            _serviceTableDS,
            serviceIdField);
    }
    return numberSeqFormHandler;
}
```

4. Next, we will need to write the methods that control what happens when the various data source event methods are run. Write the methods as follows:

```
public void formMethodClose()
{
    if (numberSeqFormHandler)
    {
        numberSeqFormHandler.formMethodClose();
    }
}
public void formMethodDataSourceCreate(FormRun _element,
FormDataSource _serviceTableDS)
{
    this.numberSeqFormHandler(_element,
     _serviceTableDS).formMethodDataSourceCreate();
}
```

```
public void formMethodDataSourceDelete(
    FormRun _element,
    FormDataSource _serviceTableDS,
    boolean _forced = false)
{
    this.numberSeqFormHandler(_element,
        _serviceTableDS).formMethodDataSourceDelete(_forced);
}
public void formMethodDataSourceLinkActive(FormRun _element,
FormDataSource _serviceTableDS)
{
    this.numberSeqFormHandler(_element,
     _serviceTableDS).formMethodDataSourceLinkActive();
}
public boolean formMethodDataSourceValidateWrite(
    FormRun _element, FormDataSource _serviceTableDS)
{
    boolean ret = true;
    if (!this.numberSeqFormHandler(
        _element,
        _serviceTableDS).formMethodDataSourceValidateWrite())
    {
        ret = false;
    }
    return ret;
}
public void formMethodDataSourceWrite( FormRun _element,
FormDataSource _serviceTableDS)
{
    this.numberSeqFormHandler(_element,
     _serviceTableDS).formMethodDataSourceWrite();
}
```

 This code does seem like a lot, but it is largely the same in most implementations and, with some refactoring, it can simply be copied. The `SalesTableType` class uses this pattern.

5. The next task is to override certain methods on the `ConVMSVehicleServiceTable` form in order to call the methods we have just written.

When reading the following steps, it may seem quicker and easier to call `ConVMSVehicleServiceTable.type().formMethodDataSourceWrite()`. This will carry a significant performance overhead, as the handler will be constructed whenever a method is called.

6. Create a global variable for the form by opening the `classDeclaration` node of the form and typing the following, just after the first opening brace:

```
ConVMSVehicleServiceTableType serviceTableType;
```

7. Now, we need to hook up the data source event methods to our handler class. The naming scheme for the number sequence methods tells us which to use on each data source event method. The first is `formMethodClose`, so we will need to override the `Close` method at the form level. To do so, enter the following code:

```
public void close()
{
    if (!serviceTableType)
    {
        serviceTableType = ConVMSVehicleServiceTable.type();
    }
    serviceTableType.formMethodClose();
    super();
}
```

 The reason for the code that reads `if (!serviceTableType){...}` is to only create a new `serviceTableType` instance if required. You could change this so that the code is in a separate method named, for example, `protected ConVMSServiceTableType ServiceTableType()`. The `close` method would then be one line, `element.ServiceTableType().formMethodClose(); –` of course, followed by `super();`.

8. The rest override the methods on the `ConVMSVehicleServiceTable` data source. To save time, override the following methods:

- `Create`
- `Delete`
- `LinkActive`
- `ValidateWrite`
- `Write`

9. These methods should be written as follows:

```
public void create(boolean _append = false)
{
    /// this line is from Chapter 3, and is not part of the number
    /// sequence code
element.viewOptionHelper().setViewOption(FormViewOption::Details);
    super(_append);
    if (!serviceTableType)
    {
        serviceTableType = ConVMSVehicleServiceTable.type();
    }
    serviceTableType.formMethodDataSourceCreate(element, this);
}

public void delete()
{
    if (!serviceTableType)
    {
        serviceTableType = ConVMSVehicleServiceTable.type();
    }
    serviceTableType.formMethodDataSourceDelete(element, this);
    super();
}

public void linkActive()
{
    if (!serviceTableType)
    {
        serviceTableType = ConVMSVehicleServiceTable.type();
    }
    serviceTableType.formMethodDataSourceLinkActive(element, this);
    super();
}

public boolean validateWrite()
{
    boolean ret;
    ret = super();
    if (!serviceTableType)
    {
        serviceTableType = ConVMSVehicleServiceTable.type();
    }
    ret = ret &&
    serviceTableType.formMethodDataSourceValidateWrite(element,
     this);
    return ret;
}
```

```
public void write()
{
    if (!serviceTableType)
    {
        serviceTableType = ConVMSVehicleServiceTable.type();
    }
    serviceTableType.formMethodDataSourceWrite(element,
     this);
    super();
}
```

10. Save and close all designers, and build the package.
11. Although we should test at each stage, this requires setting up a number sequence. The following steps are a rough guide, just so we can test the form's behavior.
12. In the web client, open the Vehicle management workspace and click on parameters.

This is to trigger the NumberSeqApplicationModule::loadAll() method.

13. Once open, check that the two records appear in the grid in the **Number sequences** tab.

If they do not, either we missed adding the call to NumberSeqApplicationModule::loadAll() in our init method or the delegate subscription in our NumberSeqModule_ConVMS class is incorrect.

14. Navigate to **Organizational administration** | **Number sequences** | **Number sequences**.
15. Click on **New**.
16. Enter ConVMSServ in the **Number sequence code** field (the prefix helps group sequences together) and Vehicle service id as **Name**.
17. Set **Scope** to Company and enter the current company ID as **Company**.
18. Configure the **Segments** grid by removing the company row and changing the Constant to VS.

The numbers that this will generate read top to bottom. So, VS followed by ###### will create numbers VS000001, VS000002, and so on.

19. Change the value for Largest to 999999 in the **General** tab.
20. The next part is the first test; expand **References** and click on **Add**.
21. Select the module from the **Area** tab, in our case Vehicle management, and then Service ID. Click on **OK**.
22. Next, open Vehicle management workspace and create a new service order record to test that the various events work correctly.

How it works...

The process is done in three parts:

- Writing a number sequence definition class that registers our EDT in the number sequence framework
- Updating the parameter form so that we can maintain the new number sequence
- Integrating the service order form with the number sequence framework

The number sequence framework is not just a way to get a new number in a prescribed format. It also automatically handles what happens should the record not be saved, and what should happen if we delete a record.

Number sequence setup

Whenever we need a number sequence, we will always use the number sequence framework to declare and maintain the number sequence we need. The first thing we did was create a class that extends the NumberSeqApplicationModule class. This allows us to define the number sequences, and also set up the event that will generate the number sequence setup data.

This makes the number sequence available, and we can create the sequence using the Number Sequence form found in **Organizational administration** | **Number Sequences** | **Number Sequences**. We can create one manually and refer to the sequence defined in our class, or use the **Generate** button.

If we take a look at the `NumberSeqModule` base enum, we will see that the extension is seamlessly applied to the base type, even though the extension is named `NumberSeqModule.ConVMS`. This would only work in the packages that reference it. We have not modified `NumberSeqModule`. The second point to note is that the `ConVMS` prefix we added to the element is required, as all elements inside an enum must be unique across all extensions to it.

It is the convention to be able to see and maintain the number of sequences for the module that they belong to. This is why we modified our parameters form. This nicely shows the link to the number sequence reference and the number sequence code that defines how the numbers will be generated and maintained by the framework.

The scope in our case was one module, as defined by the enum; however, we can include more, should we have more complicated requirements. The implementation in the `InventParameters` form demonstrates how this would be done. The `TmpIdRef` temporary table is used to generate the query used by the `NumberSequenceReference` data source. This was done in the `executeQuery` method.

A new concept was demonstrated in the code for the `NumberSequenceReference` data source. The `NumberSequenceCodeId` field is actually a `RecId` relation but is displayed as human-readable. This is done by using a control of the `FormReferenceFieldGroupControl` type. The data source field methods, `lookupReference` and `resolveReference`, will facilitate this process.

Hooking up the number sequence

The code to tie the various forms for the data source events to the number sequence framework was done in its most abstracted method. This allows the service order to be extended. For example, if we added a service order type field, we could have a different sequence per type of service order without having to rework the code very much.

In these methods, we used the `element` and `this` keywords. On a form, the `this` keyword is the most confusing one as it changes depending on where it is used. This is because we have nested class definitions inside the main form class. So, in the context where we used it, `this` means `ConVMSVehicleServiceTable_DS`. Within the form's root methods, `this` means the `FormRun` object that is created when the form is run. We would tend to use `element` in favor of `this`, even in the form's root methods. This adds clarity as `element` is always the `FormRun` instance.

There's more...

We should add number sequence handling logic to the `ConVMSVehicleTable` form.

We don't need a form handler class in this case; we can add the methods directly to the `ConVMSVehicleTable` form. Declare the `NumberSeqFormHandler` class global to the form and write the initialize method also at the form level. Call the method after the `super()` call in `init`. In each data source method we changed in this recipe, just call `numberSeqFormHandler(element, ConVMSVehicleTable_DS).<method>` directly.

The `CustTable` form is a good example of this.

You can also create a type class for this. This isn't usually required for `Main` tables as the business logic on these tables is not as complicated.

Feel free to challenge yourself on this. To save time, we can copy the `ConVMSVehicleServiceTableType` class and refactor it to our purposes. The following steps cover how to add number sequence handling logic to the form. In this case, they are summarized, as the tasks are very similar to the recipes we have already covered. To do this, follow these steps:

1. Open the code for the `ConVMSParameters` table.
2. Copy and paste the `NumRefServiceId` method, changing it so that it reads as follows:

   ```
   public static NumberSequenceReference NumRefVehicleId()
   {
       return NumberSeqReference::findReference(extendedTypeNum(
       ConVMSVehicleId));
   }
   ```

3. Save and close the editor.
4. Create a new class named `ConVMSVehicleTableType`.
5. Copy the contents of `ConVMSVehicleServiceTableType` (everything inside the outermost braces) and paste it into our new class.

6. Now for a series of find and replace. Double-click on
`ConVMSVehicleServiceTable` so that it's highlighted and press *Ctrl + H*.
Enter `ConVMSVehicleTable` in the second textbox and ensure Match case is
selected – it should look as follows:

7. The two icons to the right of the second textbox are `Replace next` and `Replace
all`. In our case, replacing all occurrences is fine, and you can do this by pressing
Alt + A.

8. Do the same to replace `serviceTable` with `vehicleTable`, ensuring that case-
sensitivity is selected.

9. Then, replace all occurrences of Service with Vehicle, following by service with
vehicle.

It is always prudent to look at the code to check that it will only affect the
code that you want it to. The code editor will highlight the changes in
yellow.

10. Edit the remaining methods so that the validate methods all just return `true` and
remove the code from the `modifeidField` method. The only methods with code
should be the number sequence methods, the `Construct` method, and
the `ParmConVMSVehicleTable` method.

11. Just like we did for `ConVMSVehicleServiceTable`, create the `Type` method and
override
the `insert`, `delete`, `update`, `validateField`, `validateWrite`, `validateDel
ete`, and `modifiedField` methods to be able to call the methods on
the `ParmConVMSVehicleTableType` class. You can copy and paste these
methods if desired and rename them as required. Remove the four `CanEdit`
methods as they are not required in this class:

```
We have already modified the validateField method, so this should
be migrated to the type class.
```

12. Finally, modify the `ConVMSVehicleTable` form as we did the `ConVMSVehicleServiceTable` form in order to hook up the number sequence. The only difference is the `Create` method since we don't have a create form. We just need to call the `formMethodDataSourceCreate` method and place the following code after the `super()` call on the overridden create data source method:

```
if (!vehicleTableType)
{
    vehicleTableType = ConVMSVehicleTable.type();
}
vehicleTableType.formMethodDataSourceCreate( element, this);
```

The remaining methods are simple refactored copies from the `ConVMSVehicleServiceTable` form. In order to test this, a number sequence should be created and associated with `Vehicle Service Id`. It should honor all the settings on the number sequence.

 Take care when refactoring. The order of find and replace is important and it will only affect the code we want to and that the casing is respected.

Creating a create dialog for details transaction forms

In this recipe, we will create a dialog that brings together the key information needed in order to create the header fields on our details transaction (order entry) form. This is often different than the fields on the header portion of the lines view of the form. This is because it is common that some fields that are entered at the point of creation aren't needed after their creation.

Getting ready

For this recipe, we need to have created a details transaction style form. This was covered in Chapter 3, *Creating the User Interface*, in the *Creating a details transaction (order entry) form* recipe.

How to do it...

To create the Create form, follow these steps:

1. We need to make some changes to the `ConVMSVehicleServiceTableForm` class in order to pass state information between the main form and the create form. Open the class and add the following:

```
// global variables
ConVMSVehicleServiceTable serviceTableCreated;
// new methods
public ConVMSVehicleServiceTable ParmServiceTableCreated(
    ConVMSVehicleServiceTable _serviceTableCreated =
    serviceTableCreated)
{
    serviceTableCreated = _serviceTableCreated;
    return serviceTableCreated;
}
public ConVMSVehicleServiceTable CurrentRecord()
{
    return conVMSVehicleServiceTable_ds.cursor();
}
```

2. Create a new form, suffixing the detail's form name with Create, for example, `ConVMSVehicleServiceTableCreate`.

3. Drag the table(s) associated with the header record to the form's **Data Source** node. In our example, this is the `ConVMSVehicleServiceTable` table.

4. Set the properties for the `ConVMSVehicleServiceTable` data source as follows:

Property	Value
Allow Delete	No.
Allow Notify	No; we want this to act as a single record dialog and disable most of the events that the data source performs for us.
Auto Search	No.
Insert At End	No.
Insert If Empty	No.
Delay Active	No.

We will need to control the behavior of the data source in this case as it will be called from another, so we have to disable certain user options and events.

5. Override the form's `init` method and write the following piece of code:

```
// global to the form / element
ConVMSVehicleServiceTableForm serviceTableForm;
ConVMSVehicleServiceTableType serviceTableType;
/// <summary>
/// the form must be called with a form handler class
/// </summary>
public void init()
{
    if (element.args())
    {
        if (element.args().caller() is
         ConVMSVehicleServiceTableForm)
        {
            serviceTableForm = element.args().caller();
        }
    }
    if (!serviceTableForm)
    {
        //Form was incorrectly called
        throw error ("@SYS22996");
    }
    super();
    serviceTableType = ConVMSVehicleServiceTable.type();
}
```

6. Continue to override the run and close form methods with the following lines of code:

- Run method:

```
public void run()
{
    ConVMSVehicleServiceTable.clear();
    ConVMSVehicleServiceTable_DS.create();
    super();
}
```

- Close method:

```
public void close()
{
    if(serviceTableType)
    {
        serviceTableType.formMethodClose();
    }
```

```
        super();
    }
```

7. Now, we need to adjust some of the `ConVMSVehicleserviceTable` data source's methods. Start this process by overriding the `research` method and writing the following code:

```
public void research(boolean _retainPosition = false)
{
    //super(_retainPosition) Disable the refresh feature.
}
public void reread()
{
    //  Allow the DS to reread only if saved
    if (ConVMSVehicleServiceTable.RecId)
    {
        super();
    }
}
void write()
{
    // this ensures that the form close if
    // the number sequence can't be used
    // and passes a null record back
    try
    {
        serviceTableType.formMethodDataSourceWrite(element, this);
        super();
    }
    catch (Exception::Error)
    {
        ConVMSVehicleServiceTable.RecId = 0;
        serviceTableForm.ParmServiceTableCreated(
         ConVMSVehicleServiceTable);
        element.close();
        throw Exception::Error;
    }
    this.reread();
    this.refresh();
    // update the handler form with the new record.
    serviceTableForm.ParmServiceTableCreated(
     ConVMSVehicleServiceTable);
}
void create(boolean append = false)
{
    // only allow create if the current record hasn't been saved
    if (!ConVMSVehicleServiceTable.ServiceId)
    {
```

```
        super(append);
        serviceTableType.formMethodDataSourceCreate(element, this);
    }
}
```

8. Apply the `Dialog - basic` pattern to the **Design** node.
9. Complete the **Design** properties, but set the **Caption** property to a label for `New vehicle service order`.
10. Complete the form layout according to the pattern. Use the following as a guide:

    - Within the **Dialog Commit Content** pattern element, add a new group using the `Fields and Field Groups` pattern, and add fields and field groups as desired.
    - The **OK** and **Cancel** buttons in the pattern are `Command Buttons`, and the pattern will hide the **Command** property. Make the **OK** button the default button. These will need labels to be set for the **Text** property.

11. Next, open the `ConVMSVehicleServiceTableForm` class and add the following methods:

```
public str CreateFormName()
{
    return formStr(ConVMSVehicleServiceTableCreate);
}
public boolean create()
{
    Args args = new Args();
    args.name(this.CreateFormName());
    args.caller(this);
    FormRun createFormRun = classfactory.formRunClass(args);
    createFormRun.init();
    createFormRun.run();
    if (!createFormRun.closed())
    {
        createFormRun.wait();
    }
    if (createFormRun.closedOk())
    {
        return true;
    }
    //else - set the record to the calling current record and
    // return false
    serviceTableCreated = this.currentRecord();
    return false;
}
```

12. Open the `ConVMSVehicleServiceTable` form, open the code for the
    `ConVMSVehicleServiceTable.create` method, and change it so that it reads
    as follows:

```
public void create(boolean _append = false)
{
    ConVMSVehicleServiceTable newServiceTable;
    if(formHandler.create())
    {
        newServiceTable = formHandler.ParmServiceTableCreated();
        if (newServiceTable)
        {
            super(_append);
            ConVMSVehicleServiceTable.data(newServiceTable);
            this.setCurrent();
        }
    }
}
```

13. Now, we should save all, build, and test. You should test the `New` button on the
    `Vehicle service` form, as well as the `New` button on the workspace.

How it works...

When the user clicks **New** (or the form is opened with a menu item that has **Open Mode** set
to **Yes**), the form triggers a task that calls the current data source's `Create` method. In our
case, we must let the data source do this; however, at this point, we will open the create
dialog using the `Create` method we wrote on the form handler.

The `Create` method is a standard way to call any form from code. Never use the form
name as a string literal without using a compile-time function, in this case `formStr`.

This calls the create dialog, which is set up so that the normal form events no longer fire.
We will initialize the form from the form handler class in order to pass the new record back.

Once control returns to our details form, we will replace the data of the record with the
record we created with the create dialog; this was done in the `data([Common])` method.

The key activities can be seen in this diagram:

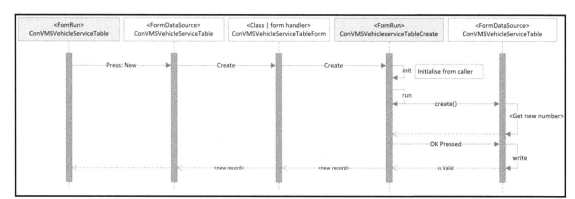

Understanding the control flow for form events is important when writing code. It is very easy to get unexpected results, should we not follow this pattern. Some examples are that the newly created record is not shown to the user after the record has been created by the `Create` form or that a blank record is shown if the user presses cancel on the create form.

Updating form controls at runtime

Sometimes, the form needs to be adjusted beyond allowing the user to edit a record or field or allowing a button to be pressed. Let's say we wish to add custom fields, where the label is decided by information only known at runtime. The example that will be used in this recipe is intended to be seen as a starting point, showing a way in which we can dynamically control the form.

Getting ready

Ideally, we should have a form with a grid view, such as the `ConVMSVehicleServiceTable` form.

How to do it...

To iterate through a container control in order to interact with its controls, follow these steps:

1. Open the `ConVMSVehicleServiceTableForm` handler class.

2. First, let's write a method that can set a form control's label:

```
private void SetControlLabel(FormControl _formControl, str _label)
{
    if (_formControl is FormStringControl)
    {
        FormStringControl stringCtrl = _formControl;
        stringCtrl.label(_label);
    }
    if (_formControl is FormRealControl)
    {
        FormRealControl realControl = _formControl;
        realControl.label(_label);
    }
    // etc for FormIntControl, FormInt64Control, FormDateControl
}
```

3. Next, we will write a method that will add some logic so that we can get the label and call the method in *step 2* to set the label property:

```
private void ProcessControl(FormControl _control)
{
    if (_control.fieldBinding() != null)
    {
        // we only handle bound controls in this example;
        RefFieldName fieldName =
         _control.fieldBinding().fieldName();
        str label = 'Field: ' + fieldName;
        this.SetControlLabel(_control, label);
    }
}
```

4. Finally, write the method that will process a container control that is either a grid or group control:

```
public void ProcessGridControl(FormGridControl _containerControl)
{
    int controls = _containerControl.controlCount();
    Counter controlNum;
    for (controlNum = 1; controlNum <= controls; controlNum++)
    {
        FormControl formControl =
         _containerControl.controlNum(controlNum);
        // we can now do something with the control on the grid or
        // group control
        this.ProcessControl(formControl);
    }
}
```

FormControl is a base type that other controls extend, and therefore only contains a subset of properties. A "number of decimal places" property makes no sense on a string control, and a grid cannot have a label.

To use this method, we need to add a call to it during the form's init method, after the call to super().

How it works...

The code is split into three methods for readability and usability. It is always good practice to keep methods concise with a clear purpose.

The first method, SetControlLabel, will accept a FormControl object and a label in order to set its label property. FormControl is the base type for form controls, which is useful, but it does not contain the label property. We could write a method for each type of control, accepting a FormStringControl, FormRealControl, and so on, but this results in a lot of duplicated code.

In order to set the label property, we must check the control's type and then cast it, as shown in the following code:

```
if (_formControl is FormStringControl)
{
    FormStringControl stringCtrl = _formControl;
    stringCtrl.label(_label);
}
```

The other option we have, which seems more elegant, is to use code similar to the following:

```
switch (_formControl.type())
{
    case FormControlType::String:
        FormStringControl stringCtrl = _formControl;
        stringCtrl.label(_label);
        break;
    // etc.
}
```

This is not documented officially, so this wasn't used here. The ideal method would be an interface where we would write something like the following:

```
if (_formControl is FormControlLabelI)
{
    FormControlLabelI labelCtrl = _formControl;
    labelCtrl.label(_label);
}
```

Sadly, there is no such interface, but should one be made, it would be a simple process to change our code in order to use it. This is one of the many reasons why interfaces are so useful and why we should use them more and more in our code.

The second method, `ProcessControl`, has the task of accepting a `FormControl` object and determining if the label should be changed and what the label should be.

We might evolve this so that we have a setup table that contains a list of fields and the desired label. The following code should be used to get the field name so that this new label can be looked up:

```
RefFieldName fieldName = _control.fieldBinding().fieldName();
```

In our case, we will just use the field name to add it to the label, in order to show that the concept works.

The final `ProcessGridControl` method shows a standard pattern of iterating through a container control in order to access the controls within it. Groups and grids are both container controls, and the pattern in this method can be used with both types of container control.

When this technique is used properly, it can prove very useful. Some examples are as follows:

- Custom fields where the purpose is not known at design time.
- To show rolling balances where the months are relative to today.
- On some setup forms where the fields are reused. An example is a business event's endpoints where the URL field changes based on endpoint type.

This should be done to change labels for standard elements as this can lead to problems with supporting users, as well as form load time.

5
Application Extensibility

Application extensibility has always been a strong feature from the initial origins of Microsoft Dynamics 365 for Finance and Supply Chain Management. What was Axapta that later became Dynamics AX. It had a clever layer system to isolate modifications between development parties. When editing a standard object, such as a class, the element being changed (such as a method) would be copied to the developer's current layer where it was modified. The compiler would look down from the top layer (from the USR, VAR, and ISV through to the base SYS layer) to build the solution. This made upgrades much simpler and carried a lower risk than its peers. When coupled with a very advanced development environment, the cost of implementation and maintenance was a major selling point of the system.

Despite all of this advanced technology, some customers still found themselves almost version-locked as the cost of an upgrade was still significant—and the longer the delay, the higher the cost. Even with clever code isolation, a code upgrade still had to be done. Tables and classes were relatively easy, but forms were difficult to the point where it could be quicker just to rewrite them.

This type of change is referred to as over-layering, where we use the *Customize* option when editing code in a different package. Layers don't really play a part in **Supply Chain Management (SCM)**, but this is where the term over-layering originates. Over-layering is no longer allowed on standard packages. Some **Independent Software Vendors (ISVs)** may allow it, but we still should not over-layer as this requires a code-upgrade process each time the source package is updated.

One of the goals of SCM was to maintain the ability to provide customized solutions while allowing customers to be always up to date. With the launch of the *One version* release of SCM, this goal has matured.

This chapter focuses on how we extended SCM without an over-layer, using the advanced features of the SCM development environment to make our solutions a close fit for our user's business requirements. This chapter will use real-world examples to cover the key extensibility features in SCM:

- Adding fields to a standard table
- Writing data-event handlers
- Using a Chain of Command to initialize data
- How to customize a document layout without an over-layer
- Modifying a standard form
- Using a Chain of Command with a form
- Replacing a standard lookup with our own
- Adding a form display method to a standard form

Technical requirement

You can find the code files for this chapter at the following GitHub links:

- `https://github.com/PacktPublishing/Extending-Microsoft-Dynamics-365-Finance-and-Supply-Chain-Management-Cookbook-Second-Edition/blob/master/Chapter%205%20-%20ConVMSReports.axpp`
- `https://github.com/PacktPublishing/Extending-Microsoft-Dynamics-365-Finance-and-Supply-Chain-Management-Cookbook-Second-Edition/blob/master/Chapter%205%20-%20ConVehicleManagement.axpp`

Adding fields to a standard table

Adding fields to standard tables is the most common change we do, and in this recipe we will add a field to the `SalesConfirmHeaderTmp` table, which we will use in the *How to customize a document layout without an over-layer* recipe. The requirement for this is to add the order sales pool to the report.

Getting ready

In order to do this, we need a solution. Since we are writing a new requirement—a change to a report—we will create a new project within our `ConVehicleManagement` package. Separating requirements into separate projects allows software development to be planned more easily. It results in easier code maintenance as there is less trawling through a mammoth project to find the code that needs to be changed.

Create a new project (in a new solution) and name it `ConVMSSalesReports`; this shows the project is for sales order documents. One project per report seems excessive, and one project for all reports defeats the purpose of separating work by project.

Ensure that the new project is placed in the folder mapped to the Trunk's project folder. In `Chapter 1`, *Starting a New Project*, we created a development branch named `Dev` and mapped it to `C:\Trunk\Dev`. In this case, our project should be placed in `C:\Trunk\Dev\Projects`. Ensure that **Add to Source Control** is checked before pressing **OK**.

Before adding any new elements, check that the model is correct (the name in brackets after the project name), and if it isn't, open the project properties and change it to the desired model—such as `Contoso - vehicle management`.

How to do it...

Follow the steps given below:

1. Locate the `SalesConfirmHeaderTmp` table in the **Application Explorer**.
2. Right-click on it, and choose **Create extension**.
3. Remember that all element names must be globally unique; in our case, our project and package have the same name so we don't have to rename the extension portion of the name this time.
4. Open the new table extension in the designer.
5. Locate the **Name** EDT in the **Application Explorer** and drag it to the table extension's **Fields** node.
6. Rename the field to `ConVMSSalesReportsPoolName`.
7. Set the **Label** property to `@SYS84547` (sales pool).
8. Save and close the designer.

How it works...

This recipe is closely linked to the next two recipes, and some explanation is required as to how we know which tables to modify. To keep this information in one place, this explanation is in the *There's more...* section of the *How to customize a document layout without an over-layer* recipe.

When an extension is created, an artifact is created that contains the changes to the element being extended. This is true of all extensions. There is no copying from layer to layer; it is a reference and a list of changes.

The actual source of the table extension is shown in the following piece of code:

```
<?xml version="1.0" encoding="utf-8"?>
<AxTableExtension xmlns:i="http://www.w3.org/2001/XMLSchema-instance">
  <Name>SalesConfirmHeaderTmp.ConVMSSalesReports</Name>
  <FieldGroupExtensions />
  <FieldGroups />
  <FieldModifications />
  <Fields>
    <AxTableField xmlns=""
      i:type="AxTableFieldString">
      <Name>ConVMSSalesReportsSalesPoolName</Name>
      <ExtendedDataType>Name</ExtendedDataType>
      <Label>@SYS84547</Label>
    </AxTableField>
  </Fields>
  <Indexes />
  <Mappings />
  <PropertyModifications />
  <Relations />
</AxTableExtension>
```

When the project is built and the database synchronization is done, the `SalesConfirmHeaderTmp` physical table will have the base fields plus the fields in all of its extensions. This is why the field name needs to be prefixed. Adding VMS as part of the prefix for the project and project elements is interesting. `ConSalesReports` would be enough for a customer-specific implementation developed by the customer or partner. If we are delivering a vertical then we should use VMS as well to separate it from other solutions we may write. We can, therefore, have two sales order confirmations, and the decision as to which gets used will be done by configuring the print management.

There's more...

You can also extend field groups. This allows us to add fields to a field group that is used in forms to keep the presentation consistent and reduce the number of changes and the amount of code maintenance work.

We can also add indexes and relations.

 Indexes are created within the physical table in SQL, so these must also be prefixed to ensure that we don't cause any collisions (by duplicating names).

More on structuring packages and projects

Using the AX 2012 development paradigm, where one is tempted to deploy models to production independently, we might decide to create a package for reports. This would mean we could deliver reports to production, so it may seem natural to create a package that references the main development package. There's some logic to this, but there are two critical problems that mean this method must not be used.

The first problem with this is that any new fields need to be in one package. This could be the main package, requiring one requirement to span packages, or in the reporting package. Any changes in a higher package can't be seen by lower packages: the reference only goes one way.

The second, but much larger problem, is that it would bypass the application life cycle management process. Unless we deploy all packages to the sandbox for testing, we can't be sure that there isn't a change in one package that breaks code in a referenced package. We could even end up with tests passing in a sandbox, but breaking in production. Even though this has been used in AX 2012 to expedite fixes and updates, this was never the recommended approach; the risk is too high. When firefighting software issues, we often cause more fires than we put out in our haste.

The better solution is to create one main package and split the work via projects. One per technical design document is usually a good plan. We should, therefore, create a project that contains the changes we need.

Writing data-event handlers

Data-event handlers deal with delegates exposed on every table. These delegates are listed under the **Events** node.

 These events do not fire if the associated method (for example, `insert`) is overridden on the table and `super()` is not called.

How event handler methods are organized is up to the developer, but they do need to be placed logically so that others will find them easily. A good naming convention (from experience) is to use the following convention: `TableName_Project_DataHandler`, so in our case it would be `SalesConfirmHeaderTmp_ConVMSSalesReports_DataHandler`.

It would be tempting to name it `ConVMSSalesReportsDataHandlers`, and stick them all in one class, but when we eventually have many projects with data-events, it can get hard to see what events are firing. Having one class for all table events means that it becomes a library class, and our code from different requirements gets merged, leading to other issues when reading the code should regression occur.

How to do it...

To create a data-event handler, follow these steps:

1. Create a new `SalesConfirmHeaderTmp_ConVMSSalesReports_DataHandler` class.
2. Open the table design for the table in question; in our case, double-click on the `SalesConfirmHeaderTmp.ConVMSSalesReports` table extension.
3. Expand **Events** and locate **onInserting**.

 The **onInserted** event is too late as we want to fill in a field before the record is written; if we subscribe to **onInserted**, the data will not be saved.

4. Right-click on the **Event** and choose the **Copy event handler method**. This will create a code snippet, and place it in the paste buffer.

5. Open the
   `SalesConfirmHeaderTmp_ConVMSSalesReports_DataHandler` class, and
   paste in the code snippet generated in *step 4* into the class body, as shown here:

```
class SalesConfirmHeaderTmp_ConVMSSalesReports_DataHandler
{
    [DataEventHandler(tableStr(SalesConfirmHeaderTmp),
     DataEventType::Inserting)]
    public static void SalesConfirmHeaderTmp_onInserting(Common
     sender, DataEventArgs e)
    {
    }
}
```

 Look at the event declaration: it references the table, not the extension.
This is important, as the extension is not a table, and the system correctly
creates the subscription to the table.

6. Next, we will need to write the code; the obvious code to write may seem to be as
   follows:

```
SalesConfirmHeaderTmp header = sender;
SalesTable salesTable;

select SalesPoolId
  from salesTable
  where salesTable.SalesId == header.SalesId;

header.ConVMSSalesReportsSalesPoolName =
SalesPool::find(salesTable.SalesPoolId).Name;
```

 This would be wrong, as we assume that the sales order record will never
be deleted; however, and once invoiced, they can be deleted. What we
should do is add the `SalesPoolId` to the `CustConfirmJour` table, which
is a permanent record of the confirmation.

7. Create an extension of the `CustConfirmJour` table, called
   `CustConfirmJour.ConVMSSalesReports`.

8. Drag the `SalesPoolId` EDT from the **Application Explorer**, and rename it to
   `ConVMSSalesReportsSalesPoolId`.

9. Right-click on the **onInserting** event and choose **Copy event handler method**.

10. Create a new class called
    `CustConfirmJour_ConVMSSalesReports_DataHandler` and paste in the
    method created in *step 9* - **Copy event handler method** and update the code as
    follows:

```
/// <summary>
/// Handles the inserting event of <c>CustConfirmJour</c>
/// </summary>
/// <param name="sender"></param>
/// <param name="e"></param>
[DataEventHandler(tableStr(CustConfirmJour),
DataEventType::Inserting)]
public static void CustConfirmJour_onInserting(Common sender,
DataEventArgs e)
{
    CustConfirmJour jour = sender;
    jour.ConVMSSalesReportsSalesPoolId=
      jour.salesTable().SalesPoolId;
}
```

 The record is passed by reference so we don't return the updated record,
we must also not call `insert` or `update`.

11. Finally, our event handler method in
    `SalesConfirmHeaderTmp_ConVMSSalesReports_DataHandler` should
    actually read as follows:

```
/// <summary>
/// Handles inserting event <c>SalesConfirmHeaderTmp</c>
/// </summary>
/// <param name="sender">The calling record</param>
/// <param name="e"></param>
[DataEventHandler(tableStr(SalesConfirmHeaderTmp),
DataEventType::Inserting),
 SuppressBPWarning('BPParameterNotUsed', 'Parameter e is part of
 the delegate signature, but is not required by the method')]
 public static void SalesConfirmHeaderTmp_onInserting(Common
 sender, DataEventArgs e)
{
    SalesConfirmHeaderTmp header = sender;
    CustConfirmJour jour;
    select ConVMSSalesReportsSalesPoolId
        from jour
        where jour.RecId == header.JournalRecId;
```

```
header.ConVMSSalesReportsSalesPoolName =
    SalesPool::find(jour.ConVMSSalesReportsSalesPoolId).Name;
}
```

 The `SuppressBPWarning` attribute suppresses a BP warning to the effect that we didn't use the `e` parameter.

12. Save and close the designer.
13. To test this, perform a full build including a database sync and create a sales confirmation.

We should test that the `SalesPoolId` field was populated in the `CustConfirmJour` table:

1. Create a new sales order, and remember the sales order ID (in my case it is `000784`), ensuring that the sales pool is populated on the sales order.

2. Create a sales order confirmation (in the sales order form choose **SELL** | **GENERATE** | **Confirm sales order**) and press **OK**—you don't need to print it for this test.

3. Open **SQL Management studio** as an administrator (if possible, currently only local VMs can do this).

4. Connect to the local VM database server (using `.` as the server name will do this).

5. Expand **Databases** and right-click on `AxDB` to select **New Query**.

6. Write the following `transact-sql` code:

```
SELECT SALESID, CONVMSSALESREPORTSSALESPOOLID
    FROM CustConfirmJour
    WHERE SALESID='000784'
```

7. You should see the following in the **Results** grid:

	SALESID	CONVMSSALESREPORTSSALESPOOLID
1	000784	04

8. Then try the following code:

```
SELECT SALESID, CONVMSSALESREPORTSSALESPOOLNAME
    FROM SALESCONFIRMHEADERTMP
    WHERE SALESID='000784'
```

This revealed no results. This is because it is marked as a temporary table in the table's definition in SCM—temporary tables are not physical tables. The table is a real table, but the data is cleaned up after use. This is needed because of the way data is passed to the report.

How it works...

The event handlers we wrote in this recipe are bound when the package is built; no changes are made to the base packages; we can ship the package as a `deployable package` to a different system, and it should all work fine.

The subscribers are not called in any order, and this cannot be relied upon. So, the code must be written in a way that doesn't make this assumption. When considering transaction durability, events are called within the transaction of the caller—and throwing an exception will cause the whole transaction to be aborted.

There's more...

Adding fields as an extension is relatively straightforward, but we also need to handle events such as `modifiedField` and `validateField`. This is done in the same way, by right-clicking on the **Event** and choosing the **Copy event handler method** option.

The problem is that we don't know the field being handled. The `DataEventArgs` object that is passed in to the method is a based class that can be cast to the correct type within the method; for example, you would write the following code in a `ValidateField` handler:

```
[DataEventHandler(tableStr(InventTable), DataEventType::ValidatedField)]
public static void InventTable_onValidatedField(Common sender,
DataEventArgs e)
{
    ValidateFieldEventArgs fieldArgs = e;
```

We can then use the `fieldArgs.parmFieldId()` accessor method in a switch statement.

ing delegates are called before the action is done (prior to `super()`), and ed delegates are called after the action. They only fire on `super()`; so, if the developer doesn't call `super()` in the method, the event will not fire. This was the case in `SalesLine`, `SalesTable`, `PurchLine`, and `PurchTable`, but Microsoft has refactored them so that they do call `super()`.

Other specialized classes under `DataEventArgs` that are useful are as follows:

Class	Usage
`ValidateFieldEventArgs`	onValidatedField onValidatingField
`ValidateEventArgs`	onValidateWrite onValidatingWrite onValidateDelete onValidateingDelete
`ModifyFieldEventArgs`	onModifiedField onModifyingField

Deciding between data-events or Chain of Command

When writing data-event handlers, we must also take into account Chain of Command extensions. The *Using Chain of Command to initialize data* recipe shows an alternative to using data-events.

In this specific case, I would opt for Chain of Command, and the decision is based on many factors, including the following:

- Looking up data in order tables, where there is an `InitFrom` method for that table that can be used instead.
- Is the data likely to be inserted using a set-based operation with triggers disabled, such as `insert_recordset`? These are common in journal and transaction tables, and when data is inserted or updated through a data entity.

Data-events are ideal on main and worksheet tables, but care should be taken when using this on journal or transaction tables. Code-based delegates should be safe, as are the `public` methods that are designed to initialize data. Although we have discussed test projects, writing tests for this purpose can seem pointless. However, it is a common source for regression as Microsoft can change the way data is written to improve performance.

Pre- and post-event Handlers

Pre-and post event handlers are the last resort when we need to hook into standard code. They are very prone to breaking changes, and can often compile and then fail at runtime. They are mentioned here for completeness.

The only time you should encounter pre-post handlers is in code upgraded from AX 2012. In these cases, we should change the code so that it either handles a delegate or uses a Chain of Command.

Using a Chain of Command to initialize data

A Chain of Command can be used as an alternative method to copy the value from our new field to the report's data table. This is a preference for reports as it will usually avoid looking up the source table in the data-event. Sometimes data is inserted using a set-based operation, and could mean the event is never fired.

A Chain of Command is done by creating a `final class` that references the class it augments, using a class attribute. These classes do not extend the class; they augment it. This is explained further in the *How this works* section of this recipe.

Getting ready

We will continue with our reporting project, `ConVMSSalesReports`, in this recipe.

How to do it...

To create an extension class, follow these steps:

1. Create a new class called `SalesConfirmDP_ConVMSSalesReports_Extension`. It must end with the extension, should start with the class name, and have a unique project name.

2. Change the class declaration so that it reads as follows:

```
[ExtensionOf(classStr(SalesConfirmDP))]
public final class SalesConfirmDP_ConVMSSalesReports_Extension
{
}
```

3. Press *F12* on `SalesConfirmDP`, so we can see which methods we need to hook into it. Then look for the `initializeSalesOrderConfirmationHeader` method. This method is suitable because its purpose is to copy data from the `CustConfirmJour` table to a new instance of the reporting dataset table.

4. Copy the method declaration, and paste it into our class, as follows:

```
protected SalesConfirmHeaderTmp
initializeSalesOrderConfirmationHeader()
{
}
```

We will get a compilation error when we save this, stating that Chain of Command methods must call `next`. Note that `next` must be called once, unconditionally.

5. The standard method accepts no parameters but returns a `SalesConfirmHeaderTmp` table buffer. We, therefore, need the standard code to run before we add our initialization to it, so we'll change the method so that it reads as follows:

```
protected SalesConfirmHeaderTmp
initializeSalesOrderConfirmationHeader()
{
    SalesConfirmHeaderTmp localTmp = next
     initializeSalesOrderConfirmationHeader();
    localTmp.ConVMSSalesReportsSalesPoolName =
     SalesPool::find(this.parmCustConfirmJour()
     .ConVMSSalesReportsSalesPoolId).Name;
    return localTmp;
}
```

6. We shouldn't have both methods enabled, so disable the event handler by commenting out the `DataEventHandler` attribute declaration from the method. You don't need to close the project for this; you can just open it from the **Application Explorer**.

7. Save and close all tabs. Since we modified a class that is not in our project, we will need to use the **Build models** option to build the entire package. When doing this, check the package to build, and press **Build**.

How this works...

The term extension is used specifically to avoid confusion with the `extends` keyword. Extension classes are augmentation classes that are automatically instantiated in place of the standard class. There is no access to private methods, but we can add state variables and access them along with the form's public variables and methods.

The class name starts with the class name we are augmenting, by convention. This is, in part, so that we can easily see all of the extension classes together in the **Application Explorer**; the middle part of the name is so that we can easily see which package and project the class belongs to.

Extension classes started out as augmentations (decoration) to standard classes, and we would add state variables (`private` or `public`— and protected has no relevance in final classes). We can add methods too, which could be display methods if we are creating an extension to a form (using `[ExtensionOf(formStr(<form>))]`) or a table (using `[ExtensionOf(formStr(<table>))]`). When we add controls, we see them as an option in the drop-down list against the form control's **Data method** property.

Extension classes must be final, and these classes are instantiated automatically in our package, in place of the standard class. We will use the term augment as opposed to extend to avoid confusion. They can be thought of as the system merging both classes together to create one class.

This is great but fails to allow us to hook into business logic. We must not place event handlers in these classes (they would be self-referencing), leaving extension classes with only specific uses, such as display methods.

When adding new methods, they must be unique, even among other extension classes in our package and any other package. Care should be taken when naming them: `public ItemName DisplayItemName_ConReports()` is a good example of this.

This is where the Chain of Command comes in. This also allows our class extension to hook into the business logic of any wrappable `protected` or `public` methods that aren't marked as internal. `Wrappable` is an attribute sometimes added to the `protected` or `public` methods to prevent the Chain of Command. This is done using the `[Wrappable (false)]` attribute.

The rules of these methods are as follows:

- Must always call `next`.
- `next` must not be conditional (placed in a condition block).
- `next` must only be called once.

There is one exception to the preceding rules. If the original method is marked with `[Replaceable(true)]`, we don't have to call `next`. This is rare, as it is always preferable to use a delegate pattern in such a case. The delegate pattern is where you pass a parameter class as a variable to send and receive state information from the delegate's subscriber.

We can choose to call `next` anywhere in the method.

We can, therefore, have many classes using a Chain of Command. Let's say we have MyClass with the DoFoo method:

```
public class MyClass
{
    public void DoFoo()
    {
        info('Original Foo');
    }
}
```

We might then have two extension classes, the first augmenting with food:

```
[ExtensionOf(classStr(MyClass))]
public final class MyClass_ConFood_Extension
{
    public void DoFoo()
    {
        info('Augment foo with food');
        next DoFoo();
    }
}
```

Then a second that augments with foot:

```
[ExtensionOf(classStr(MyClass))]
public final class MyClass_ConFoot_Extension
{
    public void DoFoo()
    {
        info('Augment foo with foot');
        next DoFoo();
    }
}
```

When MyClass.DoFoo is executed, the following output is produced:

1. Augment foo with food.
2. Augment foo with foot.
3. Original Foo.

The first two can be in any order, but since `next` is last in the method, the original will always be last. Should we debug the code, we will see that when we step into the brace on `MyClass.DoFoo`, it will call either of the two extension methods (regardless of where `next` is in the method). It will then process the code until it finds the `next` command. At this point, it calls the `next` method in the Chain of Command list; if there are now more methods, it will call the standard method before returning control back to the first method.

How to customize a document layout without an over-layer

The example here adds an extension field to a print-managed standard document without over-layering the report. We will use the sales order confirmation report to add the sales order pool name to the report.

There are two main types of reports: listing reports and documents. The documents, such as the sales order confirmation document, use temporary tables to make the layout easier to write. Any report can use this technique, but it is more common on document layouts and complicated listing reports.

We've already discussed the older method of keeping reports: a separate package. This is not ideal in SCM as the only benefit is the ability to deploy separately to the main package. Due to the fact that packages reference in one direction, we can't use fields written for a *reporting package* in the main package. This means making changes in multiple projects to add a new field to a report; they should all be in the same package, especially if the new field stems from a need to show it on a report, as in our case.

We won't cover the actual report design in this recipe, as report design is beyond the scope of this book, but we will cover all other areas. We have already added fields and event handlers in earlier recipes; we just need to add the field to the report.

How to do it...

To add the new field to the report, follow these steps:

1. Locate the `SalesConfirm` report in the **Application Explorer**.
2. Right-click on the report and choose **Duplicate in project**.
3. Rename the report to `ConVMSSalesReportsSalesConfirm`.

4. Open the report in the designer and expand the **Datasets** and `SalesConformHeaderDS` nodes. Then, look for the new extension field in the **Fields** node. If this does not appear, right-click on each dataset and choose **Restore**.

5. You can now proceed to design the report as per your requirements.

The next stage is integrating the report so that our new report is used instead of the standard report. To do this, follow these steps:

1. We will need to add an event handler to a delegate exposed by Microsoft on the `PrintMgmtDocType` class called `getDefaultReportFormatDelegate` .

2. Create a class named in the usual pattern (such as `PrintMgmtDocType_ConVMSSalesReports_Handler`). The following code does this (you can start by copying the event handler method from `getDefaultReportFormatDeletgate` in the `PrintMgmtDocumentType` class):

```
/// <summary>
/// Allows the SSRS Report used for the Print management based
/// reports to be overridden
/// </summary>
/// <param name = "_docType">The PrintMgmtDocumentType</param>
/// <param name = "_result">The EventHandlerResult</param>
[SubscribesTo(classstr(PrintMgmtDocType),
 delegatestr(PrintMgmtDocType, getDefaultReportFormatDelegate))]
public static void DefaultReportFormat(PrintMgmtDocumentType
_docType, EventHandlerResult _result)
{
    switch (_docType)
    {
        case PrintMgmtDocumentType::SalesOrderConfirmation:
            _result.result(ssrsReportStr(
              ConVMSSalesReportsSalesConfirm, Report));
            break;
    }
}
```

We used to use the `notifyPopulate` delegate in the `PrintMgmtReportFormatPublisher` class to add our report to print management. This required us to write a custom `add` method as `PrintMgmtReportFormatSubscriber::add` was `private`. We should not have to do this since Step 6 should handle adding the new report to print management.

3. Save and close the designer, and build the project.

4. You will need to deploy the report once this is done in order to test it. To do this, right-click on the report and choose **Deploy reports**. You will also need to configure print management to use the new report design.

How it works...

Even though the dataset in the report is the base table, it shows our extension fields. It will also show all extension fields for packages that the reports package references. The process of report design is straightforward from that point onward.

The integration has been well thought out by Microsoft and has, therefore, exposed a delegate that they handle. In the method that calls this delegate, the code determines if it has been handled, and will use the result arguments for the report name.

We have re-asserted a few times that we have the following naming convention of `<TypeNameBeingHandled>_<ProjectName>_<TypeOfHandler>`. From the experience in trying to see which other code is running inline with an event or method call, this helps a lot. It gives the class a definite purpose: `PrintMgmtDocType_ConVMSSalesReports_Handler` is handling delegates/events in the `PrintMgmtDocType` class for the purpose of the `sales reports` for the `Contoso vehicle management solution`. But what if we want to see all of our code together? This is partly why we have purpose/requirement-specific solutions/projects, and you can see all elements in the **Model** by right-clicking on the **AOT** (**Application Object Tree**) node in the **Application Explorer** and choosing **Model view**. Prefixing our code in order to see it listed together alphabetically is no longer as important.

 AOT is a legacy name used in Dynamics AX 2012 that goes all the way back to Damgaard Axapta. It stands for **Application Object Tree**, describing the tree view of objects. It can now just be thought of as the root node of the **Application Explorer**. You may see in some documentation a phrase such as **Locate the SalesTable table in the AOT;** this is synonymous with **Application Explorer** in this context.

There's more...

Some knowledge of the database was required in order to know to which tables we had to add extension fields, and just reading the code is not only daunting but also impractical. This example was chosen specifically as it isn't easy to find. This recipe is much easier when the field is to be added to a form. We can see the menu item in the URL in the client, and from there find the form and the table.

The temporary tables used were found simply by opening the `SalesConfirm` report and looking at the data sources it uses. We knew which report it was, based on our consistent name conventions.

Sales documents start with `Sales`, and are followed by the document type, as shown here:

- SalesQuotation
- SalesConfirm
- SalesPackingSlip
- SalesInvoice

Purchasing documents start with `Purch`, and are also suffixed with the document type:

- PurchPurchaseOrder
- PurchReceiptsList
- PurchPackingSlip
- PurchInvoice

These documents are created through the `FormLetter` framework. The pattern is that each document has a header and lines table that forms the permanent data, allowing reports to be reproduced exactly as they were when first printed, even if the order has been changed or deleted. These are referenced as journals. Tables follow a similar convention, as shown in the following table:

Document	Journal header table	Journal line table
SalesQuotation	CustQuotationJour	CustQuotationTrans
SalesConfirm	CustConfirmJour	CustConfirmTrans
SalesPackingSlip	CustPackingSlipJour	CustPackingSlipTrans
SalesInvoice	CustInvoiceJour	CustInvoiceTrans
PurchPurchaseOrder	VendPurchOrderJour	None
PurchReceiptsList	VendReceiptsListJour	VendReceiptsListTrans
PurchPackingSlip	VendPackingSlipJour	VendPackingSlipTrans
PurchInvoice	VendInvoiceJour	VendInvoiceTrans

When we use the **Copy event handler method** option on the event, this merely creates a valid method declaration for use. It does not modify the source table or add any reference. The code can, therefore, be added manually; using the **Copy event handler method** function saves time and has no drawbacks. The reference is created when the project is built.

More on report formats and print management

Reports are added to print management using `PrintMgmtReportFormatPopulator`. This has all the base code to add report formats. There is a protected method that has no code, `addDocuments()`. This seems odd as it isn't a delegate, and appears to be unused. This is because this is designed to be overridden using Chain of Command, which we will discuss later in this chapter.

Chain of Command allows us to augment a class and also wrap methods with our code; you can see this in the `PrintMgmtReportFormatPopulatorAppSuite_Extension` class. It has a method called `addDocuments`, but has no attribute to link it to the class it is augmenting. The code is worth looking at:

```
protected void addDocuments()
{
    // Purchasing documents
    this.addPurchaseDocuments();
    // and so on for each set of documents..
    next addDocuments();
}
```

The new keyword here is `next`, which calls the next extension class or the method itself once the chain is processed.

To use this, we would simply follow this pattern. If the report is a standard report (the event is our customized sales confirmation), we would use `addStandard`—our delegate handler to `PrintMgmtDocType.getDefaultREportFormatDelegate` will be used to get the correct **SQL Server Reporting Services (SSRS)** report name.

Modifying a standard form

Adjusting the layout of a form, as an extension, has been made very easy for us. This is covered in the first part of the recipe. We will also cover a new technique to work with form code.

Getting ready

Re-open the main development project, ConVehicleManagement, for this. Before we start using the *Adding fields to a standard table* recipe to add a field to the SalesTable table for the ConVMSVehicleServiceId EDT, also add a relationship to ConVMSVehicleServiceTable. Create a field group also called ConVMSServiceGroup with a label for Service details.

How to do it...

To write a form extension for the sales order form, SalesTable, follow these steps:

1. Locate the desired form (SalesTable) in the **Application Explorer**, right-click on it, and choose **Create extension**. This will add a new form extension to our project.
2. Locate the new form extension in our project, and rename it so it will remain globally unique, for example, SalesTable.ConVehicleManagement.
3. Open the form extension in the designer.

 We can now drag any field or field group, including extension fields that are available to the current package, to the design.

4. Find ConVMSServiceGroup in the SalesTable data source **Field Group** node (usually at the bottom).
5. Next find a place to put it; for example, expand **MainTab** | **TagPageDetails** | **DetailsTab** | **LineView** | **LineViewTab** and the **LineViewHeader** tab page.
6. Drag the ConVMSServiceGroup field group on top of the LineViewHeader node.
7. You can also add the ConVMSVehicleServiceId field to the main grid, which is **TagPageGrid** | **GridHeader**.

Remember that, whilst doing this, all changes should be at the lowest level possible as this ensures consistency and minimizes maintenance effort. Data validation is done in tables and the UI is handled on forms (or form handler classes). We can also choose to change the properties of the controls on the form's design. The rule here is that, if it lets you change, it will work.

8. Next, try to do the same for the sales order to create the dialog form, which is `SalesCreateOrder`. To test this, you need to build the solution and synchronize the database.

How it works...

The form extension works like any other extension; they are delta changes that are applied alongside other form extensions in order to build the form the user sees.

This is a great idea and should prevent forms from being a hindrance to an upgrade. Sometimes, however, the group that our extension is added to can be renamed or removed. The code-upgrade tool in **LCS** (**Life-cycle services**) will spot many issues where new patterns are used, and will often change our code in order to fit. In cases where control is orphaned, the tool will create a task for us to fix it. The form will not build until it is fixed.

Sometimes, we edit the XML to remove the control, and then re-add the control using the form designer. The usual reason for this is that form group controls are changed (or corrected in my opinion) to be based on table field groups. The actual fix in these cases is to extend the table and add our field there instead, removing the field from the form extension.

There's more...

There are many more types of extension that we can perform, but all follow the same theme. Ensure that the element is named correctly and is unique (and certainly doesn't have the `.extension` suffix).

You can tell which objects can have extensions due to the **Application Explorer** having specific extension nodes; for example, **Menu Items** is followed by the **Menu Item Extensions** node. Or simply: if you can select `Create extension`, you can!

Using Chain of Command with a form

The forms in SCM can contain a lot of code that we may wish to augment to suit a specific requirement. We have added a service ID field to the sales order, so it may seem a fair requirement to default the service ID if it were called from a service order.

When a form is opened, an `args` object is passed. If we add the `SalesTable` menu item to our service order form, and set the dataset to the service order, the `args` object will be constructed with a reference to this record. We can use this to filter a list of sales orders or use it in the form to set defaults on a new sales order record.

How to do it...

First, we will add the sales order menu item to our service order, and then use the Chain of Command to integrate it into our solution. To add the menu item, follow these steps:

1. Open the `ConVMSVehicleServiceTable` form.
2. Right-click on the `HeaderActionPane` action pane control, and choose **New** | **Button Group**. Name it `FormActions`.

Button groups appear directly in the action pane, without a label. Action pane controls are separate sections that the user can select; they need a label and contain Button groups. The decision as to which to follow depends on how many actions we have.

3. Locate `SalesTableGrid` in the **Application Explorer** (**User interface** | **Menu items** | **Display**), and drag it the `FormActions` button group. This creates a `Menu item button` control, with the main properties set for us.

This is chosen as the **FormViewOption** property on the menu item is Grid, making the form open in Grid view. We could just use the plan `SalesTable` menu item, and make this setting on the menu item button on our form.

4. On the new menu item button control, change the **Data source** property to `ConVMSVehicleServiceTable`.
5. Save and close all design tabs. Build the project, and test the new button. It should open the sales order form and show all sales orders in a grid view.

The next stage is to filter the sales orders if the sales order form was opened from a service order record. We will use an extension class and use the Chain of Command to handle the `init` method of the sales order form:

1. Create a class called `SalesTable_ConVehicleManagement_Form_Extension`.

    We added `Form` into the class name in order to ensure that it is unique. We could later add an extension of the `SalesTable` table but we would need to differentiate between them. To avoid this, we would therefore always add `form` into the class name if the extension is for a form. This is because tables and classes are types and are globally unique.

2. We will first add a `private` variable to hold the calling service order record; write this as follows:

   ```
   [ExtensionOf(formStr(SalesTable))]
   public final class SalesTable_ConVehicleManagement_Form_Extension
   {
       // add private as the default is protected
       private ConVMSVehicleServiceTable conVMS_CallerServiceTable;
   }
   ```

3. We need to filter our sales order based on this, in order to filter the sales orders if the form was opened from a service order—that is, if the `conVMS_CallerServiceTable` table instance has a record. Write the following method:

   ```
   public void ConVMSVehicleServiceTableFilter()
   {
       if (conVMS_CallerServiceTable.RecId != 0)
       {
           FormDataSource localSalestable_ds = SalesTable_ds;
           QueryBuildDataSource localQBDS =
            localSalestable_ds.queryBuildDataSource();
           QueryBuildRange localQBR = SysQuery::findOrCreateRange(
            localQBDS, fieldNum(SalesTable,
            ConVMSVehicleServiceId));
           localQBR.value(conVMS_CallerServiceTable.ServiceId);
       }
   }
   ```

4. Next, we will handle the `init` method. Remembering that we are augmenting the code, we will write it so that we only handle our specific need—when opened from a service order. We want to intercept the `init` method, so locate the `init` method on the `SalesTable` form, copy the method's declaration, and paste it into our extension class. Complete the code as follows:

```
public void init()
{
    next init();
}
```

For the next steps, remember that we are augmenting `SalesTable` form and it is an augmented version of `SalesTable` form; therefore, we have full access to all protected and public methods and variables. Private methods are made unavailable to protect us from possible regression due to an upgrade.

5. We will then add the following code so that we handle our specific case:

```
public void init()
{
    next init();
    switch (this.args().dataset())
    {
        case tableNum(ConVMSVehicleServiceTable):
            conVMS_CallerServiceTable = this.args().record();
            this.ConVMSVehicleServiceTableFilter();
            break;
    }
}
```

6. We should save our work, build the solution, and test it. It should open a sales order list page with no records.

You may find you have the following error path:
`[dynamics://View/RetailSalesTableChannelAttributeView]:En um type 'RetailChannelAttributeModifier' for the field 'Modifier' is not found.`
The `RetailChannelAttributeModifier` enum is in the `Retail` package.We must add this to our reference list in order to build our solution.

7. Next, we will write code to default the service order ID when a new sales order is created.

The natural thing is to write an accessor (`Parm`) method on our extension class and then an event handler to the form's `initValue` event. But forms are types so we can't call the extension method.

8. In our case, there is a method that has been written for use with a Chain of Command: `salesTableCreated`. Write the following method:

```
protected void salesTableCreated()
{
    next salesTableCreated();
    if (conVMS_CallerServiceTable.RecId != 0)
    {
        SalesTable.ConVMSVehicleServiceId =
        conVMS_CallerServiceTable.ServiceId;
    }
}
```

9. Save and close all designers, and build the solution. In this type of change, we should test the following:

- **Test 1**: When opening the sales orders from a service order, only orders for that service order are shown.
- **Test 2**: When creating a new sales order, the service order is populated on the new sales order.
- **Test 3**: When not opening the sales order list from a service, test that creating the order normally is not affected by our change.

How it works...

There isn't anything new in the first section, so we will focus on the extension part of the recipe.

The declaration is interesting. Compile-time functions such as `formStr` and `tableStr` just return a string, and are used to cause a compilation error should the element not exist. In the case of extensions, they serve a second purpose: to determine the type of the element. This is needed as forms can have the same name as a class or table.

The naming convention we used for global variables and methods results in long names, which may seem to contain unnecessary prefixes. We are not creating a new class. We are creating an extension class that augments the element referred to in the `ExtensionOf` attribute.

Every method and variable we declare has to be unique not only in relation to the element we are augmenting but also with every other extension of that element, including those in other packages. This is also why every local variable is prefixed with `local`.

 If we were editing the original class directly, it would be obvious that all global variables and method names must be unique. It would also be obvious that local variable names in the methods can't have the same name as any global variable. This is how we should think, but also to take further with this thought process further we want our code to sit nicely along side any other extension package the customer may wish to install.

There is a known fault in the current platform release (Platform 31 at the time of writing) that means we can't always access the right side of declared types. This is why we created a new type of `FormDataSource` as a copy (by reference) of `SalesTable_ds`. At some point, this will be fixed, so we can use this workaround until it is. There is no performance penalty as we are only copying a reference to it.

It may appear that we broke a convention when we used `this` instead of `element` in the `init` method. By convention, we would always use `element` when referring to the form instance, even in methods at the root of the form declaration—the form's own methods. This makes it very clear that we mean the form when we type `element`; `this` can vary given that the form has nest classes for data sources, fields, and controls.

In the extension class, `this` and `element` are the same thing, but they are handled differently by the compiler. The `element` instance is treated as a class variable, and there has been a problem accessing the right side of class variables in extension classes. We can't declare a local variable for `element` as there is no type to declare it as, except `FormRun` (which is of no use here). In this case, it is fine to use `this`. So, as it stands, this is currently not a problem; we can only use a Chain of Command with the base form declaration.

We most likely had to add a reference to `Retail` in order to build the project. This does seem odd until we consider how packages are built. We are now referencing the sales order form in our package; we, therefore, must reference the immediate dependencies. This is a view that contains a field that is based on this type.

The last part, defaulting the service ID field on the sales order table, wasn't as elegant as it should be. The technique relied on hooking into an extension point that was added by Microsoft. The ideal way to access forms as typed is to implement an interface, which is a great way to access a form's methods. We cannot add interfaces through an extension; if we need access to a method or variable defined at form level, we will need to access this using the following technique:

```
Object thisObj = this;
if (formHasMethod(this, ParmMyNewMethod))
{
    MyVariable myVar = thisObj.ParmMyNewMethod();
}
```

With the `Object` class, you can call any method, and it will compile—it just has to exist at run-time. This is a last resort, and prone to regression where code will fail or behave incorrectly, without any warning from the compiler. In our case, we would not have used this method; it would be preferable to write an event handler method, which has a `formRun()` method. From there, we can access its `args` object, and therefore the `dataset()` and `record()` methods.

Access form level methods can be done elegantly with our own forms, by implementing an interface we wrote as a code contract and writing code similar to the following:

```
public class MyForm extends FormRun implements MyNewMethodableI
{
    // this method was defined on the MyNewMethodableI interface
    public void MyNewMethod()
    {
        info("My new method was called");
    }
}
```

So, when we only have access to an instance of `FormRun`, we could write the following:

```
if (formRun is MyMethodableI)
{
    MyMethodableI instance = formRun;
    instance.MyNewMethod();
}
```

Using the interface means we can access the form code as if it were a type, which is much safer than using `Object`.

Replacing a standard lookup with our own

Sometimes we will need to add a field to a lookup or change the way it filters the list shown to the user. In this example, we will change the item lookup on the sales order line data source so that it only lists items that are on a related service order. This recipe will show you how to write a lookup, add a filter and an exists join, and prevent the standard lookup from being displayed.

We will be writing this lookup against a lookup event for the `ItemId` field on the `SalesLine` data source, on the `SalesTable` form.

How to do it...

To create a new lookup handler event, follow these steps:

1. Since this handles the lookup event on the `SalesTable` form, create a class named `SalesTable_ConVehicleManagement_FormHandler`.

2. Open the `SalesTable` form design, and expand `Data Sources`, `SalesLine`, and then `ItemId`.

    You will see there is no lookup event here, which means we can't override the lookup so that all controls based on this field will be affected. We can't use the Chain of Command on the lookup method because it does not support nested objects, and this forces us to override the lookup at the control level.

3. Next, find the `SalesLineGrid` grid control, and expand the `SalesLine_ItemId` control to see the events that it has.

4. Right-click on `OnLookup` and choose **Copy event handler method**.

5. Paste the method into our class, which should look like the following:

```
[FormControlEventHandler(formControlStr(SalesTable,
SalesLine_ItemId), FormControlEventType::Lookup)]
public static void SalesLine_ItemId_OnLookup(FormControl sender,
FormControlEventArgs e)
{
}
```

6. The lookup we want should only run if it is called from a service order, so we need to get this. Add the following code into our new method:

```
SalesLine salesLine = sender.dataSourceObject().cursor();
ConVMSVehicleServiceId serviceId =
salesLine.salesTable().ConVMSVehicleServiceId;
if (serviceId != '')
{

}
```

7. We now know we have a service order so we should cancel the super call (which triggers the standard lookup). As we have seen in other event handlers, the `args` object is a generic base class and isn't particularly useful. We want to be able to cancel the super call, which is possible for some events such as lookups. To do this, we simply cast the `FormControlEventArgs` object as `FormControlCancelableSuperEventArgs`, shown as follows:

```
FormControlCancelableSuperEventArgs cancelable = e;
cancelable.CancelSuperCall();
```

8. To make the code easier to write, we should write a new method to perform the lookup. Start the method with the following code, which constructs the basic lookup object we need:

```
public static void ItemIdLookup(ConVMSVehicleServiceId _serviceId,
FormControl _control)
{
    SysTableLookup lookup =
     SysTableLookup::newParameters(tableNum(InventTable),
    _control);
}
```

9. Next, we need to add a data source to the lookup, which is usually done by creating a `Query` object and calling its `addDataSource()` method. In our case, we need the `QueryBuildDataSource` object it returns in order to add an exists join to the service order lines. The code is as follows:

```
Query q = new Query();
QueryBuildDataSource inventTableQBDS =
q.addDataSource(tableNum(InventTable));
QueryBuildDataSource serviceLineQBDS =
inventTableQBDS.addDataSource(tableNum(ConVMSVehicleServiceLine));
```

10. We then need to tell it the type of join and add a relationship, which is done as follows:

```
serviceLineQBDS.joinMode(JoinMode::ExistsJoin);
serviceLineQBDS.addLink(fieldNum(InventTable, ItemId),
fieldNum(ConVMSVehicleServiceLine, ItemId));
```

11. We can then add our range to filter on the service ID, which is done by the following lines of code:

```
QueryBuildRange serviceIdRange = SysQuery::findOrCreateRange(
    serviceLineQBDS,
    fieldNum(ConVMSVehicleServiceLine, ServiceId));
serviceIdRange.value(_serviceId);
```

12. Now tell the lookup the query to use and then add fields to the lookup. Adding fields to the lookup is done using the addLookupField and addLookupMethod methods on the lookup instance of SysTableLookup:

```
lookup.parmQuery(q);

lookup.addLookupfield(fieldNum(InventTable, ItemId));
lookup.addLookupMethod(tableMethodStr(InventTable, itemName));
lookup.addLookupfield(fieldNum(InventTable, ItemType));
```

13. We then add a call to perform the lookup (lookup.performFormLookup()), the entire method should read as follows:

```
public static void ItemIdLookup(ConVMSVehicleServiceId _serviceId,
FormControl _control)
{
    SysTableLookup lookup =
     SysTableLookup::newParameters(tableNum(InventTable),
     _control);
    //build the query
    Query q = new Query();
    QueryBuildDataSource inventTableQBDS =
     q.addDataSource(tableNum(InventTable));
    QueryBuildDataSource serviceLineQBDS =
     inventTableQBDS.addDataSource(
        tableNum(ConVMSVehicleServiceLine));
    // set the relation
    serviceLineQBDS.joinMode(JoinMode::ExistsJoin);
    serviceLineQBDS.addLink(fieldNum(InventTable, ItemId),
    fieldNum(ConVMSVehicleServiceLine, ItemId));
    QueryBuildRange serviceIdRange = SysQuery::findOrCreateRange(
     serviceLineQBDS, fieldNum(ConVMSVehicleServiceLine,
```

```
        ServiceId));
    serviceIdRange.value(_serviceId);

    //tell the lookup the query to use
    lookup.parmQuery(q);

    //add field to the lookup grid
    lookup.addLookupfield(fieldNum(InventTable, ItemId));
    lookup.addLookupMethod(tableMethodStr(InventTable, itemName));
    lookup.addLookupfield(fieldNum(InventTable, ItemType));

    //perform the lookup
    lookup.performFormLookup();
}
```

14. Finally, add a call to our lookup in our event handler, where the entire event handler method should read as follows:

```
[FormControlEventHandler(formControlStr(SalesTable,
SalesLine_ItemId), FormControlEventType::Lookup)]
public static void SalesLine_ItemId_OnLookup(FormControl sender,
FormControlEventArgs e)
{
    SalesLine salesLine = sender.dataSourceObject().cursor();
    ConVMSVehicleServiceId serviceId =
     salesLine.salesTable().ConVMSVehicleServiceId;
    if (serviceId != '')
    {
        FormControlCancelableSuperEventArgs cancelable = e;
        cancelable.CancelSuperCall();
        SalesTable_ConVehicleManagement_FormHandler::ItemIdLookup
        (serviceId, sender);
    }
}
```

15. Close and save all tabs, and build the project in order to test the lookup. Test cases where the lookup should show and where it should not.

 The build may fail with **SourceDocumentTypes is required to compile this module**. This is because we are the referencing sales line directly in our package. Add a reference to this package.

How it works...

There are two new topics here: an event where the super can be canceled and the lookup code. We just know that `FormControlEventArgs` can be cast to `FormControlCancelableSuperEventArgs`. If it isn't, we will get an error at run-time.

We have made three assumptions, which we could test for and throw an exception at runtime:

- The control is bound to a data source.
- The bound data source is a `SalesLine` record.
- `FormControlEventArgs` can be cast to `FormControlCancelableSuperEventArgs`.

We could make the code more robust by considering the following:

- Testing that the control is bound:

  ```
  if (sender.dataSourceObject() != null)
  ```

- Test that the bound data source is based on `SalesLine`:

  ```
  if (sender.dataSourceObject().cursor().tableId ==
  tableNum(SalesLine))
  ```

- Testing that `FormControlEventArgs` can be cast to `FormControlCancelableSuperEventArgs` by:

  ```
  if ( !(FormControlEventArgs isFormControlCancelableSuperEventArgs))
  {
      // throw a suitable error e.g. "<class>.<method> was called
      // incorrectly"
  }
  ```

In many cases, the assumptions are appropriate because the code can only be called if these assumptions are true anyway. A table data-event sender parameter will always be the table it is handling.

Lookup code is common for most lookups. Lookups would usually be written on the table that we are applying the lookup to, but in our case this isn't possible. The form event handler class is sufficient in this case as the lookup is specific to a form of control.

We had two other options for writing the lookup and query. One was to use an inner join—this would allow us to add fields from the service order line to the lookup grid. This would also cause duplication if the same item was added to a service order. The other option we had was to make the lookup simply use the `ConVMSVehicleServiceLine` table, and just add a range.

Adding a form display method to a standard form

We can add display methods to tables and forms using extension classes. The table route is preferred, as tables are reusable. We sometimes need to add display methods to a form because some information is only available when the form is built, such as data on the form's data sources.

This is a limitation in that the display methods on forms cannot be added to the data source object, and they don't currently accept a record as a parameter. For this reason, they can only use the current record of a data source and cannot, therefore, be used as on-grid controls—they would show the same values on all rows.

In our case, we will write a display method to show information from a service order, in order to state that new orders will be attached to the service order. Of course, if this is intended as a warning, it needs to be more prominent and also display on the Create dialog. The aim here is to show how to write a display method using a form extension.

How to do it...

To write a display method via a form extension, follow these steps:

1. Open the form extension class we created earlier
   (`SalesTable_ConVehicleManagement_Form_Extension`).
2. Write the following method:

```
public display str DispConVMSServiceMessage()
{
    if (conVMS_CallerServiceTable.RecId == 0)
    {
        // New sales orders will not be linked to a service order
        return '';
    }
    //Service %1
```

```
        return strFmt("@ConVMS:ServiceMsg",
    conVMS_CallerServiceTable.ServiceId);
    }
```

 There is no need for an `else` block; this takes up CPU time and the result will be the same as in the preceding code block. `Str` will suffice as the return type as we don't want a label in this case.

3. Open the `SalesTable.ConVehicleManagement` form extension designer.
4. Add a **String** control to the `EntityStatus` field group in **TabPageDetails | HeaderInfo**.
5. Name the **String** control `CtrlDispConVMSServiceMessage`, remembering that this must be globally unique across all models.
6. We are using a form display method, so we will not populate the **Data Source** property. Click the drop-down menu for the **Data Method** property, which will show the following in the list: `SalesTable_ConVehicleManagement_Form_Extension.DispConVMSServiceMessage`. Select this, and then close and save all editor tabs.
7. Build the solution, and test the form when opened both from the menu and from a service order.

How it works...

This further reinforces that extension classes are augmentations of the form or class we created the extension for. Our display method appears (albeit qualified with the extension class name) as if it is on the form code itself. It also seems that the method itself doesn't have to be unique after all. This is not true, we will get a compilation error if we create a second extension class on the same object with a method of the same name. The automatic prefix of the class name is there to help us find the method.

There's more...

The code in our display method returns an empty string, and it doesn't look great having a pointless empty control on the form. We should hide it.

To do this, we would usually use the `formControlStr` compile time function as shown below the control instance:

```
int controlId = this.controlId(formControlStr(SalesTable,
SalesLine_ItemId));
FormStringControl = this.control(controlId);
```

We can't use this with extension fields, so we need to make the control automatically declare itself. Find the `CtrlDispConVMSServiceMessage` control and set the **Auto Declaration** property to **Yes**. Save and close the form.

We can now write an `EnableFields` method to control its visibility on our form extension class:

```
public void ConVMSEnableFields()
{
    boolean localIsService = (conVMS_CallerServiceTable.RecId != 0);
    FormStringControl localDispConVMSServiceMessage =
     this.CtrlDispConVMSServiceMessage;
    localDispConVMSServiceMessage.visible(localIsService);
}
```

We had to assign the control to a local variable as we sometimes can't access the right side of the main element's objects.

Add a call to this method in the Chain of Command `init` method we wrote earlier:

```
public void init()
{
    next init();
    switch (this.args().dataset())
    {
        case tableNum(ConVMSVehicleServiceTable):
            conVMS_CallerServiceTable = this.args().record();
            this.ConVMSVehicleServiceTableFilter();
            this.ConVMSEnableFields();
            break;
    }
}
```

In this call, the standard `init()` method is called first, along with any other Chain of Command extensions that haven't yet been called, and then our code is run. Remember that our code is not guaranteed to be run last, even though `next` is at the start of the method. It only guarantees that the standard code will be run first.

6
Writing for Extensibility

Any solution we write should be written in a way that it is extendable with minimal impact on the existing code. When writing a solution as an **Independent Software Vendor (ISV)**, it is critical to avoid situations where our customers are forced to use inelegant workarounds in order to make the vertical solution fit their specific requirements.

Writing for extensibility takes the form of writing delegates, with relevant and careful consideration of whether to assign private, protected, or public to our methods. We would also split out code into more methods, which is good practice in any case but also serves a purpose in enabling Chain of Command. The recipes in this chapter are focused on topics that help us create extendable solutions.

In this chapter, we'll cover the following recipes:

- Writing and using delegates
- Using the attribute framework to construct classes
- Creating a purchase order programmatically
- Creating a facade
- Defining business actions in data
- Creating a SysOperation process
- Adding an interface to the SysOperation framework
- Using SysOperationSandbox

Technical requirements

You can find the code files of this chapter on GitHub at `https://github.com/PacktPublishing/Extending-Microsoft-Dynamics-365-Finance-and-Supply-Chain-Management-Cookbook-Second-Edition/blob/master/Chapter%206.axpp`.

Writing and using delegates

Delegates are written specifically for other parties to hook into our code. This is either through an extensibility request, or because we envisage that it will be required. All the events in the tables are actually delegates, and if we write a delegate on a table, they will also appear in the events list.

One thing that delegates can't do is return a value, and we will use an example where information is passed back to the caller from the delegate. This is done by passing a value that is passed by reference—such as a table or a class.

In our example, we will write a delegate to be called when the status changes.

How to do it...

Although delegates can be written with a simple set of parameters (or none at all), our example requires data to be passed back. To do this, perform the following steps:

1. Create a new parameter class called `ConVMSVehicleStatusChangeResponseParameters`; this is a normal class with a set of `public` variables. The class should be as follows:

```
class ConVMSVehicleStatusChangeResponseParameters
{
    public boolean delegateWashandled;
    public boolean success;
    public str message;
}
```

 We are only handling the response; the outbound parameters will be on the delegate declaration itself.

2. Let's write our delegate, which will be passed the previous and new service status and the service order record. It will have the past tense to highlight to the consumer that the service order has already been updated.
   Open `ConVMSVehicleServiceTable` and write the following new method:

```
delegate void
ServiceStatusChanged(ConVMSVehicleStatusChangeResponseParameters
_parameters, ConVMSVehicleServiceStatus _previousStatus,
ConVMSVehicleServiceStatus _newStatus) {}
```

3. We need to know the previous and current version of the service table record, so we have to use the table's update method for this. Find this method (or override if this is not yet overridden) and add the following line of code to the top of the method:

```
ConVMSVehicleServiceTable thisOrig = this.orig();
```

4. Now we have the original state of the record, we can write the following code to test whether the status has changed:

```
if (thisOrig.ServiceStatus != this.ServiceStatus)
{

}
```

 This must be placed after the `super()` call because we want to be sure the record is written. The ideal place is just before the end of the method.

5. We can now construct our parameter class and write the code to call the delegate, as follows:

```
ConVMSVehicleStatusChangeResponseParameters params = new
ConVMSVehicleStatusChangeResponseParameters();
this.ServiceStatusChanged(params, thisOrig.ServiceStatus,
this.ServiceStatus);
```

6. We should then handle the situation where the call was not successful, which is done in the following lines of code:

```
if (params.delegateWashandled && !params.success)
{
    throw error(params.message);
}
```

7. We should make the whole update block into a transaction so that the whole transaction fails if the delegate fails. The completed code for the method will be as follows:

```
public void update()
{
    ConVMSVehicleServiceTable thisOrig = this.orig();
    ttsbegin;
    this.Type().Updating(); // existing code from previous chapter
                            // - not part of this example
    super();
    this.Type().Updated(); // existing code from previous chapter -
                            // not part of this example

    if (thisOrig.ServiceStatus != this.ServiceStatus)
    {
        ConVMSVehicleStatusChangeResponseParameters params =
            new ConVMSVehicleStatusChangeResponseParameters();
        this.ServiceStatusChanged(params, thisOrig.ServiceStatus,
        this.ServiceStatus);
        if (params.delegateWashandled && !params.success)
        {
            throw error(params.message);
        }
    }
    ttscommit;
}
```

 The following steps are an example of how to subscribe to a delegate. We wouldn't normally use this technique for elements in our project or package; we would simply add a call to the method.

8. Create a class named `ConVMSVehicleServiceStatusChangeCheck`.

9. Open the table designer for `ConVMSVehicleServiceTable` and expand the **Events** node.

10. At the top should be our new delegate; right-click on it and choose **Copy event handler method**.

11. Select the code editor for the new `ConVMSVehicleServiceStatusChangeCheck` class and paste in our method—it should be as follows:

```
[SubscribesTo(
    tableStr(ConVMSVehicleServiceTable),
```

```
        delegateStr(ConVMSVehicleServiceTable, ServiceStatusChanged))]
public static void ConVMSVehicleServiceTable_ServiceStatusChanged(
    ConVMSVehicleStatusChangeResponseParameters _parameters,
    ConVMSVehicleServiceStatus _previousStatus,
    ConVMSVehicleServiceStatus _newStatus)
{
}
```

12. We should next determine whether another handler has been run and failed; we don't want to interfere with someone else's logic:

```
// if another handler has run and failed, do not continue
if (_parameters.delegateWashandled && !_parameters.success)
{
    return;
}
```

13. Then we write our code:

```
// perform our check
if (_previousStatus == ConVMSVehicleServiceStatus::Complete &&
_newStatus == ConVMSVehicleServiceStatus::Cancelled)
{
 _parameters.delegateWashandled = true;
 _parameters.success = false;
 _parameters.message =
 strFmt("@ConVMS:CompleteServiceOrdersCannotBeCancelled");
}
```

14. That's it; just compile and test that this behaves as expected. You will need to make the ServiceStatus field editable in order to test this in the UI.

How it works...

This technique allows us to create our own *events* and is not restricted to tables. It can be used for classes and forms also. Delegates are straightforward enough: write a method stub as delegate void <MethodName> (<optional parameters>) and just call it in the code. If there are any subscribers, they will all be called—but in no particular order. This is why, in our example of the parameter class, we check whether it has already been handled before continuing.

We should always write delegates for anything we consider to be an event; another option could be delegates such as `ServiceOrderCompleted` and `ServiceOrderCancelled`. The aim here is to provide a method so that other developers, who may be working in a package that just references our own, can safely interact and extend our code. Even when writing a vertical solution, the fit can't be assumed to be 100%—so extensibility should be considered a key selling point of our solution.

The choice over what data to send is important; the same thought should go into this decision when we decide whether a variable is `public`, `protected`, or `private`. If we passed the service order record, the subscriber could change it—which may not be desirable. At the same time, if our subscriber wished to create a sales order from the service order when it reaches the status *completed*, they would struggle; the subscriber can only access the parameters sent with the event.

In our case, we could write a new `ServiceOrderCompleted` method that has the parameter class and the service order record. When we do this, we must handle the situation where the subscriber has altered our table using the following code:

```
if (FormDataUtil::isFormDataSource(this)) // this or the table instance if
                                          // not on the table itself
{
    // again, this or the table instance if not on the table itself
    FormDataUtil::getFormDataSource(this).reread();
}
```

The preceding code should avoid any **Another user has altered...** messages.

There's more...

We can also use this method in order to construct classes when retrofitting extensibility to a class structure constructed through a switch statement.

These constructors are usually written as follows:

```
ConVMSVehicleServiceStatusBase instance;
switch (_status)
{
    case ConVMSVehicleServiceStatus::None:
        instance = new ConVMSVehicleServiceStatus_None();
        break;
    case ConVMSVehicleServiceStatus::Confirmed:
        instance = new ConVMSVehicleServiceStatus_Confirmed();
        break;
    // etc.
```

```
    default:
        throw error("<Status not implemented error>");
}
```

In this case, the parameter class would be written as follows:

```
class ConVMSVehicleServiceStatusConstructResponseParameters
{
    public boolean delegateWashandled;
    public ConVMSVehicleServiceStatusBase instance;
}
```

The delegate would be declare static:

```
static delegate void serviceStatusContruct(
    ConVMSVehicleServiceStatusConstructResponseParameters _parm,
    ConVMSVehicleServiceStatus_status) {}
```

The constructor is then written as follows:

```
ConVMSVehicleServiceStatusBase instance;
switch (_status)
{
    case ConVMSVehicleServiceStatus::None:
        instance = new ConVMSVehicleServiceStatus_None();
        break;
    case ConVMSVehicleServiceStatus::Confirmed:
        instance = new ConVMSVehicleServiceStatus_Confirmed();
        break;
}
if (!instance)
{
    ConVMSVehicleServiceStatusConstructResponseParameters parm;
    parm = new ConVMSVehicleServiceStatusConstructResponseParameters();
    ConVMSVehicleServiceTable::ConVMSVehicleServiceStatus(parm, _status);
    if (!parm.delegateWasHandled())
    {
        throw error("<Status is not implemented>");
    }
    instance = parm.instance;
}
return instance;
```

This pattern has been used in the standard code, where the risk of regression errors is high and the code has been used by customers and end-user organizations and it would result in a breaking change. This is not as elegant as the attribute factory framework, which is demonstrated next.

Using the attribute framework to construct classes

In `Chapter 4`, *Working with Form Logic and Frameworks,* we wrote the `ConVMSVehicleServiceTableType` class. This had a method that determined whether or not the record can be edited. It used a `CanEdit` method, which in turn called a `CanEditStatus` method. There was nothing obviously wrong here, but what if our customer wanted to add a status? They could use Chain of Command, which is okay, but this also means we didn't design the solution to be extended in this way. There are two ways to structure the logic in this case:

- Use a switch statement on the status
- Write a class per status that is constructed based on the record's status

The latter option is used by `SalesLineType`. This is much simpler to read, especially when the code in each case is more than one line. It is also much easier to extend. The traditional way to write this would be a switch-based constructor. This is even harder to extend by our customers, and we would need to call a delegate and pass a data contract by reference in order for it to communicate back the object that should be constructed.

 We will refactor our code to use the attribute framework, which is more code, but it is much elegant and easier to maintain going forward.

Having decided on a class per status, we still have structural choices to make, such as which of the following options to choose:

- `ConVMSVehicleServiceTableType_None`, `ConVMSVehicleServiceTableType_Confirmed`, and so on
- `ConVMSVehicleServiceStatusType_None`, `ConVMSVehicleServiceStatusType_Confirmed`, and so on

The second option would have one `ConVMSVehicleServiceTableType` class with a `CreateStatusInstance` method that returns the appropriate class for the status value. This is ideal when we only intend to specialize one area of code into separate classes. The `ConVMSVehicleServiceTableType` class handles table events and number sequences, which we don't want to have the option to be changed by service status. We will, therefore, create a structure based on the service status; the second option.

So we will have the following structure:

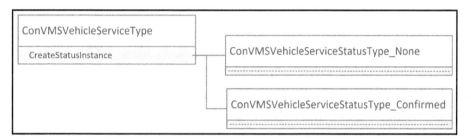

CreateStatusInstance must return a base class or an interface. A base class that is abstract would work, as this enforces that everything that extends it must implement the required methods—again we are thinking that our code will be extended by others when designing this. If we want to provide base class functionality, the choice would be an abstract base class, and if we want to decouple the two completely and only place a demand that the class implements one or more methods, we would use an interface.

How to do it...

We will first construct an attribute class that will be used to tell the framework which class should be made for the status value; this is done with the following steps:

1. Create a new class named ConVMSVehicleServiceStatusAttribute.
2. The contents of this class is nearly the same for all attribute classes, and we can use a string or base enum. In this case, we are using the ConVMSVehicleServiceStatus enum, so write the following code:

```
class ConVMSVehicleServiceStatusAttribute
    extends SysAttribute
    implements SysExtensionIAttribute
{
    ConVMSVehicleServiceStatus serviceStatus;
    public void new(ConVMSVehicleServiceStatus _serviceStatus)
    {
        serviceStatus = _serviceStatus;
    }
    public str parmCacheKey()
    {
        // This key must be invariant across languages, so use
        // int2str() instead of enum2str()
        return classStr(
        ConVMSVehicleServiceStatusAttribute)+';'
```

```
            +int2str(enum2int(serviceStatus));
    }

    public boolean useSingleton()
    {
        // if the class using this attribute is immutable, consider
        // returning true in most cases it is safer to return
        // false.
        return false;
    }
}
```

3. We will now create an interface to act as a code contract; create a new interface named `ConVMSVehicleServiceStatusTypeI`.

4. We will ensure that the implementations have the ability to check whether a service can be edited or deleted. Complete the interface so that it reads as follows:

```
interface ConVMSVehicleServiceStatusTypeI
{
    public boolean CanEdit()
    {
    }
    public boolean CanDelete()
    {
    }
}
```

 When creating the interface in the add dialog, the interface artifact type must be selected. Choosing class and changing the class to read as above will cause a problem later as this will create the metadata with the **Is Interface** property set to `false`.

5. We can now write the create instance method; create a new method on `ConVMSVehicleServiceTableType` with the following declaration:

```
public ConVMSVehicleServiceStatusTypeI CreateStatusTypeInstance()
{
}
```

6. We use the `SysExtensionAppClassFactory::getClassFromSysAttribute` method to construct our instance; this takes an argument of a class that extends `SysAttribute` and a base class name. So we construct our attribute class first, as follows:

```
ConVMSVehicleServiceStatusAttribute attr = new
ConVMSVehicleServiceStatusAttribute(serviceTable.ServiceStatus);
```

 Since the main type class is constructed with a service status, we will use this to construct the attribute class.

7. To construct our instance that implements `ConVMSVehicleServiceStatusTypeI`, we write the following code:

```
ConVMSVehicleServiceStatusTypeI instance =
SysExtensionAppClassFactory::getClassFromSysAttribute(classStr(ConV
MSVehicleServiceStatusTypeI), attr);
```

8. We could just return `instance`, but this would cause a `null` reference exception until all concrete implementations are written (the classes that implement our interface). So we should throw and exception if `instance` is `null` or is not `ConVMSVehicleServiceStatusTypeI`. Sometimes the cache can be out of sync with the code (for example, if we rename a base enum element name), so we will first try to clear the cache and then throw an exception if this fails. The completed method is as follows:

```
public ConVMSVehicleServiceStatusTypeI CreateStatusTypeInstance()
{
    // we want to construct this based on the current status of the
    // record, not the value we may be changing it to.
    ConVMSVehicleServiceStatus localServiceStatus =
     serviceTable.ServiceStatus;
    ConVMSVehicleServiceTable origServiceTable =
     serviceTable.orig();
    if (origServiceTable.RecId != 0)
    {
        localServiceStatus = origServiceTable.ServiceStatus;
    }

    ConVMSVehicleServiceStatusAttribute attr = new
     ConVMSVehicleServiceStatusAttribute(localServiceStatus);
    ConVMSVehicleServiceStatusTypeI instance =
```

```
        SysExtensionAppClassFactory::getClassFromSysAttribute(
         classStr(ConVMSVehicleServiceStatusTypeI), attr);
        if (!instance || !(instance is
         ConVMSVehicleServiceStatusTypeI))
        {
            SysExtensionCache::clearAllScopes();
            instance =
            SysExtensionAppClassFactory::getClassFromSysAttribute(
             classStr(ConVMSVehicleServiceStatusTypeI), attr);
            if (!instance || !(instance is
             ConVMSVehicleServiceStatusTypeI))
            {
                throw error(Error::wrongUseOfFunction(funcName()));
            }
        }
        // additional information can be passed if the interface has
        // parm methods,
        // contracts or parameter classes work best with interfaces
        return instance;
    }
```

9. Let's refactor our code; change the `CanEditStatus` method to read as follows:

```
public boolean CanEditStatus()
{
 return this.CreateStatusTypeInstance().CanEdit();
}
```

10. Then write an equivalent `CanDeleteStatus()` method and `CheckCanDeleteStatus()` method (you will need to create a label for this also):

```
public boolean CanDeleteStatus()
{
    return this.CreateStatusTypeInstance().CanDelete();
}
public boolean CheckCanDeleteStatus()
{
    if (!this.CanDeleteStatus())
    {
        return checkFailed(strFmt("@ConVMS:ServiceCannotBeDeleted",
         serviceTable.ServiceId, serviceTable.ServiceStatus));
    }
    return true;
}
```

11. The final step in the `ConVMSVehicleServiceType` class is to change the `ValidateDelete()` method to use the new method, for example:

```
public boolean ValidateDelete()
{
    boolean canDelete = true;
    // this pattern is normal as the method will often contain m
    canDelete = canDelete && this.CheckCanDeleteStatus();
    return canDelete;
}
```

 We can use the interface in code even though there are no concrete implementations.

12. Next, we will write the classes that do the actual work. We will write a class for each status value in the format `ConVMSVehicleServiceStatusType_<status element name>`. The first class's declaration should be written as follows:

```
[ConVMSVehicleServiceStatusAttribute(ConVMSVehicleServiceStatus::
 None)]
class ConVMSVehicleServiceStatusType_None implements
ConVMSVehicleServiceStatusTypeI
```

13. Next, copy the two method declarations from the interface, and paste them into the class body. At status `None`, we can both edit and delete, so the completed class will be as follows:

```
[ConVMSVehicleServiceStatusAttribute(ConVMSVehicleServiceStatus::
 None)]
class ConVMSVehicleServiceStatusType_None implements
ConVMSVehicleServiceStatusTypeI
{
    public boolean CanEdit()
    {
        return true;
    }
    public boolean CanDelete()
    {
        return true;
    }
}
```

Use copy and paste to create the interface method stubs. They are not case-sensitive at compile time, but they are at runtime. Do *not* copy the interface and rename the class declaration to class. This will not change the **Is interface** metadata property to false.

14. Save and close this class.

15. We can now duplicate this first class for the statuses `Confirmed`,`Complete`, and `Cancelled`. Just use copy and paste in Solution Explorer—we should now have four classes:

    - `ConVMSVehicleServiceStatusType_None`
    - `ConVMSVehicleServiceStatusType_Confirmed`
    - `ConVMSVehicleServiceStatusType_Complete`
    - `ConVMSVehicleServiceStatusType_Cancelled`

16. Change each class so that each conforms to the following table:

Class	ConVMSVehicleServiceStatusAttribute	CanEdit	CanDelete
ConVMSVehicleServiceStatusType_None	ConVMSVehicleServiceStatus::None	true	true
ConVMSVehicleServiceStatusType_Confirmed	ConVMSVehicleServiceStatus::Confirmed	true	false
ConVMSVehicleServiceStatusType_Complete	ConVMSVehicleServiceStatus::Complete	false	false
ConVMSVehicleServiceStatusType_Cancelled	ConVMSVehicleServiceStatus::Cancelled	false	true

17. Double-check each class to ensure that the attribute declaration, `ConVMSVehicleServiceStatusAttribute`, is correct and that each class implements `ConVMSVehicleServiceStatusTypeI`.

18. Save and close all editors and then build the project and test each status to ensure that they work correctly.

How it works...

The first question that might be asked is *why?* We wrote five classes and an interface when a few lines of code in a switch statement was required and would have been much quicker to write.

The first reason is that switch statements are naturally hard to extend through extensibility. With this method, we can use Chain of Command on the classes and add a new status element very easily. We just add the new base enum element as usual, and then write the class to handle it. This is no code to change in the `ConVMSVehicleServiceTableType` class. The attribute pattern is designed to be extended by developers working on our package and those working for our customers in their own packages.

Another reason is that the status logic is now decoupled from the place it is used (the `ConVMSVehicleServiceTableType` class). We can now use this code elsewhere, with very little effort. The usage of the code is simplified as we don't have to think about the code that is being called and the implementation is simplified as we only have to conform to the interface.

To speed up the development time, the attribute class can be simply copied and edited to suit your needs as can the create instance methods.

There is a comment in the `CreateStatusInstance` method that states additional information can be passed to the instance after it is instantiated. When using an interface method, use a parameter class, and not parameter (`Parm<Value>`) methods. The interface is a contract and every class that implements it must implement every method in the interface. If we add a new method to the interface because we have a case that needs additional information, we will break every other class. This will result in breaking customer solutions where they have used the interface; however, adding a new `public` variable to our parameter class will not break our customer solutions.

A parameter class would be similar to the following code:

```
public class ConVMSVehicleServiceActionParameters()
{
    // add a public variable declaration for each variable we need
    // variable1, et at are just unimaginative examples
    public boolean variable1;
    public boolean variable2;
}
```

We wouldn't use `parm` methods in this scenario, as the class is just a way to pass parameters. This also is a nice way to avoid using containers to return more than one variable.

There are two main sections to this pattern: declaring the attribute and then making a call to create the instance using the attribute class. The purpose of the attribute class is twofold. The first purpose is to decorate the instance classes in order for the framework to locate the correct class through a metadata search. The other is to create a cache key in order to avoid repeated metadata searches.

When the `SysExtensionAppClassFactory::getClassFromSysAttribute` method runs, it will construct a cache key string that includes the attribute's `parmCacheKey` method and the base class parameter (in our case, the `ConVMSVehicleServiceStatusTypeI` interface). With this key, it will see whether an instance has previously been constructed and placed in the global cache. If it has, the cached value is returned, which is very quick. Should the cache key not be found, the framework will perform a metadata search for classes with the appropriate attribute declaration and will also implement the correct interface.

We could also use a base class instead of an interface, should this pattern be used. In this case, the search will determine that it is a class and look for classes that extend this base class. This uses the metadata property **Is interface** that is set when the class or interface is created to know whether it is a class or an interface—it does not use the class declaration of class or interface!

This also seems to have a lot of overhead, and we would intuitively think this must be slower. Try debugging it; even when it does the metadata search, no delay is noticeable and if it is already in the global cache, the performance difference seems negligible.

Creating a purchase order programmatically

This recipe focuses on the creation of a purchase order in code. This is actually the first of three recipes that will extend our service status change handling over the next few recipes into a framework that allows the functional consultant more control over the business logic that is executed. One of the problems in solution design is that the business rules are often coded into the solution, and each iteration in the implementation evolves these rules and results in a change to the code. Writing business logic in a succinct class designed for that purpose results in code that is easier to read, maintain, and change. One common problem is when we are asked to write code that links user-defined data to code. Here's an example:

> *When an item of the* `Audio` *Item Group is bought from an import vendor, it must print the* `Audio` *specification document at the receipt stage.*

A common solution is the following:

```
if (purchLine.inventTable().ItemGroupId() == 'Audio' && isImport)
{
    MyCustomPrintService::PrintAudioSpecication(purchLine);
}
```

This is made better with a parameter added to a parameter table, so the consultant can decide or change the item group for `Audio`. What tends to happen next is that there are two `Audio` item groups, so we end up with a switch statement and two parameter fields in the parameter table.

The solution to this problem is adding a checkbox to the item group table for `IsAudio`; this can be sufficient until we discover a requirement for a `Visual` specification document; the company decided to buy visual products during the implementation.

 This tends to happen most when the business process is determined to have low maturity during the solution design process. A hidden risk is that a process can seem to have deceptively high maturity when a process is even subtly changed through the introduction of a new system.

In our case, we have been given the following requirements:

Create a purchase order for items at status `Confirmed` *for Bikes in group "Over 500cc".*

We are then told a future requirement is to allow the user to create a purchase order manually for items added after the service order is confirmed. The solution to this would be to do the following:

1. Write a class that can create a purchase order from a list
2. Write a facade (explained later in the chapter) to the purchase order
3. Create class to create a purchase order from a service order
4. Design a method to call the new facade for a vehicle group at a specific service order status

In this recipe, we will focus on writing the service class to create a purchase order from a list. The class will need to feed back to the caller the purchase order lines created for each element in the list. This will need a correlation identifier and a reference to the purchase order line. The source record's `RecId` field is a good correlation identifier, and since the `InventTransId` field is a unique key on purchase order lines, this will be the reference we will return.

Getting ready

To save time during this recipe, ensure that the package references the `Calendar` package. This is because the `PurchTable` table contains the field `AccountingDate` field, which is in the `Calendar` package.

The purchase order line generation code also uses elements from the following packages, so these must also be referenced:

- `SourceDocumenation`
- `ContactPerson`
- `Tax`
- `FiscalBooks`

How to do it...

To create the classes required to create a purchase order, follow these steps:

1. First, we will create a data contract class for what is required. We need a correlation identity (the source record's `RecId`), `ItemId`, and the quantity required. The class should be created as follows:

```
[DataContract]
class ConVMSPurchOrderGenerateRequestLineContract
{
    RefRecId sourceRecId;
    ItemId itemId;
    PurchQty purchQty;
    [DataMember]
    public RefRecId SourceRecId(RefRecId _sourceRecId =
     sourceRecId)
    {
        sourceRecId = _sourceRecId;
        return sourceRecId;
    }
    [DataMember]
    public ItemId ItemId(ItemId _itemId = itemId)
    {
        itemId = _itemId;
        return itemId;
    }
    [DataMember]
    public PurchQty PurchQty(PurchQty _purchQty = purchQty)
    {
        purchQty = _purchQty;
        return purchQty;
    }
}
```

2. Next, we will create a response contract using the following steps:

```
[DataContract]
class ConVMSPurchOrderGenerateResponseContract
{
    RefRecId sourceRecId;
    InventTransId createdInventTransId;
    [DataMember]
    public RefRecId SourceRecId(RefRecId _sourceRecId =
     sourceRecId)
    {
        sourceRecId = _sourceRecId;
        return sourceRecId;;
    }
    [DataMember]
    public InventTransId CreatedInventTransId(
        InventTransId _createdInventTransId = createdInventTransId)
    {
        createdInventTransId = _createdInventTransId;
        return createdInventTransId;
    }
}
```

3. Next, we will create the purchase order generation class, create a class
   named `ConVMSPurchOrderGenerate`, and create a public constructor as
   follows:

```
class ConVMSPurchOrderGenerate
{
    List responseList = new List(Types::Class);
    List requestList;
    Map vendPurchIdMap; // needed when splitting the lines into
                        // purchase orders per vendor
    /// <summary>
    /// protect from being constructed directly
    /// </summary>
    protected void new()
    {
    }

    /// <summary>
    /// Construct instance of ConVMSPurchOrderGenerate from a
    /// list of ConVMSPurchOrderGenerateRequestLineContract objects
    /// </summary>
    /// <param name = "_requestList">List of
        ConVMSPurchOrderGenerateRequestLineContract</param>
    /// <returns>instance of ConVMSPurchOrderGenerate</returns>
    public static ConVMSPurchOrderGenerate NewFromRequestList(List
```

```
_requestList)
{
    ConVMSPurchOrderGenerate instance = new
     ConVMSPurchOrderGenerate();
    instance.requestList = _requestList;
    return instance;
}
}
```

 We override the new method in order to prevent the class from being constructed directly. The code can fail unless it is constructed correctly.

4. The next part has a little complexity; we don't know the supplier yet, so we should first prepare the data so we know the vendors we need, and therefore how many purchase orders. The following method will create a Map of supplier and purchase order ID from the request list:

```
private void CreateVendPurchIdMap()
{
    vendPurchIdMap = new Map(Types::String, Types::String);
    ListEnumerator le = requestList.getEnumerator();
    while (le.moveNext())
    {
        var currentValue = le.current();
        // first test that the list contains the correct type
        if ( !(currentValue is
         ConVMSPurchOrderGenerateRequestLineContract))
        {
            throw error(error::wrongUseOfFunction(classStr(
             ConVMSPurchOrderGenerateRequestLineContract)));
        }
        ConVMSPurchOrderGenerateRequestLineContract requestLine =
         currentValue;
        VendAccount vendAccount =
         InventTable::find(requestLine.ItemId()).primaryVendorId();
        if (VendAccount == '')
        {
            // Item %1 has no default vendor set up
            throw error(strFmt("@ConVMS:ItemHasNoDefaultVend",
             requestLine.ItemId()));
        }
        // no need to check if it exists already, map keys are
        // unique
        // and this will simply replace the existing value
        vendPurchIdMap.insert(VendAccount, '');
```

```
        }
    }
```

5. The purchase order header will be created from default values; it just needs the vendor account. The method is created as follows:

```
protected PurchTable CreatePurchTable(VendAccount _vendAccount)
{
    PurchTable purchTable;
    purchTable.clear();
    purchTable.initValue(PurchaseType::Purch);
    NumberSeq num =
     NumberSeq::newGetNum(PurchParameters::numRefPurchId(), false);
    purchTable.PurchId = num.num();
    VendTable vendTable = VendTable::find(_vendAccount);
    purchTable.initFromVendTable(vendTable);
    purchTable.PurchName = vendTable.name();
    if (!purchTable.validateWrite())
    {
        throw error("@SYS23020");
    }
    purchTable.insert();
    return purchTable;
}
```

This method is protected in case it needs to be extended through a Chain of Command extension.

6. Next, we will create the code that will create the purchase order line; this is done as follows:

```
protected InventTransId CreatePurchLine(
    PurchTable _purchTable,
    ConVMSPurchOrderGenerateRequestLineContract _requestLine)
{
    PurchLine purchLine;
    purchLine.initValue(PurchaseType::Purch);
    purchLine.initFromPurchTable(_purchTable);
    purchLine.ItemId = _requestLine.ItemId();
    purchLine.itemIdChanged();
    purchLine.PurchQty = _requestLine.PurchQty();
    purchLine.createLine(true, true, true, true, true, true);
    return purchLine.InventTransId;
}
```

7. We could just write everything else in one method, but this would be hard to read. We will create a method that will use the map created in `CreateVendPurchIdMap` and an `ConVMSPurchOrderGenerateRequestLineContract` object to check or create the purchase order record, which is done by the following method:

```
private PurchTable
CheckCreatePurchTable(ConVMSPurchOrderGenerateRequestLineContract
_request)
{
    if (!InventTable::exist(_request.ItemId()))
    {
        throw error(strFmt(InventTable::txtNotExist(),
         _request.ItemId()));
    }
    VendAccount vendAccount =
     InventTable::find(_request.ItemId()).primaryVendorId();
    PurchTable purchTable;
    PurchId purchId;
    // this should always be true, given that
    // the CreateVendPurchIdMap method didn't
    // throw an error - but guard in case
    // this method was changed or someone
    // caused the state to change through CoC
    if (vendPurchIdMap.exists(vendAccount))
    {
        purchId = vendPurchIdMap.lookup(vendAccount);
    }
    if (purchId == '')
    {
        purchTable = this.CreatePurchTable(vendAccount);
        vendPurchIdMap.insert(vendAccount, purchTable.PurchId);
    }
    else
    {
        purchTable = PurchTable::find(purchId);
    }
    return purchTable;
}
```

8. We should also write a helper method to add the results to the list. This will be as follows:

```
protected void AddToResponseList(RefRecId _sourceRecId,
InventTransId _inventTransId)
{
    ConVMSPurchOrderGenerateResponseContract response =
```

```
        new ConVMSPurchOrderGenerateResponseContract();
        response.SourceRecId(_sourceRecId);
        response.CreatedInventTransId(_inventTransId);
        responseList.addEnd(response);
    }
```

9. Now, we just need to iterate through the list and call the methods we have just created in a new `public Run` method, which is written as follows:

```
public void Run()
{
    Microsoft.Dynamics.Ax.Xpp.ErrorException exception;
    try
    {
        this.CreateVendPurchIdMap();
        ListEnumerator requests = requestList.getEnumerator();
        ttsbegin;
        while (requests.moveNext())
        {
            ConVMSPurchOrderGenerateRequestLineContract request =
             requests.current();
            PurchTable purchTable =
             this.CheckCreatePurchTable(request);
            InventTransId inventTransId =
             this.CreatePurchLine(purchTable, request);
            if (inventTransId == '')
            {
                throw
                 error(strFmt("@ConVMS:FailedToCreatePurchLine",
                   request.ItemId(), purchTable.OrderAccount));
            }
            this.AddtoResponseList(request.SourceRecId(),
             inventTransId);
        }
        ttscommit;
    }
    catch (exception)
    {
        responseList = new List(Types::Class);
        error(exception.Message);
    }
    catch
    {
        responseList = new List(Types::Class);
        error("@SYS23020");
    }
}
```

10. Finally, we should provide a method to get the response list, which is done by the following method:

```
/// <summary>
/// returns the response list
/// </summary>
/// <returns>list of
ConVMSPurchOrderGenerateResponseContract</returns>
public List ParmResponseList()
{
    return responseList;
}
```

11. Save and close all code editors, and build the project.

How it works...

We have written a generic way to create purchase orders from a list that we can use in many places.

This is the first time we have used a `Map` object. Maps are key/value sets where the key is guaranteed to be unique. We can iterate over them using the map's `getEnumerator()` method, which returns a `MapEnumerator` object.

We also used `var` for the first time. This behaves the same as the C# `var`. This can be any type and must be assigned to be an instance of a type when it is declared. It is very useful when we don't know the type at design time.

These are very useful, and sometimes risky unless used correctly. For example, we must always check whether an element exists before using the lookup method, otherwise it throws an exception. You can store simple types such as strings, or even records and class instances, but the key should always be a basic type such as a number or string. When storing classes in a map, be careful when trying to serialize it to the container as you will need to create a static `Create` method on the class in order to deserialize it to an instance again.

In our case, we used them to create a map entry for each vendor that we needed to create a purchase order for. The `map` object was initialized and then used to check whether we had created a purchase order for the current request's vendor, the primary vendor from the item.

Create methods don't have any new concepts as such. The only element of note here is that we used the createLine method on the purchase order line. The SalesLine table also has this method, and is the preferred method to insert a new order line. The only downside is that we only know whether the order was created or not based on the InventTransId field being populated. This is why the Run method had a throw exception if this was returned blank.

The Run method itself was fairly standard. We added some exception handling in this method, which is needed to ensure that the method runs as an ACID transaction. Although all data that was updated within the ttsbegin/ttscommit commands will either commit or roll back if an exception occurs, the ttsbegin and ttscommit commands do not affect the state of internal variables. This is why the catch reinitialized the response list.

ACID is an acronym that states that a transaction must be the following:

Atomic	The transaction either succeeds completely or fails completely.
Consistent	In terms of a database transaction, the transaction must ensure the result of the transaction brings the database to a consistent state.
Isolated	The changes made by this transaction are isolated from other changes by other processes. This means that the changes a transaction makes are not visible to other processes until it completes.
Durable	Once committed, the change cannot be reversed as it is the new state.

A lot of the implementation of the preceding is provided by SQL Server, which will also handle power failure by rolling forward or back transactions to ensure that the database is in a consistent state. ACID was coined mainly to described database transactions, and is extended to include state variables. But we don't have a beginning and end for application processes; we have to write code to compensate for this failure—which is the code we write in the catch block or code that is run to process a resulting success or failure state variable.

When it comes to handling when to throw and when to continue, it depends on what we are trying to achieve. We may want to simply skip lines that fail, and return the result (by adding success and a message parameter method) in the response list. We would then catch each error within the loop.

Sometimes we can't have full control over the resulting state, such as integrations to other systems or web service calls; and sometimes we may wish to submit complicated processes asynchronously (for example, submitting as a batch job). This would require us to use a compensation principle, which is like when we queue for coffee, we order it while in the queue, pay, and receive it afterwards. Should the asynchronous process fail (the coffee was not made), we need to compensate the transaction in some way. When it comes to asynchronous processes, we would just need a way to communicate the failure (read a response into a log table, for example) and handle it appropriately.

Creating a facade

The previous recipe requires an amount of preparation in order to be called, and in these cases, we would often write a facade to simplify the class's usage. They usually consist of one or more static methods for each use case that is required. Although we will have a specific use case, they are usually generic. To see examples of facade classes in standard code, type `type:"class" facade` into Application Explorer's search text box.

For more information on searching in SCM, please see the following links:

- Metadata search in Visual Studio: `https://docs.microsoft.com/en-us/ dynamics365/fin-ops-core/dev-itpro/dev-tools/metadata-search-visual- studio`
- Filtering Application Explorer: `https://docs.microsoft.com/en-us/ dynamics365/fin-ops-core/dev-itpro/dev-tools/application-explorer`

The facade will be specific to a target service class (in our case, the `ConVMSPurchOrderGenerate` class) and will be named after this class suffixed with `Facade`.

Facades do not have to focus on one class at a time but should focus on a topic or framework.

How to do it...

To create the facade class, follow these steps:

1. Our service order line table does not currently have a quantity field, so one should be added using the EDT `PurchQty`. Ensure that this also appears on the service order form's line grid, by adding it to the `Overview` field group on the table. You will also need to refresh the data source on the form (right-click on it and choose **Restore**).
2. Create a new class named `ConVMSPurchOrderGenerateFacade`.
3. Create a new static method called `CreateOrderFromServiceOrder`, as follows:

```
public static List
CreateOrderFromServiceOrder(ConVMSVehicleServiceTable
_serviceOrder)
{
    ConVMSVehicleServiceLine lines;
    List requestList = new List(Types::Class);
    ttsbegin;
```

```
while select lines
    where lines.ServiceId == _serviceOrder.ServiceId
{
    ConVMSPurchOrderGenerateRequestLineContract contract =
        new ConVMSPurchOrderGenerateRequestLineContract();
    contract.ItemId(lines.ItemId);
    contract.PurchQty(lines.PurchQty);
    contract.SourceRecId(lines.RecId);
    requestList.addEnd(contract);
}
ConVMSPurchOrderGenerate generate =
 ConVMSPurchOrderGenerate::NewFromRequestList(requestList);
generate.Run();
List responseList = generate.ParmResponseList();
ttscommit;
return responseList;
}
```

4. Save and close the designer, and build the project.

How it works...

It was tempting to simply write a purchase order generation that worked directly from a service order. This would have been slightly quicker to write and there would be no need to pass data back and forth to the order generation class. This also means that the code is less flexible and cannot be reused. By having code in a more granular level, it is also easier for others to extend it. We can decide exactly what should be protected from changes by other developers and allow extensions at specific points to ensure that our code is not broken.

Once we have released code that has either protected or public methods, we are to an extent locked. Other developers could be using the public methods, as they should and extending classes with a Chain of Command on protected methods. Only private methods are safe to change without causing our customers' code to break.

Defining business actions in data

So far, we have thought of extensibility in terms of other developers; this enables them to extend and augment our code safely and easily. What happens when we want different actions to occur based on something known at runtime? The traditional method would be a series of checkboxes on a parameter form, and the code would have conditions that would be written to test each of these settings.

Another option would be to allow the consultant to add features in a plugin pattern, for example, deciding on which code should run under what condition.

The pattern for this would be to have the following components:

- A base enum that is used on the user interface: the type of action required
- An interface so that we can write code without the actual concrete implementation
- A service class to allow us to construct and interact with the concrete implementation through the attribute framework

Let's go back to our requirement:

> *Create a purchase order for items at status* `Confirmed` *for Bikes in group "Over 500cc".*

A reasonable solution would be to have a table with three fields:

- `ConVMSVehicleServiceStatus`
- `ConVMSVehicleGroupId`
- `ConVMSVehicleServiceAction`

We could also use a query object that is packed to a container and saved as a container field on the table, which would be the ultimate flexibility. An example of this is the **Location directives** form in **Warehouse management** | **Setup** | **Location directives**. Performance must be considered, as executing a query to check whether the record meets a condition takes far longer than a simple `if` statement. For our requirement of determining an action based on the service order status, a query is not a bad idea because the delay would not be noticeable by the user. However, we will stick to using a table with static fields so as to not detract from the main purpose of this recipe.

How to do it...

To create this new framework, follow these steps:

1. Create a new base enum called `ConVMSVehicleServiceAction` that is also extensible with one element, `CreatePurchaseOrder`.

   If we are creating a framework designed to be extended, the action enum must be extensible.

2. Create labels for the base enum and the element—these are to be used on the user interface.

3. Create a new table called `ConVMSVehicleServiceActionTable` as per best practice for a group table, and add the following fields:

Field name	Type
VehicleGroupId	ConVMSVehicleGroupId
VehicleServiceStatus	ConVMSVehicleServiceStatus
VehicleServiceAction	ConVMSVehicleServiceAction

4. Create a unique index for the `VehicleGroupId` and `VehicleServiceStatus` fields; name it `ConstraintIdx`.

5. Write a `Find` method that accepts the `VehicleGroupId` and `VehicleServiceStatus` fields

6. Write a new form named `ConVMSVehicleServiceActionTable` as a simple list form pattern for our new table.

7. Create a display menu item and add it to the menu as usual.

   Alternatively, given that the number of records will be small, this could be added as a tab on the parameter form.

8. Next, we need an interface that defines what the action requires. Create a new interface named `ConVMSVehicleServiceActionableI`. Complete it as follows:

```
interface ConVMSVehicleServiceActionableI
{
    public Description Description()
    {
    }
 public boolean PerformAction(ConVMSVehicleServiceTable
   _serviceOrder)
    {
    }
}
```

9. Now we can create our service class, the class that processes the actions. Create a class named `ConVMSVehicleServiceActionService`.

10. Create a copy of the `ConVMSVehicleServiceStatusAttribute` (copy and paste) and rename the copy to `ConVMSVehicleServiceActionAttribute`. The code should be changed to read as follows:

```
ConVMSVehicleServiceAction action;
public void new(ConVMSVehicleServiceAction _action)
{
    action = _action;
```

```
    }
    public str parmCacheKey()
    {
        return
    classStr(ConVMSVehicleServiceActionAttribute)+';'+int2str(enum2int(
        action));
    }
    public boolean useSingleton()
    {
        return false;
    }
```

When copying attribute classes, be very careful. It may still compile and result in errant data in the global cache.

11. We need an instance to work with, so start by creating a `CreateInstance` method on the `ConVMSVehicleServiceActionService` class. The method should be as follows:

```
    public ConVMSVehicleServiceActionableI
    CreateInstance(ConVMSVehicleServiceAction _action)
    {
        ConVMSVehicleServiceActionAttribute attr = new
         ConVMSVehicleServiceActionAttribute(_action);
        ConVMSVehicleServiceActionableI instance =
         SysExtensionAppClassFactory::getClassFromSysAttribute(
          classStr(ConVMSVehicleServiceActionableI), attr);
        if (!instance || !(instance is
         ConVMSVehicleServiceActionableI))
        {
            SysExtensionCache::clearAllScopes();
            instance =
             SysExtensionAppClassFactory::getClassFromSysAttribute(
              classStr(ConVMSVehicleServiceActionableI), attr);
            if (!instance || !(instance is
             ConVMSVehicleServiceActionableI))
            {
                return null; // don't throw, we want to handle this in
                             // the calling method
            }
        }
        return instance;
    }
```

12. Create a `Construct` method (no parameters) and override the new method so that it is protected:

```
protected void new()
{
}
public static ConVMSVehicleServiceActionService Construct()
{
    return new ConVMSVehicleServiceActionService();
}
```

13. Let's write a method we can use on the user interface, to get the description from the action class. Write a method named `GetDescription` as shown in the following code:

```
public Description GetDescription(ConVMSVehicleGroupId _groupId,
ConVMSVehicleServiceStatus _status)
{
    ConVMSVehicleServiceActionTable actionTable =
        ConVMSVehicleServiceActionTable::Find(_groupId, _status);
    if (actionTable.RecId != 0)
    {
        ConVMSVehicleServiceActionableI action =
         this.CreateInstance(actionTable.VehicleServiceAction);
        if (action != null)
        {
            return action.Description();
        }
    }
    return ''; // or a warning - the instance cannot be created, so
              // it will fail at runtime
}
```

14. We can now write the code that will trigger the action to be performed. This will use the current service order to determine the vehicle group and status and then use `CreateInstance` in order to construct the action class and run the `PerformAction` method:

```
public void ProcessServiceTable(ConVMSVehicleServiceTable _service)
{
    ConVMSVehicleGroupId groupId =
     ConVMSVehicleTable::Find(_service.VehicleId).VehicleGroupId;
    ConVMSVehicleServiceActionTable actionTable =
     ConVMSVehicleServiceActionTable::Find(groupId,
     _service.ServiceStatus);
    if (actionTable.RecId != 0)
    {
```

```
ConVMSVehicleServiceActionableI action =
 this.CreateInstance(actionTable.VehicleServiceAction);
if (action != null)
{
    action.PerformAction(_service);
}
}
}
```

15. The final step is to hook this up to the status change. Earlier we wrote some code to call a delegate in the `Update` method of `ConVMSVehicleServiceTable`. Open the `Update` method, and change the code so the code added earlier is changed to read as follows:

```
if (thisOrig.ServiceStatus != this.ServiceStatus)
{

    ConVMSVehicleStatusChangeResponseParameters params = new
        ConVMSVehicleStatusChangeResponseParameters();
    this.ServiceStatusChanged(params, thisOrig.ServiceStatus,
     this.ServiceStatus);
    if (params.delegateWashandled && !params.success)
    {
        throw error(params.message);
    }
    // This line is added so that the change is status on update is
    // handled by our new functionality
ConVMSVehicleServiceActionService::Construct().ProcessServiceTable(
    this);
}
```

16. We now need to write a class that implements the `CreatePurchaseOrder` enum option. The class is part of our `ConVMSVehicleServiceAction` framework, so it should be named `ConVMSVehicleServiceAction_CreatePurchaseOrder`.

 Even if we were extending this framework in a different package, it should still start with `ConVMSVehicleServiceAction`—but the suffix should be made unique by inserting our project/package name to ensure that it will be globally unique now and in the future, for example, `ConVMSVehicleServiceAction_<MyPrefixAndProject>_Cr eateSalesOrder`.

17. We then need to decorate the class with our attribute and ensure that it implements `ConVMSVehicleServiceActionableI`. Do this as follows:

```
[ConVMSVehicleServiceActionAttribute(ConVMSVehicleServiceAction::
 CreatePurchaseOrder)]
```

```
class ConVMSVehicleServiceAction_CreatePurchaseOrder implements
 ConVMSVehicleServiceActionableI
{
}
```

18. Finally, implement the required methods, which should read as follows:

```
public Description Description()
{
    return "@ConVMS:CreatePurchaseOrder";
}
public boolean PerformAction(ConVMSVehicleServiceTable
_serviceOrder)
{
    List responseList =
     ConVMSPurchOrderGenerateFacade::CreateOrderFromServiceOrder
     (_serviceOrder);
    if (responseList.elements() > 0)
    {
        return true;
    }
    return false;
}
```

 This is simplistic, but will suffice to demonstrate how to write the pattern. We will expand on this in the *There's more...* section.

19. Save and close all forms, and build the project. You should also synchronize the database as we have created new fields and a table.

How it works...

We have just used the concepts from the start of the chapter to implement a pattern that is designed to be extended. We could have written the previous three recipes in one step and in one class, which is often the case. By separating the code into distinct classes, we have created a reusable purchase order generation class, a facade to ease its usage, and a framework to allow a functional consultant to determine how it is used. Should the customer change their mind on which conditions the code should run, it is done without changing code.

This should reinforce why interfaces are useful. We were able to write the whole framework without implementing the specific create purchase order action.

There will be cases where a code change is made, but this would be to enable a scenario and not write that scenario into code.

There's more...

There are a few logical extensions we could add here. The purchase order generation can return a list of responses that linked the source service order line to the purchase order line. We could, therefore, add a field to the service order line to allow us to know which lines have a purchase order.

To do this, we need to add a new field from using the `InventTransId` EDT and add a relation to `PurchLine`. We would then add code to our action class to iterate through the response list, as follows:

```
public boolean PerformAction(ConVMSVehicleServiceTable _serviceOrder)
{
    List responseList =
     ConVMSPurchOrderGenerateFacade::CreateOrderFromServiceOrder
     (_serviceOrder);
    if (responseList.elements() == 0) // this is reversed from the code in
                                      // the How do it section.
    {
        return false;
    }
    ListEnumerator le = responseList.getEnumerator();
    ttsbegin;
    while (le.moveNext())
    {
        ConVMSPurchOrderGenerateResponseContract response = le.current();
        ConVMSVehicleServiceLine line;
        select forupdate line where line.RecId == response.SourceRecId();
        if (line.RecId != 0)
        {
            line.PurchInventTransId = response.CreatedInventTransId();
            line.update();
        }
    }
    ttscommit;
    return true;
}
```

There are a few issues here. We are starting to fall for the temptation to couple the action to the service order code. For example, what happens when we delete the purchase order? We would want to clear the reference on the service order line. The relation will, therefore, fail best practice checks unless we tell it how to handle this (the **On Delete** relation property).

Purchase order lines don't physically get deleted; they soft delete by setting the **Deleted** field to **Yes**.

The temptation is to add a data event handler in our action implementation. This would be wrong, as the purpose of this class is to implement the create purchase order action, and that is it. Should we want to handle the deletion of order lines, this would be a new class.

Creating a SysOperation process

This framework provides a simple method to allow us to write routines that can be synchronous or asynchronous with no further effort to allow this to happen.

The complexity in creating a routine that is run in a batch process is how to store the various parameters that the routine may require. This was done in the previous version using the RunBaseBatch framework. This older framework stored this data in a loosely typed blob, and required special handling should the developer add or change the parameters. It had other problems, including the fact that the data and process were tightly coupled.

The SysOperation framework provides a new and simpler way to create processes. It decouples the data (or parameters) from the process by using a data contract. The data contract is a class that is the parameter for the entry point to the class that performs the process. The framework adds further help in automatically creating a dialog from the data contract, which will use the EDTs in the contract to provide the label and even drop-down lists based on the table reference on the EDT.

To use the framework, we will need the following three classes:

- **Controller**: This is a class that extends SysOperationServiceController, which controls both the UI and the instantiation of the processing class.
- **Data contract**: This is a class that contains the properties required by the process class.
- **Processing**: This is the class that actually does the work.

We can use this to create any process, and the following pattern can be reused for your own needs. In this recipe, we will create a process that the user can use to change the vehicle's group.

How to do it...

The first part of this is to create the data contract, which is done by following these steps:

1. Create a new class named `ConVMSVehicleGroupChangeContract`.

2. Complete the declaration as follows:

```
[DataContract]
class ConVMSVehicleGroupChangeContract
    extends SysOperationDataContractBase
    implements SysOperationValidatable
{
    ConVMSVehicleId vehicleId;
    ConVMSVehicleGroupId vehicleGroupId;
}
```

3. Then add the data member methods as follows:

```
[DataMember]
public ConVMSVehicleId vehicleId(ConVMSVehicleId _vehicleId =
 vehicleId)
{
    vehicleId = _vehicleId;
    return vehicleId;
}
[DataMember]
public ConVMSVehicleGroupId vehicleGroupId( ConVMSVehicleGroupId
_vehicleGroupId = vehicleGroupId)
{
    vehicleGroupId = _vehicleGroupId;
    return vehicleGroupId;
}
```

4. Next, implement the `validate` method from `SysOperationValidatable`:

```
public boolean validate()
{
    if (vehicleId == '')
    {
        //Vehicle Id must be specified
        return checkFailed("@ConVMS:VehicleIdRequired");
    }
    if (!ConVMSVehicleTable::Exist(vehicleId))
    {
        //Vehicle %1 does not exist
        return checkFailed(strFmt("@ConVMS:VehicleIdNotExist",
         vehicleId));
```

```
    }
    if (vehicleGroupId == '')
    {
        //Vehicle group is required
        return checkFailed("@ConVMS:VehicleGroupRequired");
    }
    if (!ConVMSVehicleGroup::Exist(vehicleGroupId))
    {
        //Vehicle group %1 does not exist
        return checkFailed(strFmt("@ConVMS:VehicleGroupNotExist",
         vehicleGroupId));
    }
    return true;
}
```

The `validate` method name must be lowercase as this is the casing used in `SysOperationValidatable`. This will build and compile without errors even if the case is different, but it will fail at runtime, stating that the class does not implement the `validate()` method. You can use **Go to reference** (*F12*) on the interface name to copy the correct signature, and avoid this type of error.

Now, to create the class that performs the update, let's follow these steps:

1. Create a new class named `ConVMSVehicleGroupChange`.

2. Within the class, declare the following global variables:

```
ConVMSVehicleId vehicleId;
ConVMSVehicleGroupId vehicleGroupId;
```

3. Let's write a method to initialize from the contract; this should be protected so that it can be extended should another developer need to do so:

```
protected void InitFromContract(ConVMSVehicleGroupChangeContract
_contract)
{
    vehicleId = _contract.vehicleId();
    vehicleGroupId = _contract.vehicleGroupId();
}
```

4. Next, we will write the method to make the change, which is done as follows:

```
protected void UpdateVehicleGroup()
{
    ConVMSVehicleTable vehicle =
     ConVMSVehicleTable::Find(vehicleId, true);
    if(vehicle.RecId != 0)
```

```
        {
            vehicle.VehicleGroupId = vehicleGroupId;
            vehicle.update();
        }
    }
```

5. We should write a `validate` method. Even though the contract can do this, the class might have further validation requirements in a future version—or a customer may wish to extend this through Chain of Command:

```
public boolean Validate()
{
    return true;
}
```

6. Let's write the entry `Run` method, which will be called from the `SysOperation` process:

```
public void Run(ConVMSVehicleGroupChangeContract _contract)
{
    if (!_contract.validate())
    {
        return;
    }
    this.InitFromContract(_contract);
    if (!this.Validate())
    {
        return;
    }
    ttsbegin;
    this.UpdateVehicleGroup();
    ttscommit;
}
```

 We want the errors to not be caught. If the process was run in a batch, we want the batch framework to catch the error and mark the batch task as a status error.

The next part of the process is to create the controller class, which is done as follows:

1. Create a new class called `ConVMSVehicleGroupChangeController`.
2. Modify `classDeclaration` so that it extends `SysOperationServiceController`.

3. Finally, we will need an entry point, which is a `main` method. The method should be created as per the following lines of code:

```
public static void main(Args _args)
{
    ConVMSVehicleGroupChangeController controller;
    controller = new ConVMSVehicleGroupChangeController(
        classStr(ConVMSVehicleGroupChange),
        methodStr(ConVMSVehicleGroupChange,Run),
        SysOperationExecutionMode::Synchronous);
    controller.parmDialogCaption("@ConVMS:VehicleGroupChange");
    controller.startOperation();
}
```

4. Next, create an **Action menu item** named `ConVMSVehicleGroupChangeController`.
5. Set the **Label** property to a label for `Vehicle group change`. Change the **Object Type** property to `Class` and the **Object** property to `ConVMSVehicleGroupChangeController`.
6. Add this to the `PeriodicTask` submenu of the `ConVMSVehicleManagement` menu and build the project.

How it works...

We will get a dialog where the dialog fields are created automatically from the contract. We can even submit it to the batch queue. Pretty cool, and very little additional effort.

A lot is happening here, and this requires an explanation.

As our class extends `SysOperationServiceController`, we get a lot of functionality, the first being that it can construct a dialog from the data contract. However, how did it know?

When the new method executed, the framework looked at the `Run` method and determined the contract from the method's input parameter.

The call to `startOperation` caused the system to build the user interface and handle the code execution based on what the user does. The dialog is constructed using the EDTs specified in the data member methods. Since we constructed the EDTs correctly with reference to the main table, it can also provide a simple lookup for us.

As part of the dialog handling, the framework will test whether the data contract class implements `SysOperationValidateable`. If it does, it will call this method when the user clicks **OK**, and handle it appropriately.

This explains why the new method requires the class and method names, but the third parameter is an execution mode. This comes into its own if we execute the controller programmatically. Synchronous means it will run in line with the current process, unless the user has elected to Run in the background. If this was chosen, the execution method would have changed to ScheduledBatch.

 The classStr and methodStr compile-time functions, as explained in the previous chapters, are used to check whether the element the functions refer to exists at compile time.

If you run this process twice, you will see the previous options are remembered and act as defaults. This is because the contract is serialized to a container and stored in the user's usage data.

There's more...

To force the process through the batch framework, we will use the execution modes ReliableAsynchronous and ScheduledBatch.

Both of these methods submit jobs to the batch server for execution, where the ReliableAsynchronous method auto-deletes the jobs after execution.

The jobs do not execute immediately, but within a minute of submission; the batch server polls for waiting jobs every minute. We should use this method to perform asynchronous or scheduled jobs that require heavy processing.

Programmatically speaking, we wouldn't normally use the ScheduledBatch mode. This would be set based on the user choosing to run it as a background task.

To submit the task as ReliableAsynchronous, simply change the code that constructs the controller to use this execution mode. On execution, you may notice that the information message indicates that nothing was done, but if you wait for about a minute and check the vehicle record, you will see that it has succeeded. You can also see the batch history for this.

Calling the process from a form

The example in this recipe simply demonstrates the framework, but the example is not particularly useful. To do so, it would be better to call the process from the vehicle form and default the parameters to the current vehicles.

To do this, we will need to fetch the constructed contract and update it with the record set by the caller from the `Args` object like this:

```
public static void main(Args _args)
{
    ConVMSVehicleTable vehicle;
    switch (_args.dataset())
    {
        case tableNum(ConVMSVehicleTable):
            vehicle = _args.record();
            break;
    }
    ConVMSVehicleGroupChangeController controller;
    controller = new ConVMSVehicleGroupChangeController(
        classStr(ConVMSVehicleGroupChange),
        methodStr(ConVMSVehicleGroupChange, Run),
        SysOperationExecutionMode::Synchronous);

    controller.parmDialogCaption("@ConVMS:VehicleGroupChange");
    if(vehicle.RecId != 0)
    {
        // this line is unpleasant as there is not compile-time function
        // we can easily use to check that the parameter is correct
        ConVMSVehicleGroupChangeContract contract;
        contract = controller.getDataContractObject('_contract');
        if (!contract)
        {
            //Function %1 was called with an invalid value
            throw error (strFmt("@SYS23264",
                classStr(ConVMSVehicleGroupChangeController)));
        }
        contract.VehicleGroupId(vehicle.VehicleGroupId);
        contract.VehicleId(vehicle.VehicleId);
    }
    controller.startOperation();
    if(FormDataUtil::isFormDataSource(vehicle))
    {
        //This will call the table's data source's research
        //method to refresh the data from the table.
        //The true parameter will keep the current record
        FormDataUtil::getFormDataSource(vehicle).research(true);
    }
}
```

We will then need to add the action menu item to our vehicle form. On the main `FormActionPane` control, add a new `Action Pane Tab`, and set the **Caption** property to a label for `Vehicles`. Create a button group with the **Caption** property set to `@SYS9342`.

Finally, drag the action menu item to the button group and set the following properties:

Property	Value
Data Source	`ConVMSVehicleTable`: this sets `args.Record()`.
Needs Record	`Yes`: this disables the button if there is not a current record.
Save Record	`Yes`: this is the default, and is needed in order to avoid a potential concurrency error.
Multi Select	`No`: our code does not handle multiple records, so we must not allow the user to select more than one when pressing this button.

These properties are important. The **Needs Record** and **Multi Select** properties are controlled when the button is enabled, and the **Save Record** will call the data source's write method when clicked, if the buffer needs to be saved. We need to ensure we are dealing with the correct data source, so we specifically set this on buttons to ensure that this is correct. When the button is clicked, the current buffer will be sent in an `Args` object and accessed through the `Args.Record()` method, along with a reference to the data source.

Using the data contract to make changes to the dialog

Let's take a step back. When the `main` method of `ConVMSVehicleGroupChangeController` is called, the framework constructs the user interface based on the data members of the data contract. The system will use the EDT returned by the method to determine the type and label of the form control it creates. Sometimes we may wish to alter this standard behavior. This is done by adding attributes to the data member methods.

The system then builds the user interface using the data contract. It reads the metadata from the data contract and adds each data method as a control on the dialog. We can adjust some of this by adding attributes to the data methods. The following table shows some of the most common attributes:

`SysOperationLabel`	Overrides the label for the control
`SysOperationHelpText`	Overrides the help text on the control
`SysOperationDisplayOrder`	Allows us to control the order in which the controls are built on the form

The following code provides an example of the completed code:

```
[DataMember, SysOperationControlVisibility(false)]
public ConVMSVehicleId VehicleId(ConVMSVehicleId _vehicleId = vehicleId)
{
 vehicleId = _vehicleId;
 return vehicleId;
}
//New vehicle group
//Please select a new vehicle group for the vehicle
[DataMember,
 SysOperationLabel(literalStr("@ConVMS:NewVehGroup")),
 SysOperationHelpText(literalStr("@ConVMS:NewVehGroupHT")),
 SysOperationDisplayOrder('1')]
public ConVMSVehicleGroupId VehicleGroupId( ConVMSVehicleGroupId
_vehicleGroupId = vehicleGroupId)
{
    vehicleGroupId = _vehicleGroupId;
    return vehicleGroupId;
}
```

By making the vehicle ID field not visible, we have broken the action menu item we added to the periodic menu. The user won't be able to specify the vehicle and the `validate` method will return `false`. It would be worse if the user had previously tested it, as the vehicle ID from the last test would be used.

Adding an interface to the SysOperation framework

We can do a lot by just decorating the contract data methods but, sometimes, we need more control. This recipe steps through adding more control to the user interface created by the `SysOperation` framework.

Getting ready

We just need an existing `SysOperation` process class that we wish to add a customized interface to.

If you are following on from the previous recipe, remove the `SysOperationControlVisibility` attribute from the `VehicleId` data method.

How to do it...

To add the user interface, please follow these steps:

1. Create a class named `ConVMSVehicleGroupChangeUIBuilder`. Add `extends SysOperationAutomaticUIBuilder` to the class declaration.

2. We need two dialog fields that we will later bind to the data contract; the completed class declaration should look like this:

```
class ConVMSVehicleGroupChangeUIBuilder extends
SysOperationAutomaticUIBuilder
{
    DialogField vehicleIdField;
    DialogField vehGroupIdField;
}
```

3. We will now need to bind the contract's data member methods to the dialog fields. This is done in the `postBuild` method. Override the `postBuild` method with the following piece of code:

```
public void postBuild()
{
    ConVMSVehicleGroupChangeContract contract;
    super();
    contract = this.dataContractObject();
    vehicleIdField = this.bindInfo().getDialogField(
        contract,
        methodStr(ConVMSVehicleGroupChangeContract, VehicleId));
        vehGroupIdField = this.bindInfo().getDialogField(
          contract,
        methodStr(ConVMSVehicleGroupChangeContract,
        VehicleGroupId));
}
```

4. In order to handle dialog field events, we will need to create suitable methods and register them as an override. Create a method called `validateVehicleGroup`, as shown here:

```
public boolean ValidateVehicleGroupId(FormStringControl _control)
{
    ConVMSVehicleGroupChangeContract localContract;
    localContract = new ConVMSVehicleGroupChangeContract();
    localContract.vehicleId(vehicleIdField.value());
    localContract.vehicleGroupId(_control.valueStr());
    return localContract.validate();
}
```

The method declaration has to match the method we will register as an override. We can achieve this by overriding the required method on a form control of the right type. The first parameter will always be the form control object that triggered the event.

5. Now that we have a `validate` method, we will need to hook it to the dialog field's event. In the `postBuild` method overridden earlier, add the following lines at the end of the method:

```
vehGroupIdField.registerOverrideMethod(
    methodStr(FormStringControl, validate),
    methodStr(ConVMSVehicleGroupChangeUIBuilder,
     validateVehicleGroupId),
    this);
```

Nearly done! However, we haven't handled hiding the vehicle ID field if it was called from a vehicle record. We can't determine this from within the UI builder class; only the controller's main method knows this. This means we will need a mechanism to tell the UI builder whether or not to hide the field. Since we attach the UI builder to the data contract, we will add a hidden field to the data contract, as follows:

1. First, change the decoration in a class declaration of `ConVMSVehicleGroupChangecontract` so that it is associated with the UI builder:

```
[DataContract,
SysOperationContractProcessing(classStr(ConVMSVehicleGroupChangeUIB
uilder))]
```

2. Then add a variable declaration to the class declaration, as follows:

```
NoYesId hideVehicleId;
```

3. Add a data member method for the variable with the visibility attribute:

```
[DataMemberAttribute,
 SysOperationControlVisibilityAttribute(false)]
public NoYesId HideVehicleId(NoYesId _hideVehicleId =
 hideVehicleId)
{
    hideVehicleId = _hideVehicleId;
    return hideVehicleId;
}
```

This is used to communicate to the UI builder class whether the vehicle ID should be visible to the UI builder class.

4. Open `ConVMSVehicleGroupChangeUIBuilder` and edit the `PostBuild` method to add the following code at the end:

```
if (contract.HideVehicleId() == NoYes::Yes)
{
    vehicleIdField.visible(false);
}
```

5. Finally, we will need to modify our controller's main method to handle the case where it was called from a vehicle record; the completed code is as follows:

```
public static void main(Args _args)
{
    ConVMSVehicleTable vehicle;
    switch (_args.dataset())
    {
        case tableNum(ConVMSVehicleTable):
            vehicle = _args.record();
            break;
    }
    ConVMSVehicleGroupChangeController controller;
    controller = new ConVMSVehicleGroupChangeController(
        classStr(ConVMSVehicleGroupChange),
        methodStr(ConVMSVehicleGroupChange,Run),
        SysOperationExecutionMode::Synchronous);

    controller.parmDialogCaption("@ConVMS:VehicleGroupChange");
    // this line is unpleasant as there is not compile-time
    // function
    // we can easily use to check that the parameter is correct
    ConVMSVehicleGroupChangeContract contract =
     controller.getDataContractObject('_contract');
    if(!contract)
    {
        //Function %1 was called with an invalid value
        throw error (strFmt("@SYS23264",
         classStr(ConVMSVehicleGroupChangeController)));
    }
    contract.HideVehicleId(NoYes::No);
    if(vehicle.RecId != 0)
    {
        contract.VehicleGroupId(vehicle.VehicleGroupId);
```

```
            contract.VehicleId(vehicle.VehicleId);
            contract.HideVehicleId(NoYes::Yes);
    }
    controller.startOperation();
    if(FormDataUtil::isFormDataSource(vehicle))
    {
        //This will call the table's data source's research
        //method to refresh the data from the table.
        //The true parameter will keep the current record
        FormDataUtil::getFormDataSource(vehicle).research(true);
    }
}
```

6. Save and close all editors, and build the project to test our changes.

How it works...

By using this method, we have added a coupling to the process class structure by means of the binding to the UI builder. This seems to make it so the data contract is no longer reusable for other purposes—but this is actually desirable in this case. When writing processes that use the SysOperation framework, the data contract is used to both pass data and also create the user interface. The only time we might have some sharing is when we are designing a set of processes that share a set of common properties, and in that case, we would use a data contract base class that each specialization would extend.

The process may seem a little complicated at first but, when we break this down, it will become clearer what is actually happening.

The first task was to declare to the DialogField variables that we want added to the resulting dialog, and then to bind them to the data contract data methods. However, in order for this to work, we had to bind the UI builder class to the data contract. We did this by adding the SysOperationContractProcessing attribute to the data contract.

Once this is done, the DialogField variables are now bound to the data contract methods. We then wrote a method to validate the vehicle group control, and bound this to the control's validate event using the control's registerOverrideMethod method.

Once this is all done, the dialog created by the framework can be validated interactively, allowing the user to correct any errors without having to start again.

The changes to the main method were to handle the situation when the vehicle ID should be hidden. We want the vehicle ID to show by default and only be hidden when it is called with a vehicle record. So we set the HideVehicleId data member to **No** as a default, setting it to **Yes** if it was called from a vehicle record.

Using SysOperationSandbox

The SysOperationSandbox class provides a way to start a process that doesn't block the client. Any long-running process will show a message that states the system is busy and does not allow the user to cancel the process. The SysOperationSandbox allows a process to be started that the user can cancel, which causes the process to abort and roll back.

To do this, we need two static methods: one that initiates the process and one to act as a callback class that the framework will call to perform the desired action.

This is only suited to processes that we expect to take over a minute. We will adjust our vehicle group change class to make it use SysOperationSandbox.

How to do it...

To use SysOperationSandbox, follow these steps:

1. Open the ConVMSVehicleGroupChange class.
2. Add a new method that acts as the callback for the operation, which is done with the following code:

```
private static void ProcessSandboxCallback(container _parms)
{
    ConVMSVehicleId vehicleId;
    ConVMSVehicleGroupId vehicleGroupId;
    [vehicleId, vehicleGroupId] = _parms;

    ConVMSVehicleGroupChangeContract contract = new
     ConVMSVehicleGroupChangeContract();
    contract.VehicleId(vehicleId);
    contract.VehicleGroupId(vehicleGroupId);

    ConVMSVehicleGroupChange groupChange = new
     ConVMSVehicleGroupChange();
    groupChange.InitFromContract(contract);
    groupChange.Run(contract);
}
```

3. Write the method to trigger the process as follows:

```
private static void ProcessSandbox(ConVMSVehicleGroupChangeContract
_contract)
{
    ConVMSVehicleId vehicleId = _contract.VehicleId();
    ConVMSVehicleGroupId vehicleGroupId =
    _contract.VehicleGroupId();
    container parms = [vehicleId, vehicleGroupId];
    SysOperationSandbox::callStaticMethod(
        classNum(ConVMSVehicleGroupChange), // class to call
        staticMethodStr(ConVMSVehicleGroupChange,
         ProcessSandboxCallback), // the call back method
        parms, // the parameters as a container
        "@ConVMS:VehicleGroupChange"); // the waiting message
}
```

The call accepts three prompt parameters, of which the waiting message is mandatory. You can also specify a completion and cancellation message.

4. Write a new entry point method so we can run this as an asynchronous operation. We cannot use this process when the routine is running in a batch, so to minimize the impact, create a new entry point method as follows:

```
public void RunAsOperation(ConVMSVehicleGroupChangeContract
_contract)
{
    if (isRunningOnBatch())
    {
        this.Run(_contract);
    }
    else
    {
        ConVMSVehicleGroupChange::ProcessSandbox(_contract);
    }
}
```

5. Change the controller class so that it calls the RunAsOperation method instead of Run, and build and test the result.

How it works...

We wrote the `static` methods as `private` for a reason. We don't want to allow the code to be run out of our control. Should another developer try to use the `Sandbox` method, it could cause an error if the process was running in batch.

The other reason they are `private` is that we are using a container object to pass the variables. This is unsafe, as containers can contain virtually anything. We need to be sure that it contains our variables and in the correct order. This is the only way to use the `Sandbox`, so we need to be careful. Even if our method does not need any parameters, the callback method must have a container as a input parameter, which it will simply ignore.

We would normally place the code in this recipe in a separate class, in order to simplify the use cases, for example, `ConVMSVehicleGroupChangeService`.

Advanced Data Handling 7

This chapter focuses on the more advanced elements of data structures and how we interact with them. The topics that will be covered in this chapter should be considered a toolbox that we can call on, should the standard development patterns not be suitable.

Data structures represent physical entities in the SQL Server database, which means they are much harder to change later – especially after they contain data. Due to this, we need to make the right design choices during the design phase. Knowing the benefits and drawbacks of using inheritance and date-time effectiveness is important when designing a technical solution.

In this chapter, we will cover the following recipes:

- Implementing table inheritance
- Using menu items to create a record for a table that uses inheritance
- Using date-time effectiveness
- Creating a view with a query and computed columns

Technical requirements

You can find the code files for this chapter in this book's GitHub repository at `https://github.com/PacktPublishing/Extending-Microsoft-Dynamics-365-Finance-and-Supply-Chain-Management-Cookbook-Second-Edition/blob/master/Chapter%207.axpp`.

Implementing table inheritance

Table inheritance can be implemented so that we have a base table with common attributes, as well as specializations that extend that table and add their own attributes and methods. This is similar to classes, but only in concept—although the base table can have many child tables, only one physical table is created in the SQL Server. The physical table in the SQL Server contains all of the fields from the base table and its child tables.

A good candidate for this is the vehicle table, where we could have a base vehicle table and a child table for each type, such as Bike, Car, and Truck. This is suitable as long as we are sure these can be considered physical data structures, and not a categorization. For example, we can change a product from inventory to non-inventoried by changing the inventory model group, but we cannot change a vehicle from a Bike to a Car after the record has been created if we used table inheritance.

If we choose to use table inheritance, the result is a logical data structure that is represented as different tables in the **Application Explorer** but is physically stored as one table in the SQL Server. As far as we are concerned, though, these are different tables. This means that the user must choose the type of vehicle they are creating before filling in any data. This also means that it is difficult to retrofit if data has been created. Once we have started to use table inheritance, we can't remove it later.

In our case, we will alter `ConVMSVehicleTable` in order to use inheritance.

Getting ready

Before we start, if you haven't done so already, you should use the *Creating a table handler class* and *Hooking up a number sequence* recipes in `Chapter 4`, *Working with Form Logic and Frameworks*, to create a type class for `ConVMSVehicleTable`. The *There's more...* section of the *Hooking up a number sequence* recipe shows a summarized list of steps regarding how to do this.

How to do it...

To implement table inheritance, follow these steps:

1. Open the `ConVMSVehicleTable` table and locate the **Support inheritance** property.
2. Change the property value from **No** to **Yes**. This will automatically create a new field called `InstanceRelationType`.

This field is used to select the various subtypes of a record. Therefore, we need to add an index to this table. Even though this logically replaces the need to have a vehicle type field, the vehicle type field is useful and should also have an index.

3. Create two indexes that allow duplicates, one for `InstanceRelationType` and the other for `VehicleType`. The name of the index should be the field name suffixed with `Idx`, for example, `InstanceRelationTypeIdx`.

4. As a side task, save all the changes to `ConVMSVehicleTable` and build the project. We need to synchronize, so right-click on the project in the Solution Explorer and choose **Synchronise ConVMSVehicleManagement**.

5. Open a web browser to Dynamics SCM and open the `Vehicle table` form. If you receive SQL Server errors, it means the database was not synchronized.

6. Click the **+ New** button. Nothing will happen, apart from a record being created. There is only one type, the base, so this is not unexpected.

7. Go back to Visual Studio and create a new table named `ConVMSVehicleTableTruck`.

8. Change the **Support Inheritance** property to **Yes** and complete the **Extends** property so that it's `ConVMSVehicleTable`.

Completing the **Extends** property removes `InstanceRelationType` and adds a relation to the parent table on `RecId`.

9. Create a label for the table called `Trucks`.

10. Create a new enum called `ConVMSVehicleTruckType` that has the elements `Fixed`, `Articulated`, and `Tanker` and add this as a field on the table.

11. Build the project and synchronize the database.

12. Open `SQL Server Management Studio`. Connect to the local database server, select `AxDB` from the *Databases* list, and press *Alt+N* (or right-click on the `AxDB` database and select **New Query**).

13. Type in the following transact-SQL:

```
select * from CONVMSVEHICLETABLE
```

14. Press *Ctrl + E* (or click **Execute**) and scroll to the right of the results list; the field that we added to the `ConVMSVehicleTableTruck` table will be there. Also, there is no physical table that is named `ConVMSVehicleTableTruck`.

15. Open a browser window to Dynamics SCM and try to create a new vehicle. We will be presented with a dialog asking us to decide between a vehicle type, that is, `Vehicles` or `Trucks`.

> The label for the record type is taken from the **Label** property of the table.

16. As you create the record, the new field is not visible to the form, and the `Vehicle type` field is not related to the record type. To associate the type of record type to the `Vehicle type` field, we must use code.

17. Open the `ConVMSVehicleTable` form. Expand **Data Sources** and right-click on the `ConVMSVehicleTable` table. From there, choose **Restore**.

> This refreshes the data source, adding `ConVMSVehicleTableTruck` under the **Derived Data Sources** node.

18. Under the `DetailsTab` tab control, create a new tab page named `TruckDetailsPage`. Use the `Fields and Field Groups` pattern and add the `TruckType` field from the `ConVMSVehicleTable_ConVMSVehicleTableTruck` derived data source.

19. **Save all** and build the project. In SCM, create two vehicles, one as `Vehicles` and the other as `Trucks`.

> The only time the new field is enabled is if it is a `Truck`.

20. Now, create a table for `Bikes` and `Cars` in order to complete the required types.

On the base table, we can also set a property called **Abstract**. This is similar in concept to classes, which means that you can't create an instance of it. Base tables that are marked as abstract won't be listed as types to select from when we create a new record. In our case, abstract isn't a bad idea if we don't want to allow *generic* vehicles that aren't `Bike`, `Car`, or `Truck`.

This works OK, but the `Vehicle type` field has to be manually set in order for it to make sense. We could just remove it, but it is useful if you want to allow the user to create a filter on `Bikes`, for example. We should maintain this field automatically.

21. `Vehicle type` is extensible, so a simple `switch` is not appropriate. Instead, we need to create a parameter class so that we can pass data to and from a delegate, as shown in the following code:

```
class ConVMSVehicleTypeParameter
{
    public ConVMSVehicleTable vehicleTable;
    public ConVMSVehicleType vehicleType;
    public boolean vehicleTypeSet = false;
}
```

22. Open the `ConVMSVehicleTableType` class and write a delegate that we will call, should our `switch` not return a value:

```
delegate void GetVehicleTypeDelegate(ConVMSVehicleTypeParameter
_parameters) {}
```

23. Next, create a `public` method named `GetVehicleType`. Write the method as follows:

```
public ConVMSVehicleType GetVehicleType()
{
    switch (vehicleTable.InstanceRelationType)
    {
        case tableNum(ConVMSVehicleTableTruck):
            return ConVMSVehicleType::Truck;
        case tableNum(ConVMSVehicleTableBike):
            return ConVMSVehicleType::Bike;
        case tableNum(ConVMSVehicleTableCar):
            return ConVMSVehicleType::Car;
    }
    ConVMSVehicleTypeParameter parm = new
     ConVMSVehicleTypeParameter();
    // we don't really want the user to alter this,
```

```
        // but since it is always passed by reference
        // we have little control. We could use the .data()
        // method, but this could cause unexpected behaviour
        // should the developer try to call update.
        parm.vehicleTable = vehicleTable;
        this.GetVehicleTypeDelegate(parm);
        if (parm.vehicleTypeSet)
        {
            return parm.vehicleType;
        }
        return ConVMSVehicleType::NotSelected;
}
```

 We have made the `public` method as there is no danger to the internal state, and it might be useful to other developers. We also used the delegate pattern with a parameter class to allow other developers to add new vehicle types correctly.

24. In the `Inserting` method, set the `VehicleType` field using the new method, as shown in the following code:

```
public void Inserting()
{
    vehicleTable.VehicleType = this.GetVehicleType();
}
```

25. Finally, make the `VehicleType` field read-only by setting the **Allow Edit** and **Allow Edit on Create** properties to **No**.
26. Save and close all editors, build the project, and synchronize the database.

How it works...

Table inheritance is not implemented as physical data structures as we might assume. The natural presumption of how this works is that each child table we create is represented as a physical table in the SQL Server and that there is some logical mechanism that joins them together in the application. In fact, there is only one physical table, and the fields from all the tables are stored in this table. The separation is logical and is a useful way to abstract data into logical entities.

We can see that when we issue a `SELECT * FROM <BaseTable>` in a SQL Server query window, we get all the fields in one, which implies that all the field names must be unique across the table set.

This leaves the question of why the child tables have a relation of `<childTable>.RecId = <parentTable>.RecId`. This is a self-relation, highlighting again that the child table and parent table are, in fact, the same table. The relation is there as a helper to the form engine and has no purpose in referential integrity.

We can add methods to the child tables and field groups, but we can't extend a field group on the base table so that it includes child fields. For example, in order to add fields from child tables to the main **Grid** control, we would need to remove the data group and add the fields manually from the data source. We can add fields from both the base and child tables to the grid, allowing fields from different child tables to be added. `Truck` fields will simply be blank is the current record type is a `Bike` – they are actually `NULL`, which is unusual for SCM as fields in SQL are always initialized as empty values. Even dates are 01/01/1900 00:00! This is an exception to that rule.

This is the behavior in SQL (fields not in use by the child table are `NULL`), but even these null values are displayed as the type defaults. This is why I chose to add an enum to the `Truck` table when a `Bike` is created. The field is disabled as expected but appears to have a value – the first or default option from the enum. It doesn't really have a value; it is 0 and is represented by the first option in the enum's elements.

The steps in this recipe fall into four parts:

- *Steps 1-6* were the steps required to make the base table support inheritance.
- *Steps 7-12* covered adding a new child table to the base table.
- *Steps 17-21* covered some changes to the user interface in order to show fields from the child table.
- *Steps 22-27* covered setting the vehicle type based on the table type that the user created.

As part of *Step 25*, you may also wish to add a call to the `GetVehicleType()` method to the `initValue` method of the `ConVMSVehicleTable` table. Since `initValue` is only guaranteed to be called for records that are created through the user interface, you'll need to place the call so that it is enforced on insert correctly. However, it is a nicer experience for the user to see the data as it will be before they press **Save**; otherwise, they may think they chose the wrong option.

Using menu items to create records for tables that use inheritance

When we create a new record on a form whose data source uses table inheritance, the system offers a dialog asking us to **select a record** type. This is suitable in most cases, but we may wish to add specific menu item buttons for each record type, such as **New car**, **New Bike**, and so on. If we were using a create form, the system would show two dialog forms: one for the record type selection and then the create dialog. This would be irritating to the users as it adds unnecessary clicks to the process.

We will add a menu item button to the vehicle form for each vehicle type.

Getting ready

This recipe is a continuation of the previous recipe, but to start, we need to have a table that uses table inheritance with an enum tied to the table's type, which is the vehicle type field in our case.

How to do it...

To create **New** buttons for each record type, follow these steps:

1. The changes are on the `ConVMSVehicleTable` form, so open the code for this form.
2. We need to write a method that creates a `Map` object for a vehicle type, but since we are working with an extensible enum, we need to allow other developers to add to this map to handle their new enum element. Therefore, we need a delegate that has the input parameters that the developer needs. Write this as follows:

```
/// <summary>
/// Used to handle vehicle types not handled as standard
/// </summary>
/// <param name = "_vehicleType">The type being requested</param>
/// <param name = "_dataSourceName">The data source name, use this
/// as the map key, and the child table name as the value</param>
/// <param name = "_tableTypes">Map of data source name and child
/// table name – add one element
/// if the type is to be handled, otherwise do nothing</param>
delegate void GetTableTypesMapForVehicleTypeDelegate(
```

```
ConVMSVehicleType _vehicleType, DataSourceName _dataSourceName,
 Map _tableTypes) {}
```

 The map (which is passed by reference) is a map of two strings: key is the data source name, while the value is the desired child table name.

3. Next, we can write the code that builds the table type map, as follows:

```
private Map GetTableTypesMapForVehicleType(ConVMSVehicleType
_vehicleType)
{
    Map tableType = new Map(Types::String, Types::String);

    switch(_vehicleType)
    {
        case ConVMSVehicleType::NotSelected:
            tableType.insert(ConVMSVehicleTable_DS.name(),
             tableStr(ConVMSVehicleTable));
            break;
        case ConVMSVehicleType::Truck:
            tableType.insert(ConVMSVehicleTable_DS.name(),
             tableStr(ConVMSVehicleTableTruck));
            break;
        case ConVMSVehicleType::Car:
            tableType.insert(ConVMSVehicleTable_DS.name(),
             tableStr(ConVMSVehicleTableCar));
            break;
        case ConVMSVehicleType::Bike:
            tableType.insert(ConVMSVehicleTable_DS.name(),
             tableStr(ConVMSVehicleTableBike));
            break;
        default:
            this.GetTableTypesMapForVehicleTypeDelegate(
                _vehicleType, ConVMSVehicleTable_DS.name(),
                tableType);
    }
    if (tableType.elements() == 0)
    {
        //Vehicle type %1 has not been implemented
        throw error(strFmt("@ConVMS:VehTypeNotImplemented",
         enum2str(_vehicleType)));
    }
    return tableType;
}
```

This is `private` to give us the freedom of changing the method without worrying about regression in other developers' code. We handled the extensibility requirement with the delegate.

4. Next, we need to write a `public` method so that we can call it from a command button. This can be done like so:

```
public void CreateContractRecordForType(ConVMSVehicleType
_vehicleType)
{
    Map mapTypes =
     this.GetTableTypesMapForVehicleType(_vehicleType);
    ConVMSVehicleTable_DS.createTypes(mapTypes);
}
```

5. Next, open the form designer. First, disable the standard **New** button by changing the form's Design's **Show New Button** property to **No**.
6. Add a new **Button Group** named `RecordActions` under the main `FormActionPaneControl` – the name is just to tell us why we created it and is the convention.
7. Create a new **Menu Button** as a child of the `RecordActions` button group called `NewVehicle`. Make the **Normal Image** property `New` and the **Text** property `@SYS2055`.
8. Create three buttons under the `NewVehicle` **Menu Button**. Configure them as shown in the following table:

Name	Text
NewTruck	Truck (for example, @ConVMS:Truck)
NewCar	Car
NewBike	Bike

9. Override the `clicked` method for `newTruck` and write it as follows:

```
public void clicked()
{
    super();
    element.CreateContractRecordForType(ConVMSVehicleType::Truck);
}
```

10. Do the same for the remaining two buttons, changing the vehicle type parameter as appropriate.
11. Save and close all the editors and build the project.

How it works...

When the standard new button is called, the form code populates a list of the tables that were inherited from the data source's table. If the main table is abstract, it is not added to the list. Once the user selects an option, a map is initialized. The key is the data source name, while the value is the table name to be created. The following table shows this:

User-selected option	Map->key	Map->value
Vehicles	ConVMSVehicleTable	ConVMSVehicleTable
Trucks	ConVMSVehicleTable	ConVMSVehicleTableTruck
Bikes	ConVMSVehicleTable	ConVMSVehicleTableBike
Cars	ConVMSVehicleTable	ConVMSVehicleTableCar

 The data source name is usually the same as the table name and will be the main table's data source name.

Then, it calls the form's `createTypes` method with this map, where the map will contain one element per data source, which essentially means one element. The form then calls the data source's `create` method, where the data source's buffer has been instantiated with the selected inherited table, such as `ConVMSVehicleTableBike`.

We are simply hooking into this process by populating the map with the desired option based on the vehicle type.

You can test this by adding breakpoints to the methods and see for yourself what is called and when. To do this, use the **Debug** | **Attach to process** option and select the `w3wp` process. You will need to check the **Show processes from all users** box in order to see this process.

Using date-time effectiveness

Date-time effectiveness is used to state that records are valid for a specific period of time. This can be to enforce that every change to a record is time-stamped, allowing us to see the state of the record at any point in time. It can also be used to plan future states, such as a planned pay rise.

In our case, we will create an odometer table so that the user can enter the odometer setting for the vehicle and allow them to see the current and historical states of the record.

Getting ready

The example in this recipe builds on the vehicle table and form, but we can use this pattern to create a table and form that implements date-time effectiveness in any SCM project.

How to do it...

For simplicity, we will split this recipe into sections.

Create the date-time effective table

To create a date-time effective table, follow these steps:

1. Create a new table called `ConVMSVehicleOdometerTable`.
2. Complete the table as a `Main` table, in the same way as `ConVMSVehicleTable` was created. Don't add a primary index or `Find` or `Exist` methods yet.
3. Add a `VehicleId` field based on `ConVMSVehicleId` and a foreign key relation to `ConVMSVehicleTable` on `VehicleId`.
4. Make the `VehicleId` field not visible, mandatory, and not editable.
5. Create a new Real EDT named `ConVMSVehicleOdometer` that extends `Qty`. Set the `Label` and other properties as desired.
6. Drag the new EDT to the **Fields** node of `ConVMSVehicleOdometerTable` and rename it to `Odometer`.
7. Create a field group named `Overview` and add the `Odometer` field – remember to set the **Label** to `@SYS9039 (Overview)`.
8. Now, it's time to make it date-time effective. Change the **Valid Time State Field Type** table property to `UtcDateTime`.

 Changing the **Valid Time State Field Type** to `utcDateTime` added two fields to our table, `ValidFrom` and `ValidTo`. These fields are required in order to create the primary index. The concept here is that we give the appearance that the vehicle has one odometer setting, but in fact, there can be many as each change creates a new version.

9. Create a new index named `VehicleIdx` and add the `VehicleId` field to it.
10. Change the **Alternate key** property to **Yes**. This enables the **Valid Time State Key** property.
11. Set the **Valid Time State Key** property to **Yes**.

12. Leave the **Valid Time State Mode** property as `NoGap` – this is only set to `Gap` under specific scenarios where we want there to be a gap between a `ValidTo` date-time and the next `ValidFrom` date-time. Selecting a record in this gap will return a blank record.

13. Should we build the project now, it will fail, stating that the index does not contain a `ValidFrom` column. Add the `ValidFrom` and `ValidTo` fields to the index.

14. Set the table's primary index property to `VehicleIdx`.

15. Next, we can write the `Find` methods, which have an additional parameter. Write these as follows:

```
public static ConVMSVehicleOdometerTable Find(
  ConVMSVehicleId _vehicleId,
  utcdatetime _validFrom = DateTimeUtil::utcNow(),
  utcdatetime _validTo = _validFrom,
  boolean _forUpdate = false,
  ConcurrencyModel _concurrencyModel = ConcurrencyModel::Auto)
{
    ConVMSVehicleOdometerTable odometerTable;
    odometerTable.selectForUpdate(_forUpdate );

    if (_forUpdate && _concurrencyModel != ConcurrencyModel::Auto)
    {
        odometerTable.concurrencyModel(_concurrencyModel);
    }
    if (_vehicleId)
    {
        // select based on now, which could technically be
        // different from the time when this method was called,
        // therefore use prmIsDefault to check if the parameter
        // is the default value, we should not check if
        // _validFrom is equal to Now again - this is not
        // equivalent as Now will have changed!
        if (prmisDefault(_validFrom) && prmisDefault(_validTo))
        {
            select firstonly odometerTable where
              odometerTable.VehicleId == _vehicleId;
        }
        // select based on a specific point in time
        else if (_validFrom == _validTo)
        {
            select firstonly ValidTimeState(_validFrom)
              odometerTable where odometerTable.VehicleId ==
              _vehicleId;
        }
```

```
                else
                {
                    // select records that are valid for the validFrom
                    // and validTo date range
                    select ValidTimeState(_validFrom, _validTo)
                     odometerTable where odometerTable.VehicleId ==
                     _vehicleId;
                }
            }
            return odometerTable;
        }
```

16. Write the equivalent method for `Exist`.

17. Build the project and use the project's **Synchronize** option (right-click on the project and choose `Synchronize <project name>`) to synchronize the changes in data structures while we update the vehicle form.

Adjust the vehicle details form so that it includes the new "date-time effective" odometer table

Let's look at the steps to understand how we can adjust the vehicle details form:

1. Open the `ConVMSVehicleTable` form and drag the `ConVMSVehicleOdometerTable` table onto the **Data Sources** node.

2. Set the **Join Source** to `ConVMSVehicleTable` and change the **Insert At End** property to **No**.

 We don't want to let the user add multiple odometer settings as there should only be one per vehicle.

3. Override the `ConVMSVehicleOdometerTable` data source's `initValue` method to set the `VehicleId`, as follows:

```
public void initValue()
{
    super();
    ConVMSVehicleOdometerTable.VehicleId =
     ConVMSVehicleTable.VehicleId;
}
```

4. Close the code editor.

5. Create a new tab page named `OdometerPage` under the `DetailsTab` tab control.

6. Set the label to the **Odometer** settings, set the **Caption** property to the **Odometer** settings, and apply the **Toolbar and Fields** pattern.

7. Add an **Action Pane** called `OdometerActionPane` and a **Group** control called `OdometerSettingsGroup`. Set the group to the **Fields and Field groups** pattern.

8. Drag the **Odometer** field from the `ConVMSVehicleOdometerTable` data source to the `OdometerSettingsGroup` group control.

9. Build the project and test the changes you've made so far.

Reviewing the results of updating a date-time effective table in SQL

The following are the steps to check the results of updating our table in SQL:

1. Upon testing the form, we should see our new tab page with a single control. We should be able to edit this field, and it should behave as if it is part of the vehicle field list. Change the **Odometer** value several times, pressing **Save** after each change. Nothing special will appear to happen.

2. Open **SQL Server Management Studio** and open a new query against the `AxDB` database.

3. Type the following transact-SQL:

```
SELECT * FROM CONVMSVEHICLEODOMETERTABLE
```

4. Press *Ctrl + E* (or click **Execute**). You should see results similar to the ones shown in the following table:

VEHICLEID	ODOMETER	VALIDTO	VALIDTOTZ	VALIDFROM	VALIDFROMTZ	DATAAREAID
V000000018	12.000000	2019-05-19 14:05:45.000	35001	2019-05-19 14:05:33.000	35001	usmf
V000000018	14.000000	2019-05-19 14:15:57.000	35001	2019-05-19 14:05:46.000	35001	usmf
V000000018	12.000000	2154-12-31 23:59:59.000	35001	2019-05-19 14:15:58.000	35001	usmf

Writing a form so that we can see the current and previous state of the data

The following steps show us how we can write a form to see the current and previous state of the data:

1. What we have so far is great, but we would also like to give our users access to see the state of the record. In order to do this, a new form is required. Create a form named `ConVMSVehicleOdometerTable`. Also, create a **Display menu item** to reference this form.

2. Drag the `ConVMSVehicleOdometerTable` table to the **Data Sources** node and change the **Max Access Right** property to `View`.

3. Override the form's `init` method with the following code:

    ```
    public void init()
    {
    if (element.args().dataset() != tableNum(ConVMSVehicleTable))
    {
    throw
    error(Error::missingRecord(tableStr(ConVMSVehicleTable)));
    }
    ConVMSVehicleTable vehicle = element.args().record();
    if (vehicle.RecId == 0)
    {
    throw
    error(Error::missingRecord(tableStr(ConVMSVehicleTable)));
    }
    super();
    QueryBuildDataSource qbds =
      ConVMSVehicleOdometerTable_ds.queryBuildDataSource();
    QueryBuildRange vehRange = SysQuery::findOrCreateRange(
    qbds, fieldNum(ConVMSVehicleOdometertable, VehicleId));
    vehRange.value(vehicle.VehicleId);
    }
    ```

4. Close the code editor and apply the `Simple List` pattern to the form's Design.

5. Complete the form pattern by adding controls in order to conform to the pattern. This was covered in `Chapter 4`, *Working with Form Logic and Frameworks*. Specifically, remember to set the design's **Data Source** property.

6. Ensure that the **Grid** control has the `Odometer`, `ValidFrom`, and `ValidTo` fields.

7. Close and save all editors and open the `ConVMSVehicleTable` form design.

8. Under the `OdometerPage` tab page control we created earlier, ensure we have an **Action Pane** with a **Button Group**. Drag the `ConVMSVehicleOdometerTable` display menu item to the button group.

9. Set the **Normal Image** property to `Details` and the **Data Source** property to `ConVMSVehicleTable`.

10. The ability to show the versions of the record at certain points in time is a feature of the platform. In order to implement this feature, we must implement the `IDateEffectivenessPaneCaller` interface on the form. Open the code for the `ConVMSVehicleOdometerTable` form and change the declaration so that it reads as follows:

```
public class ConVMSVehicleOdometerTable extends FormRun implements
IDateEffectivenessPaneCaller
```

11. This forces us to implement the `getDateEffectivenessController` method. First, we need to construct a `DateEffectivenessPaneController` instance. To do this, we must declare it as a global method and initialize it in the form's `init` method. The completed code is as follows:

```
DateEffectivenessPaneController dePaneController;
public void init()
{
 if (element.args().dataset() != tableNum(ConVMSVehicleTable))
 {
 throw
  error(Error::missingRecord(tableStr(ConVMSVehicleTable)));
 }
 ConVMSVehicleTable vehicle = element.args().record();
 if (vehicle.RecId == 0)
 {
 throw
  error(Error::missingRecord(tableStr(ConVMSVehicleTable)));
 }
 super();
 QueryBuildDataSource qbds =
  ConVMSVehicleOdometerTable_ds.queryBuildDataSource();
 QueryBuildRange vehRange = SysQuery::findOrCreateRange(
 qbds, fieldNum(ConVMSVehicleOdometertable, VehicleId));
 vehRange.value(vehicle.VehicleId);
 // date time controller
 dePaneController =
  DateEffectivenessPaneController::constructWithForm(this,
   ConVMSVehicleOdometerTable_ds, true, true, true);
 }
```

The last three Boolean options determine the options that are available to the user when the **As of date** dialog is displayed to the user.

12. `getDateEffectivenessController` is implemented by adding the following method:

```
public DateEffectivenessPaneController
getDateEffectivenessController()
{
    return dePaneController;
}
```

13. Save and close all editor windows and build the project.
14. When you open the **Odometer settings** for the vehicle, you will see an `As of date` drop dialog button. When you drop this down, you can choose to show the values of a particular date or to show all records.

How it works...

We saw that there is a lot of automation when we tested editing the odometer value and looked at the results in SQL. The system created a new version on every save (should anything have changed), and the fact the user has no control over this makes it great for auditing changes. It can also add significant overhead, depending on the volume.

A customer or consultant might request that date-time effectiveness is implemented on a table, and the request might seem reasonable if the requirement is to track a history of changes that have been made to a record. We also need to consider that it also adds complications to the code that we write and a significant overhead to the database – every change has to update the `ValidTo` field with the current date-time and create a new record for the change. This happens on every update to the record that's made through the user interface.

This should, therefore, be reserved for scenarios where the version is a requirement and the table type is `Main` or `Group`. This shouldn't be used for the worksheet (orders) or transaction tables. There are other patterns we would employ for this, such as the history of sales order delivery note being stored in the delivery note journal tables, that is, `CustPackingSlipJour` and `CustPackingSlipTrans`. The sales order only stores the current state of the order.

When we changed the table to a **Valid Time State** table, it added the `ValidFrom` and `ValidTo` fields automatically and forced us to create an index that contained the `ValidFrom` field. We added the `ValidTo` field in order to improve query efficiency when records are selected for a data range. The SQL statement is similar to the following when we select a valid record at a point in time:

```
SELECT *
    FROM CONVMSVEHICLEODOMETERTABLE
    WHERE '2019-05-19 14:05:45.000' BETWEEN VALIDFROM and VALIDTO
    AND VEHICLEID=N'V000000018' -- DataAreaId AND Partition have
    been omitted for clarity
```

When we wrote the `Find` method, we used an additional clause to ensure we selected the correct record based on the required date-time. The `ValidTimeState` clause has one mandatory parameter of the required date-time and an optional parameter for the valid date-time. When specifying one parameter, we only want one record – the one value at that point in time. This is why we added `firstonly`. This is to assist the database engine by telling it we only want the first result. This is good practice when we expect one result.

The `firstonly` clause was omitted when we selected for a range of dates as this can return more than one record.

The concurrency option was added in case we wanted to use pessimistic concurrency. If we are updating records in code, we sometimes want to ensure that no other process can interfere with our process. Since valid time state tables update more than one record at a time (the current and previous state records), we are more likely to get a message stating **Another user has changed the current record**. This occurs because optimistic concurrency lets more than one process select a record to update, and the first to commit updates the table's `RecVersion` field. When the subsequent processes try to write back the system checks, if the `RecVersion` has changed since the record was selected, it throws an error.

By using pessimistic concurrency, we physically lock the record and make other processes wait until we have completed the transaction. This is not good for performance but is sometimes required.

The `ConVMSVehicleOdometerTable` child form that we created to view the history of the changes was largely standard, except we implemented the `IDateEffectivenessPaneCaller` interface.

There are three important Boolean parameters that are passed to this class:

Parameter	Explanation
Use plural labels	Changes the dialog caption to `Display the` **`records`** `as at`.
Allow show all records	When the data source is displayed as a grid, set this to true to allow the user to see a history of every change that was made to the record.
Use Date-time	Must match the table's **Valid Time State Field** type. If this property is `UtcDateTime`, this parameter must be set to true.

We could have also added this to the vehicle form, but since we are only showing a single field on the vehicle table, we would construct the controller as follows:

```
dePaneController =
  DateEffectivenessPaneController::constructWithForm(this,
    ConVMSVehicleOdometerTable_ds, false, false, true);
```

The preceding code means that the dialog will be set to `Display the record as at` and there will not be an option to show all records.

Creating a view with a query and computed columns

Views are great high-performance ways to bring data from multiple tables together. We can start with a query and then add fields from that query to a field list in order to create a view that is then created in SQL and is usable as a read-only table anywhere in SCM.

This is great for fact panes, reports, and inquiries. Although we will only cover a simple view in this recipe, the key point is to show how we can create view methods that are used as computed columns in the view. Just like we could add a display method to a table, which is then used in a form, we can also do this in a view. The difference is that the work is done by the SQL Server and comes with two big advantages: they are much quicker to calculate and you can sort and filter on this calculated result. As far as SCM is concerned, this *calculated* view field is just a field.

Getting ready

This follows our vehicle management project that we have created throughout this book. The techniques that you will learn about here can be applied when creating any view in an SCM project.

How to do it...

First, we will create a simple view of service orders, which we will start as a query. To do this, follow these steps:

1. Create a new query named `ConVMSVehicleServiceDetailView`.

    This query will be used to create a view. Since this query will control the structure of our view, we want it to be obvious that this query is written as the basis for a view. If another developer made a change to the query and used it for their own purpose, it would affect the view or views that use it.

2. Drag the `ConVMSVehicleTable` table onto the **Data Sources** node of the new query.
3. On the property sheet for the new `ConVMSVehicleTable` data source, change the **Dynamics Fields** property to **Yes** and then set it to **No**.

    Choosing `yes` will populate the field list with all of the fields on the table, while changing it to **No** after will allow us to remove fields that we don't need.

4. Remove all fields except for `VehicleId`, `Name`, `VehicleGroupId`, `VehicleType`, and `VehicleRegNum`.
5. Drag the `ConVMSVehicleGroup` table onto the **Data Sources** node that lies under the `ConVMSVehicleTable` data source.
6. Set the `ConVMSVehicleGroup` data source **Dynamics Fields** property to **No**.
7. Set the **Use Relations** property to **Yes**.
8. Expand the **Fields** node (which will be empty) and then right-click on it to choose the **New | Field** option.
9. Regarding the properties for the new data source field, set the **Field** property to `Name`.

10. Now, you should have the following folder structure:

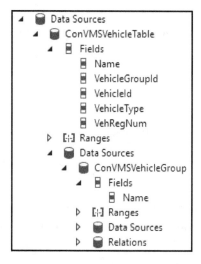

11. Save and close the editor.

This will suffice for this example. Next, we will create a view from this query. Let's get started:

1. Create a new `View` with the same name as our query, `ConVMSVehicleServiceDetailView`.

2. In the property sheet for the new view, set the **Query** property to `ConVMSVehicleServiceDetailView`.

3. This is now referenced in the view's **View Metadata** node.

4. Expand the **View Metadata** node, and then the **Fields** nodes within the `ConVMSVehicleTable` node. Click on the first field, and then *shift*-click on the last field. Once all the fields have been selected, press *Ctrl + C*.

5. Collapse the **View Metadata** node and click on the **Fields** node of the view. Press *Ctrl + V* to paste the fields from the data source to the view's field list.

6. Then, locate the `Name` field from the `ConVMSVehicleGroup` data source in the **View Metadata**. Copy it and paste it into the view's **Field** node.

7. This will be named `Name1` in the field list. Rename it to `VehicleGroupName`. You can also specify a label here since we have two fields with the same label: `Vehicle Name` and `Vehicle Group Name`.

8. Save and close the view editor. Build the project and synchronize the database.

9. Next, we should open the SQL Server Management Studio application.

10. Once open, connect to the local machine's SQL Server as usual and select the AxDB database from the **Databases** node.

11. Press *Alt* + *N* to create a new query window. Then, type in the following code:

```
SELECT * FROM ConVMSVehicleServiceDetailView
```

 We do this to test the view. This will also spot most cases where a Cartesian join has been created. A Cartesian join is created when we don't specify a relation between two data sources, for example, SELECT * FROM SALESTABLE A JOIN SALESLINE B. The result set is the number of records in SALESTABLE to the power of the number of records in SALESLINE.

Next, we will add a computed column to the view. This is based on a view method that returns the transact-SQL code that the column is based on. The transact-SQL statement we are looking to create is as follows:

```
SELECT TOP 1
CASE WHEN CST.ServiceDateConfirmed = {ts '1900-01-01 00:00:00.000'}
    THEN CST.ServiceDateReq ELSE CST.ServiceDateConfirmed END
FROM ConVMSVehicleServiceTable CST
WHERE T1.DATAAREAID = CST.DataAreaId AND T1.PARTITION =
CST.Partition
AND T1.VEHICLEID = CST.VehicleId AND CST.ServiceStatus = 2
ORDER BY CASE WHEN CST.ServiceDateConfirmed = {ts '1900-01-01
00:00:00.000'}
    THEN CST.ServiceDateReq ELSE CST.ServiceDateConfirmed END DESC
```

The following may seem counter-intuitive at first, so once this is complete, please refer to the *How it works...* section for clarification. To write the computed column method, continue with these steps:

1. Go back to Visual Studio and to our view editor.

2. Right-click on the **Methods** node and click on **New Method**.

3. Create the method as a private static method (it has no purpose outside of this view) named LastServiceDate and that returns str as its type.

4. We need to gain access to the view's metadata to get the view's field name, which will be different from the field name in the view's field definition. This is done with the following code:

```
DictView dv = new
DictView(tableNum(ConVMSVehicleServiceDetailView));
```

5. We need to join the `DataAreaId` and `Partition` system fields, so we need to get the field names from the view's metadata:

```
str vehicleDataAreaIdField = dv.computedColumnString(
    tableStr(ConVMSVehicleTable), fieldStr(ConVMSVehicleTable,
    DataAreaId),
    FieldNameGenerationMode::WhereClause);
str vehiclePartitionField = dv.computedColumnString(
    tableStr(ConVMSVehicleTable), fieldStr(ConVMSVehicleTable,
    Partition),
    FieldNameGenerationMode::WhereClause);
```

6. We need to get the field name for the vehicle ID so that we can use it as part of the `where` clause. This is done using the following code:

```
str vehicleIdField = dv.computedColumnString(
    tableStr(ConVMSVehicleTable), fieldStr(ConVMSVehicleTable,
    VehicleId),
    FieldNameGenerationMode::WhereClause);
```

7. Next, we will get the vehicle service table name, which is done using the standard `tableStr` compile-time function, as shown here:

```
str serviceTableName = tableStr(ConVMSVehicleServiceTable);
```

8. We need an alias for the vehicle service table. This can be anything – we just need to ensure that it is unique within the context of the view. Create this like so:

```
str serviceTableAlias = 'CST'; // short for Contoso Service table
```

9. Now, we need the `VehicleId`, `DataAreaId`, and `Partition` from this table, which need to be prefixed with the alias, as shown here (it is the period or full stop symbol in the single quotes):

```
str serviceVehicleIdField = serviceTableAlias + '.' +
fieldStr(ConVMSVehicleServiceTable, VehicleId);
str serviceDataAreaIdField = serviceTableAlias + '.' +
fieldStr(ConVMSVehicleServiceTable, DataAreaId);
str servicePartitionField = serviceTableAlias + '.' +
fieldStr(ConVMSVehicleServiceTable, Partition);
```

10. We have the necessary fields in order to join the vehicle table with the vehicle service table. Now, we need to find out the field names for the service dates and service status. The service status is straightforward. This is another simple `fieldStr` compile-time function:

```
str serviceStatusField = serviceTableAlias + '.' +
fieldStr(ConVMSVehicleServiceTable, ServiceStatus);
```

11. We have two dates (requested and confirmed) where we will use the confirmed date if it's been populated; otherwise, the requested date will be used. Use the following lines of code to do this:

```
str serviceDateReqField = serviceTableAlias + '.' +
fieldStr(ConVMSVehicleServiceTable, ServiceDateReq);
str serviceDateConfirmedField =
 serviceTableAlias + '.' + fieldStr(ConVMSVehicleServiceTable,
ServiceDateConfirmed);

str serviceDateToUse = SysComputedColumn::if(
 SysComputedColumn::equalExpression(
 serviceDateConfirmedField,
SysComputedColumn::returnLiteral(dateNull())),
 serviceDateReqField,
 serviceDateConfirmedField);
```

12. Let's put this together and build the inline SQL statement that we will use as a field in the view definition. This is done as follows:

```
// SELECT TOP 1 <date to_use> from ConVMSVehicleServiceTable CST
str sql = strFmt('SELECT MAX(%1) FROM %2 %3', serviceDateToUse,
serviceTableName, serviceTableAlias);

// WHERE A.DataAreaId = CST.DataAreaId AND A.Partition =
CST.Partition
// AND A.VehicleId = CST.VehicleId
sql += strFmt(' WHERE %1 = %2 AND %3 = %4 AND %5 = %6',
    vehicleDataAreaIdField, serviceDataAreaIdField,
    vehiclePartitionField, servicePartitionField,
    vehicleIdField, serviceVehicleIdField);

// AND CST.ServiceStatus = 2 -- if this is what the value is for
completed
sql += strFmt(' AND %1 = %2',
    serviceStatusField,
    int2str(enum2int(ConVMSVehicleServiceStatus::Complete)));
```

13. Complete the method by returning the `sql` string using the following command:

    ```
    return sql;
    ```

14. Save and close the code editor. Now, we can add our computed column to the field list of our view. Right-click on the **Fields** node and choose **New** | **Date Computed Column**.

15. Change the new field's **View Method** property to `LastServiceDate` using the drop-down list. If the list is empty, it is because the code was not saved or the method declaration was not `public static str LastServiceDate()`. Only `private static` methods that have no parameters and return type string are shown here.

16. Change the **Name** property to `LastServiceDate`.

17. If we had an EDT for this field, we would fill this in here in order to control how this field is displayed on a form. Alternatively, we can use the existing `ConVMSVehicleServiceDateReq` EDT but manually enter a new label into the **Label** property, for example, *Last service date*.

18. Save and close all windows, build the project, and synchronize the database.

19. Create two service orders against two different vehicles to test the confirmed and requested date logic. In one service order, complete only the requested field, and in the second, complete both dates. Ensure that both service orders are set to `Complete`.

20. Open the SQL Server management studio, and, against the `AxDB` database, write a new query, as shown in the following code:

    ```
    select * from ConVMSVehicleServiceDetailView
    ```

How it works...

The first part of this recipe was to create a query and then a view, based on that query. Although we can create views directly, creating a query first allows greater control. For simple views like this, there isn't an obvious benefit, and it is acceptable to just add the tables manually to the view. When we start adding more levels to the view, or if we wish to perform aggregations on child records, the queries become a necessity. When adding data sources manually to views, there can only be one data source per level. This results in some deep levels in the data source tree view and relations that are not all intuitive.

When a view is built from a query, changes that are made to the query will affect the view. This is why the query was named the same as the view. This serves to show that changes to the query will affect a view.

When we added the `ConVMSVehicleGroup` table to the query, we didn't specify the relationship specifically. We just set the **Use Relations** property to **Yes**. This will use the table's metadata to determine the relationship. The only problem with this is that we don't get an error if no relationship is found between the tables. This is why we tested the view if it didn't add a relation. Here, we would end up with a Cartesian join of all vehicles to all vehicle groups.

The next part of this recipe was to add the computed column.

The first thing to remember here is that the method returns a piece of transact-SQL that is written into the view definition when the database is synchronized. This is a common misconception of what a computed column is, in that it is often thought of as a method that executes at runtime. It is executed once when the view is created as part of the database synchronization.

Computed columns are perfect for simple calculations where the information is available within the view's result set. For example, in the following method, we can return the value of the vehicle registration number if it is filled in. If the vehicle registration number is not filled in, the vehicle ID is returned:

```
private str VehicleRegOrId()
{
    DictView dv = new DictView(tableNum(ConVMSVehicleServiceDetailView));
    return SysComputedColumn::if(
            SysComputedColumn::equalExpression(
                dv.computedColumnString(tableStr(ConVMSVehicleTable),
                                        fieldStr(ConVMSVehicleTable,
                                        VehRegNum)), ''),
        dv.computedColumnString(tableStr(ConVMSVehicleTable),
         fieldStr(ConVMSVehicleTable, VehicleId)),
        dv.computedColumnString(tableStr(ConVMSVehicleTable),
         fieldStr(ConVMSVehicleTable, VehRegNum)));
}
```

This returns the following text:

```
CASE T1.VehRegNo = '' THEN T1.VehicleId ELSE T1.VehRegNo END
```

We could just return the preceding code as a string and it will most likely work fine. We use the `SysComputedColumn` functions as these will return the correct transact-SQL command, which could change with new editions of SQL Server.

The `DictView` class, like other `Dict` classes, is used to gain access to the view metadata and metadata functions. The `computedColumnString` method is used to get the SQL field name prefixed with the alias of the table. For example, if the `ConVMSVehicleTable` table was created with the alias `T1`, the method will return `T1.VehicleId` for the `VehicleId` field.

When views are created by SCM, it uses aliases for each table starting with `T1` and goes up from there. The reason for needing an alias is best explained by example. The following code is perfectly valid in transact-SQL:

```
SELECT TOP 1 SALESID, SALESNAME FROM SALESTABLE -- caps is an unfortunate
convention in transact-SQL.
```

The following line of code is not valid:

```
SELECT SALESID, ITEMID FROM SALESTABLE JOIN SALESLINE ON SALESID = SALESID
```

The join on `DataAreaId` and `Partition` was omitted for clarity, but all joins written in SQL or a computed column method must always join on `Partition` and `DataAreaId` if the tables contain these fields.

The reason it is not valid is that the compiler doesn't know which table `SALESID` belongs to. The following code is valid:

```
SELECT ST.SALESID, ITEMID FROM SALESTABLE ST JOIN SALESLINE SL ON
ST.SALESID = SL.SALESID
```

The `ITEMID` field is valid in this case because `SALESTABLE` does not contain a field named `ITEMID`. Even so, we should **always** add an alias.

Some common mistakes can occur when creating computed columns. The following method is a good example of a common mistake:

```
private static str BadExample1()
{
    ConVMSParameters parm = ConVMSParameters::Find();
    DictView dv = new DictView(tableNum(ConVMSVehicleServiceDetailView));
    return SysComputedColumn::if(
        SysComputedColumn::equalExpression(
            dv.computedColumnString(tableStr(ConVMSVehicleTable),
                fieldStr(ConVMSVehicleTable, VehicleGroupId)),
            parm.DefaultVehicleGroupId),
        'Is Default',
        'Is not default');
}
```

This would create the following transact-SQL as the view column:

```
CASE WHEN T1.VehicleGroupId = 'Default' THEN 'Is Default' ELSE 'Is not
default' END
```

The preceding code wrote the value from the parameter table at the point the database was synchronized. This is because the method is only ever called when the database is synchronized, in order to create the view. Any change to the value of the parameter would have no effect on the view. To write this code, you could add the ConVMSParameters table to the query without a join, and then use the metadata method to compare the two fields. The result you actually want is as follows (if T2 was the alias for ConVMSParameters):

```
CASE WHEN T1.VehicleGroupId = T2.DefaultVehicleGroupId THEN 'Is Default'
ELSE 'Is not default' END
```

This brings us to the example that was used in the method. The first part of our method was to create variables for the fields we will use when constructing the transact-SQL statement. This is for clarity as we build the transact-SQL statement.

We used the DictView metadata class for the field name variables and used compile-time functions to set the field names from the ConVMSVehicleServiceTable table.

The transact-SQL we wish to return is as follows:

```
SELECT TOP 1
CASE WHEN CST.ServiceDateConfirmed = {ts '1900-01-01 00:00:00.000'}
    THEN CST.ServiceDateReq ELSE CST.ServiceDateConfirmed END
FROM ConVMSVehicleServiceTable CST
WHERE T1.DATAAREAID = CST.DataAreaId AND T1.PARTITION = CST.Partition
AND T1.VEHICLEID = CST.VehicleId AND CST.ServiceStatus = 2
ORDER BY CASE WHEN CST.ServiceDateConfirmed = {ts '1900-01-01
00:00:00.000'}
    THEN CST.ServiceDateReq ELSE CST.ServiceDateConfirmed END DESC
```

In the preceding code, the alias CST was used. This is suitable as there is little chance of a clash between this and the standard table aliases.

How we build the transact-SQL string variable is up to us, but we do want it to be readable. We could use one large strFmt command to concatenate the various elements together, but it is easy to make mistakes in the parameter order. Using strFmt is fine when we are building one phrase at a time.

There's more...

This example was chosen to show a more complicated computed column that demonstrates more than one concept at once. The other reason was to also show an example of something we sometimes want to avoid. Depending on the execution plan that's generated by the database engine, it is possible that the inline (subquery) select statement can be executed for each row that's returned from the main view. This is undesirable, but thanks to the intelligence of the database engine, this is not often the case. When a view seems to perform poorly, a computed column is often the cause.

Let's look at the view that we created in SQL Server Management Studio. Locate the AxDB database and locate the view from within the **Views** node. Right-click on the **view** and choose **Script View as** | **CREATE to** | **New Query Editor Window**. Delete the lines until the CREATE VIEW statement and delete the text that reads CREATE VIEW [dbo].[CONVMSVEHICLESERVICEDETAILVIEW] AS.

The first word should be SELECT. The following is the code for this. It's been formatted so that it is readable:

```
SELECT
  T1.NAME AS NAME, T1.VEHICLEGROUPID AS VEHICLEGROUPID, T1.VEHICLEID AS
VEHICLEID,
  T1.VEHICLETYPE AS VEHICLETYPE, T1.VEHREGNUM AS VEHREGNUM, T1.DATAAREAID
AS DATAAREAID,
  T1.PARTITION AS PARTITION, T1.RECID AS RECID, T2.NAME AS
VEHICLEGROUPNAME,
  T2.DATAAREAID AS DATAAREAID#2, T2.PARTITION AS PARTITION#2,
  (CAST ((
    SELECT MAX(
      CASE
        WHEN CST.ServiceDateConfirmed = {ts '1900-01-01 00:00:00.000'}
        THEN CST.ServiceDateReq
        ELSE CST.ServiceDateConfirmed
      END)
    FROM ConVMSVehicleServiceTable CST
    WHERE T1.DATAAREAID = CST.DataAreaId
    AND T1.PARTITION = CST.Partition
    AND T1.VEHICLEID = CST.VehicleId
    AND CST.ServiceStatus = 2) AS DATETIME)) AS LASTSERVICEDATE
  FROM CONVMSVEHICLETABLE T1
  CROSS JOIN CONVMSVEHICLEGROUP T2
  WHERE ((( T1.VEHICLEGROUPID = T2.VEHICLEGROUPID)
      AND ( T1.DATAAREAID = T2.DATAAREAID)) AND ( T1.PARTITION =
        T2.PARTITION))
```

Although we naturally think of a view as the entity we are working with, the SQL Server database engine is not limited by this abstraction. The choice of execution plan is based on the entire select statement. In our case it would merge the preceding transact-SQL with the outer statement, such as `SELECT VehicleId FROM CONVMSVEHICLESERVICEDETAILVIEW WHERE VehicleGroupId = 'Default'`. There is more to this, but it helps to think of it this way when designing and using views.

This query looks inefficient at first glance as it looks like it performs a `SELECT` statement for each row in `ConVMSVehicleTable`.

The small dataset that we have can't be used to investigate query execution plans. When we have only a few rows, the database engine will often prefer to not use an index or even just scan it. This is the same as using an index to find a result when there's only one page.

For this test, I inserted the data using a SQL script using a `DataAreaId` that was not in use so that I could easily clean up afterward. This transact-SQL script I used was as follows:

```
DECLARE @vehId int
SELECT @vehId = 1
WHILE @vehId < 10000
BEGIN
    INSERT INTO CONVMSVEHICLETABLE
        (VEHICLEID, VEHICLEGROUPID, [NAME], DATAAREAID)
        VALUES ('V'+cast(@vehId AS nvarchar), '1', 'Test name', 'ZZZ')
    DECLARE @servId int
    SELECT @servId = 1
    WHILE @servId < 50
    BEGIN
        INSERT INTO CONVMSVEHICLESERVICETABLE
            (VEHICLEID, SERVICEID, SERVICESTATUS, SERVICEDATEREQ,
            DATAAREAID)
            VALUES ('V'+cast(@vehId AS nvarchar), 'S'+cast(@vehId * @servId
            as nvarchar), 2, GETUTCDATE(), 'ZZZ')
        SELECT @servId = @servId + 1
    END
    SELECT @vehId = @vehId + 1
END
INSERT into CONVMSVEHICLEGROUP (VEHICLEGROUPID, [NAME], DATAAREAID) VALUES
('1', 'Veh Group name', 'ZZZ')
```

For simplicity, type the following into a query window:

```
SELECT *  FROM [AxDB].[dbo].[CONVMSVEHICLESERVICEDETAILVIEW]   where
DATAAREAID = 'zzz' AND Partition=5637144576
```

5637144576 is the default partition. The partition number is only different from 5637144576 under certain testing scenarios when running a test case.

Let's look at the execution plan for the query. Go back to the query window and select **Include Actual Execution Plan** from **Query**. Execute the query to generate the result set and the execution plan. The database engine has worked out a reasonable plan. However, it shows that most of the cost (the percentage) is in fetching the data from a clustered index on ConVMSVehicleServiceTable. Depending on how much data there is, you will probably see suggested indexes of VehicleId, ServiceStatus, DataAreaId, and Partition on ConVMSVehicleServiceTable. This is a good suggestion, but is improved further by also adding the two dates we need. We should have thought of this, so add this as a non-unique index – of course, we need to build and synchronize the database once we're done.

When we run the query again, the plan looks good and the result set comes back quickly, even for several thousand records.

 If we see a missing index message and the suggested index didn't include DataAreaId and Partition, it means that we have a fault in our view method, in that we forgot the join on these two fields.

There is another way to do this, that is, to construct the query so that we join ConVMSVehicleServiceTable in the main query, thereby removing the need for a computed column. To do this, we would do the following:

1. Create a duplicate of the ConVMSVehicleServiceDetailView query and name it ConVMSVehicleServiceDatesView.
2. Expand the ConVMSVehicleTable data source and drag the ConVMSVehicleServiceTable table to the **Data Sources** node so that it is a sibling of ConVMSVehicleGroup.
3. Change the **Use Relations** property to **Yes** and set the **Dynamics Fields** property to **No**.
4. Set the **Join Mode** property to Outer Join.
5. Right-click on the **Fields** node under ConVMSVehicleServiceTable and choose **New | Max**. In the property sheet for the new field, choose ServiceDateReq as the **Field** property value.

6. Repeat this for `ServiceDateConfirmed`.

7. Add the `VehicleId` field from `ConVMSVehicleServiceTable` to the **Group By** node.

8. Create a new view named `ConVMSVehicleServiceDatesView` as we did in this recipe, this time using the `ConVMSVehicleServiceDatesView` query.

9. Add the main fields as desired, but not the new aggregate data fields for now (you can't drag or use copy and paste on these fields).

10. All `GROUP BY` fields must be in the view, so add the `VehicleId` field from `ConVMSVehicleServiceTable` to the view's **Field** node.

11. Right-click on the view's **Fields** node and choose **New | Field**. Choose `ConVMSVehicleServiceTable` from the **Data Source** property and set the **Field Name** and **Name** properties to `ServiceDateConfirmed`.

 It would be reasonable to presume that since we made the field `Max` in the query this will carry through; however, it doesn't. There will be no aggregation and the result will show a result per service order.

12. Change the **Aggregation** property to `Max` and change the **Name** property to `LastServiceDateConfirmed`.

Should we build and synchronize the database, the view will be created from the following statement:

```
SELECT T1.NAME AS NAME, T1.VEHICLEGROUPID AS VEHICLEGROUPID, T1.VEHICLEID
AS VEHICLEID,
 T1.VEHICLETYPE AS VEHICLETYPE, T1.VEHREGNUM AS VEHREGNUM,
 MAX(T3.SERVICEDATECONFIRMED) AS LASTSERVICEDATECONFIRMED
FROM CONVMSVEHICLETABLE T1
CROSS JOIN CONVMSVEHICLEGROUP T2
LEFT OUTER JOIN CONVMSVEHICLESERVICETABLE T3
 ON ((( T1.VEHICLEID = T3.VEHICLEID)
   AND ( T1.DATAAREAID = T3.DATAAREAID))
   AND ( T1.PARTITION = T3.PARTITION))
WHERE((( T1.VEHICLEGROUPID = T2.VEHICLEGROUPID)
   AND ( T1.DATAAREAID = T2.DATAAREAID))
   AND ( T1.PARTITION = T2.PARTITION))
GROUP BY T1.VEHICLEID, T1.NAME, T1.VEHICLEGROUPID, T1.VEHICLETYPE,
   T1.VEHREGNUM, T1.DATAAREAID, T1.PARTITION, T2.DATAAREAID,
    T2.PARTITION, T3.DATAAREAID, T3.PARTITION
```

This seems to look better until we see the GROUP BY at the bottom. This is because we used an aggregation. Even though we only added the field to group on, the view generation will add all the fields that don't have an aggregation to the GROUP BY clause.

The execution plan, in this case, is different, in that the results from the three tables are fed directly back to the sort operation. This is caused by GROUP BY, and most of the cost is in a sort. This seems odd as, intuitively, this query should be more efficient. The query for the computed column looks like it is calculated for each row, but this isn't actually the case. The database engine constructs the best plan it can, and the actual execution is not always done as we might expect. The actual performance, in this case, is not very different, with the computed column method being slightly faster.

The point to take away, in this case, is that we should pay close attention when creating views in order to get the best performance, even though the computed column performed slightly faster in this case.

If we have a view with several computed columns that aggregate (SUM) data from the same table but with different criteria, for example, if we build a view to mimic InventSum, the computed column method will perform poorly. Adding InventSum multiple times to the view, filtered on the status, will usually make it perform much better.

8
Business Events

Business events are a relatively new feature, available as a flight in Platform 24 and generally available from Platform 26. The concept is to allow a business event to be defined that can be sent to an external target. This would stem from a requirement such as this:

> *"When a sales order is confirmed, send a message to the customer."*

Alternatively, it could be this:

> *"When a Bill of materials is approved in Finance and **Supply Chain Management** (**SCM**), send a message to the production manager for secondary approval, and if approved, create a formula in the on-premise production control system."*

Both of these can be done with very little coding, and most of the work is done via configuration. The framework is designed for performance, and the method by which the messages are sent is asynchronous. Even though this normally means there is a one-minute delay caused by the batch server process, the business events framework will send the messages immediately, without delaying the business logic that triggered the event.

We will split the steps of this into the following recipes:

- Creating a new business event
- Creating an Azure Service Bus queue
- Configuring the business event to use a Service Bus queue
- Setting up Microsoft Flow to receive the Service Bus queue message
- Receiving messages in SCM from the Service Bus

Technical requirements

For this recipe, you will need the following in order to perform the tasks:

- Administrator rights to an Azure Active Directory
- Access to Microsoft Flow

You can find the code files for this chapter on GitHub at `https://github.com/`
`PacktPublishing/Extending-Microsoft-Dynamics-365-Finance-and-Supply-Chain-`
`Management-Cookbook-Second-Edition/blob/master/Chapter%208.axpp`.

Creating a new business event

We will create the `Bill of materials is approved` business event in this recipe, and also add a summary of how to create the `sales order confirmed` business event in the *There's more...* section.

For this chapter, we will create a new package. Even though a reasonable example would be to create a vehicle service order approval process using Microsoft Flow, the real-world challenge would come from hooking into standard processes such as the Bill of materials approval.

Getting ready

Before we start, we should create a new package and model named `ConProductionIntegration`, and then create a project with the same name. Use the recipes in `Chapter 1`, *Starting a New Project*, as guidance, and remember to reference the appropriate packages. For this recipe, the following packages must be referenced:

- `ApplicationSuite`
- `ApplicationFoundation`
- `ApplicationPlatform`
- `ApplicationCommon`
- `UnitOfMeasure`

How to do it...

The first part is to create the contract, which is the data that is sent to an endpoint by the business event. This is done as follows:

1. This event has a nested data contract, so we will create the bill of material lines contract first. Create a class named `ConPIBOMLineContract` that must be decorated as a `DataContract`. The completed class should be as follows:

```
[DataContract]
class ConPIBOMLineContract
{
    ItemId itemId;
    Qty qty;
    BOMUnitId bomUnitId;
    [DataMember('ItemId'), BusinessEventsDataMember('Material Id')]
    public ItemId ParmItemId(ItemId _itemId = itemId)
    {
        itemId = _itemId;
        return itemId;
    }
    [DataMember('Qty'), BusinessEventsDataMember('Quantity')]
    public Qty ParmQty(Qty _qty = qty)
    {
        qty = _qty;
        return qty;
    }
    [DataMember('BOMUnitId'), BusinessEventsDataMember('Unit')]
    public BOMUnitId ParmBOMUnitId(BOMUnitId _bomUnitId =
     bomUnitId)
    {
        bomUnitId = _bomUnitId;
        return bomUnitId;
    }
}
```

The methods are prefixed with `Parm` as this assists the JSON serialize, so use the `DataMember` attribute to return the data member name without the `Parm` prefix so that the resulting JSON does not include the `Parm` prefix. The `BusinessEventsDataMember` is required and is used by the user interface when configuring the event.

2. Create a new class named `ConPIBillOfMaterialsApprovedBusinessEventContract`, which must extend `BusinessEventsContract` and be decorated as a `DataContract`.

3. Add key member variables, such as `BOMId`, `Name`, and `InventSiteId`, and a list for the lines of the Bill of materials; the code should be as follows:

```
[DataContract]
class ConPIBillOfMaterialsApprovedBusinessEventContract extends
BusinessEventsContract
{
    BOMId bomId;
    Name bomName;
    InventSiteId siteId;
    // List of ConPIBOMLineContract
    List bomLines;
}
```

4. Next, we need data member methods, which are similar to the data methods created in the lines data contract; add the following methods:

```
[DataMember('BOMId'), BusinessEventsDataMember("BOM Id")]
public BOMId ParmBOMId(BOMId _bomId = bomId)
{
    bomId = _bomId;
    return bomId;
}


[DataMember('BomName'), BusinessEventsDataMember("Bill of materials
Name")]
public Name ParmBomName(Name _bomName = bomName)
{
    bomName = _bomName;
    return bomName;
}


[DataMember('SiteId'), BusinessEventsDataMember("Site")]
public InventSiteId ParmSiteId(InventSiteId _siteId = siteId)
{
    siteId = _siteId;
    return siteId;
}

[DataMember('BOMLines'),
 BusinessEventsDataMember("BOM lines"),
 DataCollectionAttribute(Types::Class,
classStr(ConPIBOMLineContract))]
public List ParmBOMLines(List _bomLines = bomLines)
{
    bomLines = _bomLines;
    return bomLines;
}
```

This completes the contract. In many guides, the contract contains the code that instantiates it; this will work but will complicate the code—it is far better to write an interaction class to populate the data contract.

5. Create a class named ConPIBillOfMaterialsApprovedBusinessEventContractInteraction, and add the following method:

```
class ConPIBillOfMaterialsApprovedBusinessEventContractInteraction
{
    public static ConPIBillOfMaterialsApprovedBusinessEventContract
        newFromBomVersion(BOMVersion _bomVersion)
    {
        ConPIBillOfMaterialsApprovedBusinessEventContract
         contract = new
          ConPIBillOfMaterialsApprovedBusinessEventContract();
        contract.ParmBOMId(_bomVersion.BOMId);
        contract.ParmBomName(_bomVersion.Name);
        contract.ParmSiteId(_bomVersion.inventSiteId());
        List lines = new List(Types::Class);
        BOM bomLines;
        while select bomLines where bomLines.BOMId ==
         _bomVersion.BOMId
        {
            ConPIBOMLineContract lineContract = new
             ConPIBOMLineContract();
            lineContract.ParmItemId(bomLines.ItemId);
            lineContract.ParmQty(bomLines.BOMQty);
            lineContract.ParmBOMUnitId(bomLines.UnitId);
            lines.addEnd(lineContract);
        }
        contract.ParmBOMLines(lines);
        return contract;
    }
}
```

6. We will need a label for our event so that the user sees a description in the user interface when configuring the event. Create the label for the Bill of materials approved text. You will need a new label file for this, as this is a new package. Make the ID BOMApprovedEventName, so that we know that this is the purpose of the label.

7. Next, we can create our business event; create a class named
   `ConPIBOMApprovedBusinessEvent`, and complete the definition, shown as
   follows:

```
[BusinessEvents(classStr(ConPIBillOfMaterialsApprovedBusinessEventC
ontract),
 'ConProductionIntegration:BOMApprovedEventName',
 'ConProductionIntegration:BOMApprovedEventName',
 ModuleAxapta::BOM)]
class ConPIBOMApprovedBusinessEvent extends BusinessEventsBase
{
}
```

 The `ConProductionIntegration:BOMApprovedEventName` text is a
language-invariant label, which may seem confusing given the purpose of
a label file. This is currently only used in business events when the event
is created in data, and the label is written into this table as static text.

8. Our event is to process the action of approving a **Bill of materials** (**BOM**); the
   `BOMVersion` table will, therefore, be the data that this event will be based on.
   Create a `private` variable for the `BOMVersion` table record and a private `Parm`
   method for this.
9. Override the new constructor and make it `private`.
10. Then create a `static` constructor that takes a `BOMVersion` record and constructs
    the class.
11. Finally, write and override of `buildContract` that will construct the
    `ConPIBillOfMaterialsApprovedBusinessEventContract` data contract
    using the
    `ConPIBillOfMaterialsApprovedBusinessEventContractInteraction`
    class. The completed content of the class is given in the following code snippet:

```
private BOMVersion bomVersion;
protected void new()
{
}
private BOMVersion ParmBOMVersion(BOMVersion _bomVersion =
bomVersion)
{
    bomVersion = _bomVersion;
    return bomVersion;
}
static public ConPIBOMApprovedBusinessEvent
NewFromBOMVersion(BOMVersion _bomVersion)
{
```

```
ConPIBOMApprovedBusinessEvent businessEvent = new
 ConPIBOMApprovedBusinessEvent();
businessEvent.ParmBOMVersion(_bomVersion);
return businessEvent;
}
public BusinessEventsContract buildContract()
{
    return
ConPIBillOfMaterialsApprovedBusinessEventContractInteraction::newFr
omBomVersion(bomVersion);
}
```

12. The final part of the code is to create a hook in the application code that means our event has occurred. In our case, the best place is the run method of the BOMVersionApprove class. Create an extension class of BOMVersionApprove, and complete as follows:

```
[ExtensionOf(classStr(BomVersionApprove))]
public final class
BomVersionApprove_ConProductionIntegration_Extension
{
    public void run()
    {
        next run();
        if (this.parmRemove() == NoYes::No)
        {
ConPIBOMApprovedBusinessEvent::NewFromBOMVersion(BOMVersion::findRe
cId(recId)).send();
        }
    }
}
```

13. Whenever we create a new business event, we must perform data synchronization, even if we haven't made any changes to any data structures. First, build the project, and then perform database sync.

How it works...

This framework is very well designed, especially in terms of how to integrate with it.

There are four main steps, and the pattern is virtually the same for all business events we create:

1. Create a data contract class that extends BusinessEventsContract.
2. Create an interaction class to simplify its creation.

3. Create the business events class that extends BusinesEventsBase and can instantiate from a caller (usually a record).

4. Create a class to handle the application event via a delegate subscription or an extension.

The data contract we created was the payload that the business event will process. The data contract has some additional attributes that tell the framework how to read the data contract. This is for the purposes of serializing the data contract to a JSON string and also for showing the user the content of the payload, using labels that the user can understand. The interaction class is just to simplify the creation of the data contract set from the BOMVersion record.

The business event class ties all this together. The BusinesSEvents attribute ties the event to the data contract and sets the label that is displayed to the user when the event is configured. All we need to do then is to create a constructor that instantiates the data contract, and to override the buildContract method.

All we need to do to fire the event is to construct the business event and call send(). So, at the point in the code where we want this event to fire, we place the call to construct and send.

In this case, the run method is run for both when the Bill of materials is approved and when approval is removed. So we add a line of code to check if the parmRemove parameter is, **No**—that is we are not removing the approval.

The following steps are processed as part of sending a business event:

1. Business event steps that run synchronously, and must, therefore, run quickly:
    1. Construct the Business event, which builds the data contract.
    2. Send the Business event, which serializes the data contract to JSON and inserts it into the BusinesSEventsCommitLog table.

2. Business event steps that run asynchronously for each record in the business events commit log, BusinessEventsCommitLog:
    1. Build the endpoint adapter, in this case, the Service Bus adapter.
    2. Send the message.
    3. On transient failure (timeout), retry.
    4. On non-transient failure, mark the message as failed.

The last point, where the message failed, reminds us of the compensation principle of handling transactions. If this was part of an approval system, where we want a response, we would have unhandled dead letters. When using this method, there are many places where a message could get stuck, and thinking of writing compensating code for each scenario then becomes an anti-pattern – we are using the wrong technical solution. We shouldn't use business events for application synchronization.

A batch routine is not used to send business events, and the events are processed almost immediately after they are inserted into the queue.

There's more...

When developing business events we must consider any performance impact the event might cause. As part of the `send` method, the contract is initialized and serialized to a JSON string. We therefore only want this code to run if required.

We can wrap the call to this using the following code:

```
if
(BusinessEventsConfigurationReader::isBusinessEventEnabled(classStr(ConPIBO
MApprovedBusinessEvent)))
{
}
```

This will reduce the impact if the current company does not have the event configured. The other important factor is that the business event payload must be as small as possible, and having a nested payload would usually be avoided. Should a large payload be required, consider using the business event to simply let the target know that there is something to collect. The subscriber could then use the information in the event to get the document.

The business events must have a clear purpose, such as the Bill of materials being approved. It must only send the event when we are sure that it was indeed approved and there is little or no chance that the process was rolled back due to validation failures in SCM. We should not use business events to send data through a batch routine in order to drip-feed information to a target system. We would need data entities in order to do this.

See also

The following link is the official documentation on business events development; there may be some differences since the time of writing:

- In the official guide, the `buildContract` is marked as replaceable and hookable. This is not required, or desirable. These attributes make it so we can use a pre-post event handler and also avoid the call to next when using a Chain of Command. Pre-post event handlers should be avoided if possible, and if we do want this to be replaceable, we should use a delegate instead, as this allows extensions to play nice with each other.
- The official guide places the contract initialization in the contract itself. This isn't uncommon, but it is much cleaner to leave the data contract as just data members. This will be serialized to JSON so we only want elements in this contract that we want to serialize.

The business events development documentation can be found at: `https://docs.microsoft.com/en-us/dynamics365/unified-operations/dev-itpro/business-events/business-events-dev-doc`.

Creating an Azure Service Bus queue

A Service Bus queue is arguably the best target for a business event. This acts as a message queue, where the subscriber can read the messages in the queue. We can easily configure Microsoft Flow to read from the Service Bus.

If you have a person whose role it is to create Azure resources, they need to create a Service Bus topic and provide the following information:

- Queue name
- Application ID
- Azure application secret
- Primary connection string
- Key Vault DNS name
- Key Vault secret name

In order to do this, you need to be given the appropriate rights to create Azure resources and link them to a subscription. There is a small cost to this, so the subscription will need a credit in order to proceed.

For this recipe, we will be using the `https://portal.azure.com` site.

How to do it...

To create a Service Bus, starting from a Resource Group for the services, follow these steps:

1. Create a Notepad document to temporarily store the keys; do not save this document, as it will contain secrets that must be only stored in encrypted form. Start the document with the following text:

   ```
   Queue name:
   Application Id:
   Azure Application secret:
   Key Vault DNS Name:
   Key Vault secret name:
   Primary connection string:
   ```

2. Open the main portal page at `https://portal.azure.com` and log in with an account with privileges to create and maintain resources, and associate with an internal subscription with a credit available.

First, we need to create an application registration:

1. Select **Azure Active Directory** and then navigate to **App registrations**.

You may find that the user interface changes over time; at the time of writing, you select **App registrations** from the burger menu. The concepts here will stay the same, but the interface will change as it is improved in usability as features are added.

2. Enter `BusinessEventsCon` in the name and click **Create**.
3. Copy the **Application (client) ID** value into the document next to `Application Id`.

4. Click **Certificates and Secrets**.

5. Click **New client secret**, name it `BusinessEventsConSecret`, and set the expiry as desired and **Add**.

6. You must copy the **Value** and paste it into your Notepad document, next to `Azure Application secret`.

7. Next, click **API permissions**. You should see a button named `Grant admin consent for <Directory name>`; click this button and follow the instructions. Before continuing, wait for the status to update to `Granted for <directory name>`.

If you do not see this, you are not an administrator, and you must, therefore, ask an Azure administrator to do this for you.

To create a Resource Group for the Service Bus, follow these steps:

1. Use the interface to locate **Resource Groups**; click on it and then press **Add** on the pane that opens. This should be visible when you select the burger menu (again, true at the time of writing).

If you cannot see this option, click **All resources**, and use the search to find `Resource Groups`. Add this to favorites so it appears on the left-hand list.

2. In the dialog that opens, select the **Subscription** to use, and enter the name of the **Resource Group**. Enter the name `AZR-BusEvents-Prod`. Click **Review + Create** and then **Create**.

3. In the **Resource Groups** pane, press **Refresh**, and then click on `AZR-BusEvents-Prod`. This opens the details of the Resource Group. The left part of the dialog shows the various sections, where **Overview** is currently selected, and the right side shows the details of that section. This is shown in the following screenshot:

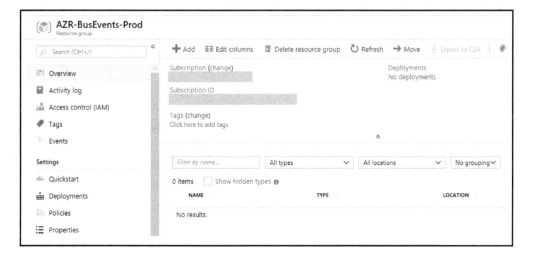

To create a Service Bus, follow these steps:

1. We need to add a Service Bus namespace. Click **Add**, and type `Service Bus` in the search bar. In the results list, locate **Service Bus**, and click on it.
2. On the Service Bus details page that has now opened, press **Create**.
3. Enter `AZR-BusEvents-Prod-ServiceBus` as the **Name**.
4. Choose a **Pricing** tier, select **Standard**, which is the lowest we can use for business events, and press **Create**. This can take a minute to process.

To get the primary connection string for the Service Bus, follow these steps:

1. Go to the new Service Bus we just created, and select **Shared access policies**, shown as follows:

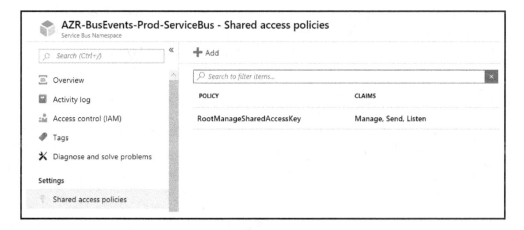

2. Click on the **RootManageSharedAccessKey** Policy, and in the dialog that opens, copy the value for **Primary Connection String** into Notepad next to the primary connection string.

To create a Service Bus queue, follow these steps:

1. We now need to add a queue to our Service Bus. In the overview of the AZR-BusEvents-Prod-ServiceBus Service Bus, click **+ Queue**. Do not enable **Sessions**, and the defaults are usually fine.
2. In the **Name** field, enter AZR-BusEvents-Prod-BOM because this is where we will send our BOM Approval event to. Press **Create** to create a new Service Bus queue.
3. Enter AZR-BusEvents-Prod-BOM in our Notepad document next to Queue name.

To create a secret in a new Key Vault, follow these steps:

1. Go back to the AZR-BusEvents-Prod Resource Group, click **Add,** and this time search for Key Vault. Select this in the list, and click **Create**. Name this AZR-BusEvents-Prod-Vault, and press **Create**. This can take a few minutes to complete.
2. Open the details of the new Key Vault, and copy the DNS Name value (starting with and including https) into the Notepad document next to Key Vault DNS Name.
3. Click on the **Secrets** section on the section list, which is under **Settings**, and click **Generate / Import**.
4. Enter AZR-BusEvents-Prod-Secret into the **Name** field. Also paste this into the Notepad document next to Key value secret name.
5. Copy the value for Primary connection string from the Notepad document, and paste it into the **Value** field.
6. Type Primary connection string into the **Content type** field.
7. Press **Create**.

Follow these steps to allow the app registration to access the Key Vault:

1. From the section list on the Key Vault, select **Access policies**.
2. Click **Add Access Policy**.

3. Leave the **Configure from template (optional)** option blank, and select **Get** and **List** from the **Secret permissions** list.

> Care should be taken here: only apply the access that the application requires. For our purposes, it only needs to get and list secrets.

4. Under the **Select principle** list, select BusinessEventsCon, which is the application registered earlier.
5. Press **Add** on the dialog, and then press **Save** on the **Access Polices** page.

How it works...

The preceding process results in a secure way to access the Service Bus from SCM. There are many steps but we can break them down into the following:

1. Create an App registration.
2. Create a Resource Group.
3. Create a Service Bus in the Resource Group.
4. Create a new Service Bus queue in the Service Bus.
5. Create a new key value for the Service Bus.
6. Add a new secret, using the primary connections string as the value.
7. Allow the App registration to access the Key Vault.

The result of this is a new Service Bus queue and the information SCM requires in order to access it.

See also

The following article is also useful and shows the link between Azure and SCM. It doesn't, at the time of writing, cover the creation of a service bus queue as it assumes this has already be done by an Azure administrator, as discussed at: https://docs.microsoft.com/en-us/dynamics365/unified-operations/dev-itpro/business-events/home-page#managing-endpoints.

Configuring the business event to use a Service Bus queue

In this recipe, we will configure our Bill of materials approved business event to be sent to our new Service Bus queue.

The configuration of a business event is company-specific, so the events can be enabled by the company and have a different endpoint per company.

You will need the following information created in the previous recipe in order to complete this:

- Service Bus queue name
- Application ID
- Azure Application secret
- Key Vault DNS name
- Key Vault secret name

How to do it...

To configure the business event, follow these steps:

1. Open SCM in the browser on our Development **Virtual Machine** (**VM**), and navigate to **System administration** | **Setup** |**Business events** | **Business events catalog**.
2. Select the **Endpoints** tab, and click **New**.
3. On the **Configure new endpoint** dialog, select `Azure Service Bus queue`, and press **Next**.
4. For convenience, paste in the `Service Bus queue Name` value into the **Endpoint name** and **Queue name**.
5. Paste in the remaining values from the Notepad document.
6. Press **OK**. This will validate the information by connecting to Azure with the supplied information.

 If you get an error, it will likely be a copy and paste error or a missed step. Go back to the *Creating a Service Bus queue* recipe, and check the steps.

7. Click the **Business events Catalog** tab page.

8. Try to locate the `Bill of materials approved` business event, and if this is not in the list choose **MANAGE | Rebuild business events catalog**.

> If it still does not appear, build the package in Visual Studio and synchronize the database.

9. Select the `Bill of materials approved` business event, and click **Activate**.

10. Select the current company in the **Legal entity** field, which will be USMF in the demonstration dataset.

11. Select the endpoint created in *steps 1 to 6*, and press **OK**.

12. If you receive the `Unable to configure business event ConPIBOMApprovedBusinessEvent for company usmf because it has reached the limit of 0 configured endpoints` error, it is because the demonstration data was created prior to Platform 25. In order to fix this, run the following Transact-SQL in SQL Server management studio:

```
USE AXDB -- this is the default database name
GO
UPDATE BUSINESSEVENTSPARAMETERS
SET ENDPOINTSPEREVENT = 10,
BUNDLESIZE = 50,
ENABLED = 0
```

> This will update the parameters table (for which there is no form) so that each event can have up to 10 endpoints. You may need to restart **Internet Information Service (IIS)** in order to flush the cache for this to take effect. The ENABLED flag relates to batch processing, which is not used in later platforms to send business events. A parameters form may become available in future platform updates; if available, this should be used instead of running a manual Transact-SQL script.

How it works...

This recipe is relatively straightforward. It simply states that the business event is to be sent to the Azure Service Bus queue. At this point, the event is active, and every time we approve a Bill of materials, the event will be processed.

When looking at the event in the business events workspace, you may notice that the right pane contains the details of data contract we created, and from this we can also click **Download Schema**. This doesn't, at this point, download a schema. It downloads an instance of the serialized data contract with default values. In our case, it is not useful as the Bill of materials lines section is a null object; again, it is not a schema but a sample JSON file with no values.

The last recipe can be used so that you can read this message by hooking it up to read the queue that the event is sending the message to. You can see this also by using a Service Bus queue explorer utility, or set up Microsoft Flow to receive data from the queue.

Creating a Microsoft Flow to receive the Service Bus queue message

Microsoft Flow is a great tool for an organization to create logic flows that take data from a source, and based on a condition send a message to an onward service.

In this case, we will create a flow to read our Service Bus queue, decode the payload, and send it to a user for approval. We will extend this in the next recipe.

How to do it...

To configure Microsoft Flow, follow these steps:

1. In a web browser, navigate to `https://flow.microsoft.com`.
2. Sign in using your organizational account.
3. Expand **Data** on the left, and select **Connections**.
4. Click **New Connection**.
5. Click the **Search** option, and type `Service Bus`. There will be one result; click the + symbol.
6. Enter the primary connection string for the Service Bus queue (see the *Get the primary connection string for the Service Bus* section in the *Creating an Azure Service Bus queue* recipe).
7. Press **Create**.
8. Refresh the list, and select **Edit** from the **...** button. Set the name to the Service Bus queue name (for reference), and paste in the primary connection string again.
9. Select **My Flows** on the left hand list.

10. Click **New** | **Automated-from blank**.
11. In the **Flow name**, enter `Process BOM Approval`.
12. Enter `Service Bus` in the **Search all triggers** text box.
13. Select `Service Bus - When a message is received in a queue (auto complete)` - you may have to hover the mouse of the entry in order to see the full name.
14. Press **Create**.
15. For the queue name, press the drop-down list to select the Service Bus connection created earlier.
16. Click **New step**.
17. In the search box, type `initialize variable`, and then in the **Actions** list choose **Initialize Variable**.
18. Enter `BOMApprovalContent` as the **Name**.
19. Select **String** as the **Type**.
20. Click the **Value** field, and then click on the option **Content** on the right-hand list that appears.
21. In the search box, type `Parse JSON`, and select this option from the **Actions** list, shown as follows:

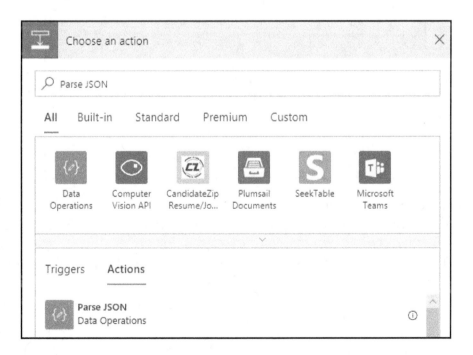

22. In the **Content** field, click **Add dynamic content** and then select the `BOMApprovalContent` variable.

23. We now need a schema. Open the business events form in SCM, locate the business event and click **Download Schema**, and copy the text into the paste buffer.

> This is not a JSON schema, but a sample file that has all element defaults set to empty or zero.

24. Now we have the text of a sample message, click **Generate from sample**, paste in the text, and press done, the result will be shown as follows:

25. Click **Save** on the top right.

26. Click **My Flows** on the left-hand list to see the list of flows again. On our flow, select the vertical **...** button, and click on **Run history**.

27. You should see an instance of the flow that ran, expand the Initialize variable block, and copy the contents of the **Value** field, this will look like the following:

```
{"BOMId":"D0001BOM","BOMLines":[{"BOMUnitId":"ea","ItemId":"M0001",
"Qty":1.0},{"BOMUnitId":"ea","ItemId":"M0002","Qty":1.0},{"BOMUnitI
d":"ea","ItemId":"M0003","Qty":1.0},{"BOMUnitId":"ea","ItemId":"M00
04","Qty":1.0},{"BOMUnitId":"ea","ItemId":"D0002","Qty":1.0}],"BomN
```

```
ame":"Mid-Range
Speaker","BusinessEventId":"ConPIBOMApprovedBusinessEvent","Control
Number":5637150576,"EventId":"C0D16056-46B0-4E4C-901B-
AA25E84B3695","EventTime":"/Date(1560101558000)/","MajorVersion":0,
"MinorVersion":0,"SiteId":"1"}
```

This was created when we tested the business event, and is a better example to use to generate the schema.

28. Click **Edit** on the top right.
29. On the `Parse JSON` step, click **Generate from sample**.
30. Paste in the value taken from *step 27*.
31. You should now see that the `BOM Lines` section is properly formatted.
32. Save the flow.

How it works...

There are a few steps here, some iterative. The basic steps are as follows:

1. Create a connection to the Service Bus with the connection string.
2. Create a flow to read the Service Bus.
3. Use the `initialize variable` task in order to cast the inbound message as a string. This is because the Service Bus message will be `base64` encoded, which the `Parse JSON` task cannot read.
4. Use `Parse JSON` in order to deserialize the data into information that we can use later in the flow.

We can create approvals, send a formatted email, or send the data to the production control system.

The last part can be difficult when we consider security implications. As Microsoft Flow runs in the cloud, we would, therefore, send a message to a different **Service Bus** queue in order for that application to process it. With this method, we could write a service in C# or X++ that reads the Service Bus in order to process a response from a flow.

Another option, which is more useful in on-premise systems that can't connect to Azure Service Bus, is the on-premise connector. This allows the flow to write data to a table that is installed on the same server as the connector. No ports need to be opened for this, as the on-premise connector establishes contact with Microsoft Flow using the organizational credential used when it was installed.

See also

It pays off to understand more about Azure Service Bus and Microsoft Flow. The following links should be useful in understanding the capabilities of these services:

- Microsoft Flow documentation, at: `https://docs.microsoft.com/en-us/flow/`
- Azure Service Bus Messaging documentation, at: `https://docs.microsoft.com/en-gb/azure/service-bus-messaging/`
- Service Bus authentication and authorization, at: `https://docs.microsoft.com/en-us/azure/service-bus-messaging/service-bus-authentication-and-authorization`

Receiving messages in SCM from the Service Bus

We now have a method to send a business event when a Bill of materials is approved. What would be useful is to close the loop, and use Microsoft Flow to approve the BOM that would then make the BOM active.

We don't have a way to read the bus in SCM, so we will need to write one. The main purpose of this recipe is to show how we can read the Service Bus in SCM. When writing a solution for inbound actions, we should use a similar pattern to business events, where the process is simply in reverse.

In this recipe, we will only have one adapter and a form to store the connection details. Again, this is a technical demonstration and does not deal with the security impact of storing connection strings and secrets in a table.

The main recipe stops when we can successfully read the message from the queue– this will be extended later. This is done this way as the code to read the Service Bus contains new concepts that we need to focus on.

Getting started

This follows on from the earlier recipes, and the code written here should be added to the same project: `ConProductionIntegration` in this case.

How to do it...

To write a solution to read the Service Bus, follow these steps:

1. First, create an enum named `ConPIInboundActionType`. This will form the type of action. Label this `Inbound action`.
2. Add an element named `ActivateBillOfMaterials`.
3. Create a string **Extended Data Type (EDT)** named `ConPIInboundActionId` and extend `Num` and with a label.
4. Create a table named `ConPIInboundActionTable`.
5. Add the following fields:

Name	EDT/Enum
ActionId	ConPIInboundActionId
Name	Name
ActionType	ConPIInboundActionType
ServiceBusQueueName	BusinessEventsServiceBusQueueEndpointQueueName
ConnectionString	SysConnectionString

6. Add a field group for `Overview` (`ActionId`, `Name`, or `ActionType`).
7. Add a field group for `ConnectionDetails` (ServiceBusQueueName or ConnectionString).
8. Complete the table, as per best practices, as a `Group` table.
9. Before writing the form, we will write the code to read the Service Bus queue so we can use it as part of validation and testing. Create a class named `ConPIServiceBusReader`.
10. At the top of the class, add the following `using` statements:

```
using System.IO;
using System.Text;
using Microsoft.ServiceBus;
using Microsoft.ServiceBus.Messaging;
```

11. Set up the class variables, and write the constructor code, shown as follows:

```
private str queueName;
private str connectionString;

protected void new(str _queueName, str _connectionString)
{
    queueName = _queueName;
    connectionString = _connectionString;
```

```
}
public static ConPIServiceBusReader
Construct(ConPIInboundActionTable _action)
{
    return new ConPIServiceBusReader(_action.ServiceBusQueueName,
    _action.ConnectionString);
}
```

 We aren't using the key vault in this case, for simplicity. A more secure method would be to use the build in `Key Vault` mechanism, which is configured in **System Administration** | **Setup** | **Key Vault parameters**.

12. Next, we will write a `validate` method; this simply tries to construct a queue client on the Service Bus to test if a connection can be made. It can be done using the following code:

```
public boolean Validate()
{
    System.Exception exc;
    try
    {
        var receiverFactory = MessagingFactory::
         CreateFromConnectionString(connectionString);
        var receiver =
         receiverFactory.CreateQueueClient(queueName);
    }
    catch (exc)
    {
        return checkFailed(exc.Message);
    }
    return true;
}
```

The final method is to write the code to read the Service Bus queue, but we have a problem – we need to call `<T>BrokeredMessage.GetBody()`. This is a generic type, which is not supported in X++. To solve this without resorting to reflection, we need to create a C# library project.

13. Right-click on the solution in the **Solution Explorer,** and choose Add | New Project..

14. Choose **Class library** and then **Visual C#**, and name the project `ConServiceBus`.

15. Rename the `class1.cs` to `ServiceBusFacade.cs`, and click **Yes** to rename the references.
16. Right-click on the **References** node, and choose **Add reference**.
17. Click **Browse**, and search in the `C:\AOSService\PackagesLocalDirectory\Bin` folder.

 This might be `K:` on Azure-based Development VMs.

18. Look for the `Microsoft.ServiceBus.dll` file, select it, and press **Add** and then **OK** on the **Reference manager** dialog.
19. Open the `ServiceBusFacade` class.
20. Alter the class so that it reads as follows:

```
using Microsoft.ServiceBus.Messaging;
using System.IO;
namespace ConServiceBus
{
    public class ServiceBusFacade
    {
        public static Stream GetBodyStream(BrokeredMessage
         _message)
        {
            return _message.GetBody<Stream>();
        }
    }
}
```

21. Build the C# project.
22. Back in the `ConProductionIntegration` X++ project, add a reference to the `ConServicebus` C# project by right-clicking on the **References** node, and choose the `ConServiceBus` project from the **Projects** tab page.
23. Open the `ConPIServiceBusReader` class, and add the following to the top of the class:

```
using ConServiceBus;
```

24. Write the `read` method shown as follows:

```
public str Read(boolean _peek = false)
{
    if (!this.Validate())
    {
        return '';
    }
    str messageBody = '';
    var receiverFactory = MessagingFactory::
     CreateFromConnectionString(connectionString);
    Microsoft.ServiceBus.Messaging.ReceiveMode receiveMode;
    receiveMode = Microsoft.ServiceBus.Messaging.ReceiveMode::
     ReceiveAndDelete;
    if (_peek)
    {
        receiveMode = Microsoft.ServiceBus.Messaging.ReceiveMode::
         PeekLock;
    }
    var queueClient = receiverFactory.CreateQueueClient(queueName,
     receiveMode);
    using (var message = queueClient.Receive())
    {
        if (message != null)
        {
            System.Exception exc;
            try
            {
                // The correct way, when X++ supports generic types
                // System.IO.Stream inputStream =
                // message.GetBody<Stream>();
                System.IO.Stream inputStream
                    = ConServiceBus.ServiceBusFacade::
                       GetBodyStream(message);
                using (System.IO.StreamReader reader
                    = new System.IO.StreamReader(inputStream))
                {
                    messageBody = reader.ReadToEnd();
                }
                if (_peek)
                {
                    message.Abandon();
                }
                else
                {
                    message.Complete();
                }
            }
```

```
            catch(exc)
            {
                    message.Abandon();
                    Error(exc.Message);
            }
        }
        queueClient.Close();
    }
    return messageBody;
}
```

 The code in bold uses reflection to call <T>GetBody(); this is because X++ does not support generic types. The safe way to do this is to use a C# library, and this is covered in the *There's more...* section. Outside of testing and prototyping scenarios, reflection should be avoided.

25. The final part is to create a form for the table using the Simple list and Details - List Grid pattern.

26. Follow the normal pattern, adding a tab page for the connection details.

27. Write a display method and a form method to test the current record and display the results. Write the following code:

```
[FormObservable]
Notes resultText;
public display Notes ResultText()
{
    return resultText;
}
public void DoTest()
{
    ConPIServiceBusReader reader
        = ConPIServiceBusReader::
            Construct(ConPIInboundActionTable);
    resultText = reader.Read(true);
}
```

28. Create a Button Group and Button called TestButton on the action pane at the top, and override the clicked event method to call element.DoTest();.

29. Add a new tab page, using the Fill Text patter, and add a string control using ResultText() as the **Data Method** property.

30. The form should look like the following screenshot:

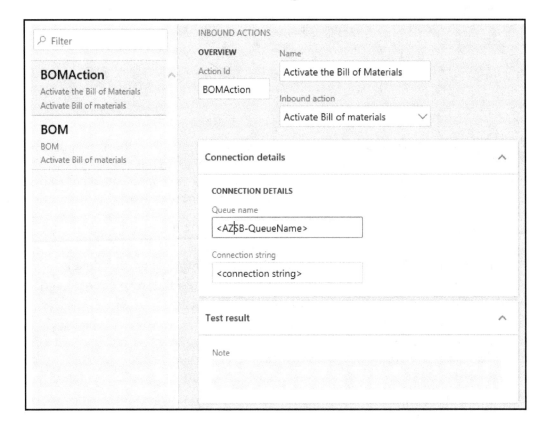

31. Add the menu item to an extension of `OrganizationAdministration`, under `Setup`.
32. Close and save all documents, build the package, and synchronize the database.

How it works...

Before getting into the detail, a new attribute was used on the `[FormObservable]` form. When this is placed above a form variable, any display method will be executed whenever that variable changes.

Let's test this first by reading the `Bill of Material Approved` business event that is being sent to the Service Bus. To do this, disable the flow (as this consumes the message), and configure the inbound actions form with the queue name and connection string we used when setting up the Service Bus queue for the `Bill of Material Approved` event.

Approve any Bill of materials, and go to the Azure portal (`https://portal.azure.com`), check the queue's **Overview** and you will see a dashboard, such as the following:

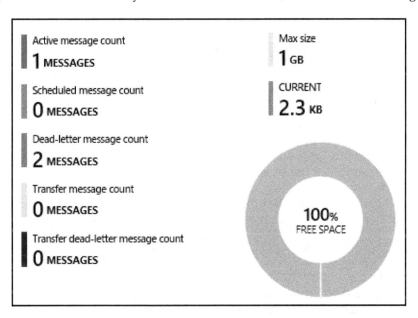

This shows that **1 message** is in the queue, and **2** have failed as **Dead-letter messages**. The dead letters were failed attempts created while testing the code in this recipe.

Using the new inbound action form, press **Test**. You should see the results as shown in the following screenshot:

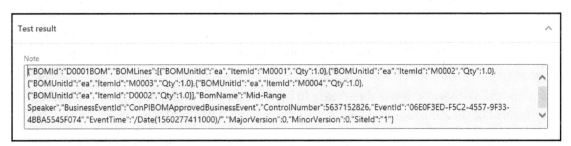

This is exactly what we expected: the data contract serialized to a JSON string.

The new concept in this recipe is the code in the `Read` method of `ConPIServiceBusReader`.

The first part is to construct a `QueueClient`, which is done using `Microsoft.ServiceBus.Messaging.MessagingFactory`. This just needs the connection string.

We then determine whether we are going to get a peek lock or consume the message. For testing, we just want to peek the message so we will peek and later abandon the message in order to leave it in the queue. Consuming is the enum value `ReadAndDelete`, and the term **Complete** is used to mean that the message is read and then deleted from the queue. Within Flow, you see the **Auto complete** option that means that the message is read with `ReadAndDelete`.

The `QueueClient` is constructed using the `MessagingFactory` instance, using the Service Bus queue name and the receive mode (`Peek` or `Receive` and `Delete`).

Once we have `QueueClient`, the following line of code constructs a `var` of the `Microsoft.ServiceBus.Messaging.BrokeredMessage` type:

```
using (var message = queueClient.Receive())
```

Since `BrokeredMessage` implements `iDisposable`, we can use the `using` clause to automatically dispose it when out of the scope of the using code block. We would then like to get the message body. This would normally be done using `message.GetBody<Stream>()`, but since generic types aren't supported in X++, we have to create a C# library to call this method. We could have done this through reflection, but this would be a bad idea when we consider potential regression.

 Although it is preferable for code management to keep all code in X++, reflection adds a risk of regression. With the one-version release of SCM, the update cycles are automatic with an option to temporarily pause the update. Reducing the risk of regression should, therefore, be a key part of our decision making when designing a solution. So, we should avoid reflection, and use a C# library instead.

From this point on, we can use the stream to build `StreamReader`, and use `ReadToEnd` to get the message as a string.

The final part is to decide whether to complete the message or abandon it. If we are peeking, we always want to abandon the peek lock placed earlier. We now have a JSON string. At this point, we can then de-serialize it to a data contract class in order to process the message.

There's more...

To complete the solution, we have a batch routine that does the following for each record in the inbound actions table:

1. Calls `ConPIServiceBusReader`
2. Constructs a class using the attribute factory pattern to process the message (using the action type of the inbound action table)

We have covered all of the concepts required to complete this already, so we should now challenge ourselves to complete the solution using the following steps as a guide:

1. Create a Service Bus queue for the message back to SCM. This should be added to the same Service Bus resource as the one created for the business event.
2. Add an `Approval` step to Microsoft Flow that results in a message being sent to the Service Bus queue.
3. Write an interface that acts as a code contract so that all classes implement `ProcessMessage(string _jsonString)`.
4. Write a `SysOperation` class that creates an instance using the attribute factory from the inbound action's `Action type`.
5. Write an attribute class based around the `ConPIInboundActionType` enum, such as `ConPIInboundActionTypeAttribute`.
6. Write a data contract class to handle each message expected from the Service Bus – you can see how this is done by looking at the output of the data contract written to send the business event – simply, the `DataMethods` must have the same name and be of the correct type.
7. Write an implementation of each action type, implementing the interface created in *step 3* and decorated with the attribute class created in *step 5*.

The code that constructs the data contract class from the message body is `FormJsonSerialiser::deserialiseObject(classNum(<DataContractClass>, messageBody);`.

If our JSON string was as follows:

```
{"BOMId":"D0001BOM", "ApprovedBy":"CEN"}
```

Then the data contract would be as follows:

```
[DataContract]
public class ConPIBomActivateContract
{
    private BOMId bomId;
    private str approvedBy;
    [DataMethod]
    public BOMId BOMId(BOMId _bomId = bomId)
    {
        bomId = _bomId;
        return bomId;
    }
    [DataMethod]
    public str ApprovedBy(str _approvedBy = approvedBy)
    {
        approvedBy = _approvedBy;
        return approvedBy;
    }
}
```

This method can equally be used for on-premises (local business data) and cloud deployments, because we are always calling out from SCM to the cloud.

9
Security

The security model in SCM is role-based. This is similar to the way in which we produce the solution design, where we design processes alongside the role that would perform them. The security model is designed using roles and duties, which in turn have the required privileges. The phrasing of a functional requirement would be written as *The service order clerk will create new service orders*. The role is `Service order clerk`, while the duty is `Create new service orders`. The duty implies that the user needs to have a `create` privilege on the service order table.

Whenever a solution is designed, even **independent software vendor (ISV)** solutions, we will have roles and duties in mind so that we can create security elements when the solution is written. So far, we haven't created any security elements so that we could focus on the recipes' tasks.

This does not mean that the customers have no control themselves, and we will nearly always find that the security requirements will need to be adjusted for each implementation. This is done by the customer in the security design process in SCM and does not affect the deployed code. In this chapter, we will focus on writing AOT security elements.

The security model in SCM can be broken down into the following structure:

- Roles
- Duties
- Privileges
- Policies

The primary structure of the security model includes process cycles, roles, duties, and privileges. We will explore these first, before taking a look at Policies and Code Permissions.

Entry points define the access level that's granted to methods of entry to SCM functionality, such as menu items and services.

Permissions define access to tables and fields, server methods (such as a service call where the code won't run under the user's security context), and form controls (buttons, fields, or other controls placed on a form).

As a part of the functional requirements definition, the business processes are analyzed, along with the roles that perform them. The business processes will then be mapped to the Operations system processes. This is used for many purposes, including gap fit level, training plans, testing plans, and so on. This method of analyzing roles and processes also fits nicely into the Operations security model, allowing the security model to be designed based on this.

The security model that we design and implement should always be simple to use and follow the pattern of the standard roles provided by Microsoft. An important design principle is to think of the user's roles, and not to think of specific users, which should result in the following outcomes:

- Reduced number of roles
- Less complicated assignment of users to roles
- Roles are easier to maintain, with reduced risk of errors, such as the unintended assignment of privilege to a user

In this chapter, we will cover the following recipes:

- Creating privileges
- Creating duties
- Creating security roles
- Creating policies

Technical requirements

You can find the code files for this chapter on GitHub at `https://github.com/PacktPublishing/Extending-Microsoft-Dynamics-365-Finance-and-Supply-Chain-Management-Cookbook-Second-Edition/blob/master/Chapter%2010.axpp`.

Creating privileges

Privileges are normally created for each menu item (display, output, or action) for an access level. Every menu item should be in a privilege, but you can add more than one menu item to a privilege if they must never be assigned different permissions, such as menu items that point to the same form. This is the most granular level and will be grouped into duties and roles later.

Since the privilege assigns the access level, we will usually have two: one that provides a view only and one that maintains (full) access rights.

Getting ready

We will need an SCM project open in Visual Studio to complete this recipe.

How to do it...

To create a privilege to provide view access to the vehicle form, follow these steps:

1. Choose to add a new item to the project.
2. In the **Add New Item** dialog, select **Security** from the left-hand list and **Security Privilege** from the right.
3. Enter `ConVMSVehicleTableView` in the **Name** field and click on **Add**.
4. Complete the **Description** property. This should describe to the security administrator what this privilege grants access to.
5. Complete the **Label** property by giving it a short description for the security administrator, such as `View vehicle records`.

> It can be a good idea to include some text or even a prefix in the text to uniquely identify which module this security element relates to. The security administrator will only be able to easily see the **Label** and **Description** properties, and it could be easy to confuse the security element with another.

6. In the designer, drag the `ConVMSVehicleTable` menu item onto the **Entry Points** node. If you have created menu items for the inherited tables, add these too.

At this point, consider the other menu items that must be added to this privilege, such as the Odometer. Also, remember to keep the scope of a privilege as small as possible as this is the lowest level of granularity.

7. Change the entry point's **Access Level** property to `Read`.
8. To create the privilege to maintain the vehicle table, create a new privilege named `ConVMSVehicleTableMaintain`.
9. Complete the **Description** property.
10. Complete the **Label** property, for example, `Maintain vehicle records`.
11. In the designer, drag the `ConVMSVehicleTable` menu item onto the **Entry Points** node.
12. Change the entry point's **Access Level** property to `Delete`.
13. Should the form have any associated data entities, such as those that allow us to edit the form's data in Excel, they should also be added to the privilege under the **Data Entity Permissions** node with the appropriate access level.

How it works...

The privileges are simply a way to grant permissions to an entry point, which can be services to a duty, role, or even directly to a user. Typically, we only add entry points to a privilege, such as menu items. In order to grant access to the user, the system applies the access level to form controls and data sources.

Since we can't extend security privileges, we always create a new privilege. This is not a real restriction and helps enforce good practices; we can't get more granular than a privilege in terms of assigning permissions to a user. We should never over-layer (customize) an existing security privilege as there is no need to – duties and roles are extensible.

There's more...

On the vehicle form, we have a button that allows us to change the vehicle group, and this should be hidden for the view's privilege. When adding controls to forms where the system can't determine the needed permission, we must set it on the control while designing the form. In our case, the button was created with a **Needed Permission** property of `Update`. So, the button will be hidden when the privileges that are granted to the user are less than `Update`.

In some cases, we may wish to elevate the permission level above that of the privilege's access level. This is a very special case and is done by following these steps:

1. Locate the `ConVMSVehicleGroupChangeController` control on the `ConVMSVehicleTable` form.
2. Change the **Needed permission** property to `Update`. This will hide the button if the permission used to enter the form was less than `Update`.
3. Open the `ConVMSVehicleTableMaintain` privilege and expand the **Entry Points** node and the `ConVMSVehicleTable` entry point.
4. Right-click on the **Controls** node and choose **New Control**.
5. In the **Name** property, type in the name of the control, such as `ConVMSVehicleGroupChangeController`.
6. Select the appropriate **Grant** property. To grant access, make it `Update`.

Impact on licensing

Operations is licensed based on named users. Based on your organization's requirements, a mix of **client access license (CAL)** types can be bought.

The user's CAL type is determined by the entry points (effectively, the menu items) that they have read access to, or higher. For each menu item, we have two properties that control which license type will be required:

- `ViewUserLicense`: This is when a user is given `Read` access to this menu item
- `MaintainUserLicense`: This is when a user is given `Update` or higher access to this menu item

The CAL type is determined by the highest user license type that the user is assigned to. We are not forced to enter values in these menu item properties, but it would be a breach of the license agreement to create a menu item to open a standard form if we don't match the user license type of the original menu item. Microsoft reserves the right, at their expense, to inspect the system.

 Security administrators should plan a cyclic approach to security. Check with the **Named User License Counts** report and adapt the security setup to ensure that you are complying with the license. Checking and maintaining license compliance is the license holder's responsibility.

See also

To find out more about *Security and data entities,* you can refer
to https://docs.microsoft.com/en-us/dynamics365/operations/dev-itpro/data-entit
ies/security-data-entities.

Creating duties

A duty is a collection of one or more privileges. The paradigm is that we are creating a list
of duties that the role will perform and, therefore, add the required privilege in order for
the role to be able to perform that duty.

It is common to have only one privilege in duty, but more can be added; for example, the
setup forms may be added to one duty.

Duty names are suffixed with a verb to denote the action the duty will allow the role to
perform; common suffixes include Maintain, Inquire, and Approve. In order to determine
the correct suffix, look at the standard duties and suffix your duties using the same naming
convention.

How to do it...

To create a duty, follow these steps:

1. Choose to add a new item to the project.
2. In the **Add New Item** dialog, select **Security** from the left-hand list and **Security Duty** from the right.
3. Enter ConVMSVehicleTableInquire in the **Name** field and click on **Add**.
4. Complete the **Description** property; this should describe to the security administrator what this duty does, such as Responsible for responding to vehicle detail information requests.
5. Complete the **Label** property by providing a short description of the security administrator, such as Inquires into vehicle records.
6. In the designer, drag the ConVMSVehicleTableView security privilege onto the **Privileges** node.
7. Repeat this for all the duties required; for example, a ConVMSVehicleTableMaintain duty that will have the ConVMSVehicleTableMaintain privilege.

How it works...

You can consider that a duty is a collection of security privileges, which it is; however, when designing the security model, we would do this the other way around – we would design the role with the required duties and then add the required security privilege to support the duty.

When extending the standard application, we often create new forms and therefore new menu items. The security privilege may, therefore, be required for an existing duty. In this case, we would create an extension of the required duty. To do this, we would right-click on that duty, and choose **Create extension**, remembering to change the .extension suffix to one that relates to the model we are developing: application elements belong to a model, and models belong to a package. Then, we can just drag the privilege from the project onto the duty. This same process would be followed should we wish to add a new duty and a standard role – or an existing role in a different package.

Creating security roles

A role is a collection of duties and privileges. The role is what we associate with a user, which can be done automatically based on the employee's information, such as their position in the company. Security roles should be thought of in terms of the personas that first appeared with Dynamics AX 2012. This change intends to move the thinking away from creating groups of functionality to designing the roles based on how the organization is structured. For example, a sales manager would be in a sales manager role, which will have duties assigned to it. The duties have privileges, which in turn give access to the sales manager in order to perform that role.

In our case, we could consider that they have three roles: vehicle management supervisor, vehicle service supervisor, and vehicle service entry clerk. When defining these roles, we do so by defining the duties that each role will have. The naming convention is similar to other objects and suffixed with the type of role. These types include Supervisor, Manager, Clerk, or others, should these not fit the required role; for example, `ConVMSVehicleManager` would have the `Maintain` duties for vehicle master data.

We can add privileges directly to a role, but we should be strict and only add duties directly to a role. This assists in maintenance. Additionally, it is a best practice to have all the privileges in one or more duties. All the duties must be in one or more roles.

We can also add roles as a subrole. This may help in rare cases, but, again, try to avoid this. It makes maintenance a little more restrictive for the security manager. They may want to grant or restrict access to the subrole without changing the rights of the parent role.

How to do it...

To create a role, follow these steps:

1. Choose to add a new item to the project.
2. In the **Add New Item** dialog, select **Security** from the left-hand list and **Security Role** from the right.
3. Enter `ConVMSVehicleManager` in the **Name** field and click on **Add**.
4. Complete the **Label** property; this should describe to the security administrator what this duty does, such as `Managers vehicle master data`.
5. Complete the **Description** property by providing a short description to the security administrator, such as `Responsible for the maintenance of vehicle records and associated set up data`.
6. In the designer, drag the duties that provide full rights to the vehicle and set up menu items on the **Duties** node.
7. Repeat this for all the roles.

How it works...

Technically, this is straightforward. The complicated part is designing the security model with the customer in order to have a common view of security from a human resource perspective. When security roles are synchronized with the organizational hierarchy, security becomes more of a human resource management process than an IT administrator role.

You may notice that you can add privileges directly to a role, but this should be avoided. When adding privileges directly, we usually end up with a higher maintenance load when changes are required. Adding or removing privileges from a duty affects all the roles that the duty is added to.

See also

For more information on *role-based security*, you can refer to https://docs.microsoft.com/en-us/dynamics365/operations/dev-itpro/sysadmin/role-based-security.

Creating policies

The term *security policies* is a slight misnomer. It is also known under a more accurate term of **Extensible Data Security** (**XDS**). It is an evolution of record-level security that was deprecated from AX 2012: you could still do this, but it wasn't a recommended approach.

In this scenario, we will create a policy that only allows access to vehicles of the truck type. We will have a team that only has access to trucks when creating service orders.

How to do it...

To create a role, follow these steps:

1. Choose to add a new item to the project.
2. In the **Add New Item** dialog, select **Data Model** from the left-hand list and **Query** from the right.
3. Enter `ConVMSVehicleTruckPolicy` in the **Name** field and click on **Add**.
4. In our new query, drag the `ConVMSVehicleTable` table to the **Data Sources** node.
5. Set the **Dynamic Fields** property to **No** and then add the `VehicleType` field to the **Fields** list by right-clicking on the **Fields** node and choosing **New** | **Field**.
6. Drag the field onto the **Ranges** node.
7. On the new `VehicleType` range, change the **Value** property to `Truck`.

 When deployed, this will be updated for us. We can also use the enum's value as the type is not extensible.

8. Save and close the query designer.
9. In the **Add New Item** dialog, select **Security** from the left-hand list and **Security Policy** from the right.
10. Enter `ConVMSVehicleTruckPolicy` in the **Name** field and click on **Add**.
11. Set **Label** to `Vehicle management clerk vehicle table truck access policy`.
12. Set **Help Text** to `Restricts access to the vehicle table so that only trucks can be selected`.
13. Set **Primary Table** to `ConVMSVehicleTable`. This tells Operations the name of the primary table in the **Query** property.

14. Enter `ConVMSVehicleTruckPolicy` into the **Query** property.
15. Leave **Use Not Exist Join** as **No**. Otherwise, this would have the effect of making the policy allow inactive vehicles only.
16. Set **Constrained Table** to **Yes** to state that this table's records will be constrained by the policy.
17. Leave **Operation** as `Select`; we intend this policy to come into effect when selecting records.
18. While implementing the *Creating security roles* recipe, create a role for a `Truck` service entry clerk called `ConVMSVehicleTruckServiceClerk`.
19. Now, on the security policy, set **Context Type** to `RoleName` and enter `ConVMSVehicleTruckServiceClerk` in the **Role Name** property.
20. Finally, set the **Enabled** property to **Yes**.

How it works...

When the user in the policy's role opens a form, or when a drop-down is displayed, the system will create a query that combines the form's data source with the policy's query definition as an `Exists` or `Not Exists` join. This query cannot be changed by the user and is enforced at the kernel level.

Here's a word of caution: since the data policy is defined using a query, it could add significant server load, especially when the query is not written efficiently. In order to use policies, there should be a clear business case, and it may be more appropriate to have a secondary list page instead. These policies should be based on business process rules, where access must be restricted for security purposes. See the link in the *See also* section for more details.

So, creating a policy that is based on data the user enters, such as vehicles for a particular vehicle group, indicates that it isn't a policy but a filter on the vehicles list page. Policies are normally based on rules that are unaffected by user setup, such as an enum.

This could very easily have an impact on performance, so the ranges and joins we create in the query must be written correctly and covered by the appropriate indexes.

There's more...

We can also constrain related tables and views; for example, we could restrain access to vehicle service records that are not linked to vehicles of the `Truck` type.

We can do this in two ways – tables that have a relation defined, and those that don't, which includes views.

To add a constrained table, follow these steps:

1. Right-click on the **Constrained Tables** node and choose **New** | **Constrained Table**.
2. Set the **Constrained** property to **Yes**.

 Constrained tables can be nested, and we can add intermediary tables to eventually get to the table we want to constrain. We may not want these intermediary tables to be constrained, and would, therefore, leave this value as **No**.

3. Set the **Name** property to `ConVMSVehicleServiceTable`.
4. Select `ConVMSVehicleTable` in the **Table Relation** property.

To add a view or a table without a relation, use the Constrain Expression option instead. In this case, we have a **Value** property, where we enter the relation, for example, `ConVMSVehicleTable.VehicleId == ConVMSVehicleServiceTable.VehicleId`. This value hasn't been validated, so we must ensure that it is correct.

See also

You can refer to the following links to find out more about the topics that were covered in this chapter:

- *Best Practices, Tips, and Tricks for Implementing XDS (Extensible Data Security) policies:* `https://blogs.msdn.microsoft.com/daxserver/2013/06/26/best-prac tices-tips-and-tricks-for-implementing-xds-extensible-data-security-policies/`
- *Security Architecture:* `https://docs.microsoft.com/en-us/dynamics365/operations/dev -itpro/sysadmin/security-architecture`
- *Security Policies Properties for AX 2012:* `https://msdn.microsoft.com/en-us/library/gg731857.aspx`

These links are still relevant for Dynamics 365 for Finance and Supply Chain Management.

10
Data Management, OData, and Office

Data integration with other applications is a very important part of Finance and **Supply Chain Management** (**SCM**). It is a cloud-first ERP solution, and this means that it has to provide secure ways to manage its data. As part of the implementation data usually has to be imported, and after that, we will often wish to import and export data from SCM, we may also wish to integrate with other applications, such as Excel, or access data from SCM in our internal on-premise applications.

Although SCM provides many data integration features out of the box, we will usually have to extend or write new entities. The topics covered in this chapter provide the recipes that are commonly used to access our data in terms of both integration and for use in Edit in Excel experiences. The following topics are covered:

- Creating a data entity with an Edit in Excel experience
- Extending standard data entities
- Importing data through the Data Import/Export Framework
- Reading, writing, and updating data through OData

Technical requirement

You can find the code files of this chapter on GitHub at the links given here:

- `https://github.com/PacktPublishing/Extending-Microsoft-Dynamics-365-Finance-and-Supply-Chain-Management-Cookbook-Second-Edition/blob/master/Chapter%2010%20ConODataTest.zip`
- `https://github.com/PacktPublishing/Extending-Microsoft-Dynamics-365-Finance-and-Supply-Chain-Management-Cookbook-Second-Edition/blob/master/Chapter%2010.axpp`

Introduction

Since Microsoft Dynamics 365 Finance and Supply Chain Management is a cloud solution, we can't integrate directly with our local area network. Even though ports could be opened in order to do this, it opens an unnecessary security risk. Even when deployed on a local business data (on-premise), we should still use the same patterns as used in the cloud. This would aid fail-over scenarios should Azure be our **Disaster Recovery** (**DR**) solution or should we wish to move to the cloud at a later date.

All integrations should have a service endpoint that will be accessed by SCM.

To facilitate writing integrations that are agnostic of the local network resources, Microsoft has evolved the **Data Import/Export Framework** (**DIXF**) in this release to help resolve many of the integrations issues we often face. It also opens up a much more integrated way in which we can communicate with Microsoft Office.

In this chapter, we will cover the usage and extensibility options for data entities, and also how to interact programmatically with our data entities through OData.

Creating a data entity with an Edit in Excel experience

In this task, we will create a data entity for our vehicle table, which we will extend in order to demonstrate how data entities can be used. We will also use this to allow us to maintain vehicle data through the Office add-in and make it a public OData entity.

Getting ready

We will just need to have an SCM project open, and a table for which we want to create a data entity.

How to do it...

To create the data entity, follow these steps:

1. Before we start, we need to check that the table we are going to use has a natural key. We can either configure an alternate key, or simply choose a single key unique index as the table's primary key. Open the designer for the ConVMSVehicleTable table, and check that the **Primary Key** property is set to VehicleIdx.

2. In the project, add a new item. Within the **Add New Item** dialog, select **Data Model** from the left-hand list, and then **Data Entity** from the right.

3. Enter ConVMSVehicleTableEntity as **Name** and press **Add**.

4. We will then get a **Data Entity Wizard** dialog and select ConVMSVehicleTable in the **Primary datasource** drop-down list.

> As you scroll down, the drop-down list can resize, causing an item to be selected by mistake. It is, therefore, easier to use the *Page Up* and *Page Down* keys to locate the table.

The **Entity** category is not correct by default, and in our example, it should be Master; you can use the following table as a guide to select the correct category:

Table group	Entity category
Main, Group	Master
Worksheet (all types)	Document
Transaction (all types)	Transaction
Parameter	Parameter
Reference	Reference

5. The dialog made a guess that `Con` was a prefix and stripped this from the **Public entity name** and **Public collection name** fields; the prefix should be put back to avoid the chance of a naming collision.

The defaults will create a public interface for access by other applications, such as Microsoft Office, a staging table for use with the DIXF, and security privileges in order to control who has access to this entity.

6. Click on **Next**, which will open the **Add Fields** page after a short delay.

On this page, we can add related data sources and virtual fields. In our case, this is not required, and we will cover this option in the *There's more...* section.

7. If we check **Convert labels to field names**, it will use the field's labels for the field names. This is not usually desirable; the label may need the context of a field group in order for us to know which field it relates to. Do not check this checkbox. The following grid is created based on the table's definition, which will be used as the settings used to generate the data entity. These settings are usually correct; in our case, the grid is as follows:

Field name	Data entity field name	Data type	EDT type name	Is Mandatory	Label Id	Label
☑ VehicleId	VehicleId	String	ConVMSVehicleId	☑	@ConVMS:VehicleId	Vehicle id
☑ Name	Name	String	Name	☐	@SYS7399	Name
☑ VehicleGroupId	VehicleGroupId	String	ConVMSVehicleGroupId	☑	@ConVMS:VehicleGroupId	Vehicle group
☑ VehicleType	VehicleType	Enum		☐	@ConVMS:VehicleType	Vehicle type
☑ VehRegNum	VehRegNum	String	ConVMSVehRegNum	☐	@ConVMS:VehRegNum	Registration
☑ AcquiredDate	AcquiredDate	Date	ConVMSAcquiredDate	☐	@ConVMS:DateAcquired	Date acquired
☑ InstanceRelationType	InstanceRelationType	Int64		☐		
☐ DataAreaId	DataAreaId3	String	DataAreaId	☐	Company	Company
☐ CreatedBy	CreatedBy	String	CreatedBy	☐	Created by	Created by
☐ CreatedDateTime	CreatedDateTime	UtcDateTime	CreatedDateTime	☐	Created date and time	Created date and time
☐ ModifiedBy	ModifiedBy	String	ModifiedBy	☐	Modified by	Modified by
☐ ModifiedDateTime	ModifiedDateTime	UtcDateTime	ModifiedDateTime	☐	Modified date and time	Modified date and time

We can make additional fields mandatory; however, if we decide to uncheck a mandatory field, we will get an error unless it is specified in code before the actual record is inserted or updated. This can be useful when the mandatory field is inferred from another field in the data entity.

8. Click on **Finish**.

The wizard has created the following objects for us:

Element	Description
ConVMSVehicleTableEntity	This is the data entity.
ConVMSVehicleTableStaging	This is a table used to stage data when importing via the DIXF.
ConVMSVehicleTableEntityMaintain	This is a security privilege to allow us full access to the data entity.
ConVMSVehicleTableEntityView	This is a security privilege to allow view-only access to the data entity.

9. Build the project and synchronize it with the database.

10. Open the main form for the data entity, in our case, the `Vehicles` form, which can be accessed directly using the following URL:
    `https://usnconeboxax1aos.cloud.onebox.dynamics.com/?cmp=usmf&mi=ConVMSVehicleTable`

11. On the top right of the screen, the Office icon has a new option, **OPEN IN EXCEL**, as shown in the following screenshot:

12. If you hover the mouse over the **Vehicle table (usmf)** link, you will see that it is our entity, as shown in the following screenshot:

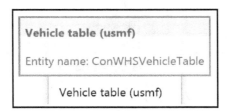

13. This is the public entity name we specified in the wizard, and we can change it by changing the **Public Entity Name** property on the data entity.
14. Click on the **Vehicle table (usmf)** link, and then click **Download** in the **Open in Excel** dialog.
15. Once Microsoft Excel opens, you may get the following warning:

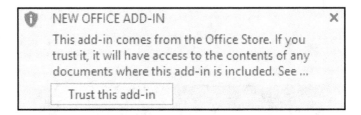

16. Click on **Trust this add-in**.
17. Next, click on **Sign in**, and sign in using the same account you used for logging into Dynamics 365 for Operations.

 Once signed in, it will populate a sheet with the data from the ConVMSVehicleTable table, but only add the mandatory fields. To test the entity, we should add a few fields.

18. In the add-in, click on **Design** and then click on the edit icon next to the Vehicles table, as shown in the following screenshot:

19. On the next page, select all of the fields (except `InstanceRelationType`, if the table was configured to use inheritance) in the **Available fields** list and press the **Add** button that is just above the **Selected fields** list.
20. Click on **Update**, and then click **Yes** in response to the warning.
21. Click on **Done**, which takes us out of the design experience, and then press **Refresh** to fetch the new data.
22. Our sheet should now have the data from the vehicle table, as shown in the following screenshot:

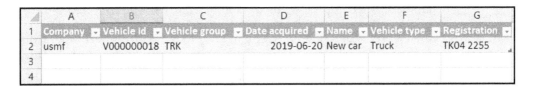

	A	B	C	D	E	F	G
1	Company	Vehicle id	Vehicle group	Date acquired	Name	Vehicle type	Registration
2	usmf	V000000018	TRK	2019-06-20	New car	Truck	TK04 2255
3							
4							

The headings are labels in your user's language and the enumerated types are also translated.

23. Edit one or more of the fields using the add-in to select the values when they have a drop-down list or date picker. Do not change the **Vehicle Id** value, but you can test this yourself in a different test to see what happens.
24. Click on **New** in the add-in in order to add a new vehicle, and complete the sheet as required. Once done, the result should be similar to the following screenshot:

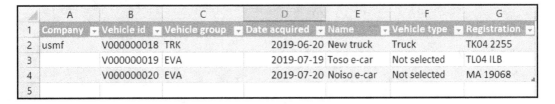

	A	B	C	D	E	F	G
1	Company	Vehicle id	Vehicle group	Date acquired	Name	Vehicle type	Registration
2	usmf	V000000018	TRK	2019-06-20	New truck	Truck	TK04 2255
3		V000000019	EVA	2019-07-19	Toso e-car	Not selected	TL04 ILB
4		V000000020	EVA	2019-07-20	Noiso e-car	Not selected	MA 19068
5							

The **Company** column was left blank, and we should actually remove this column from the sheet. If you remember, the link had the company within the link's name, so this connection is bound using that company ID.

25. Once done, click on **Publish**; the entity will be refreshed with the company ID that was actually used when the records were created.

26. Finally, refresh the **Vehicles** form in SCM, and you will see the records within the vehicles list page.
27. Close the Excel worksheet.
28. Ideally, we would want to control which fields are available, so open the `ConVMSVehicleTableEntity` data entity in the designer.

 The properties are very similar to those of a table, and the nodes in the design share those of both queries and tables. In fact, this is created in the SQL Server database as a view, and, if we synchronized the database, we could view the data in SQL Server Management Studio.

29. Add the fields you would like to see by default to the **AutoReport** field group.
30. You may also have noticed that the `VehicleGroupId` field did not have a drop-down list in Excel, and the foreign key relation does not help in this case. We will need a custom lookup, as shown in the following piece of code:

```
[SysODataAction(
    'ConVMSVehicleTableEntityVehicleGroupLookup', false),
    SysODataCollection('_fields', Types::String),
    SysODataFieldLookup(fieldStr(ConVMSVehicleTableEntity,
    VehicleGroupId))]
public static str LookupVehicleGroupId(Array _fields)
{
    RefFieldName vehicleGroupIdFld;
    vehicleGroupIdFld = fieldStr(ConVMSVehicleTableEntity,
                            VehicleGroupId);

    Map fieldMap;
    fieldMap = OfficeAppCustomLookupHelper::getFieldMap(
        tableStr(ConVMSVehicleTableEntity), _fields);

    DataAreaId dataAreaId = curExt();
    RefFieldName dataAreaIdFld;
    dataAreaIdFld = fieldStr(ConVMSVehicleTableEntity,
                            DataAreaId);
    if (fieldMap.exists(dataAreaIdFld))
    {
        dataAreaId = fieldMap.lookup(dataAreaIdFld);
    }

    OfficeAppCustomLookupListResult result;
    result = new OfficeAppCustomLookupListResult();
    result.determinationFields().value(1,
                            vehicleGroupIdFld);
    str resultString;
```

```
if (OfficeAppCustomLookupHelper::fieldsBound(
  result.determinationFields(), fieldMap))
{
    int counter = 1;
    changecompany(dataAreaId)
    {
        ConWHSVehicleGroup vehicleGroups;
        while select VehicleGroupId
            from vehicleGroups
            order by VehicleGroupId
        {
            result.items().value(counter,
                        vehicleGroups.VehicleGroupId);
            counter++;
        }
    }
    resultString = result.serialize();
}
return resultString;
}
```

31. Rebuild the project and test the add-in again; you will get the fields that you added to the field group along with the drop-down list on the **Vehicle group** column.

How it works...

When we create a data entity with a public interface, it actually creates a service that Microsoft Excel communicates with. The Excel file we downloaded was just to allow connection to the data entity using OData. We aren't reading records directly; the records are read from SCM and are written back when we publish the changes.

The authentication goes through our Microsoft Office 365 account, and, when hosted in Azure, the add-in takes care of the complexities of this integration for us. It is secure (and it also honors XDS data policies), yet is available everywhere.

Until we got to writing the lookup, the process was remarkably easy, if we take into account the result we achieve with such little effort. It, therefore, stood out that we had to write quite a complicated method for the lookup.

The method does look a little daunting; however, when broken down, it becomes easier to understand.

The first key part of the method is the `SysODataFieldLookup` decoration, this declaration declares that the method is bound to the `VehicleGroupId` field and is a string data type. The `_fields` parameter provides both metadata and the value of each field in the dataset. This is converted into the `fieldMap` map for ease of use.

We will need this in order to work out which company we are working in, so we will return data from that company. This differs from other static methods; in that, it is called with a company context. This is done by looking up the value of the `dataAreaId` field as follows:

```
dataAreaIdFld = fieldStr(ConVMSVehicleTableEntity, DataAreaId);
if(fieldMap.exists(dataAreaIdFld))
{
    dataAreaId = fieldMap.lookup(dataAreaIdFld);
}
```

 We have to check if it exists before we look it up; if not, it will throw an error if the key doesn't exist on the map.

Before adding the values to the array, we should check that the `VehicleGroupId` field is bound (that is, it is in the `_fields` array). This was done using the `OfficeAppCustomLookupHelper::fieldsBound()` method call. In our case, it is semantically equivalent to checking that the field exists in the `fieldMap` map.

The actual lookup data is constructed by the following line of code:

```
result.items().value(counter, vehicleGroups.VehicleGroupId);
```

The `result.items()` function is an array or string values. Since we have access to the enter array of fields on the current *line,* we have the ability to filter the result by data in other columns.

To return the data, it has to be serialized to a string, which was done by the following line of code:

```
resultString = result.serialize();
```

The result is then interpreted by the office add-in, and the options displayed in the right-hand pane.

There's more...

There are a few special methods that are used when writing a data entity. They are as follows:

Method	Description
updateEntityDataSource	This is called when updating an existing record.
deleteEntityDataSource	This is called when deleting a record.
insertEntityDataSource	This is called when inserting a new record.
initializeEntityDataSource	This is called when a record is initialized.

These methods are used so that we can update related records that are not directly affected by the tables in the entity. A good example is when a table is related to DirPartyTable. We can't simply delete the related party record in this case when the parent is deleted, as it may be used in other roles.

The following are sample methods for a fictitious ConVMSHaulierTableEntity, which has a main data source, ConWHSHaulierTable, and a child data source, DirPartyBaseEntity:

- In this method, we will check if the entity is the DirPartyBaseEntity data source, and, if it is, it executes logic to handle the DirPartyTable and LogisticsPostalAddress tables. These tables are part of complicated structures, and the helper ensures that they are inserted correctly:

```
public boolean insertEntityDataSource(
        DataEntityRuntimeContext _entityCtx,
        DataEntityDataSourceRuntimeContext _dataSourceCtx)
{
    boolean ret;

    switch (_dataSourceCtx.name())
    {
        case dataEntityDataSourceStr(ConVMSHaulierTableEntity,
                                DirPartyBaseEntity):
            DirPartyBaseEntityHelper partyHelper;
            partyHelper = new DirPartyBaseEntityHelper();
            partyHelper.preInsertEntityDataSource(_entityCtx,
                                                _dataSourceCtx,
                    dataEntityDataSourceStr(
                            ConVMSHaulierTableEntity,
                            LogisticsPostalAddressBaseEntity)));

            ret = super(_entityCtx, _dataSourceCtx);
```

```
            if (ret)
            {
                partyHelper.postInsertEntityDataSource(_entityCtx,
                            _dataSourceCtx,
                    dataEntityDataSourceStr(
                            ConVMSHaulierTableEntity,
                            LogisticsPostalAddressBaseEntity));
            }
            break;
        default:
            ret = super(_entityCtx, _dataSourceCtx);
    }
    return ret;
}
```

- The following code handles the deletion logic and will correctly handle the update to the global address book (`DirPartyTable`), removing the links correctly for us:

```
public boolean deleteEntityDataSource(
            DataEntityRuntimeContext _entityCtx,
            DataEntityDataSourceRuntimeContext _dataSourceCtx)
{
    boolean ret;

    switch (_dataSourceCtx.name())
    {
        case dataEntityDataSourceStr(ConVMSHaulierTableEntity,
                            DirPartyBaseEntity)):
            DirPartyBaseEntityHelper partyHelper;
            partyHelper = new DirPartyBaseEntityHelper();
            partyHelper.deleteEntityDataSource(_dataSourceCtx);
            break;
        default:
            ret = super(_entityCtx, _dataSourceCtx);
    }
    return ret;
}
```

The final method in this set is the code to handle what happens when records are updated. This is identical to the `insertEntityDataSource` method except that this method is called `updateEntityDataSource`.

- The following method is called when the record is initialized; the code in this method is used correctly to initialize the global address book data structures:

```
public void initializeEntityDataSource(DataEntityRuntimeContext
_entityCtx, DataEntityDataSourceRuntimeContext _dataSourceCtx)
{
    super(_entityCtx, _dataSourceCtx);

    if (_dataSourceCtx.name() ==
            dataEntityDataSourceStr(ConWHSHaulierTableEntity,
                                    DirPartyBaseEntity))
    {
        // Takes care of maintaining the reference to existing
        // parties if this record provides a party number. This is
        // because, even though we may be inserting the customer
        // record, the party may already exist.
        DirPartyBaseEntity::
                initializeDirPartyBaseEntityDataSource(
                                        _entityCtx,
                                        _dataSourceCtx);

    }
}
```

You can see examples of how these are used in many of the standard entities; a good example is `CustCustomerEntity`.

Data entities on tables that use inheritance

When we created new records, the vehicle type field reverted to Not selected. This is because the insert method used the table type to determine the vehicle type field, which is correct yet unhelpful in this scenario.

First, we need to add a method to get the `InstanceRelationType` (the table ID of the table instance) from the vehicle type, open the code for the `ConVMSVehicleTableType` class, and add the following method:

```
public RefTableId GetInstanceRelationFromType(
    ConVMSVehicleType _vehicleType)
{
    RefTableId instanceType = tableNum(ConVMSVehicleTable);
    switch (vehicleTable.InstanceRelationType)
    {
        case ConVMSVehicleType::Truck:
            instanceType = tableNum(ConVMSVehicleTableTruck);
            break;
        case ConVMSVehicleType::Bike:
```

```
            instanceType = tableNum(ConVMSVehicleTableBike);
            break;
        case ConVMSVehicleType::Car:
            instanceType = tableNum(ConVMSVehicleTableCar);
            break;
    }
    return instanceType;
}
```

This is the reverse of the method we wrote when we changed the vehicle table to use inheritance. The sample code that can be downloaded goes a little further by adding a delegate to handle vehicle types added by a customer or partner.

The next step would be to make the vehicle type field editable when using the entity. Open the designer for the `ConVMSVehicleTableEntity` data entity, and select the `VehicleType` field from the **Fields** list.

To complete the changes, you would then change the **Allow edit on create** property from **Automatic** to **Yes**. Then right-click on `ConVMSVehicleTableEntity` in the design and choose **Update staging table**. Whenever we make structural changes to the data entity, we must always update or regenerate the staging table.

See also

The following links provide some guidance on related features and some background to data entities and OData:

- *Add templates to Open lines in Excel menu* (https://docs.microsoft.com/en-us/dynamics365/unified-operations/dev-itpro/user-interface/add-templates-open-lines-excel-menu)
- *Publish journal lines and documents from Excel* (https://docs.microsoft.com/en-us/dynamics365/unified-operations/financials/general-ledger/open-lines-excel-journals-documents)
- *Create Open in Excel experiences* (https://docs.microsoft.com/en-us/dynamics365/unified-operations/dev-itpro/office-integration/office-integration-edit-excel)

 The preceding link shows how to create a lookup using a pattern that differs from how it is used within standard software and in this recipe. I chose to use the pattern from the standard software instead of the version used at this URL.

- *Troubleshoot Office integration* (https://docs.microsoft.com/en-us/ dynamics365/unified-operations/dev-itpro/office-integration/office-integration-troubleshooting)

- *Security and data entities* (https://docs.microsoft.com/en-us/dynamics365/ unified-operations/dev-itpro/data-entities/security-data-entities)

Extending standard data entities

Extensibility is becoming more and more pervasive in the development paradigm of Dynamics 365 for Finance and Supply Chain Management, and it is important to be able to have extensible data entities; otherwise, we would have to write new ones to be able to use a field we added to a table as an extension.

In this example, we will create an extension for the Released product creation entity, named `EcoResReleasedProductCreationEntity`.

Getting ready

Part of this recipe is to add an extension field so we can import data into it, so the first part is to create an extension for the `InventTable` table with a new field. This is optional but is included in order to demonstrate how this is done.

To follow this optional step, create a table extension for the `InventTable` table and add a new field of type `Name` called `ConVMSAdditionalName`. Also, add this to a form extension so we can see the results.

How to do it...

To create a data entity extension, follow these steps:

1. In the Application Explorer, expand **Data Model** and then **Data Entities**. Right-click on `EcoResReleasedProductCreationV2Entity` and select **Create extension**.
2. To add more context to this extension, rename the extension part (after the dot) to the project's name, such as `ConVMSVehicleManagement`. Although in our case the project and the package have a very similar name, this is not usually the case, so it is good practice to think that we would always change the extension portion of the name.

After examining the **Data Sources** node, we can see that it is not based directly on `InventTable`, but on a data entity. We will, therefore, need to create an extension for this before we can add the field.

3. Right-click on the `EcoResReleasedProductV2Entity` entity and click **Create extension**, and then rename the `Extension` suffix to `ConVehicleManagement`.
4. Expand the **Data Sources** nodes and then **InventTable**, and then locate the extension field (`ConWHSAdditionalName`). Right-click on the field and choose **Copy**.
5. Collapse the **Data Sources** node and right-click on the entity's root **Fields** node. Right-click on the **Fields** node and select **Paste**.

Alternatively, you can right-click on the **Fields** node, choose **New | Mapped Field**, and complete the property sheet.

6. Save and close the data entity.
7. Open the `EcoResReleasedProductCreationV2Entity.ConVehicleManagement` data extension in the designer and expand the **Data Sources** and **EcoResReleasedProductV2Entity** nodes.
8. Locate the `ConVMSAdditionalName` field and use copy and paste to add it to the data entity's **Fields** node.
9. We also will need to add the new field to the relevant data entities' staging tables. This cannot be done automatically as we are working with an extension—the system can't add fields to the standard table as that would result in an over-layer.
10. Locate the `EcoResReleasedProductCreationV2Staging` table and create an extension; name it appropriately.
11. Add the `ConVMSAdditionalName` field as we did on `InventTable`; you can use copy and paste to do this.
12. Create an extension of `EcoResReleasedProductV2Staging` in the same way and add the `ConVMSAdditionalName` field there as well.

We can work out which table is the staging table by looking at the **Data Management Staging Table** property of the original data entity, which is `EcoResReleasedProductCreationStaging` in this case.

13. Save everything and build the project.

 You will need to add a reference to `Dimensions` and `UnitOfMeasure` to your package in order for the build to succeed.

14. Finally, synchronize the project with the database.

How it works...

The data entity extension works in a similar way to any other extension—it stores a delta change in an XML definition file that is merged with the base entity when the project is built. Should we look at the entity within the client, which we'll do in the next recipe, we will see that the fields exist as if they were part of the entity.

As it is a mapped field, we don't need to write any special code in order to persist this through the staging table to the target table. The mapping is done based on the field name, and should we forget to add the field to the staging table we will not get a warning. Since this data entity is not public, it can't be used with the Office add-in or through OData; it is intended to be used within the DIXF.

You may have noticed that the entity we used had `V2` in its name. Adding `V2` to the name shows a limitation caused by a rule from Microsoft whereby breaking changes are not allowed for extensible objects without a formal deprecation process. The problem, though, is that the data entities that were extended in the previous version will not have the changes or improvements that were added to the new version.

There's more...

The extent to which application objects (such as forms, tables, and data entities) are extensible will evolve with each release. Currently, we can add data sources, ranges, relations, field groups, and table maps to data entities. We cannot add new methods or change existing ones, as this would result in no practical difference to an over-layer (except it could be worse, as no tooling would exist for conflict management). Instead, we would use a chain of command or preferably subscribe to the many event delegates.

When subscribing to events, you will need to read the original code. Sometimes the data is transferred using an `insert_recordset` statement, where the fields are written literally into the code.

This causes two problems:

- Adding fields to the entity and staging table will not work as expected as the fields are transferred in a set-based operation that only transfers the specifically mentioned fields.
- Should new fields be added, and to avoid breaking changes, there tends to be a new version created.

For the first issue, we just need to perform an `update_recordset` command in an event or delegate subscription. The second issue is a problem for extensions to data entities. It seems Microsoft's rule of "No breaking changes" means that our extensions will simply get deprecated as the prior version is added to the deprecation path. Deprecated objects can still be used, but it does mean that the next release can make it obsolete and will fail to build. The reason that the `EcoResReleasedProductCreationV2Entity` was used to highlight this potential issue.

Importing data through the Data Import/Export Framework

This recipe is usually a system administration function but is needed in order to test our data entities. It also gives us more insight into understanding how our data entities work.

Getting ready

This recipe follows on from the previous one, where we are testing a data entity extension. The steps here can be used with any data entity.

How to do it...

To import and export data using the DIXF, follow these steps:

1. Open Dynamics 365 for Finance and Supply Chain Management in a supported browser (IE, Edge, or Chrome).

2. The first step, after making any change to the data entities, is to refresh the entity list. This can happen automatically, but, to ensure it is refreshed, open the **Data management** workspace, select **Framework parameters**, and click on **Refresh entity list** in the **Entity settings** tab page. This happens asynchronously, and you will get a message when it is complete; you may need to click in and out of forms for the message to appear.

3. Depending on the platform version you are using, you may be using the deprecated version of data management. On the **Framework parameters** form, select the **General** tab and set the **View defaults** field to Enhanced view; then close the form and the data management workspace. Once reopened, you will see an option to select the Standard view.

 This step is required because simply selecting the **Enhanced view** doesn't change the Export form to use the **Enhanced view**, which we will use later in this recipe.

4. Next, we will need to check that the fields exist and are mapped correctly on the **Data management** workspace; click on **Data entities**.

 If you get the message that **C:\Temp\Dixf does not exist**, create this folder using Windows Explorer.

5. Type in Released products into the filter control and select **Entity: "Released products V2"** from the drop-down list.

6. Click on **Target fields** and check that the field exists in the list. If not, you need to rebuild the project and synchronize the project to the database. A full build in Visual Studio using **Dynamics 365 | Build models** may be required if this persists.

7. Then, close the **Target fields** form and click on **Modify target mapping**. The grid may be empty, and if we haven't specified any specific mapping previously, we can use the **Generate mapping** button to create the default field mapping for us. This step is only required if the field list is empty or if our new field(s) are not on the list.

8. If we have specified specific mapping in this previously, clicking on **Generate mapping** will delete it. You can click on **New** and complete the line, or use the **MAPPING VISUALIZATION** tab page. In this form, drag the field from the right-hand list to the corresponding field on the left.

9. Now the mapping is done, let's export some data. On the **Data management** workspace, click on **Export**.

 It may seem odd to export a data entity that is used to create data, but the following steps are used to create an import template used later in the recipe.

10. If this is the first export created, you will be presented with an empty form. Complete the header section as shown in the following screenshot:

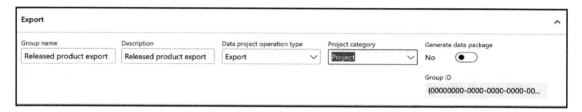

11. On the lines section, click **Add entity**, complete the form as shown in the following screenshot, and press **Add**:

12. Finally, click on **Export** from the top-button ribbon. This will start the export that is performed asynchronously, click the **Refresh** button after a few seconds to check the status, and, eventually, it will change to **Succeeded**. You can download the file by clicking **Download file** as shown in the following screenshot:

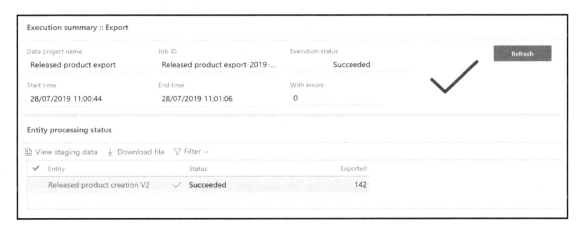

13. This downloads the Excel file, which we can use as an import template.
14. Copy the spreadsheet, and, in the copy, remove all rows except the first two (the header and the first product row), as we will use the first product as a template to save having to look up valid values: we are only testing that it works for now.
15. Change the **ItemNumber** and **ProductNumber** columns to X1000 (an item number that has not yet been used).
16. Fill in the **ConVMSAdditionalName** column with something useful.
17. Save to the Documents folder and close the spreadsheet.
18. Go back to the Dynamics 365 for Finance and Supply Chain Management client, and navigate back to the **Data management** workspace. Click on **Import**.
19. Complete the header portion of the form as we did for the export, then click **Add file**.

20. The **Add file** dialog differs from the export version. Fill the right-hand side in first, and then click **Upload and add** to add the Excel workbook we created earlier. The form should be as shown, before **Upload and add** is clicked:

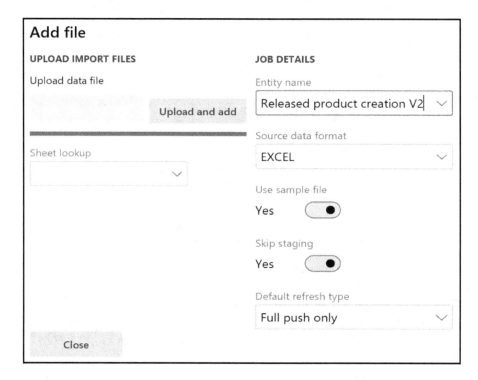

21. You should see that a record is created in the lines grid once the file is imported. Click **Close** once done.
22. Click **Import**, and then you can click **Refresh** as we did when exporting the sample file. Once complete, you should be able to see that the product was successfully created and the new field was populated.

How it works...

There is a lot to the DIXF, some of which we will cover further in the next recipe.

The main step we took in this recipe was to refresh the data entities. This builds the data entity tables from the metadata of the data entity that was defined in code. Without this step, the entity might not appear if it is new, or if it was changed, the data entity could be out of date with the physical entity and staging table data structures.

The next step was to export a sample dataset to Excel. This is to provide us with a spreadsheet that we can use to populate new records.

Once we had populated the spreadsheet, we then created a new import project to import the spreadsheet. The file is imported as a blob into the import project. The import process involves the following steps:

1. Start an asynchronous process to start the import.
2. Read the spreadsheet into the staging table using the mapping in the import project definition, which is, by default, based on the field names matching the column headers on the spreadsheet.
3. Process the staging table into the target, which in this case was the product tables.

This is a good example of why we need data entities. To create a product we need to write data into many tables, and the links between these tables are not obvious. Sometimes it is a natural key, such as Item ID, and for others, it is a record ID that is not known until the record is created in SCM.

See also

You can refer to the following pages to find out more:

- *Data entities and packages framework* (https://ax.help.dynamics.com/en/wiki/using-data-entities-and-data-packages/)
- *Data entities home page* (https://ax.help.dynamics.com/en/wiki/data-entities-home-page/)

Reading, writing, and updating data through OData

In this example, we will create a sample OData console application in order to demonstrate how to connect to and communicate through OData.

In order to start, you will need to create an application within your organization's Azure ID. You will need the application ID—an official guide as to how to do this is available at `https://docs.microsoft.com/en-us/dynamics365/fin-ops-core/dev-itpro/data-entities/services-home-page`.

Getting ready

The following doesn't have to be done in the Dynamics 365 for Finance and Supply Chain Management development virtual machine. However, it will need to have access to the URL.

How to do it...

To import and export data using the OData, follow these steps:

1. Create a new project but, this time, choose Visual C# from the `Templates` node and then `Console Application` from the right. Name the project `ConODataTest` and place it in the `project` folder that we set up for source control. Ensure that the namespace is also `ConODataTest`.

2. We will now need to install some NuGet packages. Within Visual Studio, navigate to **Tools** | **NuGet Package Manager** | **Package Manager Console**.

   > *"NuGet is the package manager for the Microsoft development platform including .NET. The NuGet client tools provide the ability to produce and consume packages. The NuGet Gallery is the central package repository used by all package authors and consumers."*   - *(Source:* `https://www.nuget.org/`*)*

3. In the Package Manager console, type the following commands:
   - `Install-Package Microsoft.Bcl.Build`
   - `Install-Package Microsoft.Bcl`
   - `Install-Package Microsoft.Net.Http`
   - `Install-Package Microsoft.OData.Core -Version 6.15.0`
   - `Install-Package Simple.OData.Client -Version 4.24.0.1`
   - `Install-Package Microsoft.Data.OData`
   - `Install-Package Microsoft.OData.Client`
   - `Install-Package Microsoft.IdentityModel.Clients.ActiveDirectory`

Simple.OData.Client is added as an alternative and is not used in this example. This is why the specific 6.15.0 version of Microsoft.OData.Core was used. If Simple.OData.Client is not being used, the version need not be specified.

4. This may take some time to install, and once it is complete, restart Visual Studio, making sure you save your project. If Visual Studio is not restarted, the build will fail without any message as to why. Once Visual Studio is opened, ensure to open the ConODataTest project before continuing.

5. Next, we will need an add-in for Visual Studio in order to read the metadata and generate types for us. Navigate to **Tools | Extensions and Updates**.

6. Click on **Online** on the left and type OData Client Code in the **Search Visual Studio Gallery** text box.

7. Select **OData v4 Client Code Generator** from the list and click on **Download**.

8. Then, choose to add a new item to the project. Select **OData Client** from the list. Name it OdataClient.tt and click on **Add**.

A tt file is a transformation file, and its purpose will become more apparent as we progress.

9. Check that you have access to https://usnconeboxax1aos.cloud.onebox.dynamics.com/ in the browser and that you can log in. Minimize (but do not close) the browser and go back to Visual Studio.

10. Open the new OdataClient.tt file in Visual Studio, and click **OK** on the security warning message. Toward the top of this file, you will see the following line:

```
public const string MetadataDocumentUri = "";
```

11. Change it so that it reads as follows:

```
public const string MetadataDocumentUri =
"https://usnconeboxax1aos.cloud.onebox.dynamics.com/data/$metadata"
;
```

12. As standard, the code generation stores a large amount of XML in a string constant, which will cause a build error. To avoid this, locate the following line:

```
public const string TempFilePath = "";
```

Change it to read as follows:

```
public const string TempFilePath = "C:\\temp\\Test.xml";
```

13. You can now click **Save** or press *Ctrl + S*. You will receive a security warning—click on **OK** to proceed. This will take a few minutes to proceed, as it is a generated client and type the code for all public entities.

 Once complete, you will see a new `ODataClient.cs` file nested under the `ODataClient.tt` file with many methods. The file is around 40 MB, so opening it will take a while and is best avoided. Should you find that Visual Studio starts to perform slowly, ensure that you have closed `ODataClient.tt` and `ODataCilent.cs` and then restart Visual Studio.

14. We can now start writing the code for our test; add a new class to the project named `ODataTest`.

15. Add the following `using` statements to the top of the file:

```
using System;
using System.Threading.Tasks;
using Microsoft.IdentityModel.Clients.ActiveDirectory;
using Microsoft.OData.Client;
using ConODataTest.Microsoft.Dynamics.DataEntities;
```

16. To simplify the process, create the following data contract classes in order to aid passing parameters. Add them inside the `namespace ConODataTest` statement, just above the `ODataTest` class definition:

```
class ODataUserContract
{
    public string userName;
    public string password;
    public string domain;
}
class ODataApplicationContract
{
    public string applicationId;
    public string resource;
    public string result;
}
public class ODataRequestContract
{
    public string company;
}
```

We would usually use get/set methods here, but I used public variables to save space for this test.

17. In the class body, declare the following class variables:

```
class ODataTest
{
    public const string OAuthHeader = "Authorization";
    public ODataUserContract userContract;
    public ODataApplicationContract appContract;
    public ODataRequestContract request;

    string authenticationHeader;
    public string response;
```

The `OAuthHeader` and `authenticationHeader` variables are key to the process of authentication with Dynamics 365 for Finance and Supply Chain Management.

18. The code to authenticate with Azure AD is as follows:

```
private AuthenticationResult GetAuthorization()
{
    UriBuilder uri = new UriBuilder("https://login.windows.net/" +
     userContract.domain);

    AuthenticationContext authenticationContext
        = new AuthenticationContext(uri.ToString());
    UserPasswordCredential credential = new
        UserPasswordCredential(
        userContract.userName, userContract.password);

    Task<AuthenticationResult> task =
     authenticationContext.AcquireTokenAsync(
        appContract.resource, appContract.applicationId,
        credential);

    task.Wait();
    AuthenticationResult
        authenticationResult = task.Result;
    return authenticationResult;
}
```

19. Now, create a `public` method that will be called in order to log on:

```
public Boolean Authenticate()
{
    AuthenticationResult authenticationResult;
    try
    {
        authenticationResult = GetAuthorization();
        //this gets the authorization token, this
        // must be set on the Http header for all requests
        authenticationHeader =
            authenticationResult.CreateAuthorizationHeader();
    }
    catch (Exception e)
    {
        response = "Authentication failed: " + e.Message;
        return false;
    }
    response = "OK";
    return true;
}
```

20. Each method that makes a call to SCM must set up a `Resources` instance, which has an event handler in order to set the authentication key. This method should be written as follows:

```
private Resources MakeResources()
{
    string entityRootPath = appContract.resource + "/data";
    Uri oDataUri = new Uri(entityRootPath,
                            UriKind.Absolute);
    var resources = new Resources(oDataUri);
    resources.SendingRequest2 += new
        EventHandler<SendingRequest2EventArgs>(
            delegate (object sender,
                        SendingRequest2EventArgs e)
    {
        // This event handler is needed to set
        // the authentication code we got when
        // we logged on.
        e.RequestMessage.SetHeader(OAuthHeader,
        authenticationHeader);
    });
    return resources;
}
```

21. The next three methods are to demonstrate reading, updating, and creating
records through OData:

```
public System.Collections.ArrayList GetVehicleNameList()
{
    System.Collections.ArrayList vehicleNames;
    vehicleNames = new System.Collections.ArrayList();

    var resources = this.MakeResources();
    resources.ConVMSVehicleTables.AddQueryOption(
        "DataAreaId", request.company);
    foreach (var vehicle in resources.ConVMSVehicleTables)
    {
        vehicleNames.Add(vehicle.Name);
    }
    return vehicleNames;
}
public Boolean UpdateVehicleNames()
{
    var resources = this.MakeResources();
    resources.ConVMSVehicleTables.AddQueryOption(
        "DataAreaId", request.company);
    foreach (var vehicle in resources.ConVMSVehicleTables)
    {
        vehicle.Name= vehicle.VehicleId
            + " : OData did it";
        resources.UpdateObject(vehicle);
    }
    try
    {
        resources.SaveChanges();
    }
    catch (Exception e)
    {
        response = e.InnerException.Message;
        return false;
    }
    return true;
}
public Boolean CreateNewVehicle(
    ConVMSVehicleTable _newVehicle)
{
    var resources = this.MakeResources();
    _newVehicle.DataAreaId = request.company;
    resources.AddToConVMSVehicleTables(_newVehicle);
    try
    {
        resources.SaveChanges();
```

```
    }
    catch (Exception e)
    {
        response = e.InnerException.Message;
        return false;
    }
    return true;
}
```

22. Finally, we can write our main method. Open the `Program.cs` file and ensure that we have the following `using` statements at the top:

```
using System;
using ConODataTest.Microsoft.Dynamics.DataEntities;
```

23. Write the `Main` method as follows (use the application ID you generated from your Azure AD application):

```
static void Main(string[] args)
{
    ODataApplicationContract appContract;
    appContract = new ODataApplicationContract();
    appContract.resource =
"https://usnconeboxax1aos.cloud.onebox.dynamics.com";
    appContract.applicationId = "<your application Id>";

    ODataUserContract userContract = new
        ODataUserContract();
    Console.WriteLine("Use your Microsoft Dynamics 365 Finance /
     Supply Chain Management");
    Console.Write("O365 Username: ");
    userContract.userName = Console.ReadLine();
    Console.Write("O365 Password: ");
    userContract.password = Console.ReadLine();
    Console.WriteLine("This is your tenant, such as yourdomain.com
     or <yourtenant>.onmicrosoft.com");
    Console.Write("O365 Domain: ");
    userContract.domain = Console.ReadLine();
    ODataTest test = new ConODataTest.ODataTest();
    test.userContract = userContract;
    test.appContract = appContract;
    if (!test.Authenticate())
    {
        Console.WriteLine(test.response);
    }
    test.request = new ConODataTest.ODataRequestContract();
    test.request.company = "USMF";
    System.Collections.ArrayList vehicleNames =
```

```
        test.GetVehicleNameList();
        foreach (var vehicleName in vehicleNames)
        {
            Console.WriteLine(vehicleName);
        }

        Console.WriteLine("Changing vehicle descriptions");
        test.UpdateVehicleNames();

        ConVMSVehicleTable vehicle = new ConVMSVehicleTable();

        Console.WriteLine("Create a new Vehicle");
        Console.Write("Vehicle Id: ");
        vehicle.VehicleId = Console.ReadLine();
        Console.Write("Vehicle group: ");
        vehicle.VehicleGroupId = Console.ReadLine();
        Console.Write("Description: ");
        vehicle.Name = Console.ReadLine();
        test.CreateNewVehicle(vehicle);
        Console.WriteLine("Press enter to continue.");
        Console.ReadLine();
    }
```

24. To see what is going on, add some breakpoints and use the debugger and run it (press *F5*); don't step into code that would open `ODataClient.cs`, as this can take a long time to open.

How it works...

To describe this, it is best to step through the key parts of the code.

The first part was clicking on **Save** on the `ODataClient.tt` file. This created the class by reading the URL we entered in the `metadataDocumentURI` variable. When the file is saved, it triggers the generation of code using metadata from Dynamics 365 for Finance and Supply Chain Management. If you click on **Save**, and then cancel the security warning, the `ODataClient.cs` file will be emptied. Unless we set the `TempFilePath` string constant, the entire metadata will be added to the `ODataClient.cs` file. This will not only make the file slow to open, but it can also cause errors when the project is run. There is a maximum size for string constants in C# projects that is the total for all string constants in the project.

Within the code we wrote, the first key part is the authentication, which works by authenticating with Azure AD and fetching the authentication, which is used with each submission request. The authorization code was determined in the `GetAuthorization` method.

The logon URI is always `https://login.windows.net/` plus your domain. If your O365 account was `julia@contoso.com`, the URI would be `https://login.windows.net/contoso.com`.

We can't send a username and password directly; we have to create a credential using the following code (from the `ActiveDirectory` namespace):

```
UserPasswordCredential credential = new
    UserPasswordCredential(
        userContract.userName, userContract.password);
```

The authentication is performed by the following code:

```
Task<AuthenticationResult> task = authenticationContext.AcquireTokenAsync(
    appContract.resource,
    appContract.applicationId, credential);

task.Wait();
AuthenticationResult authenticationResult = task.Result;
```

This differs from the current Microsoft sample code, as we now have to use an asynchronous call; using a task, the `task.wait()` line, essentially makes the code execute synchronously. This is OK for sample code, but it is more useful to use an asynchronous call when writing a production application as we can create a more user-responsive application.

The `Authenticate` method calls the `GetAuthorization` method and does two things. First, we have a `try catch` statement to return a nicer message to the user upon failure (we will populate the `response` public variable and return false); secondly, this is where the `authenticationHeader` variable is set. This we will need for the requests we make.

Within the `Program` class, in the `Main` method, we will construct `ODataUserContract` and complete the variables for `username`, `password`, and `domain` using the `Console.ReadLine()` method. We will construct the `ODataTest` class and call `Authenticate()`.

Once authenticated, we can work with the data. The three test methods, `GetVehicleNameList`, `UpdateVehicleNames`, and `CreateNewVehicle`, all have a similar pattern.

Each method makes a call to `MakeResources`, which is done by the following lines of code:

```
string entityRootPath = appContract.resource + "/data";
Uri oDataUri = new Uri(entityRootPath,
                       UriKind.Absolute);
var resources = new Resources(oDataUri);
resources.SendingRequest2 += new
    EventHandler<SendingRequest2EventArgs>(
       delegate (object sender,
         SendingRequest2EventArgs e)
{
    e.RequestMessage.SetHeader(OAuthHeader,
        authenticationHeader);
});
```

The `entityRootPath` variable is the SCM URL plus `data`; on the development virtual machine, this is `https://usnconeboxax1aos.cloud.onebox.dynamics.com/data`. We can specify HTTP headers on the request, so we have to add an event handler. This, essentially, sets the `Authorization` header property, which is what `OAuthHeader` constants equate to.

Each of the methods can then do what they need to; all requests are to use the `resources` object and, when each request is made, the event handler will be called to set the `Authorization` header property.

The following line sets the company; however, if we omit this, it will use the user's default company, which may be desirable in some cases:

```
resources.ConVMSVehicleTables.AddQueryOption(
    "DataAreaId",
    request.company);
```

The first example was to read `ConWHSVehicleTableEntity` into a list, which was done using the following code:

```
//System.Collections.ArrayList vehicleNames;
foreach (var vehicle in resources.ConWHSVehicleTables)
{
    vehicleNames.Add(vehicle.Description);
}
```

The request to the server is done when it reaches `resources.ConVMSVehicleTables`, which is when the data is actually read. The `vehicleNames.Add(...)` function simply adds our chosen field to a list. You may wonder why the resource's object knows to call the collection `ConVMSVehicleTables` and the singleton `ConVMSVehicleTable`. This is determined from the `PublicCollectionName` and `PublicEntityName` properties we specified when we created the `ConVMSVehicleTableEntity` data entity.

The next example was how to update data and was done by writing the following piece of code:

```
foreach (var vehicle in resources.ConVMSVehicleTables)
{
    vehicle.Description = vehicle.VehicleId +
                          " : OData did it";
    resources.UpdateObject(vehicle);
}
try
{
    resources.SaveChanges();
}
catch (Exception e)
{
    response = e.InnerException.Message;
    return false;
}
return true;
```

The `resoures.UpdateObject(object)` method records that we have made a change, but does not write this back. The changes are actually saved by the `resources.SaveChanges()` method. This will call SCM's validation logic for the record and, if this fails, it will throw an exception. The `e.InnerException.Messages` is actually JSON, and you can traverse this by giving the message back to the users.

The next example is to create a new vehicle. This is very simple code. We will just create an instance of the `ConVMSVehicelTable` class, populate it with the required values (`VehicleId`, `DataAreaId`, `VehicleGroupId`, and so on), and call the appropriate `AddTo` method. In this case, it is `AddToConVMSVehicleTables(ConVMSVehicleTable)`.

There is a lot we can do with OData, and the best way to learn is to use this example.

See also

The following links contain simple examples of OData, SOAP, and JSON. You may wish to change the code to match the patterns in this recipe as you use them:

- *Sample projects from Microsoft: Dynamics-AX-Integration* (https://github.com/Microsoft/Dynamics-AX-Integration/tree/master/ServiceSamples

- *Data management and integration by using data entities* (https://docs.microsoft.com/en-us/dynamics365/unified-operations/dev-itpro/data-entities/data-management-integration-data-entity?toc=/fin-and-ops/toc.json)

- *OData protocol* (https://docs.microsoft.com/en-us/dynamics365/unified-operations/dev-itpro/data-entities/odata?toc=/fin-and-ops/toc.json)

- *NuGet* (http://www.nuget.org/)

11
Consuming and Exposing Services

This chapter focuses on how to create services in SCM and how to consume them in external applications. This does not include OData services, which were covered in Chapter 10, *Data Management, OData, and Office*.

The creation of services within SCM is relatively straightforward and intuitive. This is a benefit of the patterns we used when writing code; for example, the code that was written to use the SysOpearation framework has a controller that constructs a data contract and a class to process that data contract. The decoupled nature of the development patterns that are used in SCM lends itself very well to the creation of services.

SCM is a cloud-first solution, which means we need to consider security. When accessing an SCM service, we also need to ensure that the consumer has access to SCM and has permission to access that web service. Even when deploying on-premises, security is still a concern, and our solutions need to work when deployed both on-premises and in the cloud.

For those migrating from Microsoft Dynamics AX 2012, the **Application Integration Framework (AIF)** has been removed in this release, so document services are not available; this has been replaced by OData. Custom services are still available, but no longer require the AIF. They are accessed using the paths defined by the Service Group, Service, and Operation levels. We will see this later in this chapter.

Another change from Dynamics AX 2012 is the move from XML to JSON, which is the preferred method of interaction with the API. JSON may be new to most X++ developers, but there is a lot of technical guidance available online regarding how to use it.

This chapter covers the following recipes:

- Creating a service
- Consuming a SOAP service in an external application
- Consuming a JSON service in an external application
- Consuming an external service within F&O

Technical requirement

You can find the code files for this chapter on GitHub at `https://github.com/ PacktPublishing/Extending-Microsoft-Dynamics-365-Finance-and-Supply-Chain- Management-Cookbook-Second-Edition/blob/master/Chapter%2011.axpp`.

Creating a service

There are three parts to creating a new service:

- Creating a class that contains the business logic
- Creating a service that has operations that reference operations to the class's methods
- Creating a service group

The service group is a collection of one or more services and acts as the service reference, should we consume it within Visual Studio. We will see how this translates to a **Uniform Resource Identifier** (**URI**) in the next recipe.

In this example, we will have two service operations: one to get a list of vehicles, and one to update a vehicle's group. The XML documentation has been omitted to save space.

Getting ready

We will just need a Dynamics 365 for Finance & Operations Visual Studio project open. Since we are continuing the development of the Vehicle Management System, these recipes are best followed with this project open. Even so, the code that needs to be written should be easy to refactor for your own purposes.

How to do it...

To create the service, follow these steps:

1. Create a new class that will hold our service methods and name it `ConVMSVehicleServices`.

2. The first service will be used to update the `Vehicle` service group, for which we have a contract and processing class already created (`ConVMSVehicleGroupChangeContract`, `ConWVMVehicleGroupChange`) to write this method. Write this method like so:

```
public void ChangeVehicleGroup(ConVMSVehicleGroupChangeContract
_contract)
{
 ConVMSVehicleGroupChange changeGroup = new
  ConVMSVehicleGroupChange();
 changeGroup.Run(_contract);
}
```

 This will work, but the consumer will not thank us for the lack of error handling. We could either return a Boolean on success or write a return contract. A return contract is the most useful way to return the result status.

3. To allow a meaningful reply, we will create a data contract class. Create a new class called `ConVMSMessageContract` and complete it as follows:

```
[DataContract]
class ConVMSMessageContract
{
    boolean success;
    str message;
    [DataMember]
    public boolean Success(boolean _success = success)
    {
        success = _success;
        return success;
    }
    [DataMember]
    public str Message(str _message = message)
    {
        message = _message;
        return message;
    }
}
```

4. Open the `ConVMSVehicleServices` class and change the `changeVehicleGroup` method, as follows:

```
public ConVMSMessageContract changeVehicleGroup(
    ConVMSVehicleGroupChangeContract _contract)
{
    ConVMSMessageContract message = new ConVMSMessageContract();
    ConVMSVehicleGroupChange changeGroup = new
     ConVMSVehicleGroupChange();

    try
    {
        if (_contract.validate() && updateGroup.Validate())
        {
            updateGroup.Run(_contract);
            message.Success(true);
        }
        else
        {
            message.Success(false);
            // Could not update vehicle %1 to vehicle group %2
            message.Message(
                strFmt("@ConVMS:CouldNotUpdateGroup",
                _contract.VehicleId(),
_contract.VehicleGroupId())));
        }
    }
    catch
    {
        message.Success(false);
        //Could not update vehicle %1 to vehicle group %2
        message.Message(
                strFmt("@ConVMS:CouldNotUpdateGroup",
                _contract.VehicleId(),
_contract.VehicleGroupId())));
    }
    return message;
}
```

5. Next, let's try and get a little adventurous and return a list of vehicles. In this method, we will return a list of contracts, each representing a vehicle record. First, we will need a contract to store vehicle data; create one as follows:

```
[DataContract]
class ConVMSVehicleTableContract
{
    ConVMSVehicleId vehicleId;
```

```
Description description;
ConVMSVehRegNum vehRegNum;
ConVMSAcquiredDate acquiredDate;
ConVMSVehicleType vehicleType;
ConVMSVehicleGroupId vehicleGroupId;

[DataMember]
public ConVMSVehicleGroupId VehicleGroupId(
     ConVMSVehicleGroupId _vehicleGroupId = vehicleGroupId)
{
    vehicleGroupId = _vehicleGroupId;
    return vehicleGroupId;
}

[DataMember]
public ConVMSAcquiredDate AcquiredDate(
    ConVMSAcquiredDate _acquiredDate = acquiredDate)
{
    acquiredDate = _acquiredDate;
    return acquiredDate;
}

[DataMember]
public ConVMSVehicleId VehicleId(
    ConVMSVehicleId _vehicleId = vehicleId)
{
    vehicleId = _vehicleId;
    return vehicleId;
}

[DataMember]
public ConVMSVehicleType VehicleType(
    ConVMSVehicleType _vehicleType = vehicleType)
{
    vehicleType = _vehicleType;
    return vehicleType;
}

[DataMember]
public ConVMSVehRegNum VehRegNum(
    ConVMSVehRegNum _vehRegNum = vehRegNum)
{
    vehRegNum = _vehRegNum;
    return vehRegNum;
}

[DataMember]
public Description Description(
```

```
        Description _description = description)
    {

        description = _description;
        return description;

    }

}
```

We could simply use the table as the contract, but using a data contract class allows us greater control over the data that's passed between F&O and the external application that is using the service.

6. Close the code window for the contract class and open the code window for the `ConVMSVehicleServices` class.

7. We cannot return an array of classes in F&O in the same way that C# can; instead, we need to construct a `List` and tell the compiler the type that the list contains. This is done by the `AifCollectionType` attribute, which was added to the start of the method. Complete the method, as follows:

```
[AifCollectionType('return', Types::Class,
classStr(ConVMSVehicleTableContract))]
public List GetVehicles()
{
    List vehicleList;
    ConVMSVehicleTable vehicles;
    ConVMSVehicleTableContract contract;

    vehicleList = new List(Types::Class);

    while select vehicles
    {
        contract = new ConVMSVehicleTableContract();
        contract.VehicleId(vehicles.VehicleId);
        contract.VehicleGroupId(vehicles.VehicleGroupId);
        contract.VehicleType(vehicles.VehicleType);
        contract.VehRegNum(vehicles.VehRegNum);
        contract.AcquiredDate(vehicles.AcquiredDate);
        vehicleList.addEnd(contract);
    }
    return vehicleList;
}
```

8. Now, we have our two methods, which will become our service methods. To create the service, add a new item to the project by choosing **Services** from the left-hand list and **Service** from the right. **Name** the service `ConVMSVehicleServices` and click on **Add**.

9. Select the root **ConVMSVehicleServices** node and set the **Class** property to `ConWHSVehicleServices` (the class we wrote).

10. Enter a description for the service, such as `Provides services for vehicles`.

11. The **External Name** property should be specified as a simpler form of the service name. As it will be within a service group, we don't need the prefix. `VehicleServices` is appropriate for this property.

12. Enter a namespace in the **Namespace** property, such as `http://schemas.contoso.com/ConVMS`. The URL does not have to exist as it is used as a namespace for the service.

13. Right-click on the **Service Operations** node and select **New Service Operation**.

14. Select one of the two methods in the **Method** property and make the **Name** property the same as the **Method** property.

15. Repeat this for the next service method.

16. Save and close the service designer window.

17. Create a new item in our project, this time, **Service Group** from the **Services** list. Name it `ConVMSServices`.

18. Enter `Contoso vehicle management services` in the **Description** property.

19. Locate the `ConVMSVehicleServices` service in the project or **Application Explorer** and drag it onto the **ConVMSServices** node in the designer. This adds the service to the service group.

20. Remove the `ConVMS` prefix from the **Name** property as this is superfluous.

21. Save and close all the designers and build the project.

How it works...

The first service we wrote simply created a facade for the class we had already written. When we write services, we usually write them in a single class that acts as a facade to other business logic. The aim of a facade is to simplify the instantiation and usage of a class. While doing this, we should keep the service methods we write within a topic, such as services methods that interact with vehicles. We wouldn't add methods that interact with service orders; these should be placed in a new class.

Since the `ConVMSVehicleGroupChange` class already accepted a contract as an input parameter to its `Run` method, the service method was relatively straightforward. In fact, we could have created a service directly to this class, but this wouldn't be good practice as this limits future extensions by tying the class directly to the service method.

The service method in our case accepted the same data contract that we passed to the `ConVMSVehicleGroupChange.Run` method, but this isn't always the case. We might have to look up some data in the method and perform more heavy lifting in the service method. The difference in our case was to construct a reply message contract that is returned to the caller.

The second method we wrote had a new concept, in that it returned a collection. In C#, we would return a typed collection or an array (`MyClass[]`), and we could use the `foreach` command to iterate through it. This is not supported in X++, so we have to return a `List` instead. Since we actually want to return a typed collection to the caller, we will use the `AifDataCollectionType` attribute to tell the compiler how to do this. You may notice that `DataCollection` is added to some data methods for the same purpose. This is correct for data contracts, but it does not work when it's used to write service methods. If we wrote an envelope data contract for the vehicle list, we would use `DataCollection` alongside the `DataMethod` decoration. An example of this is as follows:

```
[DataContract]
public class ConVMSVehicleTableListEnvelopeContract
{
    List vehicles;
    [DataMethod, DataCollection(Types::class,
     classStr(ConVMSVehicleTableContract)]
    public List Vehicles(List _vehicles = vehicles)
    {
        _vehicles = vehicles;
        return vehicles;
    }
}
```

The service method, in this case, would construct and return this data contract, and the `AifCollectionType` attribute would not be required.

The next part was to create a service and service group, which simply instructs the system to generate public services exposing the methods we added to the service.

We will see how this is used in the next recipe.

Consuming a SOAP service in an external application

In this recipe, we will create a new C# project to consume the service we created in the previous recipe.

Before we start, we should understand the Azure AD authentication concepts we explained in the *Reading, writing, and updating data through OData* recipe in `Chapter 10`, *Data Management, Odata, and Office*. Many of the concepts in the following recipes extend the concepts we covered in this chapter. In this example, we will create a SOAP service reference.

Getting ready

This is a continuation of the *Creating a service* recipe, so it must be completed before we can continue.

How to do it...

To consume an F&O service using SOAP, follow these steps:

1. Create a new project; this time, choose **Visual C#** from the **Templates** node and then **Console Application** from the right. Name the project `ConServiceTest` and place it in the project folders that we set up for source control. Ensure that the namespace is also `ConServiceTest`.

2. Now, we need to install some NuGet packages. Within Visual Studio, navigate to **Tools | NuGet Package Manager | Package Manager Console**.

3. In the Package Manager console, type in the following command:

   ```
   Install-Package Microsoft.IdentityModel.Clients.ActiveDirectory
   ```

4. Right-click on the **References** node in the project and choose **Add Service Reference**.

5. Enter `https://usnconeboxax1aos.cloud.onebox.dynamics.com/soap/services/ConVMSServices` in the **Address** field and click on **Go**.

    This is the F&O URL with `/soap/services/` added, followed by the service group name.

6. Expand the **ConVMSServices** node and select **VehicleServices**.

7. Change the **Namespace** field from `servicereference1` to `ConVMS` and click on **OK**.

8. Create a new class called `Authenticate`.

We will reuse this class to simplify this process. This also allows us to reuse the code throughout the project.

9. We will need two classes: the contract class so that we can pass data to the `Authenticate` class, and the `Authenticate` class itself.

These concepts are the same as the ones we described in the *Reading, writing, and updating data through OData* recipe of `Chapter 10`, *Data Management, Odata, and Office*; they are just separated in order to make the code reusable.

10. We need to state which references we are going to use. Replace the using statements at the top of the class with the following:

```
using System;
using System.Threading.Tasks;
using Microsoft.IdentityModel.Clients.ActiveDirectory;
```

11. Write the following piece of code:

```
public class AuthenticationContract
{
    public string UserName { get; set; }
    public string Password { get; set; }
    public string Domain { get; set; }
    public string ApplicationId { get; set; }
    public string Resource { get; set; }
    public string Response { get; set; }
}
```

12. This time, we will use property methods instead, as this allows for more flexibility. For example, if we omit the `set;` argument, the property is read-only:

```
public class Authenticate
{
    public const string OAuthHeader = "Authorization";
    string bearerkey;
    public AuthenticationContract Authentication
        { get; set; }
    public string BearerKey
    {
        get { return bearerkey;}
    }
```

```
public string GetSecurityURI()
{
    UriBuilder uri;
    uri = new UriBuilder(
        "https://login.windows.net/" +
        Authentication.Domain);
    return uri.ToString();
}
public UserPasswordCredential GetCredential()
{
    string uri = this.GetSecurityURI();
    UserPasswordCredential credential;

    credential =
        new UserPasswordCredential(
            Authentication.UserName,
            Authentication.Password);
    return credential;
}
private AuthenticationResult GetAuthorization()
{
    UserPasswordCredential credential;
    credential = GetCredential();

    AuthenticationContext context
    = new AuthenticationContext(GetSecurityURI());

    Task<AuthenticationResult> task =
        context.AcquireTokenAsync(
            Authentication.Resource.TrimEnd('/'),
            Authentication.ApplicationId,
            credential);

    task.Wait();
    return task.Result;
}

public Boolean GetAuthenticationHeader()
{
    AuthenticationResult result;
    try
    {
        result = GetAuthorization();
        // This gets the authorization token, this
        // must be set on the Http header for all
        // requests
        bearerkey =
            result.CreateAuthorizationHeader();
```

```
        }
        catch (Exception e)
        {
            if (e.InnerException != null)
            {
                Authentication.Response =
                        "Authentication failed: " +
                            e.InnerException.Message;
            }
            else
            {
                Authentication.Response =
                    "Authentication failed: " + e.Message;
            }
            return false;
        }
        Authentication.Response = "OK";
        return true;
    }
}
```

13. You can close the code editor for this class.

14. Create a new class called SOAPUtil.

 The code in this class was *inspired* by a sample utility at https://github.com/Microsoft/Dynamics-AX-Integration/blob/master/ServiceSamples/SoapUtility/SoapHelper.cs.

15. Set the using declarations like so:

```
using System;
using System.Linq;
using System.ServiceModel;
using System.ServiceModel.Channels;
```

16. To simplify usage, we will need a utility class. This should be written as follows:

```
public class SoapUtil
{
    public const string OAuthHeader = "Authorization";

    public static string GetServiceURI(
        string _service,
        string _d365URI)
    {
        string serviceName = _service.Split('.').Last();
```

```
        if (serviceName == "")
        {
            serviceName = _service;
        }

        return _d365OURI.TrimEnd('/') + "/soap/services/"
                                + serviceName;
    }
    public static EndpointAddress GetEndpointAddress(
        string _uri)
    {
        EndpointAddress address;
        address = new EndpointAddress(_uri);
        return address;
    }
    public static Binding GetBinding(
        EndpointAddress _address)
    {
        BasicHttpBinding binding;
        binding = new BasicHttpBinding(
            BasicHttpSecurityMode.Transport);

        // Set binding timeout and other configuration
        // settings
        binding.ReaderQuotas.MaxStringContentLength =
            int.MaxValue;
        binding.ReaderQuotas.MaxArrayLength = int.MaxValue;
        binding.ReaderQuotas.MaxNameTableCharCount =
            int.MaxValue;

        binding.ReceiveTimeout = TimeSpan.MaxValue;
        binding.SendTimeout = TimeSpan.MaxValue;
        binding.MaxReceivedMessageSize = int.MaxValue;

        var httpsBindingElement =
            binding.CreateBindingElements().
OfType<HttpsTransportBindingElement>().FirstOrDefault();
        if (httpsBindingElement != null)
        {
            // Largest possible is 100000, otherwise throws
            // an exception
            httpsBindingElement.MaxPendingAccepts = 10000;
        }

        var httpBindingElement =
            binding.CreateBindingElements().OfType<
             HttpTransportBindingElement>().FirstOrDefault();
        if (httpBindingElement != null)
```

```
    {
        httpBindingElement.MaxPendingAccepts = 10000;
    }
    return binding;
  }
}
```

 The `GetBinding` method is the key one here. We will authenticate through what is called a bearer key, which is implemented by setting the `Authorization` header variable. Therefore, we will write a binding manually so that the binding in `App.Config` does not interfere.

17. Close the code editor and create a new class called `UpdateVehicleGroup`.

18. Set the `using` statements as follows:

```
using System.ServiceModel.Channels;
using System.ServiceModel;
```

19. Write the following method:

```
public ConVMS.ConVMSMessageContract UpdateSOAP(
    AuthenticationContract _authContract,
    ConVMS.ConVMSVehicleGroupChangeContract _change)
{
    Authenticate auth = new Authenticate();
    auth.Authentication = _authContract;
    ConVMS.ConVMSMessageContract message;
    // If we fail to get the authorization bearer
    // key, stop and return the error through
    // the message contract
    if (!auth.GetAuthenticationHeader())
    {
        message = new ConVMS.ConVMSMessageContract();
        message.Success = false;
        message.Message = auth.Authentication.Response;
        return message;
    }
    string bearerKey = auth.BearerKey;

    string endPoint;
    endPoint = SoapUtil.GetServiceURI(
        "ConVMSServices",
        _authContract.Resource);

    EndpointAddress address;
    address= SoapUtil.GetEndpointAddress(endPoint);
```

```
Binding binding = SoapUtil.GetBinding(address);

ConVMS.VehicleServicesClient client;
client = new ConVMS.VehicleServicesClient(
            binding, address);
ConVMS.CallContext conContext;

conContext = new ConVMS.CallContext();
conContext.Company = "USMF";
conContext.Language = "en-us";
conContext.PartitionKey = "initial";

var channel = client.InnerChannel;
// we don't use the context, it is used to affect
// the channel so that we can set the outgoing
// message properties
// Using is used so that it is disposed of
// correctly.
using (OperationContextScope context
    = new OperationContextScope(channel))
{
    //Set the authentication bearer key
    HttpRequestMessageProperty requestMessage;
    requestMessage = new HttpRequestMessageProperty();
    requestMessage.Headers[SoapUtil.OAuthHeader] =
        bearerKey;
    OperationContext.Current.OutgoingMessageProperties[
        HttpRequestMessageProperty.Name] =
            requestMessage;

    // setup the message
    ConVMS.UpdateVehicleGroup update;
    update = new ConVMS.UpdateVehicleGroup();
    update._contract = _change;
    update.CallContext = conContext;
    ConVMS.UpdateVehicleGroupResponse response;
    message = new ConVMS.ConVMSMessageContract();
    response =
        ((ConVMS.VehicleServices)channel).
            UpdateVehicleGroup(update);
    // the response contains the current info log
    // and the return result, which the return type
    // we returned in the D365FO method.
    message = response.result;
}
return message;
}
```

20. Let's see if it works. In the `Program.cs` file, write the following piece of code as the `Main` method:

```
static void Main(string[] args)
{
    AuthenticationContract authContract;
    authContract = new AuthenticationContract();
    authContract.ApplicationId = "<your application Id>";
    authContract.Resource =
     "https://usnconeboxax1aos.cloud.onebox.dynamics.com/";
    Console.WriteLine("Use your Microsoft Dynamics 365 Finance /
     Supply Chain management account");
    Console.Write("O365 Username: ");
    authContract.UserName = Console.ReadLine();
    Console.Write("O365 Password: ");
    authContract.Password = Console.ReadLine();
    Console.WriteLine("This is your tenant, such as
     yourdomain.com");
    string defaultDomain =
        authContract.UserName.Split('@').Last<string>();
    Console.WriteLine("O365 Domain: ");
    Console.Write("(" + defaultDomain + ") :");
    authContract.Domain = Console.ReadLine();
    if (authContract.Domain == "")
    {
        authContract.Domain = defaultDomain;
    }

    UpdateVehicleGroup update = new UpdateVehicleGroup();
    ConVMS.ConVMSVehicleGroupChangeContract change;
    change = new ConVMS.ConVMSVehicleGroupChangeContract();
    change.VehicleId = "X0002";
    change.VehicleGroupId = "Leased";

    ConVMS.ConVMSMessageContract message;
    message = update.UpdateSOAP(authContract, change);
    if (message.Success)
    {
        Console.WriteLine("Success!");
    }
    else
    {
        Console.WriteLine(message.Message);
    }
    Console.ReadLine();
}
```

21. Build and run the project.

How it works...

When we added `Service Reference`, Visual Studio created a type for each contract the service reference uses, and a client class in order to interact with the services referenced by it. It corresponds to the Service Group within Dynamics AX 365 for Operations. This is a lot more helpful than what is provided by JSON, which is why this recipe was written before the JSON method. In the next recipe, we will see that we can deserialize SOAP types from JSON.

The `Authenticate` class is very similar to the class we wrote in `Chapter 10`, *Data Management, Odata, and Office*, just a little more elegant. We are simply getting an authentication token (known as a bearer key), which is used when the requests are made.

The `UpdateVehicleGroups` class has a little more to it. The first part is to get the authorization code, which is just a variation of the code that was used for accessing data through OData. It varies more from this point on.

When we constructed the client with `client = new ConVMS.VehicleServiceClient(binding, address);`, we used a binding that we constructed manually. We did this because we don't want the `App.Config` bindings to interfere. The bindings in `App.Config` are generated automatically for us when we create or update the service reference. In our case, we don't want anything special; we just want a basic binding. The authentication is done by setting the `Authorization` header property to the bearer key (authentication token).

The next new part is a legacy from AX 2012, that is, the `CallContext` class. This was used for setting the company, language, and also the credentials to use. This is no longer mandatory and is filled in for completeness. `Partition` is still active but is only used for certain testing scenarios. The client can no longer access any partition other than `"initial"`.

The next part looks complicated, but it's the only way we can set the request header variables. In this section, we will set up a `HttpRequestMessageProperty` instance in order to set the authorization header variable, like so:

```
HttpRequestMessageProperty requestMessage;
requestMessage = new HttpRequestMessageProperty();
requestMessage.Headers[SoapUtil.OAuthHeader] = bearerKey;
```

This is then passed to the current outgoing message properties with the following line:

```
OperationContext.Current.OutgoingMessageProperties[
    HttpRequestMessageProperty.Name] = requestMessage;
```

We will need to ensure that this is cleaned up afterward, so this is why we enclosed the code in the following using clause:

```
using (OperationContextScope context
            = new OperationContextScope(channel))
```

The code that does the actual work is as follows:

```
ConVMS.UpdateVehicleGroup update;
update = new ConVMS.UpdateVehicleGroup();
update._contract = _change;
update.CallContext = conContext;
ConVMS.UpdateVehicleGroupResponse response;
message = new ConVMS.ConWHSMessageContract();
response = ((ConVMS.VehicleService)channel).UpdateVehicleGroup(update);
message = response.result;
```

Within the ConVMS service, the reference is a class called UpdateVehicleGroup, which is the name of the service method we wrote. The declaration was as follows:

```
public ConVMSMessageContract UpdateVehicleGroup(
        ConVMSVehicleGroupChangeContract _contract)
```

Visual Studio created this class because of the input parameter. The class contains properties for the CallContext property, which is always created, as well as for the _contract method input parameter.

See also

You can refer to the following links for further information:

- Troubleshooting service authentication: https://docs.microsoft.com/en-us/dynamics365/unified-operations/dev-itpro/data-entities/troubleshoot-service-authentication.
- Service endpoints: https://docs.microsoft.com/en-us/dynamics365/unified-operations/dev-itpro/data-entities/services-home-page. This is a little generic, but it contains links to some useful code samples.

Consuming a JSON service in an external application

In this recipe, we will extend the previous C# project to consume the service using JSON.

The primary difference is that JSON will not create the contract and client classes for us; we will need to write them ourselves. We will use a NuGet package to help with the serialization and deserialization of C# classes to JSON.

Getting ready

This recipe is a continuation of the *Consuming a SOAP service in an external application* recipe, which must be completed before we can continue. This recipe builds on the existing `ConServiceTest` C# project that we created in the previous recipe.

How to do it...

To consume an F&O service using JSON, follow these steps:

1. Let's take a look at what JSON looks like. This will help the recipe make more sense as we progress. Open the following URL using Internet Explorer: `https://usnconeboxax1aos.cloud.onebox.dynamics.com/api/services/`.

2. This will ask you to open `services.json`. Click on **Open**, which opens a file in Visual Studio that contains all the services that were exposed. The file will contain our service in the following format:

   ```
   {"ServiceGroups":[ ...
   {"Name":"ConVMSServices"},{"Name":"CuesServiceGroup"}, etc.
   ```

   Now, open the following URL in Internet Explorer: `https://usnconeboxax1aos.cloud.onebox.dynamics.com/api/services/ConVMSServices`.

3. This time, the JSON file is called `CONWHSServices.json` and contains the following information:

   ```
   {"Services":[{"Name":"VehicleServices"}]}
   ```

4. You can do the same by adding `VehicleServices` to the URL, which will open a JSON file with the following lines of code:

```
{"Operations":[{"Name":"UpdateVehicleGroup"},{"Name":"GetVehicles"}
]}
```

5. The JSON for the `GetVehicles` operation is as follows (this can be seen by adding `GetVehicles` to the URL from *Step 4*):

```
{"Parameters":[],"Return":{"Name":"return","Type":"ConVMSVehicleTab
leContract[]"}}
```

6. Using the same method as in *Step 5*, we can see that the JSON for `UpdateVehicleGroup` is as follows:

```
{"Parameters":[{"Name":"_contract","Type":"ConVMSVehicleGroupChange
Contract"}],"Return":{"Name":"return","Type":"ConVMSMessageContract
"}}
```

The take away here is to note that we have three levels: `ServiceGroups`, `Services`, and `Operations`. These correlate to how we create services within F&O.

7. Open the Package Manager console from **Tools | NuGet Package Manager** and type in the following command:

```
Install-Package Newtonsoft.Json
```

8. To simplify usage, create a class named `JsonUtil`. The code in this class should be as follows:

```
using System;
using System.Linq;
using System.ServiceModel;
using System.ServiceModel.Channels;
namespace ConServiceTest.Json
{
    public class JsonUtil
    {
        public const string OAuthHeader = "Authorization";
        public static string GetServiceURI(
            string _servicePath, string _d365OURI)
        {
            return _d365OURI.TrimEnd('/')
                + "/api/services/"
                + _servicePath;
```

```
        }
        public static EndpointAddress GetEndpointAddress(string
        _uri)
        {
            EndpointAddress address = new EndpointAddress(_uri);
            return address;
        }
    }
}
```

9. Create a class named `JsonClient` for the C# classes that we will use to deserialize the JSON into.

10. Set up the following using declarations:

```
using System;
using System.Collections.Generic;
using Newtonsoft.Json;
using System.Net;
using System.IO;
```

11. Change the namespace to `ConServiceTest.Json`, as our classes may not be unique in the `ConServiceTest` namespace.

12. Remove the default class so that we only have a blank line inside the `namespace` braces.

13. First, we will write the classes for the `ServiceGroup` JSON, which was `{"ServiceGroups":[{"Name":"ConWHSServices"}, {etc.}"`. This is represented in C# as follows:

```
public class ServiceGroups
{
    [JsonProperty("ServiceGroups")]
    public List<ServiceGroup> ServiceGroupNames { get; set; }
}
public class ServiceGroup
{
    [JsonProperty("Name")]
    public string ServiceGroupName { get; set; }
}
```

The `JsonProperty` decoration maps the method to the JSON property.

14. We can continue this pattern for the Services and Operations levels, as shown in the following piece of code:

```
public class Services
{
    [JsonProperty("Services")]
    public List<Service> ServiceNames { get; set; }
}
public class Service
{
    [JsonProperty("Name")]
    public String Name { get; set; }
}
public class Operations
{
    [JsonProperty("Operations")]
    public List<Operation> OperationNames { get; set; }
}
public class Operation
{
    [JsonProperty("Name")]
    public string Name { get; set; }
}
```

15. Let's write a client to access the service and deserialize the data into our new classes. In our `JsonClient.cs` file, create a new class called `Client`.

16. Start the class with the following code. This will set up the global variables and constructor:

```
public class Client
{
    string d365OURI;
    Authenticate auth;
    public Client(string _d365OURI, Authenticate _auth)
    {
        d365OURI = _d365OURI;
        auth = _auth;
    }
}
```

17. Next, we will write two helper functions. The first will create a request for the supplier address, while the other will read the response from the request into a string. The code is as follows:

```
private HttpWebRequest CreateRequest(string _address)
{
    HttpWebRequest webRequest;
```

```
webRequest = (HttpWebRequest)HttpWebRequest.Create(_address);
webRequest.Method = "POST";
// the request will be empty.
webRequest.ContentLength = 0;
webRequest.Headers.Set(JsonUtil.OAuthHeader, auth.BearerKey);
return webRequest;
}
private string ReadJsonResponse(HttpWebRequest _request)
{
    string jsonString;

    using (HttpWebResponse webResponse =
     (HttpWebResponse)_request.GetResponse())
    {
        using (Stream stream = webResponse.GetResponseStream())
        {
            using (StreamReader reader = new StreamReader(stream))
            {
                jsonString = reader.ReadToEnd();
            }
        }
    }
    return jsonString;
}
```

18. Let's write the methods to read the metadata (the service groups, services, and operations). The code for this is as follows:

```
public ServiceGroups GetServiceGroups()
{
    string serviceGroupAddress = Json.JsonUtil.GetServiceURI("",
     d365OURI);
    HttpWebRequest webRequest =
     CreateRequest(serviceGroupAddress.TrimEnd('/'));
    // Must override the metadata request calls to GET as this is
    // not REST
    webRequest.Method = "GET";
    string jsonString = ReadJsonResponse(webRequest);
    ServiceGroups serviceGroups;
    serviceGroups =
     JsonConvert.DeserializeObject<ServiceGroups>(jsonString);
    return serviceGroups;
}
public Services GetServices(string _serviceGroup)
{
    string serviceGroupAddress =
     Json.JsonUtil.GetServiceURI(_serviceGroup, d365OURI);
```

```
    HttpWebRequest webRequest;
    webRequest = CreateRequest(serviceGroupAddress);
    // Must override the metadata request calls
    // to GET as this is not REST
    webRequest.Method = "GET";
    string jsonString = ReadJsonResponse(webRequest);

    Services services;
    services = JsonConvert.DeserializeObject<Services>(jsonString);
    return services;
}
public Operations GetOperations(string _serviceGroup, string
_vehicleService)
{
    string servicePath = _serviceGroup.TrimEnd('/') + "/" +
    _vehicleService;
    string serviceGroupAddress;
    serviceGroupAddress = Json.JsonUtil.GetServiceURI(servicePath,
    d365OURI);

    HttpWebRequest webRequest;
    webRequest = CreateRequest(serviceGroupAddress);
    // Must override the metadata request calls
    // to GET as this is not REST
    webRequest.Method = "GET";
    string jsonString = ReadJsonResponse(webRequest);

    Operations operations;
    operations =
     JsonConvert.DeserializeObject<Operations>(jsonString);
    return operations;
}
```

19. The next thing we need to do is make a call to get the vehicle list. This time, we
    are reusing the ConVMS.ConWMSVehicleTableContract type that we created
    in the previous recipe. The code for this should be written as follows:

```
public ConVMS.ConVMSVehicleTableContract[] GetVehicles(
  string _serviceGroup,
  string _service,
  string _operation)
{
    string servicePath;
    servicePath = _serviceGroup.TrimEnd('/')
        + "/" + _service.TrimEnd('/')
        + "/" + _operation;
    string serviceGroupAddress;
    serviceGroupAddress =
```

```
    Json.JsonUtil.GetServiceURI(servicePath, d365OURI);

    HttpWebRequest webRequest;
    webRequest = CreateRequest(serviceGroupAddress);
    string jsonString = ReadJsonResponse(webRequest);

    ConVMS.ConVMSVehicleTableContract[] vehicles;
    vehicles = JsonConvert.DeserializeObject
        <ConVMS.ConVMSVehicleTableContract[]>(jsonString);
    return vehicles;
}
```

You may wonder how this could possibly work. How can the
deserializer possibly know how to convert the JSON file into a class
without the JsonProperty decoration? This is because the property
methods have the same names as the property methods.

20. Let's test this now and see what happens. In the Program.cs file, comment out
the SOAP code from UpdateVehicleGroup update = ... and write the
following piece of code:

```
Authenticate auth = new Authenticate();
auth.Authentication = authContract;
if (auth.GetAuthenticationHeader())
{
    Json.Client client = new Json.Client(authContract.Resource,
     auth);

    Json.ServiceGroups serviceGroups;
    serviceGroups = client.GetServiceGroups();
    foreach (Json.ServiceGroup serviceGroup in
     serviceGroups.ServiceGroupNames)
    {
        Console.WriteLine(serviceGroup.ServiceGroupName);
    }
    Json.Services services
        = client.GetServices("ConVMSServices");
    foreach (Json.Service service
            in services.ServiceNames)
    {
        Console.WriteLine(service.Name);
    }
    Json.Operations operations = client.GetOperations(
        "ConVMSServices", "VehicleServices");
    foreach (Json.Operation operation
            in operations.OperationNames)
    {
```

```
            Console.WriteLine(operation.Name);
        }

    ConVMS.ConVMSVehicleTableContract[] vehicles =
        client.GetVehicles(
            "ConVMSServices",
            "VehicleServices",
            "GetVehicles");
    foreach (ConVMS.ConVMSVehicleTableContract vehicle
            in vehicles)
    {
        Console.WriteLine(vehicle.VehicleId);
    }
    Console.ReadKey();
}
```

21. Close the code editors and build and run the project to test it.

How it works...

The JSON method actually carries less overhead in terms of setting up the calls than SOAP. We don't need to set up any bindings; we just need to set the `Authorization` header property.

Once we have the authorization, all we need to do is send a string of JSON text to the service, which we could manually create. We use the JSON serialization and deserialize between data contract classes and text for convenience. This is generic JSON, and the code we write is the same as if we were writing for any other application that is able to use this method.

The difficult part is setting up the C# classes that we will deserialize to or serialize from. It isn't obvious at first, especially when a simple list of names, such as `ServiceGroups`, requires two classes. Thankfully, Newtonsoft has written a great NuGet package that means a lot of the work is done for us. We can also cheat a little by using SOAP to generate the contract classes, as we did for the `GetVehicles` method.

To explain this further, take the following JSON:

```
{"Services":[{"Name":"VehicleServices"}]}
```

The C# class for this was as follows:

```
public class Services
{
    [JsonProperty("Services")]
```

```
    public List<Service> ServiceNames { get; set; }
}
public class Service
{
    [JsonProperty("Name")]
    public String Name { get; set; }
}
```

The outer part of the JSON contains the `Services` property. This property is a list of `Name` properties. When the JSON is deserialized into the `Services` class, it looks for a property that is either named `Services` or has the `[JsonProperty("Services")]` decoration. In our case, `public List<Service> ServiceNames { get; set; }` has the required decoration.

This process continues. The deserializer now creates a `List` of the `Service` type. It will iterate through the JSON, mapping the `Name` JSON property to the `Service.Name` property. In this case, the `JsonProperty` decoration is not actually required as the property name is the same as the method name. The fact that it matches the name is the reason that we can use the classes created by the Service Reference.

The request is done by setting up the `HttpWebRequest` object, which sets the `Authorisation` header property to our bearer key and the `Method` property to `POST`. This is the default as most calls will be REST and these must use the `POST` method.

For metadata calls, we will set the `Method` property to `GET`, which is required for non-REST calls. Then, we will deserialize directly into the class.

The `GetVehicles` method deserializes into an array. We know this because the `GetVehicles.json` file contained the following lines of code:

```
{"Parameters":[],"Return":{"Name":"return",
 "Type":"ConVMSVehicleTableContract[]"}}
```

There's more...

Let's say we want to pass data to a JSON service, which is required by the `changeVehicleGroups` operation.

Open the following URL in Internet Explorer: `https://usnconeboxax1aos.cloud.onebox.dynamics.com/api/services /ConVMSServices/VehicleServices/changeVehicleGroup`.

The JSON file the preceding link opens contains the following lines of code:

```
{"Parameters":[{"Name":"_contract","Type":"ConVMSVehicleGroupChangeContract
"}],"Return":{"Name":"return","Type":"ConVMSMessageContract"}}
```

The actual JSON string that the request needs will follow the following pattern:

```
{"_contract":{"VehicleGroupId":"New vehicle
group","VehicleId":"X0002","hideVehicleId":0,"parmCallId":"00000000-0000-00
00-0000-000000000000","parmSessionIdx":0,"parmSessionLoginDateTime":"0001-0
1-01T00:00:00"}}
```

For this, we will need to construct a class with a `JsonProperty` of `_contract`. This is done by the following class, which should be added to `JsonClient.cs`:

```
public class UpdateVehicleParameter
{
 [JsonProperty("_contract")]
 public ConVMS.ConVMSVehicleGroupChangeContract Contract
 { get; set; }
}
```

You will need to add the following using statement to the top of the class if it hasn't been added already:

```
using Newtonsoft.Json;
```

The preceding class will now serialize to the JSON that the operation needs.

We will need a new method in our client class (which can be found in the `JsonClient.cs` file) to perform the update. This is done by writing the following piece of code:

```
public ConVMS.ConVMSMessageContract UpdateVehicleGroup(
    ConVMS.ConVMSVehicleGroupChangeContract _change,
    string _serviceGroup,
    string _service,
    string _operation)
{
    string servicePath;
    servicePath = _serviceGroup.TrimEnd('/')
        + "/" + _service.TrimEnd('/')
        + "/" + _operation;
    string serviceGroupAddress;
    serviceGroupAddress =
     Json.JsonUtil.GetServiceURI(servicePath, d365OURI);

    HttpWebRequest webRequest;
```

```
    webRequest = CreateRequest(serviceGroupAddress);

    UpdateVehicleParameter parm;
    parm = new UpdateVehicleParameter();
    parm.Contract = _change;

    string jsonOutString = JsonConvert.SerializeObject(parm);
    webRequest.ContentLength = jsonOutString.Length;

    using (Stream stream = webRequest.GetRequestStream())
    {
        using (StreamWriter writer = new StreamWriter(stream))
        {
            writer.Write(jsonOutString);
            writer.Flush();
        }
    }
    string jsonString = ReadJsonResponse(webRequest);

    ConVMS.ConVMSMessageContract msg =
     JsonConvert.DeserializeObject<
       ConVMS.ConVMSMessageContract>(jsonString);
    return msg;
}
```

The complicated part was visualizing the input parameter as a class. From that point on, the preceding method is largely the same as before. We will just write the JSON string to the web request's request stream.

Now, add a new method in the `UpdateVehicleGroup.cs` file in the `UpdateVehicleGroup` class. The method should read as follows:

```
public ConVMS.ConVMSMessageContract UpdateJSON(
    AuthenticationContract _authContract,
    ConVMS.ConVMSVehicleGroupChangeContract _change)
{
    Authenticate auth = new Authenticate();
    auth.Authentication = _authContract;
    ConVMS.ConVMSMessageContract message;
    if (!auth.GetAuthenticationHeader())
    {
        message = new ConVMS.ConVMSMessageContract();
        message.Success = false;
        message.Message = auth.Authentication.Response;
        return message;
    }
    Json.Client client = new Json.Client(_authContract.Resource, auth);
    message = client.UpdateVehicleGroup(
```

```
            _change,
            "ConVMSServices",
            "VehicleServices",
            "changeVehicleGroup");
        return message;
    }
```

This is done to simplify usage. Finally, add a section to the `Main` method of `Program.cs`, just below the existing JSON test code:

```
ConVMS.ConVMSVehicleGroupChangeContract jsonChange;
jsonChange = new ConVMS.ConVMSVehicleGroupChangeContract();
Console.Write("Vehicle Id: ");
jsonChange.VehicleId = Console.ReadLine();
Console.Write("New vehicle group: ");
jsonChange.VehicleGroupId = Console.ReadLine();

ConVMS.ConVMSMessageContract jsonMessage;
UpdateVehicleGroup jsonUpdate;
jsonUpdate = new UpdateVehicleGroup();
jsonMessage = jsonUpdate.UpdateJSON(authContract, jsonChange);
if (jsonMessage.Success)
{
    Console.WriteLine("Success!");
}
else
{
    Console.WriteLine(jsonMessage.Message);
}
```

This is just the start. You can experiment further; for example, you can deserialize the `DataSet` objects so that you can present data directly to grids in your apps.

See also...

Please refer to the following link to find out more about *Newtonsoft JSON Samples*: `http://www.newtonsoft.com/JSON/help/html/Samples.htm`.

Consuming an external service within F&O

This technique hasn't changed substantially since Dynamics AX 2012. The key difference is that we will need to manually craft the binding. We still need to create a C# project to consume the web service, and then use it as a reference within our F&O project.

The example service is a weather service provided by *Open Weather* (`https://openweathermap.org/`). There is no recommendation here. It was simply the first one I found when I searched for weather web services. The aim is to create a recipe that you can use for your web services. The chosen service, in this case, isn't relevant.

> When selecting a service to use, we must check the license terms and conditions since not all of them are free to use. Just because the license terms aren't enforced doesn't mean that the service is free to use.

Getting ready

Before we start, we need to sign up for the service. Open Weather has a free tier where you can use 60 requests per minute. This is fine for testing. To do this, open the following link and follow its instructions: `https://openweathermap.org/guide`.

Then, we just need an existing Dynamics 365 for Finance and Supply Chain Management project available with `Newtonsoft.Json` installed. This is done, as in previous recipes, by using the `Install-Package Newtonsoft.Json` command in the **NuGet Package Manager** console.

How to do it...

To create the service wrapper for the service, follow these steps:

1. Within the solution that your F&O project is held in, create a new C# Class Library project named `WeatherService`. You can do this by right-clicking on the `ConVehicleManagement` solution and choosing **Add** | **New project....**
2. Open the properties for the `WeatherService` project and change the Assembly name and Default namespace fields to `Contoso.WeatherService`.
3. Rename the `class1.cs` file to `OpenWeatherService.cs`.
4. The JSON that Open Weather provides for the Current Weather service is as follows:

```
{"coord": { "lon": 139,"lat": 35},
  "weather": [ { "id": 800, "main": "Clear",
    "description": "clear sky", "icon": "01n" } ],
  "base": "stations",
  "main": {"temp": 289.92, "pressure": 999, "humidity": 92,
    "temp_min": 288.71, "temp_max": 290.93 },
```

```
"wind": { "speed": 0.47, "deg": 107.538 },
"clouds": { "all": 2 },
"dt": 1560350192,
"sys": { "type": 3, "id": 2019346, "message": 0.0065,
  "country": "JP", "sunrise": 1560281377, "sunset": 1560333478 },
"timezone": 32400, "id": 1851632, "name": "Shuzenji", "cod": 200 }
```

5. To make this data easier to work with, we will create a class structure that matches the preceding JSON. Create a class named `OpenWeatherMap` and write the following code:

```
// required for methods added later in this recipe
using System.IO;
using NewtonSoft.Json;
public class OpenWeatherMap
{
    public OpenWeatherMapCoord coord { get; set; }
    public OpenWeatherMapMain main { get; set; }
    public string name { get; set; }
    public string country { get; set; }
}
public class OpenWeatherMapCoord
{
    public double lon { get; set; }
    public double lat { get; set; }
}
public class OpenWeatherMapMain
{
    public double temp { get; set; }
    public int pressure { get; set; }
    public int humidity { get; set; }
    public double temp_min { get; set; }
    public double temp_max { get; set; }
}
```

6. Next, we will write the code to get the current weather from the service. Create a class named `OpenWeatherService`.

7. To reduce the method's size, we will write methods to create the request and response. Write the following two methods in the new class:

```
private HttpWebRequest CreateRequest(string _address)
{
    HttpWebRequest webRequest;
    webRequest = (HttpWebRequest)HttpWebRequest.Create(_address);
    webRequest.Method = "POST";
    // the request will be empty.
    webRequest.ContentLength = 0;
```

```
        return webRequest;
    }
    private string ReadJsonResponse(HttpWebRequest _request)
    {
        string jsonString;
        using (HttpWebResponse webResponse =
         (HttpWebResponse)_request.GetResponse())
        {
            using (Stream stream = webResponse.GetResponseStream())
            {
                using (StreamReader reader = new StreamReader(stream))
                {
                    jsonString = reader.ReadToEnd();
                }
            }
        }
        return jsonString;
    }
```

8. Finally, write the method that we will use to get the current weather data, as
    follows:

    ```
    const string OpenWeatherMapAppKey = "<Your AppId key from
    OpenWeatherMap.org>";
    public OpenWeatherMap GetWeatherForLocation(double _lon, double
    _lat)
    {
        string address =
          $"http://api.openweathermap.org/data/2.5/weather?lat=
            {_lat}&lon= {_lon}&appid={OpenWeatherMapAppKey}";
        HttpWebRequest request = this.CreateRequest(address);
        string response = this.ReadJsonResponse(request);
        return JsonConvert.DeserializeObject<OpenWeatherMap>(response);
    }
    ```

9. **Save all** and build the project.
10. Next, we will use this service in our F&O project, which is, in our
    example, `ConVehicleManagement`. Right-click on the **References** node of your
    F&O project and choose **Add reference**.
11. Select the **Projects** tab and then our `WeatherService` project. Press **OK** to add
    the reference.
12. We will not hard code the link to the service, so we will use the attribute factory
    pattern. This means we need a new Base Enum and an attribute class. Create a
    new Base Enum named `ConVMSWeatherServiceType`.

13. Add an element named `OpenWeather` and create a label for the Base Enum and the `OpenWeather` element.

14. Create the attribute as per the usual pattern. The code for this should be as follows:

```
class ConVMSWeatherServiceTypeAttribute
 extends SysAttribute
 implements SysExtensionIAttribute
{
    ConVMSWeatherServiceType serviceType;
    public void new(ConVMSWeatherServiceType _serviceType)
    {
        serviceType = _serviceType;
    }
    public str parmCacheKey()
    {
        return classStr(ConVMSWeatherServiceTypeAttribute)
                        +';'+int2str(enum2int(serviceType));
    }
    public boolean useSingleton()
    {
        return false;
    }
}
```

15. Create a data contract class named `ConVMSWeatherServiceResultContract`. Add the following code to do this:

```
[DataContract]
class ConVMSWeatherServiceResultContract
{
    private real temperature;
    private real pressure;
    private real humidity;
    private real temp_min;
    private real temp_max;
    [DataMember]
    public real Temperature(real _temperature = temperature)
    {
        temperature = _temperature;
        return temperature;
    }
    [DataMember]
    public real Pressure(real _pressure = pressure)
    {
        pressure = _pressure;
        return pressure;
```

```
    }
    [DataMember]
    public real Humidity(real _humidity = humidity)
    {
        humidity = _humidity;
        return humidity;
    }
    [DataMember]
    public real Temp_min(real _temp_min = temp_min)
    {
        temp_min = _temp_min;
        return temp_min;
    }
    [DataMember]
    public real Temp_max(real _temp_max = temp_max)
    {
        temp_max = _temp_max;
        return htemp_max;
    }
}
```

16. Then, create an interface named `ConVMSWeatherServiceTypeI` and add the following code:

```
interface ConVMSWeatherServiceTypeI
{
    public ConVMSWeatherServiceResultContract GetWeather(
        LogisticsAddressLongitude _long,
        LogisticsAddressLatitude _lat)
    {
    }
}
```

17. Next, create a weather service class named `ConVMSWeatherServiceType_OpenWeather` for the **Open Weather** service, as follows:

```
using Contoso.WeatherService;
[ConVMSWeatherServiceTypeAttribute(ConVMSWeatherServiceType::OpenWe
ather)]
class ConVMSWeatherServiceType_OpenWeather implements
ConVMSWeatherServiceTypeI
{
    public ConVMSWeatherServiceResultContract GetWeather(
        LogisticsAddressLongitude _long,
         LogisticsAddressLatitude _lat)
    {
        OpenWeatherService srv = new OpenWeatherService();
```

```
                    OpenWeatherMap openWeatherMap =
                     srv.GetWeatherForLocation(_long, _lat);

                    ConVMSWeatherServiceResultContract result =
                        new ConVMSWeatherServiceResultContract();
                    result.Temperature(openWeatherMap.main.temp - 273); // this
    is
                     Kelvin, we want Celsius
                    result.Temp_min(openWeatherMap.main.temp_min - 273);
                    result.Temp_max(openWeatherMap.main.temp_max - 273);
                    result.Pressure(openWeatherMap.main.pressure);
                    result.Humidity(openWeatherMap.main.humidity);
                    return result;

                }

            }
```

18. Now, we can start to write the code that the form part will use. Create a class named `ConVMSWeatherService`. The following method is written for brevity since, normally, we would want to allow the user to select the weather service based on criteria, such as country. The following code is easy to refactor and will be used to create the instance of the weather service type:

```
LogisticsPostalAddress address; // class variable

protected ConVMSWeatherServiceType GetServiceType()
{
    // We would use the address class variable to look up a
    // configuration setting
    // in a setup table based on the country (or other as
    // required). This is omitted for brevity.
    return ConVMSWeatherServiceType::OpenWeather;
}
```

19. Next, write a create instance method that uses an attribute factory method to return an implementation of `ConVMSWeatherServiceTypeI`. Write the following code:

```
protected ConVMSWeatherServiceTypeI
CreateInstance(LogisticsPostalAddress _address)
{
    ConVMSWeatherServiceTypeAttribute attr;
    attr = new
     ConVMSWeatherServiceTypeAttribute(this.GetServiceType());
    ConVMSWeatherServiceTypeI instance;
    instance =
     SysExtensionAppClassFactory::getClassFromSysAttribute(
      classStr(ConVMSWeatherServiceTypeI), attr);
```

```
if (!instance || !(instance is ConVMSWeatherServiceTypeI))
{
    SysExtensionCache::clearAllScopes();
    instance =
     SysExtensionAppClassFactory::getClassFromSysAttribute(
      classStr(ConVMSWeatherServiceTypeI), attr);
    if (!instance || !(instance is ConVMSWeatherServiceTypeI))
    {
        return null; // don't throw, we want to handle this in
                     // the calling method
    }
}
return instance;
}
```

20. Next, override the `New` method and make it protected. We can't allow this to be instantiated without a `LogisticsPostalAddress` record.

21. Write the following constructor:

```
public static ConVMSWeatherService
NewFromLogisticsPostalAddress(LogisticsPostalAddress _address)
{
    ConVMSWeatherService service = new ConVMSWeatherService();
    service.address = _address;
    return service;
}
```

22. The final method is the code that will be used by the form part in order to get a weather results contract, as shown in the following method:

```
public ConVMSWeatherServiceResultContract GetWeather()
{
    ConVMSWeatherServiceResultContract contract = new
     ConVMSWeatherServiceResultContract();
    ConVMSWeatherServiceTypeI weatherInstance =
     this.CreateInstance();
    if (weatherInstance)
    {
        contract = weatherInstance.GetWeather(address.Longitude,
         address.Latitude);
    }
    return contract;
}
```

23. The next part is to create a form part that will render `ConVMSWeatherServiceResultContract`. First, we need some EDTs for the form controls. Create the following real EDTs:

Name	Label
ConVMSWeatherTemp	Temperature
ConVMSWeatherTempMin	Temperature (min)
ConVMSWeatherTempMax	Temperature (max)
ConVMSWeatherHumidity	Humidity
ConVMSWeatherPressure	Pressure

24. Create a form named `ConVMSWeatherPart`.

25. Apply the `Form Part Factbox Card` form pattern and add `WHSLoadTable` as a data source. Ensure that the data source properties for allow create, edit, and delete are set to No.

26. Set the form design's **Data Source** and **Title Data Source** properties to `WHSLoadTable`.

27. Add the following form variable:

    ```
    ConVMSWeatherServiceResultContract weatherContract = new
    ConVMSWeatherServiceResultContract();
    ```

28. Then, add a method to initialize the `weatherContract` variable from the `WHSLoadTable` record, as follows:

    ```
    public void InitWeather()
    {
        LogisticsPostalAddress postalAddress;
        switch (WHSLoadTable.LoadDirection)
        {
            case WHSLoadDirection::Inbound:
                postalAddress =
                  LogisticsPostalAddress::findRecId(
                  WHSLoadTable.OriginPostalAddress);
                break;
            case WHSLoadDirection::Outbound:
            case WHSLoadDirection::None:
                postalAddress =
                  LogisticsPostalAddress::findRecId(
                  WHSLoadTable.DestinationPostalAddress);
                break;
        }
        weatherContract =
    ```

```
ConVMSWeatherService::NewFromLogisticsPostalAddress(
    postalAddress).GetWeather();
}
```

29. Then, write a display method for each `weatherContract` data method. We will use the EDTs we created earlier to ensure we have a consistent interface:

```
public display ConVMSWeatherTemp DispTemparature()
{
 return weatherContract.Temperature();
}

public display ConVMSWeatherTempMin DispTemparature_min()
{
 return weatherContract.Temp_min();
}

public display ConVMSWeatherTempMax DispTemparature_max()
{
 return weatherContract.Temp_max();
}

public display ConVMSWeatherPressure DispPressure()
{
 return weatherContract.Pressure();
}

public display ConVMSWeatherHumidity DispHumidity()
{
 return weatherContract.Humidity();
}
```

30. Override the `Init` form method, as well as the `WHSLoadTable linkActive` method, to call the `InitWeather` method. The code should be as follows:

```
public void init()
{
    super();
    this.InitWeather();
}

[DataSource]
class WHSLoadTable
{
    public void linkActive()
    {
        super();
        element.InitWeather();
```

```
            }
          }
```

31. Add a `real` control for each display method and complete the **Display Method** property appropriately.
32. Create a label for the form caption property (Weather info) and then close the form designer.
33. Create a display menu item for the form part, setting the **Label** and **Object** properties as appropriate (that is, the label we just created and the form's name).
34. Then, create an extension for the `WHSLoadTable` form. Change the `extension` suffix to `ConVehicleManagement`.
35. Open `WHSLoadTable.ConVehicleManagement` in the designer. Right-click on the Parts node and add a new Form Part Reference.
36. Set the **Name** and **Menu Item Name** properties to `ConVMSWeatherPart`.
37. Select `WHSLoadTable` in the **Data Source** property and enter `SelfLink` in the **Data Source Relation** property.
38. **Save all** and build the project.

 Should you get an error regarding `WHSLoadTable.dispayTotalPieceCount,` ensure that your model references `Application Common`.

How it works...

The first key part of this recipe was to show you that we can add C# projects to an F&O solution and use the types that were created in that project within an F&O project. Even though we could have written the recipe purely in X++, it is easier to do so in C#. This is especially true if we wish to communicate with SOAP services. C# becomes even more obvious because C# projects will automatically generate the types in the project from the **Web Service Definition Language** (**WSDL**) definition provided by the service.

There are other reasons to use C#. Some include code protection, but the main reason is that it has special language features that are unique to C#.

One language feature that is missing from X++ can be seen in the following code:

```
return JsonConvert.DeserializeObject<OpenWeatherMap>(response);
```

`<OpenWeatherMap>` means that we are telling the `DesiarializeObject` method that we want an `OpenWeatherMap` type returned. The other technique would be to have a separate method per return type. We can't use this syntax in X++. It may become available in the future, but currently, it is not available. This makes using some .NET libraries more difficult and it becomes easier to write a C# project as a facade.

From that point on, the X++ code is not new to us. We used the attribute extension technique to decouple the form partly from the implementation of the weather service, allowing the actual service to be defined by the user. This could be further extended by placing service-specific configuration, such as the application ID, in a table in SCM. Each service would have its own setup table that the concrete implementation would access.

Although we embellished this recipe, the core take away elements are straightforward:

- We can add C# projects to an SCM project
- We can use the types in referenced C# projects as if they are native X++ types

12
Unit Testing

Unit testing helps ensure that the code fulfills the requirements at hand and that future changes (even in other packages) do not cause a regression. The unit test is written as a separate package that references the package it is testing. If we follow **Test-Driven Development** (**TDD**), we would write the tests early in the process, and some would argue first. TDD changes the way we think when writing code. Should we need to make a change to a project, we are forced to update the test-case code (as the tests will otherwise fail). This promotes a test-centric approach to development and naturally reduces the test cycles. Regression in other packages is caught by the build process. The build server will download all checked-in code, perform a build, and then look for tests to execute. Any tests that fail are reported and the build, depending on the build's setup, will be marked as failed.

Each partner or customer may have their own policies for unit testing. Some require that every piece of code is tested, while others will recommend that only key parts of the code are tested. It is common that the code of the unit tests has three times the amount of code as the code being tested, which may seem wrong at first. Writing test cases is an investment, the benefit of which isn't always apparent at the time of writing. This is because testing whether a piece of code works is usually pretty easy; the problem is that manual tests are not repeatable, often miss edge cases, and rarely spot regression caused by changes in other projects or a Microsoft update.

The biggest win, in my opinion, is the reduction in the risk of regression. This is where an apparently minor change (or a hotfix) is applied, and it affects a seemingly unrelated part of the system. These types of regression can easily make it into production since the testing procedures may only test that part of the system. This is compounded further by the fact that any fix will take at least a day to deploy since we are now forced to go through test and then production.

 The following link provides some good advice on achieving balance in testing
software: https://blogs.msdn.microsoft.com/dave_froslie/2016/02/03/achieving-balance-in-testing-software/.

Unit testing cannot catch everything. The test cases are preferably designed using the acceptance criteria and common patterns. Users will tend to evolve their use of the software, and modification can unknowingly break this usage scenario. This is where we could use the **Regression Suite Automation Tool** (**RSAT**). This tool uses task recordings from actual end-user scenarios that have been recorded and tested as part of the build quality management process. Although this is not in the scope of this chapter, the documentation for this from Microsoft is very good and can be found here: `https://docs.microsoft.com/en-us/dynamics365/unified-operations/fin-and-ops/get-started/hol-use-regression-suite-automation-tool`.

In this chapter, we will focus on unit testing and cover the following recipes:

- Creating a unit test project
- Creating a unit test case for code
- Creating an Acceptance test library entity class
- Creating an Acceptance test library specification class
- Creating an Acceptance test library data class
- Creating an Acceptance test library data class structure
- Creating an Acceptance test library class that ensures a process can be done

Technical requirements

You can find the code files for this chapter on GitHub at `https://github.com/PacktPublishing/Extending-Microsoft-Dynamics-365-Finance-and-Supply-Chain-Management-Cookbook-Second-Edition/blob/master/Chapter%2012%20-%20Unit%20Tests.axpp`.

Creating a unit test project

To write a test case, we need to reference the `Testing Essentials` package. This package is not deployed to sandbox or production environments, which means that any deployment that depends on the test framework will fail. Therefore, we must have a new package for our unit tests. The best way to write tests is to write them as we would write our main code. Therefore, we would add a test project to the same solution as the development project.

Let's say we created a project for a credit check change called `ConSalesCreditCheck` in the `Contoso` package. The structure would be similar to the following:

- Solution: `ConSalesCreditCheck`
  - Project: `ConSalesCreditCheck` (Package Contoso)
  - Project: `ConSalesCreditCheckTest` (Package ContosoTest)

 Test packages must always end in `Test`; normal projects must not. This is because we usually exclude test projects from the package generation on the build server using the name.

Getting ready

Open the solution we are going to write tests for, which will be `ConVMSVehicleManagement` for this example.

How to do it...

To create the unit test project, follow these steps:

1. Select **Dynamics 365 for Operations | Create model** from the top menu and complete the **Create model** form as follows:

Field	Value
Model name	ConVehicleManagementTest
Model publisher	Contoso IT
Layer	VAR
Model description	Test cases for the ConVehicleManagement package
Model display name	ConVehicleManagementTest

 The suffix is important and must always be `Test`.

2. Click on **Next**.
3. Select **Create new package** and click on **Next**.
4. Additionally, select (do not uncheck any options that are checked by default) the `ConVehicleManagement`, `ApplicationFoundation`, and `TestEssentials` packages from the **Packages [Models]** list and click on **Next**.

 Additional packages may be required, depending on the code we need to write.

5. Uncheck the default for creating a project, but leave the default option of making the new model the default for new projects. Click on **Finish**.
6. Right-click on the solution node in the Solution Explorer and choose **Add | New project....**
7. In the **New Project** window, ensure that the **Dynamics 365 for Operations** template is selected in the left-hand pane, and **Finance Operations Project** is selected in the right-hand pane. Enter `ConVehicleManagementTest` as the **Name** and click on **OK**.
8. Open the properties for the project and change the Model property to `ConVehicleManagementTest`. In our case, the names are the same, but this is a coincidence as there are usually many projects that are added to a package.

How it works...

What we did here was create a new package and model for our test cases, and added a project to the solution. It was important to change the Model property. The Model property essentially tells Visual Studio where the elements we add to the project are placed. Although we tend to always have one model per package, it is the model that governs the actual placing. Its physical structure is as follows:

```
C:\AOSService\PackagesLocalDirectory\<Package folder>\<Model folder>
```

In our case, for the `ConVehicleManagementTest` model, this will be as follows:

```
C:\AOSService\PackagesLocalDirectory\ConVehicleManagementTest\ConVehicleMan
agementTest
```

Once we have added an element to our project, we can no longer change the Model property.

Creating a unit test case for code

In this recipe, we will create three test cases, starting with two simple tests to test the vehicle and vehicle table code and then a test case for the `ConVehicleGroupChange` class. These tests should test when it should fail and when it should succeed. This process will involve programmatically creating some test data in order to perform the tests.

Getting ready

We will just need the unit test project, which we created in the previous recipe, open. Also, on the main menu, select **X64** from **Test** | **Test Setting** | **Default Processor Architecture**.

How to do it...

To create the unit test class, follow these steps:

1. Create a new class and name it `ConVMSVehicleGroupTest`. The suffix is important.
2. In the code editor, change the declaration so that it extends `SysTestCase`.
3. Next, we will need some constants for test cases that we expect to either succeed or fail. In this case, we will have the following:

   ```
   const ConVMSVehicleGroupId groupId = '%VG01%';
   const str notFound = '%ERROR%';
   ```

 The preceding strings are written as such to ensure that they don't interfere with existing records, which is possible if we instruct the test to use company data. By default, a special data partition is used for all data operations, which is removed once the test completes.

4. The next part is to set up the test case, which is done by overriding the `setUpTestCase` method with the following code:

   ```
   public void setUpTestCase()
   {
       super();
       ConVMSVehicleGroup vehGroup;
       ttsbegin;
       vehGroup.initValue();
       vehGroup.VehicleGroupId = groupId;
       vehGroup.insert();
   ```

```
    ttscommit;
}
```

We created the vehicle group record using the constants we defined earlier. We expect our tests to find these records to succeed.

5. Now, we can write our test method. The naming is important as it describes it is a test and the element that it is testing. The code should be written as follows:

```
[SysTestMethod]
public void VehicleGroupExistTest()
{
    this.assertTrue(!ConVMSVehicleGroup::Exist(groupId),
        'Vehicle group not found when it should');
    this.assertFalse(!ConVMSVehicleGroup::Exist(groupId),
        'Vehicle group found when it should not');
}
```

The `assertTrue` method will fail as the first parameter does not evaluate to true, and will show the message in the test results. If it succeeds, no message will be shown.

6. Let's execute the tests and check that they do, indeed, fail. To do this, build the project and choose **Test** | **Windows** | **Test Explorer**. Then, right-click on the **Test** and choose **Run Selected Tests**. The result should be as follows:

ConVMSVehicleGroupTest.VehicleGroupExistTest

Source: AxClass_ConVMSVehicleGroupTest.xpp line 18

❌ Test Failed - ConVMSVehicleGroupTest.VehicleGroupExistTest

Message:
Vehicle group not found when it should

Elapsed time: 422 ms

◢ StackTrace:

7. The code stops on failure, so if we have two assert calls, we need to test a false positive for each combination. Finally, change the parameter in the `assertTrue` method so that they should succeed; build and then click on **Run All**. The result should be as follows:

```
ConVMSVehicleGroupTest.VehicleGroupExistTest

  Source: AxClass_ConVMSVehicleGroupTest.xpp line 18

  ⊘ Test Passed - ConVMSVehicleGroupTest.VehicleGroupExistTest

  Elapsed time: 484 ms
```

8. Create a new class named `ConVMSVehicleTableTest` in order to test the vehicle table. The code is very similar to the vehicle group test class, so you can test this by completing this class yourself.

9. We also wrote some logic to default the vehicle group, which we should test actually happens. This works by defaulting the vehicle group on the vehicle table from the parameters table. To do this, we need to set this up, as follows:

```
const str groupId = 'TESTGROUP';
const ConVMSVehicleId vehicleId = '%V001%';
public void setUpTestCase()
{
    super();
    ttsbegin;
    ConVMSVehicleGroup grp;
    grp.initValue();
    grp.VehicleGroupId = groupId;
    grp.insert();

    ConVMSParameters parm = ConVMSParameters::Find(true);
    parm.DefaultVehicleGroupId = groupId;
    parm.update();
    ttscommit;
}
```

10. The test method simply calls `initValue` and tests that the vehicle group was set. The following code does this:

```
[SysTestMethod]
public void VehicleDefaultTest()
{
    ConVMSVehicleTable v;
    v.initValue();

    this.assertEquals(v.VehicleGroupId, groupId,
        'Vehicle group was not set as expected');
}
```

11. The final test is to test the vehicle group change class. This has two tests: a test ensuring that the contract's validation method works as designed and a test ensuring that the code actually changes the vehicle group as designed. To start, we will write a helper method to save repetition:

```
private void CheckContractValidate(
    ConVMSVehicleId _vehicleId,
    ConVMSVehicleGroupId _groupId,
    boolean _shouldBeValid)
{
    ConVMSVehicleGroupChangeContract contract;
    contract = new ConVMSVehicleGroupChangeContract();
    contract.VehicleGroupId(_groupId);
    contract.VehicleId(_vehicleId);

    boolean valid = contract.Validate();
    str validMsg = 'failed';
    if (valid)
    {
        validMsg = 'passed';
    }
    str shouldBeValidMsg = 'failed';
    if (_shouldBeValid)
    {
        shouldBeValidMsg = 'passed';
    }
    str msg = strFmt('Vehicle %1, group %2 %3 validation when it
     should have %4', _vehicleId, _groupId, validMsg,
       shouldBeValidMsg);
    this.assertEquals(_shouldBeValid ? 'Passed' :'Failed',
        valid ? 'Passed' : 'Failed', msg);
}
```

12. Now, we can complete our `VehcielGroupChangeTest` method, which should read as follows:

```
[SysTestMethod]
public void VehicleGroupContractValidationTest()
{
        // Test blank vehicle group
        this.CheckContractValidate('', '', false);
        this.CheckContractValidate(vehicleId, '', false);
        this.CheckContractValidate(notFound, '', false);
        // Test invalid vehicle group
        this.CheckContractValidate('', notFound, false);
        this.CheckContractValidate(vehicleId, notFound, false);
        this.CheckContractValidate(notFound, notFound, false);
```

```
// Test valid vehicle group
this.CheckContractValidate('', groupId, false);
this.CheckContractValidate(vehicleId, groupId, true);
this.CheckContractValidate(notFound, groupId, false);
// Test blank vehicle
this.CheckContractValidate('', '', false);
this.CheckContractValidate('', groupId, false);
this.CheckContractValidate('', notFound, false);
// Test invalid vehicle
this.CheckContractValidate(notFound, '', false);
this.CheckContractValidate(notFound, groupId, false);
// Test valid vehicle
this.CheckContractValidate(vehicleId, '', false);
this.CheckContractValidate(vehicleId, groupId, true);
this.CheckContractValidate(vehicleId, notFound, false);
}
```

13. Build the project, select the **Test Explorer** window (or reopen it if it was closed), and simply right-click on the new test and click on **Run Selected Tests**. This will build the project for us. The result should be as follows:

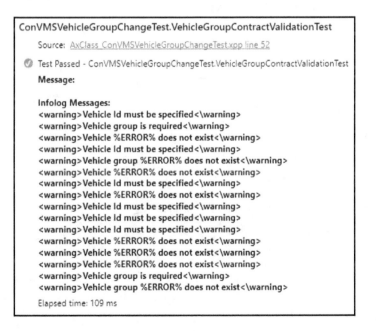

The warnings come from the target method, where it correctly failed the validation check.

14. As before, we should write the validation checks so that they fail first. You could also insert a runtime error to see how this is handled. On the line that defines the `ConVMSVehicleGroupChangeContract` class, comment out the line that instantiates it. When it executes, you will get a very verbose message stating `NullReferenceException`, showing us that even these types of errors will be caught through unit testing.

15. Now, we should write the test code to test that the vehicle group change actually runs. Like we did previously, write a helper method to save repetition:

```
private void CheckGroupChangeRun(
ConVMSVehicleId _vehicleId,
ConVMSVehicleGroupId _groupId,
boolean _shouldBeValid)
{
ConVMSVehicleGroupChangeContract contract;
contract = new ConVMSVehicleGroupChangeContract();
contract.VehicleGroupId(_groupId);
contract.VehicleId(_vehicleId);
ConVMSVehicleGroupChange change = new
ConVMSVehicleGroupChange();
change.Run(contract);

ConVMSVehicleTable vehicleTable =
ConVMSVehicleTable::Find(_vehicleId);

boolean wasChanged = (vehicleTable.VehicleGroupId ==
_groupId && vehicleTable.RecId != 0);

str didRunMsg = 'was not set';
if (wasChanged)
{
didRunMsg = 'was set';
}
str shouldRunMsg = 'not changed';
if (_shouldBeValid)
{
shouldRunMsg = 'changed';
}
str msg = strFmt('Vehicle %1, group %2 %3 when it should
 have %4', _vehicleId, _groupId, didRunMsg, shouldRunMsg);

this.assertEquals(_shouldBeValid ? 'Passed' :'Failed',
wasChanged ? 'Passed' : 'Failed', msg);
}
```

16. The actual test code is written like so:

```
[SysTestMethod]
public void VehicleGroupChangeTest()
{
    // Test blank vehicle group
    this.CheckGroupChangeRun('', '', false);
    this.CheckGroupChangeRun(vehicleId, '', false);
    this.CheckGroupChangeRun(notFound, '', false);
    // Test invalid vehicle group
    this.CheckGroupChangeRun('', notFound, false);
    this.CheckGroupChangeRun(vehicleId, notFound, false);
    this.CheckGroupChangeRun(notFound, notFound, false);
    // Test valid vehicle group
    this.CheckGroupChangeRun('', groupId, false);
    this.CheckGroupChangeRun(vehicleId, groupId, true);
    this.CheckGroupChangeRun(notFound, groupId, false);
    // Test blank vehicle
    this.CheckGroupChangeRun('', '', false);
    this.CheckGroupChangeRun('', groupId, false);
    this.CheckGroupChangeRun('', notFound, false);
    // Test invalid vehicle
    this.CheckGroupChangeRun(notFound, '', false);
    this.CheckGroupChangeRun(notFound, groupId, false);
    this.CheckGroupChangeRun(notFound, notFound, false);
    // Test valid vehicle
    this.CheckGroupChangeRun(vehicleId, '', false);
    this.CheckGroupChangeRun(vehicleId, groupId, true);
    this.CheckGroupChangeRun(vehicleId, notFound, false);
}
```

17. Now, we should run all the tests, checking both when the tests should succeed and when they should fail.

How it works...

Most of the code we wrote is relatively straightforward, but it can be a little verbose. The normal pattern for writing tests is to write them as the main code is written, starting with blank methods for the acceptance criteria specified in the technical requirements augmented with other tests that seem necessary. Often, we write tests in order to debug the code we are writing, which can easily be done by choosing **Debug selected tests**.

There are a few points that need explaining, the first being the way data is handled. When a test case is run, it uses a partition to segregate the data it creates and will tear it down once the test has completed. This occurs for each test. We must not assume an order in which the tests are run, or assume we can use data that's been created in another test method.

 The partition is a legacy feature from Dynamics AX 2012 and is a field that's used to hard-partition data as the boundaries between companies are relaxed. This partition key is now used solely for testing scenarios.

When the project was created, we referenced `ApplicationFramework` and `TestEssentials`. The discovery process works by looking for a class in the current project that extends `SysTestCase` and for methods that have the `SysTestMethod` attribute. The test method must be public, return void, and have no parameters. They should start with (or at least contain) the word test and reference the method in the class we are testing. If a test method does not appear in the Test Explorer, check that the class extends `SysTestCase` and that the test methods have the `SysTestMethod` attribute. The test will often appear before the project is built and will fail with a suitable message, should the test be run prematurely.

There's more...

There are some attributes we can add to the class declaration to alter how this behaves. In some cases, we need a lot of data in order to process the test case. These are attributes that start with `SysTestCase`.

Open one of the test classes, and at the top of the class, type `SysTestCase` in order to reveal a list of test attributes.

The following two attributes are often used in test cases:

`[SysTestCaseAutomaticNumberSequences(true)]`	This will create number sequences using defaults. The true parameter uses runtime detection to create references and code.
`[SysTestCaseDataDependency('usmf')]`	This will run the tests in the data context of the usmf company in the default partition.

The final attribute is useful when running tests on a build server that has a specific database that is restored each time a build is run.

Creating an Acceptance test library entity class

In the **Application Explorer,** there are hundreds of classes prefixed with atl. These classes are part of the Acceptance test library and are used to simplify and greatly reduce the code that's required to write test cases. Not only can these classes create setup data that is required to run a test, but also execute processes such as running a command to change the vehicle group. It may seem that we are blurring the lines between unit and integration tests. Unit tests aren't intended to test configuration data, and attempting this too early will complicate this process. At this stage, we will use atl to create some default setup data in order to write and execute unit tests. Before this framework was made available, we needed combinations of task recordings and databases that contain the base data for the tests.

The next three recipes will create a simple testing suite to test the creation of a vehicle, access its data, data validation, and write a new **Change vehicle group** test using the ATL.

Getting ready

This recipe follows the previous recipe. As a minimum, the test package we are working on must reference the following packages:

- Testing essentials
- Acceptance test library – Foundation
- Acceptance test library – Application suite (if you're using standard entities in your tests)

In our case, as we are following on from the previous recipes, we will need to add the references to the last two packages to the ConVehicleManagementTest package.

How to do it...

We will be creating tests for the vehicle table, which is a table that supports inheritance. The tool will not create a nested entity, so we must create one per type of table:

1. First, we need to create an entity for the Vehicle Group. Open the ConVMSVehicleGroup table in the designer.
2. Right-click on the table name in the designer pane and select **Add ins | Generate Atl entity**.

3. In the dialog that opens, multi-select the fields on the left and click **Add**. Change the **Destination model** to `ConVehicleManagementTest`. The result should look as follows:

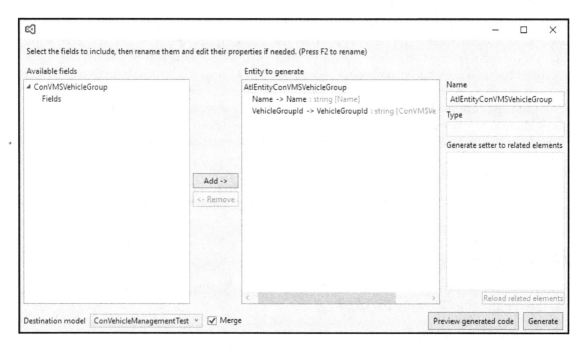

4. Click **Generate**. The tool will look for an open project that is in a package that references the **Destination model**. Select the appropriate project and click **Add to project**. If a suitable package cannot be found by the tool, you will be prompted to create a project. Clicking cancel will still result in the class being created.

 If you forgot to change the Destination model or the test package does not reference the `Acceptance test library - foundation` package, the class will create it in the `Acceptance test library - application suite` package. You will need to delete this and start this process again.

5. The next step is to create an ATL entity class for the Vehicle table. Open the `ConVMSVehicleTableCar` table in the designer.

6. Right-click on the table name in the designer pane and select **Add ins | Create Atl entity**.

7. Do the same as we did for the vehicle group table entity, but do not press **Generate**.

8. On the right-hand pane, there will be an entity named `VehicleGroupId`. There is a relation to this table, and we can generate a setter for this related table. Select **VehicleGroupId** and check the option for **setVehicleGroup**, as shown in the following screenshot:

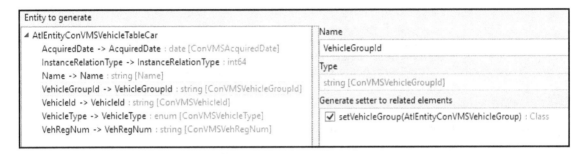

9. Ensure that the **Destination Model** is our Test model and press **Generate**.

How it works...

The entity is generated through a code generator, which creates the entity with no coding required. The code is stored as an XML file, just like any other AX class, and writes it to the folder of the **Destination Model**. This means that it is very easy to choose the wrong package and have our code in the wrong model.

This can be fixed by opening Windows Explorer and moving the file from the default folder of `C:\AOSService\PackagesLocalDirectory\ATLApplicationSuite\ATLApplicationSuite\AxClass` to the `AxClass` folder of our test package.

There's more...

The entity class allows us to interact more easily with data and allows us to use fluent coding. To demonstrate this, we can write a test class that uses this new entity class instead:

1. Create a new class in our test project named `ConVMSVehicleGroupAtlTest`.
2. Complete the code in the class like so:

```
class ConVMSVehicleGroupAtlTest extends SysTestCase
{
    const ConVMSVehicleGroupId groupId = '%VG01%';
    const str notFound = '%ERROR%';
    [SysTestMethod]
```

```
public void VehicleGroupExistAtlTest()
{
    var vehGroup =
        AtlEntityConVMSVehicleGroup::construct()
            .setVehicleGroupId(groupId)
            .setName(groupId)
            .save();
    this.assertTrue(ConVMSVehicleGroup::Exist(groupId),
        'Vehicle group not found when it should');
    this.assertFalse(ConVMSVehicleGroup::Exist(notFound),
        'Vehicle group found when it should not');
}
}
```

3. Save the new class and execute the tests.

The new concept here is the fluent coding of the set and save methods. Fluent methods return the instance of the class after the operation has completed. The set methods work by calling a base class with the field ID and the new value. The save method works by calling the base class's saveBase() method, which in turn executes the validation before and after the common.write() method is called. Common is a base type for all tables and will call insert or update, depending on whether it is a new record or not.

The other change to the way we have written code so far is the use of var. This means the test will complete, even if we change the type of the entity. The entity just needs the methods that we have used. We should not use the actual types when using the ATL framework.

Creating an Acceptance test library specification class

The specification class defines acceptance criteria and replaces the manual this.Assert...() methods. This means we can write our acceptance criteria before the tests are actually written. These are usually written in conjunction with a query class, so in this recipe, we will create both and update the test to use this new pattern.

Getting ready

This recipe follows the previous recipe. As a minimum, we need a package that references the following packages:

- Testing essentials
- Acceptance test library – Foundation
- Acceptance test library – Application suite (if using standard entities in your tests)
- An entity class for the table we are going to test, such as the one we created in the previous recipe

How to do it

To create the ATL specification class for a table, follow these steps:

1. Open the `ConVMSVehicleGroup` table in the designer.
2. Right-click on the root, table, and node and choose `Add-ins | Generate Atl Specification`.
3. This will open the following dialog:

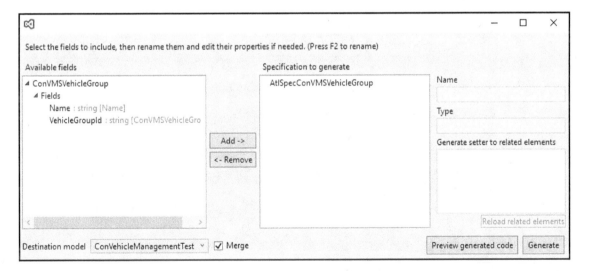

4. The methods we're adding here are specifications, which are the criterion for a successful test. Since we are going to test that the vehicle group ID is what is expected, add this field. Do this by selecting `VehicleGroupId` on the left and clicking **Add**.

5. Ensure that the **Destination model** is correct, and then click **Generate** to create the class. In the following dialog, choose **Add to project** to add it to our existing test project.

6. Now, we need to create an ATL query class. Use the Add-in option again on the `ConVMSVehicleGroup` table to generate an `Atl Query` class.

7. In the dialog, add all the necessary fields, press **Generate**, and add them to our project, just like we did in the previous steps for the specification class.

8. To change our test method so that it uses this new pattern, open the `ConVMSVehicleGroupAtlTest` class and update it so that it reads as follows:

```
[SysTestMethod]
public void VehicleGroupExistAtlTest()
{
    var vehGroup =
        AtlEntityConVMSVehicleGroup::construct()
            .setVehicleGroupId(groupId)
            .setName(groupId)
            .save();
    var groups = AtlQueryConVMSVehicleGroups::construct();

    groups.assertExpectedLines(
        AtlSpecConVMSVehicleGroup::construct()
        .withVehicleGroupId(groupId));

    groups.withVehicleGroupId(groupId).assertCount(1,
      'Expected 1 record');
    groups.withVehicleGroupId(notFound).assertCount(0,
      'Expected 0 records');
}
```

9. Build the project and execute the test. Test for a deliberate failure first by asserting that `notFound` should exist.

How it works...

This recipe showed two methods that can be used to test assertions. The `assertExpectedLines` method is the typical method you should use, but you can also use the `assertCount` method where appropriate.

When using `assertExpectedLines`, it expects an `AtlSpecification` to act as the criteria. The plain-English request we are making here is this: for a list of vehicle groups, assert that there should be a vehicle group with the ID of `groupId`.

Due to the fluent coding style, we could write all of this on one line. This is normally preferable. In this example, a var was declared for the query class in order to demonstrate a way to interact with the query class without a specification class.

In order to use the `assertCount` method, the query needs to be told the criterion before the assert is called. This is done using fluent `with` methods. We only have one criterion, but we could have several.

If we created a vehicle group with an ID of `VG1` and a name of `VG Name`, we might want to test that the vehicle group was created with the correct ID and name. In this case, we would write the following code instead:

```
groups.withVehicleGroupId('VG1').withName('VG Name').assertCount(1,
'Expected 1 record');
```

Creating an Acceptance test library data class

The data class brings the query and specification classes together, and in its simplest form, it simply constructs and returns instances of the query and specification classes. We will also pull together the previous Acceptance test library recipes to create a more typical test scenario.

In this recipe, we will complete the vehicle group test suite with an `AtlData` class, but also create a test to test the creation of a vehicle with the correct default vehicle group.

Getting ready

This recipe follows the previous recipe. As a minimum, we need a package that references the following packages:

- Testing essentials.
- Acceptance test library – Foundation.

- Acceptance test library – Application suite (if using standard entities in your tests).
- The previous Acceptance test library recipes should be completed so that you can follow along with this recipe.

How to do it...

We will split this process into sections, starting with creating a data class for the `ConVMSVehicleGroup` table:

1. Within the test project, create a new class named `AtlDataConVMSVehicleGroups`.

2. Within the editor, adjust the declaration so that it reads as follows:

```
public final class AtlDataConVMSVehicleGroups extends AtlDataNode
{
}
```

3. Then, add a method to return the query, as shown here:

```
[Hookable(false)]
public final AtlQueryConVMSVehicleGroups query()
{
    return AtlQueryConVMSVehicleGroups::construct();
}
```

4. Finally, add a method for the specification, which is as follows:

```
[Hookable(false)]
public final AtlSpecConVMSVehicleGroup spec()
{
    return AtlSpecConVMSVehicleGroup::construct();
}
```

5. Now, we can adjust our test method so that it's more readable, like so:

```
AtlEntityConVMSVehicleGroup::construct()
    .setVehicleGroupId(groupId)
    .setName(groupId)
    .save();

var vehicleGroups = new AtlDataConVMSVehicleGroups();
vehicleGroups.query()
    .assertExpectedLines(vehicleGroups.spec().withVehicleGroupId(groupI
    d));
```

```
vehicleGroups.query()
    .withVehicleGroupId(groupId)
    .assertCount(1, 'Expected 1 record');

vehicleGroups.query()
    .withVehicleGroupId(notFound)
    .assertCount(0, 'Expected 0 records');
```

How it works...

The first thing you may have noticed is that we made every class and method non-extensible by making the classes final and the methods non-hookable. This is so that no other party can affect our tests. The obvious question is, "What if the customer has used **Chain of Command (CoC)** to alter how the code behaves? Surely we have to adjust the tests so that they will pass?" The answer is no; any changes brought about through CoC should not break the standard code as this protects against future regression in our code. The standard tests should pass, even with our code changes – and our code must also pass. We are augmenting standard behavior.

By creating the AtlData class, we have simplified the creation of the test case by bringing together the specification class and query class. Now, we can write the test in one line of code. We would usually create a method to create a default record, but this involves creating a broader set of classes that would complicate this recipe. We shall cover this in the next recipe.

Creating an Acceptance test library data class structure

Now, we will create a full set of Atl classes to support the testing and creation of a vehicle. This involves integrating them into the AtlDataRoot class in order to access the suite fluently.

The class structure will be as follows:

- AtlDataConVMS: The root node for the vehicle management system:
    - VehicleGroups as the AtlDataConVMSVehicleGroups type
        - Parameters as the AtlDataConVMSParameters type
    - Cars as the AtlDataConVMSVehicleTableCars type

Getting ready

This recipe follows the previous recipe. As a minimum, we need a package that references the following packages:

- Testing essentials.
- Acceptance test library – Foundation.
- Acceptance test library – Application suite (if using standard entities in your tests).
- The previous Acceptance test library recipes should be completed in order to follow this recipe.

How to do it...

The first part is to create our root `AtlData` class and integrate it into the `AtlDataRoot` class:

1. Create the first class, `AtlDataConVMS`, as follows:

```
public final class AtlDataConVMS extends AtlDataNode
{
}
```

2. Now, we need to hook this into the `AtlDataRoot` class so that we can reference it fluently. Do this by creating an extension class named `AtlDataRootConVMS_Extension`, as shown in the following code:

```
[ExtensionOf(classStr(AtlDataRootNode))]
public final class AtlDataRootConVMS_Extension
{
    [Hookable(false)]
    public final AtlDataConVMS ConVMS()
    {
        return new AtlDataConVMS();
    }
}
```

3. First, we will work on adding the `ConVMSParameters` table into the class structure. Create an `Atl Entity` class and an `Atl Query` class for this table by following the previous recipes in this chapter. You only need to add the setter method for the `vehicleGroupId` field for the entity class.

Remember to create the `atl` entity class before the `atl` query class as the query class references the entity.

4. Next, create a class named `AtlDataConVMSParameters` that's declared as follows:

```
public final class AtlDataConVMSParameters extends AtlDataNode
```

5. We need this class to set the default vehicle group, which means we just need one method at this point. The setter methods on the `AtlData` classes are not fluent, so this is written as follows:

```
[Hookable(false)]
public final void setVehicleGroupId(ConVMSVehicleGroupId _groupId)
{
    AtlEntityConVMSParameters::construct()
        .setDefaultVehicleGroupId(_groupId)
        .save();
}
```

6. Then, add a method to access the query, as follows:

```
public final AtlQueryConVMSParameters query()
{
    return AtlQueryConVMSParameters::construct();
}
```

7. Save and close the code editor for `AtlDataConVMSParameters` and change to the tab with the code editor for `AtlDataConVMS`. Here, write the following method:

```
[Hookable(false)]
public final AtlDataConVMSParameters parameters()
{
    return new AtlDataConVMSParameters();
}
```

8. Open the `AtlDataConVMSVehicleGroup` class in the code editor and add the following declaration to the top of the class:

```
const ConVMSVehicleGroupId defaultGroupId = 'DefGroupId';
```

9. We need to create some default data if we are to ensure that we can create a vehicle. Add the following method:

```
[Hookable(false)]
public final AtlEntityConVMSVehicleGroup createDefault()
{
    AtlDataRootNode::construct()
        .ConVMS()
        .parameters()
        .setVehicleGroupId(defaultGroupId);
    return AtlEntityConVMSVehicleGroup::construct()
        .setVehicleGroupId(defaultGroupId).save();
}
```

The first line that calls AtlDataRootNode demonstrates our first usage of the AtlDataRoot structure.

10. The final part of integrating the vehicle group class set is to add a reference to the AtlDataConVMS class, which is done as follows:

```
[Hookable(false)]
public final AtlDataConVMSVehicleGroups vehicleGroups()
{
    return new AtlDataConVMSVehicleGroups();
}
```

11. This completes the class set for the vehicle groups. Now, we can alter the ConVMSVehicleGroupAtlTest test class so that it reads as follows:

```
[SysTestMethod]
public void VehicleGroupExistAtlTest()
{
    var vms = AtlDataRootNode::construct().ConVMS();
    vms.vehicleGroups().createDefault();
    ConVMSVehicleGroupId expectedGroupId = vms
        .parameters()
        .query()
        .firstEntity()
        .parmDefaultVehicleGroupId();

    vms.vehicleGroups()
        .query()
        .assertExpectedLines(
        vms.vehicleGroups().spec().withVehicleGroupId(
        expectedGroupId));
```

```
vms.vehicleGroups()
    .query()
    .withVehicleGroupId(expectedGroupId)
    .assertCount(1, 'Expected 1 record');
vms.vehicleGroups()
    .query()
    .withVehicleGroupId(notFound)
    .assertCount(0, 'Expected 0 records');
}
```

 You should compare this to the previous iterations of this method to see how it has become simpler as we have evolved it.

How it works...

The result here is that we can now access our test suite from the `AtlDataRoot` class and that all the required entities, specifications, and query classes can be accessed through calls based on this root data node.

There wasn't actually anything new here; we just brought the work we have done together and increased the benefit of the work we put in.

The next recipe shows how we can use the code we have written to simplify other tests.

Creating an Acceptance test library class that ensures a process can be done

One of the benefits of writing ATL classes is that the classes create their own data, which means we can tell them to ensure that a process can be performed.

For example, we can't create a vehicle without a vehicle group, and we know from the code that we also need a default vehicle group. Here, we need to write a method starting with `ensure`, such as `ensureCanCreateVehicle()`.

To demonstrate this, we will add `ConVMSVehicleTableCars` to our ATL data class structure.

Getting ready

This recipe follows the previous recipe. As a minimum, we need a package that references the following packages:

- Testing essentials.
- Acceptance test library – Foundation.
- Acceptance test library – Application suite (if using standard entities in your tests).
- The previous Acceptance test library recipes should be completed in order to follow along with this recipe.

How to do it

To create the ATL data class and write the `ensure` method, follow these steps:

1. Open the `ConVMSVehicleTableCar` table and generate a specification, followed by a query class. Add all the fields and the `ConVMSVehicleGroup` relation. You should have created an entity class already, but if not, create one.

 If you make a mistake, you can regenerate the class so that you can change the generated code.

2. Next, we will create a data class for the `ConVMSVehicleTableCar` table by creating a new class named `AtlDataConVMSVehicleTableCar`. The class declaration should be as follows:

```
public final class AtlDataConVMSVehicleTableCars extends
AtlDataNode
{
    // add any constants required for default values here
    const ConVMSVehicleId defaultVehicleId = 'DefaultV001';
}
```

3. Add the `spec` and `query` methods, as shown in the following code:

```
[Hookable(false)]
public final AtlQueryConVMSVehicleTableCars query()
{
    return AtlQueryConVMSVehicleTableCars::construct();
}
```

```
[Hookable(false)]
public final AtlSpecConVMSVehicleTableCar spec()
{
    return AtlSpecConVMSVehicleTableCar::construct();
}
```

4. The data class can be used to create a vehicle, but in this case, we have a dependency since we need a vehicle group. We will use a method that starts with ensure to create the necessary dependent data. Create the following method:

```
[Hookable(false)]
public final void ensureCanCreateVehicle()
{
    AtlDataRootNode::construct()
        .ConVMS()
        .vehicleGroups()
        .createDefault();
}
```

5. Next, we can create the createDefault vehicle method, which is done with the following code:

```
[Hookable(false)]
public final void createDefault()
{
    this.ensureCanCreateVehicle();
    AtlEntityConVMSVehicleTableCar::construct()
        .setVehicleId(defaultVehicleId)
        .setVehicleType(ConVMSVehicleType::Car)
        .setInstanceRelationType(tableNum(ConVMSVehicleTableCar))
        .save();
}
```

6. The final step is to add a reference in the AtlDataConVMS class. Open this class and add the following method:

```
[Hookable(false)]
public final AtlDataConVMSVehicleTableCars vehicles()
{
    return new AtlDataConVMSVehicleTableCars();
}
```

7. Now, create a class to test vehicle creation called `ConVMSVehicleTableAtlTest`.

8. Alter the declaration so that it extends `SysTestCase`. Then, write the following test method:

```
[SysTestMethod]
public void VehicleTableCreateTest()
{
    var vms = AtlDataRootNode::construct().ConVMS();

    vms.vehicles().createDefault();
    ConVMSVehicleGroupId expectedGroupId = vms.parameters().query(
    ).firstEntity().parmDefaultVehicleGroupId();
    vms.vehicles()
        .query()
        .assertExpectedLines(
        vms.vehicles().spec().withVehicleGroupId(
        expectedGroupId));
}
```

How it works...

The new concept here was the new `ensure` method. This is a simple example of making the data-generation side of testing as simple as possible. If we wanted to post a sales invoice, we would simply write `ensureCanPostSalesInvoice`. This would create the necessary data. The method can chain other `ensure` methods so that each `ensure` method remains as small as possible.

In our case, to create a vehicle, we had to just ensure that a vehicle group was created. That, in turn, created a parameter with a default vehicle group.

When we created the default, you may have noticed that we specified the `instanceRelationType` field. This is only required for tables that take part in inheritance and is the table ID of the table we are working with.

The code also lends itself to self-validating. Mistakes that are made when writing the various classes will usually show up as test failures. Even so, we should always test that the tests pass and fail as they should.

See also

The following links should be used in conjunction with these recipes and can provide further insight:

- Acceptance test library resources: `https://docs.microsoft.com/en-us/dynamics365/fin-ops-core/dev-itpro/perf-test/acceptance-test-library`
- Best practices for the Acceptance test library: `https://docs.microsoft.com/en-us/dynamics365/fin-ops-core/dev-itpro/perf-test/atl-best-practices`

13
Automated Build Management

In this chapter, we will cover the steps that are required to set up and use a build server. We touched upon some of the benefits of a build server in `Chapter 12`, *Unit Testing*, where unit tests can be executed to help reduce the risk of regression.

We shall cover two scenarios: a cloud-hosted customer implementation project deployed via LCS, and an on-premise build server, which is equivalent to an Azure server hosted under your own subscription.

If the implementation is hosted in Azure and is deployed through an LCS customer implementation project, all we need to do is set up Build Agent Pools and then supply parameters to the setup form in LCS. The process of deploying a build machine is well documented and we won't duplicate this here, especially given the pace at which updates to LCS are being made. Even if we don't set up a build server manually, the information provided in this chapter may prove useful in understanding issues that may arise with the server.

The recipes in this chapter should be used in conjunction with the released Microsoft documentation. The aim (as always) is to provide practical hands-on guidance that's intended to augment the already published documentation.

This is an area of change and improvement. Build tasks will be shortly able to deploy to LCS directly and eventually we won't need a physical build server (which, currently, is a OneBox virtual machine in the cloud subscription or one hosted in the on-premise environment).

Do not follow these steps on your development OneBox virtual machine. You should use a new virtual machine as the build process will restore a backup the first time it's run. Then, you need to download the code from Azure DevOps to the local `packages` folder.

 No code changes should ever be made directly on the build server, even though it will have Visual Studio installed.

This chapter will cover the following recipes:

- Creating a Team Services Build Agent Pool
- Setting up a build server
- Managing build operations
- Releasing a build to User Acceptance Testing

Technical requirements

You can find the code files for this chapter on GitHub at `https://github.com/PacktPublishing/Extending-Microsoft-Dynamics-365-Finance-and-Supply-Chain-Management-Cookbook-Second-Edition`

Creating a Team Services Build Agent Pool

Agent Pools contain Build agents; in SCM build server configurations, we have one Build agent for each Agent Pool and only one Agent Pool in the Azure DevOps project. Build agents act as a bridge between Azure DevOps and the physical build server. The build agent is created when we configure the build server, and that process needs to have an Agent Pool already created.

When build servers are provisioned from LCS, we will have a one-to-one relationship for this. This is because a project will typically have its own build server (which is not limited to one), and keeping queues and pools with a one-to-one relationship simplifies management.

Getting ready

You will need to have created your Azure DevOps site using TFS source control (at the time of writing) before you start this recipe.

How to do it...

To create an Agent Pool, perform the following steps:

1. Open the Azure DevOps site, for example, `<your domain / tenant>.visualstudio.com`, and open your project.
2. Click on the **Project settings** button on the bottom left of the screen, as follows in the following screenshot:

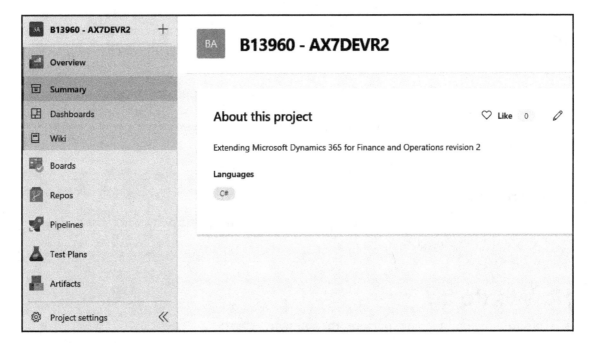

3. On the list that pops up, select **Agent Pools**.
4. On the **Agents Pools** page, click on **Add pool**.
5. The name should relate to the project; in my case, I chose `B13960-AX7DEVR2`. Choose a name that is short and makes it easy to determine which project the pool is for.

6. Uncheck **Grant access permission to all pipelines** and click on **OK**. We don't want any existing pipelines to assume access to this pool; we want to have finer control in SCM build servers.
7. We won't create an Agent at this stage as this is done from the build server.

How it works...

The Agent Pool is used while setting up of the build server in order to associate the agent, which is installed on the build server, with the queue. This way, when a build is triggered (manually or via a check-in), it knows which server to trigger the build to build on.

Setting up a build server

The build server is a one-box Dynamics 365 for Operations virtual machine, usually with demo data that is only ever used to produce builds. Even though it contains data and seems to have an application running in IIS, it cannot be used.

If we are creating a build server for a customer implementation project, most of the work will have been done for us already. We just need to specify the Agent Pool that we created in the previous recipe. This recipe will follow the ISV scenario where we install the build agent ourselves.

Getting ready

You will need a build server VM running with access to the internet, and the Agent Pool created against the project.

How to do it...

To configure the build server, perform the following steps:

1. Open the Azure DevOps site and select **Personal access tokens** from your user settings, as follows in the following screenshot:

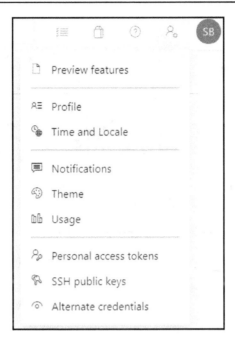

2. Click on **New Token** under the **Personal access tokens** tab that opens.

3. Enter a suitable description, such as B13960_Agent.

4. Set the expiry based on the project length. This is usually 1 year for SCM projects; you can extend this should it expire.

5. Ensure that **Full access** is selected and click on **Create**.

6. Make sure you copy the token as you will not be able to see it again!

7. Open a **PowerShell** prompt as an Administrator. This is usually a tile on the Start bar. Alternatively, you can press the *Windows* key and type Powershell. Right-click on the **PowerShell** option and choose **Run as administrator**.

8. Type the following line:

```
Cd \DynamicsSDK
```

9. Ensure that the current directory is C:\DynamicsSDK and type the following lines of code:

```
.\SetupBuildAgent.ps1 -VSO_ProjectCollection
https://<yourDomain>.visualstudio.com/DefaultCollection -
VSOAccessToken <your access token> -AgentName B13960-AX7DEVR2 -
AgentPoolName B13960-AX7DEVR2
```

10. The output should be as follows:

```
14:15:53: Configuring VSTS Agent service: B13960-AX7DEVR2
14:15:53: Setting environment variables...
14:15:54: Setting registry keys...
14:15:54: Removing existing VSTS Agent service...
14:15:55: Downloading VSTS Agent archive...
14:15:55: - Agent download URL: https://vstsagentpackage.azureedge.net/agent/2.163.1/vsts-agent-win-x64-2.163.1.zip
14:15:55: Expanding VSTS Agent archive...
14:15:55: Configuring new VSTS Agent service...
14:16:09: Configuring VSTS Agent service complete.
14:16:09: Script completed with exit code: 0
PS C:\DynamicsSDK> _
```

11. Open the Azure DevOps site and check that the agent was added to the agent queue, as follows in the following screenshot:

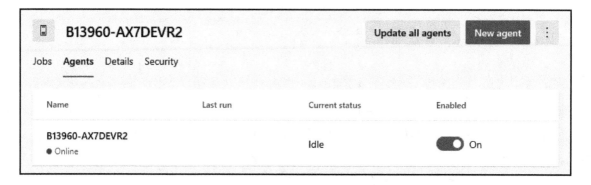

12. We still need a build definition, so go back to PowerShell and enter the following lines of code:

```
.\BuildEnvironmentReadiness.ps1 -VSO_ProjectCollection
https://<YourDomain>.visualstudio.com/DefaultCollection -
ProjectName "B13960 - AX7DEVR2" -VSOAccessToken
4jnefs3hd7dd2yc66fi2wumyuvat2rpfg5e35su6lo3he467a6ka -
AgentPoolName=B13960-AX7DEVR2
```

 The double quotes were required because the project name had spaces.

13. Open the Azure DevOps site again and open your project. Select **Pipelines** from the left navigation pane and then **Builds**. You should see the following:

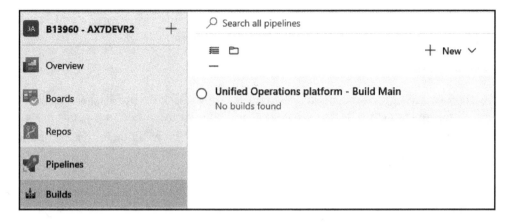

14. Click on **Edit** on the far right. This will list the Tasks that the pipeline will perform, one of which is **Generate Packages**. By looking at the arguments for this step, we can see that it uses the `PackingExclusions` variable to state which packages are to be excluded from the generated package. You can see this in the following screenshot:

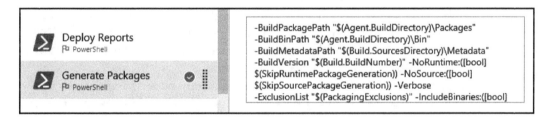

 We need to exclude any packages that reference packages that haven't been deployed to a sandbox or production environment, such as test projects. The Unit test package is not deployed and the package will, therefore, fail to deploy.

15. Click on the **Variables** tab and enter the name of the test package into the `PackagingExclusions` variable, as follows:

The PackagingExclusions variable is a comma-separated list, so each test package (not project) must be added here.

16. Before saving, we can make the name shorter. Click on the **Tasks** page, select the **Pipeline task** (the default selection), and change the name to Build - Main.

17. Click on **Save & queue** and select **Save**. On the **Save** dialog, enter a suitable comment and press **Save**.

18. This added a file called AXModulesBuild.proj to the root on the Main branch. We also need this on the Dev branch. Select **Repos** from the left navigation pane and then **Files**.

19. Expand Trunk and then Main. From the ellipses button (**...**), choose **Download** and download the file to a suitable location.

20. Click on the Dev branch and click **Upload file(s)** on the toolbar ribbon on the right-hand pane.

21. Use the **Browse** button to locate the AXModulesBuild.proj file you just downloaded and press **Check in**.

22. Select **Pipelines** from the left navigation bar. With our new pipeline selected, click on the three dots to the very right of the page and choose **Clone**. We're doing this to create a definition for continuous integration: every check-in will perform a build and run our tests.

23. After a few seconds, the page will show the definition. We should name this Build - DEV - Continuous because it is going to build the DEV branch using continuous integration.

24. From the **Tasks** page, select the Get sources option from the list. The default Server path is the Main branch, so we need to change this to Dev. This is shown in the following screenshot:

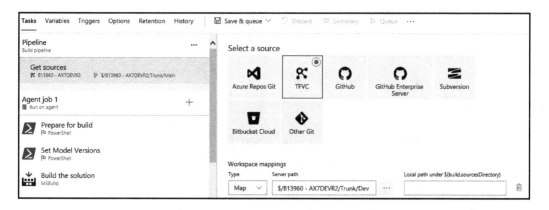

25. Select the **Build the solution** task and change the Project field so that it references Dev and not Main. In my case, I changed it from $/B13960 – AX7DEVR2/Trunk/**Main**/AXModulesBuild.proj to $/B13960 – AX7DEVR2/Trunk/**Dev**/AXModulesBuild.proj.

26. Select the **Triggers** page and enable **Continuous Integration**. The defaults are otherwise correct.

27. Select **Save** from the **Save & queue** option button.

28. Click on **Builds** again to see a list of build definitions. Then, select Build – Main and click on **Edit**.

29. Select **Triggers**, click **Add** next to the **Scheduled** heading, and create a schedule using the options that appear on the right-hand pane. This is based on your company's procedures; most companies wish to run a clean build (a complete fetch from TFS) nightly. The default schedule is usually correct.

30. Save your changes, but do not schedule a build. There is no code in Main yet as we have not integrated our Dev branch into the Main branch.

31. Select Build – DEV – Continuous and click **Queue** on the top right. On the dialog, click **Run**.

32. You should now see a console window showing the progress (very verbosely as the build is performed).

How it works...

There were five parts to this recipe:

- Getting a Personal Access Token
- Installing the build agent
- Configuring the build agent
- Uploading a build definition to the Azure DevOps project
- Configuring a build agent for clean and continuous integration

We could have downloaded the build agent manually from the Agent Queue form (you may have noticed the **Download agent** button) and then configured it using the agent's `config.cmd` script. This would be OK, but we wouldn't have been able to deploy a build definition to the project if we had done so. The next part, `BuildEnvironmentReadiness.ps1`, assumes that the agent is installed in a particular place on the drive and will, therefore, fail to run.

We ran each command with parameters rather than entering them at runtime because the script doesn't ask for optional parameters and uses the defaults.

The result of the configuration is that we have an Agent linked to our Agent queue through its configuration, and two build definitions that are both linked to the Agent queue.

Once all these have been linked and we have set up the build definitions, the build server is ready for operation.

See also

Check out the following link for more information:

- Developer topology deployment with continuous build and test automation: `https://docs.microsoft.com/en-us/dynamics365/fin-ops-core/dev-itpro/perf-test/continuous-build-test-automation`

Managing build operations

This recipe focuses on what happens when a build is triggered, and how to deal with some common issues. We will trigger a build and then monitor its progress.

Getting ready

We must have a fully functional build server and a build definition that will trigger on check-in. To reiterate the point we made at this start of this chapter, all changes must only be made on development machines, and never on the build server. Even though Visual Studio might be installed on the build server, it should never be used.

How to do it...

To manage build operations, perform the following steps:

1. Make a minor change to any code in your project and check-in the changes.
2. Then, open the Azure DevOps project and select **Builds** from the **Pipelines** menu. You should see something like the following:

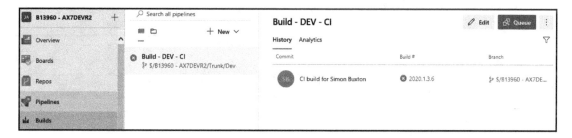

3. Clicking on the description under the **Commit** column will take us to the details of the build; click on this link.
4. This will open the details of the build operation with the Console open by default. This verbosely lists every detail of the operation as it happens. Any errors or warnings are also listed here.
5. Once complete, check for errors. These will show up on the failed task with a summary of the error displayed. At this stage, the most common error is that the model descriptor file was not checked in to source control. A typical error is **EXEC(0,0): Warning : 1:22:57 PM: No Models returned by model info provider from metadata.**

6. You may also notice that, even though no error was shown, no tests were run. The console will provide another clue:

```
No test assemblies found matching the pattern:
'C:\DynamicsSDK\VSOAgent\_work\2\Bin\**\*Test*.dll'.
```

 It is looking for DLLs that contain `Test`. We can see that naming conventions are important, albeit, in this case, possibly inelegant. It is like this because there is no way the build agent can see that the class in the DLL extends `SysTestCase`.

7. It is likely that the descriptor was not added to source control. To rectify this, begin by opening Visual Studio and selecting **Team Explorer**. From there, select **Source Control Explorer**.

8. Check whether the `Descriptor` folder is added to each package. In the following screenshot, the `Descriptor` folder is not listed under any folder. This can happen based on the version of the development tools:

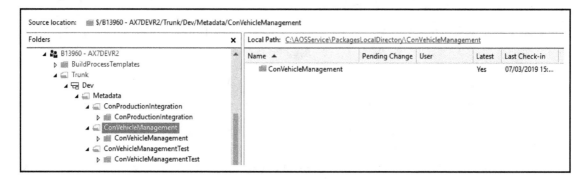

9. We add the `Descriptor` file by right-clicking on the package folder (the first **ConVehicleManagement** node, in this case) and selecting **Add Items to Folder....**. Add the **Descriptor** folder, but nothing else.

10. Once done, the list should resemble the following screenshot:

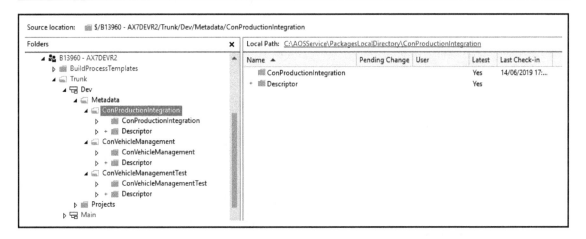

11. Checking in the changes will automatically trigger a build in the `Build - Dev - Continuous` pipeline. On the Azure DevOps site, select the `Build - Dev - Continuous` pipeline and click on the active build. This will look as follows:

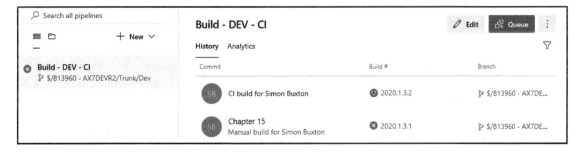

12. The build in progress has a blue circular icon. Click on its description to open the build details and look at the **Checkout** node. You should see entries similar to the following code snippet:

```
C:\DynamicsSDK\VSOAgent\_work\1\s\Metadata\ConProductionIntegration
:
Getting Descriptor
C:\DynamicsSDK\VSOAgent\_work\1\s\Metadata\ConProductionIntegration
\Descriptor:
Getting ConProductionIntegration.xml
C:\DynamicsSDK\VSOAgent\_work\1\s\Metadata\ConVehicleManagement:
Getting Descriptor
C:\DynamicsSDK\VSOAgent\_work\1\s\Metadata\ConVehicleManagement\Des
criptor:
Getting ConVehicleManagement.xml
C:\DynamicsSDK\VSOAgent\_work\1\s\Metadata\ConVehicleManagementTest
```

```
:
Getting Descriptor
C:\DynamicsSDK\VSOAgent\_work\1\s\Metadata\ConVehicleManagementTest
\Descriptor:
Getting ConVehicleManagementTest.xml
```

13. Once the build has finished, you should see the following on the build's summary page:

14. Should a test fail, we can view the output from the test case, the work item history, and the change history, and create a bug that can be assigned to a developer. This can be seen in the following screenshot:

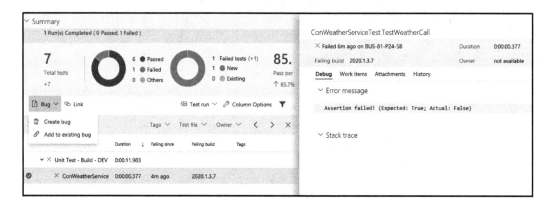

The default is to show only failed tests; to view them all, click on the outcome (for example, `Failed`) next to the **Outcome** label and choose `All`.

How it works...

When the build agent is installed, it creates a TFS workspace. This is based on the source mapping in the pipeline; for an example, refer to the following:

Source control folder	Local folder
$/B13960 – AX7DEVR2/Trunk/Dev	C:\DynamicsSDK\VSOAgent_work\1\s

It starts by downloading all changes from this folder in TFS to a local working folder. Then, it uses the descriptor file to determine what to build.

Once the files have been downloaded, the following happens:

1. Checks are made to verify whether the `DynamicsBackup` folder exists on the C drive – this will be on a backup-specific drive when the build server is deployed using LCS.
2. If it does not exist, a SQL backup is made to the `DynamicsBackup\Databases` folder and the local packages folder is copied to the `DynamicsBackup\Packages` folder.
3. If the folder exists, the SQL database is restored from this backup and the local packages folder is recreated from this folder.
4. The system will then start a full build of the system and process each step in the build definition. Most of this will call PowerShell scripts stored in the `C:\DynamcisSDK` folder.
5. Once complete, it uploads the source and resultant deployable package to the build. This will then be applied to our test server, and eventually production.

With this, we can see some of the benefits of using test cases and source control. When a test fails, we can see the change history and assign the bug fix to a developer for resolution.

When a check-in is made and there is a continuous integration pipeline, a build will be added to the queue. Once a build agent (which is running on a build server) is available, it will pick up the next build in the queue.

See also

For more information on continuous integration with SCM, please follow this link:

- Continuous delivery home page: `https://docs.microsoft.com/en-us/ dynamics365/fin-ops-core/dev-itpro/dev-tools/continuous-delivery-home- page`

Should you have third-party or ISV packages, you will be able to deploy the build process. Please see the following link for more information:

- Managing third-party models and runtime packages using source control: `https://docs.microsoft.com/en-us/dynamics365/fin-ops-core/dev-itpro/ dev-tools/manage-runtime-packages`

Releasing a build to User Acceptance Testing

At the end of the build process, a deployable package file was uploaded to the build. This file can then be applied to your user acceptance test or sandbox server.

We can apply the package manually on the test server but, for LCS-deployed **User Acceptance Testing** (**UAT**) environments, this is always done via LCS. Any release to production must be deployed to a sandbox server first and marked as a release candidate.

A simplified process for the release to UAT would involve the following steps:

1. The development team writes code and completes the tasks that are required for the next build (for example, those that are assigned to the current sprint).
2. The developers will also write unit tests and perform their own unit tests.
3. Initial testing will be done by taking a package from the Dev branch pipeline and deploying it to a OneBox. This is often done by a member of the IT or internal implementation team who has knowledge of the business process.
4. Any bugs will be rectified and retested.

5. Once you're ready to create a release, the Dev branch will be integrated into the Main branch and a build will be triggered from the Main branch.

6. The output from the Main branch is uploaded to LCS.

7. The user acceptance testing or Sandbox environment is rebuilt from production and the Main build is applied to it (via LCS).

8. The build will then undergo regression testing and test the new features that were added in this release.

9. Once passed, the build is marked as a release candidate and applied to production.

10. The Dev branch can be recreated from Main.

This recipe is split into two parts: integrating Dev back into Main and deploying the package to a UAT environment.

Getting ready

To complete this recipe, we need to have an LCS Operations server deployed through LCS. We will need a development virtual machine for the tasks required in Visual Studio. We never use Visual Studio on the build server.

How to do it...

To take a build from the Dev branch and apply it to a standalone test server, perform the following:

1. Open the Azure DevOps site, open your project, and locate `Build - Dev - Coninuous` from the **Pipelines** | **Builds** section.

2. Click on the description of the build (under the **Commit** column) and select the **Summary** tab page. You should see the following output if the build is successful:

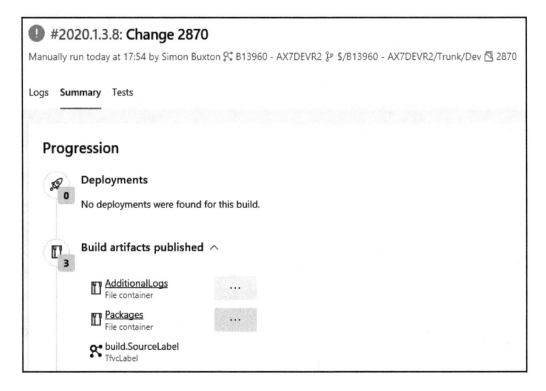

3. Click the ellipses (**...**) next to the **Packages** file container and select **View contents**.

4. Expand the **Packages** folder and click the ellipses. Choose **Download** from the list, as follows in the following screenshot:

5. Download the file and then open LCS (`https://lcs.dynamics.com/`).

6. You can apply this to a standalone OneBox using these instructions, which can be found in the **Collect topology configuration data** section: `https://docs.microsoft.com/en-us/dynamics365/fin-ops-core/dev-itpro/deployment/install-deployable-package`.

If we are to deploy a build to UAT, we need to integrate `Dev` into `Main`. Perform the following to do this:

1. Open Visual Studio.

2. Ensure that the source control mapping is configured for the `Main` and `Dev` branches, in line with the following screenshot:

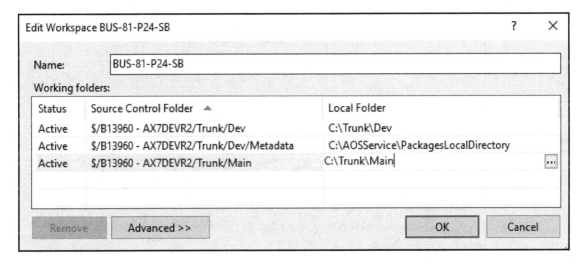

3. With this complete, we can now integrate `Dev` into `Main`. From the **Team Explorer** window, select **Source Control Explorer**.

4. Expand **Trunk**, right-click on Dev, and select **Branching and Merging** | Merge... from the popup menu, as follows in the following screenshot:

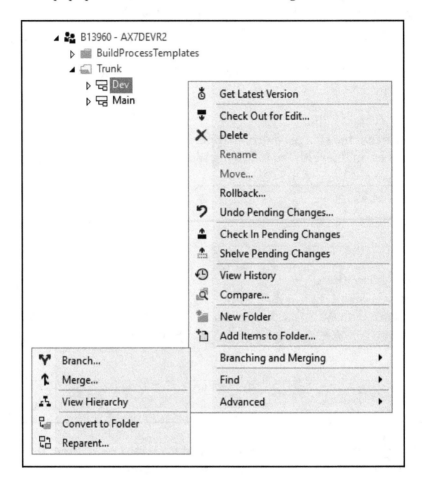

5. The next dialog box will show the **Source** as the Dev branch and the **Target** automatically as the Main branch. If it doesn't, this means we didn't create the Dev branch from Main. The dialog should look as follows:

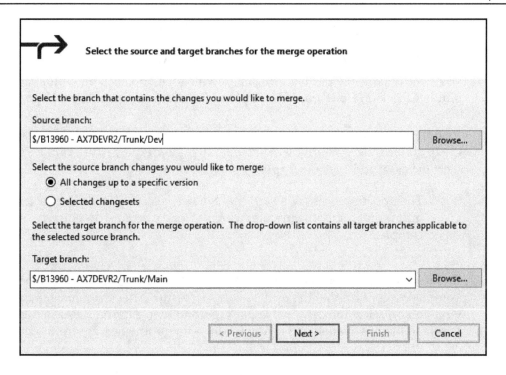

Select the source and target branches for the merge operation

Select the branch that contains the changes you would like to merge.

Source branch:

S/B13960 - AX7DEVR2/Trunk/Dev   Browse...

Select the source branch changes you would like to merge:

◉ All changes up to a specific version

○ Selected changesets

Select the target branch for the merge operation. The drop-down list contains all target branches applicable to the selected source branch.

Target branch:

S/B13960 - AX7DEVR2/Trunk/Main   Browse...

< Previous   Next >   Finish   Cancel

6. Press **Next** and then **Finish**. This will add all the changes to **Pending changes** against the Main branch.

7. Finally, choose **Check in** from **Pending changes** on the **Team Explorer** window.

8. We would usually have a task (an Azure DevOps task) for this, that states some details about the build. When we check in with a task, the code in that **Check in** is automatically associated with the **Check in**.

9. Now, you need to manually create a build for the `Build - Main` pipeline. Once you've done this, the resulting package can be used to upload to LCS.

To upload the package to LCS and apply it to the UAT environment, perform the following steps:

1. Open your LCS project and then open the Asset library. Depending on the type of project, this will be under the burger icon or a tile on the project. Do not use the Shared Asset Library.

2. In the **Asset library**, select **Software deployable package** from the left and press the plus (**+**) symbol. In the dialog, enter the build name (for example, B20191231) and a description, and then click on **Add a file**.

3. Locate the deployable package we just downloaded and click on **Upload**. Once complete, click on **Confirm** on the **Upload Software deployable package file** dialog.

4. Open the environment that this should be deployed to and choose **Maintain | Apply updates**. This will show a list of Software deployable package assets. Select the asset and click on **Apply**.

> The update process will start immediately. This will take the server offline and apply the update, which will take around an hour to complete.

5. After testing is complete, go back to the sandbox environment. You will be prompted to confirm that the update was successful. After that, go back to the Asset library, select the deployable package, and then click on **Release candidate**. Do this so that it's available to be deployed to the production environment.

How it works...

Deploying packages is performed by a PowerShell script on the target server. Agents that have been installed on LCS-deployed servers allow LCS to perform this task.

The process for this is as follows:

1. Download the deployable package to the target server or servers (the test and production environments have multiple servers and the components that are installed on each may vary).

2. Extract the deployable package.

3. Apply the update to the server using the PowerShell scripts included in the package.

4. At the end of the process, the servers' services are restarted.

This process is best used (and is, in fact, mandatory) to apply updates to customer implementation environments. You can't apply an update to production servers that haven't been applied to the sandbox server through LCS.

14
Workflow Development

Workflows in Microsoft Dynamics 365 Finance and Supply Chain Management have two main types of elements – **approvals** and **tasks** – that act on a document. This is the center of the workflow and is where tasks are triggered based on what the user decides. By *document*, we mean a record with a form that maintains it. For example, a **New customer creation** workflow would be based on the customer table using the customer details form as the document.

The workflow designer can then use conditions based on fields and display methods on tables in order to decide what happens. This solves many requirements where a great deal of flexibility in the configuration is required, but can also be misunderstood and used inappropriately. The submission of a workflow is usually started with the user pressing the **Submit** button on the form; it's which is then processed within a minute by the batch server. The minimum time it can take for a workflow to complete, if the conditions for automatic completion are met, is three minutes: up to one minute for submission, one minute for evaluation, and one minute for each subsequent workflow step. This, therefore, can't be used when the user is expecting feedback as part of the data entry process.

Even though the batch framework is likely to be desgined to enable the immediate processing of tasks, just like Business Events, it doesn't change the paradigm that workflows are asynchronous processes and no business process should rely on the immediate processing of workflow tasks. This is likely to mean that we are using workflows for the wrong purpose, and a business event or other immediate event-based technical solution is more appropriate.

In this chapter, we'll use workflow design to control the approval of a new vehicle, including a task to inspect the vehicle as part of the workflow. To do this, we will cover the following recipes:

- Creating a workflow type
- Creating a workflow approval

- Creating a manual workflow task
- Hooking up a workflow to the user interface
- Creating a sample workflow design

Technical requirements

You can find the code files for this chapter on GitHub at the following links:

- `https://github.com/PacktPublishing/Extending-Microsoft-Dynamics-365-Finance-and-Supply-Chain-Management-Cookbook-Second-Edition/blob/master/Chapter%2014%20-%20Vehicle%20management.axpp`
- **Workflows:** `https://github.com/PacktPublishing/Extending-Microsoft-Dynamics-365-Finance-and-Supply-Chain-Management-Cookbook-Second-Edition/blob/master/Chapter%2014%20-%20Workflow.axpp`

Creating a workflow type

A workflow type can be considered as a template or a document definition. It acts like an umbrella for associated workflow elements, such as approvals and tasks. When the designer starts to design a workflow, they actually select a workflow type, and the design surface will allow them to select workflow elements associated with it.

We create the workflow type first because the workflow type creation tooling will create elements that can be used in other workflow elements. We just come back to this in order to add them to the list of supported types by the workflow type.

 Be careful when naming items as this process automatically creates menu items and classes. They are all prefixed with the workflow type's name. If we have a class that exists already, it will add a 1 to the name, which is unpleasant. For this reason, the maximum length is 20 characters for all workflow types, approvals, tasks, and automated tasks.

We will create a Base Enum to persist the workflow status. In this recipe, we will only use one status field to handle the started and canceled events. The Base Enum was designed with the entire workflow in mind, which includes handling the status of workflow approval.

Getting ready

This recipe can be applied to any record that has a main form managing its data, which is the prerequisite for this recipe. The tables that workflows are typically used with are the main or worksheet table types.

How to do it...

We should create a new project for this as this is a distinct requirement within the vehicle management module. Create the project and label file as follows:

1. Create a new project (*Ctrl + Shift + N* or choose **File** | **New** | **Project/Solution...**).
2. Use the name `ConVMSVehicleWF` and ensure that the project is created under `C:\Trunk\Dev\Projects` (the folder we mapped in source control to the `projects` folder of our development branch).
3. Once the project has been created, check the project's properties to ensure that the **Model** is correct.
4. As with all new projects, create a new Label file. This should be named after the project's name, that is, `ConVMSVehicleWF`.

If we are creating a workflow type in a new module, as in our case, we need to add an element to the `ModuleAxapta` base enum and create a workflow category. The following steps can be skipped if we are adding a workflow to a module for which a workflow category has already been created. In our case, we are creating a workflow in a new module, so we will perform the following steps:

1. We need to add an element to the `ModuleAxapta` base enum. Locate the `ModuleAxapta` Base Enum and choose **Create extension** from the right-click context menu. Rename it as usual by changing the `.ConVehicleManagement` portion of the name to the project's name (`.ConVMSVehicleWF`).
2. Create a new label for `Vehicle management` and add a new element to the `ModuleAxapta` base enum named `ConVMS`, thereby completing the **Label** property.
3. To create the workflow category, we need to add a new item to our project and choose **Workflow Category** from the **Business process and Workflow** list. Enter the name `ConVMSVehicleManagement` before clicking on **Add**.

4. Create labels for the **Label** and **HelpText** properties, such as `Vehicle management` and `Vehicle management workflows`, respectively; these will be visible to the workflow designer in the user interface. Set the **Module** property to the module name, which is `ConVMS` in our case.

The following steps follow on from creating a workflow category:

1. Before we create the actual workflow type element, we need to create some base elements that are required by the workflow approval element. First, create a new query called `ConVMSVehicleWF`. To this query, add the `ConVMSVehicleTable` table, and set the **Dynamics Fields** property to `Yes`.

2. Now, we can start creating the workflow type. Choose to add a new item to the project and select **Workflow Type** from the **Business process and Workflow** list. Name the new element `ConVMSVehicleWF` and click on **Add**.

3. Complete the **Add Workflow Type** dialog, as shown in the following screenshot:

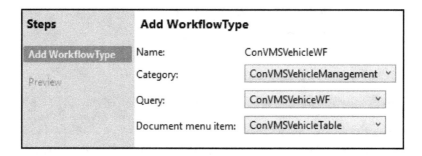

4. Click on **Next**.

5. You will see the elements that will be created; check that none are suffixed with 1 (which means that the preferred element name already exists – you should change the type's name to avoid this) and click on **Finish**.

6. Open the `ConVMSVehicleWFDocument` class and the workflow document class, and add a new method, as shown in the following code:

```
public Days ParmDaysSinceAcquired(
    CompanyId _companyId,
    TableId _tableId,
    RecId _recId)
{
    Days days;
    if(_tableId == tableNum(ConVMSVehicleTable))
    {
        ConVMSVehicleTable vehicle;
        select crosscompany AcquiredDate
```

```
              from vehicle
          where vehicle.DataAreaId == _companyId
              && vehicle.RecId == _recId;
      days = vehicle.AcquiredDate - systemDateGet();
    }
    return days;
}
```

We added the `parm` method as an example of how to add display methods that can be used in the workflow expression builder and as a placeholder in the workflow text that's presented to the user.

7. There will be two new **Action Menu Items** created, prefixed with the approval name, that is, `ConVMSVehicleWF`. These are suffixed with `CancelMenuItem` and `SubmitMenuItem`. For each of these, set the **Label** and **Help Text** properties with a suitable label, as shown in the following table:

Menu item	Label	Help Text
CancelMenuItem	Cancel	Cancel the vehicle workflow
SubmitMenuItem	Submit	Submit the vehicle to the workflow

Create the labels using names and not numbers as we will be reusing these labels in other elements.

The next step is to complete the event handler classes that were created for us by wiring up events so that their status is maintained on the vehicle. This can be done as follows:

1. We need to handle the state change, so first we need to create a Base Enum name, `ConVMSVehicleWFApprStatus`, with the following elements:

Element	Label	Description
Draft	@SYS75939	Draft – the workflow has not been submitted to the workflow yet
Waiting	Waiting	The workflow has been submitted but has not been allocated to an approver yet
Inspection	Inspection	The vehicle is being inspected
InReview	In review	The workflow has been allocated to one or more approvers
Approved	Approved	The workflow has been approved
Rejected	Rejected	The workflow was rejected by the approvers
Revised	Revised	A change was requested by an approver

These labels should be created using named label identifiers, just like we did for the menu items, since we will be reusing them on other elements.

2. Use the @SYS101302 label (**Approval Status**) in the Base Enum's **Label** property. Add the new Base Enum to the ConVMSVehicleTable table as Status and add it to the Overview field group. Make the field read-only.

3. Open the ConVMSVehicleWF workflow type and complete the **Label** and **Help Text** fields. These assist the workflow designer in selecting the correct workflow type when creating a new workflow. Good examples are as follows:

Label Id	Label
VehicleWFType	Vehicle approval workflows.
VehicleWFTypeHT	Use this workflow type to create workflows for approving new vehicles.

4. Next, create a class called ConVMSVehicleWFStatusHandler and write the following piece of code:

```
class ConVMSVehicleWFStatusHandler
{
    public static void SetStatus(
        RefRecId _vehicleRecId,
        ConVMSVehicleWFApprStatus _status)
    {
        ConVMSVehicleTable vehicle;

        ttsbegin;
        select forupdate vehicle
            where vehicle.RecId == _vehicleRecId;
        if (vehicle.RecId != 0
            && vehicle.Status != _status)
        {
            vehicle.Status = _status;
            vehicle.update();
        }
        ttscommit;
    }
}
```

Create common select statements, such as the preceding one, as a static Find method, for example, FindByRecId. When writing any select statement, check that the table has a suitable index.

5. Save and close the class.

6. Create a new class named `ConVMSVehicleWFBase` and add the following method:

```
public boolean ValidateContext(WorkflowContext _context)
{
    If (_context.parmTableId() !=
    tableNum(ConWHSVehicleTable))
    {
        //Workflow must be based on the vehicle table
        throw error("@ConVMSVehicleWF:MustBeVehicleTable");
    }
    ConVMSVehicleTable vehicle;
    select RecId from vehicle
        where vehicle.RecId == _context.parmRecId();
    if (vehicle.RecId == 0)
    {
        //Vehicle cannot be found for the workflow instance
        throw error("@ConVMSVehicleWF:VehicleNotFound");
    }
    return true;
}
```

We throw an error in the case of a validation error as we need the workflow to stop with an error should it fail; the workflow cannot continue with an invalid context.

7. Next, add a method so that the workflow type's handler class knows whether or not the supported elements actually ran. Since that final result will be approved or rejected, we can't use the same field to state that the workflow is completed. In fact, if the workflow type has been completed but nothing was done, the document should reset back to `Draft` (not submitted). Write the method as follows:

```
public boolean CanCompleteWF(WorkflowContext _context)
{
    ConVMSVehicleTable vehicle;
    select RecId from vehicle
        where vehicle.RecId == _context.parmRecId();
    if (vehicle.RecId != 0)
    {
        // Code to check if the workflow can be completed,
        // i.e. nothing in progress. We have no completion
        // conditions at present, so just return true
        return true;
```

```
    }
    return false;
}
```

8. Save and close this class and open the `ConVMSVehicleWFEventHandler` class. Alter its class declaration so that it extends `ConVMSVehicleWFBase`.

9. The class will have template methods for us to complete. Complete these as follows in order to handle the workflow type's events:

```
public void started(WorkflowEventArgs _workflowEventArgs)
{
    WorkflowContext context;
    context = _workflowEventArgs.parmWorkflowContext();
    if(this.ValidateContext(context))
    {
        ConVMSVehicleWFStatusHandler::SetStatus(
            context.parmRecId(),
            ConVMSVehicleWFApprStatus::Waiting);
    }
}

public void canceled(WorkflowEventArgs _workflowEventArgs)
{
    WorkflowContext context;
    context = _workflowEventArgs.parmWorkflowContext();
    if(this.ValidateContext(context))
    {
        ConVMSVehicleWFStatusHandler::SetStatus(
            context.parmRecId(),
            ConVMSVehicleWFApprStatus::Draft);
    }
}

public void completed(WorkflowEventArgs _workflowEventArgs)
{
    WorkflowContext context;
    context = _workflowEventArgs.parmWorkflowContext();
    if(this.ValidateContext(context))
    {
        If (!this.CanCompleteWF(context))
        {
            ConVMSVehicleWFStatusHandler::SetStatus(
                context.parmRecId(),
                ConVMSVehicleWFApprStatus::Draft);
        }
    }
}
```

The status changes here are that we move from Draft to Waiting when the workflow engine starts, and back to Draft if canceled. Should the workflow complete but fail the CanCompleteWF check, reset it back to Draft.

10. Finally, open the ConVMSVehicleWFSubmitManager class and complete the main method, as shown here:

```
public static void main(Args _args)
{
    RefRecId recId;
    CompanyId companyId;
    RefTableId tableId;
    WorkflowComment comment;
    WorkflowSubmitDialog dialog;
    WorkflowVersionTable version;

    recId = _args.record().RecId;
    tableId = _args.record().TableId;
    companyId = _args.record().DataAreaId;

    // The method has not been called correctly.
    if (tableId != tableNum(ConVMSVehicleTable)
        || recId == 0)
    {
        throw error(strfmt("@SYS19306", funcname()));
    }

    version = _args.caller().getActiveWorkflowConfiguration();
    dialog = WorkflowSubmitDialog::construct(version);
    dialog.run();

    if (dialog.parmIsClosedOK())
    {
        comment = dialog.parmWorkflowComment();

        Workflow::activateFromWorkflowConfigurationId(
            version.ConfigurationId,
            recId,
            comment,
            NoYes::No);
        // Set the workflow status to Submitted.
        ConVMSVehicleWFStatusHandler::SetStatus(
            _args.record().RecId,
            ConVMSVehicleWFApprStatus::Waiting);
    }
}
```

```
        if(FormDataUtil::isFormDataSource(_args.record()))
        {
            FormDataUtil::getFormDataSource(_args.record())
                .research(true);
        }

        _args.caller().updateWorkflowControls();
    }
```

11. Close all code editors and designers, build the project, and synchronize it with the database. The compiler will highlight any code we forgot to handle by showing TODO comments as warnings.

How it works...

The workflow type required a few elements before we created the actual workflow type. The document is defined by a query, which has a main table. This could be a query of sales orders and sales order lines, where the sales order is the main table and lets the workflow designer use fields from the query to define messages to the user, and also control how the workflow behaves. The workflow has special application element types for workflows, which point to classes that implement specific interfaces.

The workflow type is a higher level than workflow elements. Workflow elements are tasks that are assigned to the user, and they handle states such as Review, Reject, Approve, and so on. The workflow type controls whether the workflow is started, canceled, or completed.

It may seem odd that we don't map workflow event types directly to the Base Enum elements. The workflow engine doesn't read this field; it knows within itself the status of the workflow. The status field is there to allow us to easily read the status or act on a particular workflow event. For this reason, we don't actually need to handle all of the events that the workflow provides.

The ConVMSVehicleWFEventHandler class was tied to the workflow type and is used to persist the workflow's state in the target document record – the vehicle record, in our case.

The parm method on the workflow document class, ConVMSVehicleWFDocument, adds a calculated member that can be used by the workflow designer either to make decisions in the workflow design or to be displayed in messages to the users.

`parm` methods have to be written with the same input parameters as shown in the example method, and we are free to write any code we like and return the data of any base type that can be converted into a string, such as strings, dates, and Base Enums. Due to this, we cannot return types such as records, objects, or containers. Consider how the method will perform, as this will be run whenever it needs to be evaluated by the workflow engine.

See also

Check out the following links for help with setting up workflows and for further reading:

- Workflow system
  architecture: `https://docs.microsoft.com/en-us/dynamics365/operations/organization-administration/workflow-system-architecture`
- Creating workflows
  overview: `https://docs.microsoft.com/en-us/dynamics365/operations/organization-administration/create-workflow`
- Overview of the workflow system:
  `https://docs.microsoft.com/en-us/dynamics365/operations/organization-administration/overview-workflow-system` and
  `https://ax.help.dynamics.com/en/wiki/overview-of-the-workflow-system/`

- Workflow
  elements: `https://docs.microsoft.com/en-us/dynamics365/operations/organization-administration/workflow-elements`

Creating a workflow approval

A workflow approval is an element that can route the to a person or persons who can approve, reject, or request a change, or delegate an approval task. When the workflow is designed, we can use the outcome of an approval task to trigger other workflow tasks, or simply inform the user. The workflow approval status is persisted as a field on the document record (the vehicle record, in our case) in the same way that the workflow type does.

As a result of this, there are often two fields on the workflow's main table, one for the workflow document state, and another for the workflow element state. In some cases, such as human resource workflows, the Base Enum is combined into one field. This can seem confusing, but when the workflow status field is properly defined, it simplifies this process.

Getting ready

We just need to have created a workflow type or have a suitable workflow type to add the approval to.

How to do it...

To create a workflow approval, perform the following steps:

1. Add a new item to the project by selecting **Business Process and Workflow** from the left-hand list, and then **Workflow Approval** from the right. Enter ConVMSVehicleApprWF as the **Name** and click on **Add**.

2. Complete the **Add Approval** dialog, as shown here:

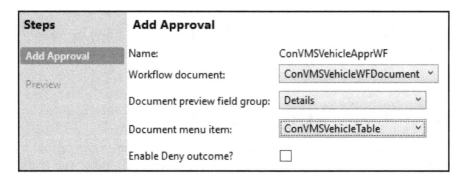

3. Click on **Next**.

4. You will be presented with all of the elements the wizard will create for us, reminding us again why the limit is 20 characters and also why the naming convention is important. Click on **Finish**.

5. Open the new ConVMSVehicleApprWF workflow approval, expand the **Outcomes** node, and note that the system has associated a workflow event handler class with **Approve**, **Reject**, and **RequestChange**. On the **Deny** outcome, change the **Enabled** property to No.

6. To complete this element, create labels for the **Label** and **HelpText** properties on the root `ConVMSVehicleApprWF` node element. The workflow designer will need this to identify the correct workflow.

7. There will be five new `Action Menu Items` created, prefixed with the approval name, `ConVMSVehicleApprWF`. These are suffixed with `Approve`, `DelegateMenuItem`, `Reject`, `RequestChange`, and `ResubmitMenuItem`. For each of these, set the **Label** and **Help Text** properties with a suitable label, as follows:

Menu item	Label	Help text
Approve	Approve	Approve the new vehicle request
DelegateMenuItem	Delegate	Delegate this approval to a colleague
Reject	Reject	Reject the new vehicle request
RequestChange	Revise	Send the request back for revision
ResubmitMenuItem	Resubmit	Resubmit the new vehicle request

For the label ID, it is a good idea to use a name that identifies what the label is, such as `Approve` for the label and `ApproveHT` for the help text.

As well as menu items, we also created an event handler class, which is named based on the workflow approval, suffixed with `EventHandler`. This class will implement seven interfaces, which ensure that a method is implemented, one per event type.

8. Open the `ConVMSVehicleApprWFEventHandler` work event handler class and alter the class declaration so that it extends `ConVMSVehicleWFBase`.

9. This class implements the `WorkflowElementDeniedEventHandler` interface, even though we chose not to in the creation dialog; remove this from the list.

10. Then, locate the `denied` method and delete it.

11. Now, we need to write some code for each method that was generated for us with a `TODO`. The sample code to write for each method is as follows:

```
public void started(WorkflowElementEventArgs
_workflowElementEventArgs)
{
    WorkflowContext context =
     _workflowElementEventArgs.parmWorkflowContext();
    if(this.ValidateContext(context))
    {
```

```
ConVMSVehicleWFStatusHandler::SetStatus(
    context.parmRecId(),
    ConVMSVehicleWFApprStatus::Waiting);
    }
}
```

12. Follow this pattern for each method while using the following table to determine which status to set:

Element	Method
Waiting	`started`
InReview	`created`
Approved	`completed`
Rejected	`returned`
Revised	`changeRequested`
Draft	`canceled`

13. For the created method, the input parameter is a different type; simply change the method, as follows:

```
public void created(WorkflowWorkItemsEventArgs
_workflowWorkItemsEventArgs)
{
    WorkflowElementEventArgs workflowArgs;
    workflowArgs =
    _workflowWorkItemsEventArgs.parmWorkflowElementEventArgs();
    WorkflowContext context = workflowArgs.parmWorkflowContext();
    if(this.ValidateContext(context))
    {
        ConVMSVehicleWFStatusHandler::SetStatus(
            context.parmRecId(),
            ConVMSVehicleWFApprStatus::InReview);
    }
}
```

14. In the previous recipe, we created the workflow type and created a method that we now can complete so that it returns whether or not the workflow can be completed. Open the `ConVMSVehicleWFBase` class and alter the method, as follows:

```
public boolean CanCompleteWF(WorkflowContext _context)
{
    ConVMSVehicleTable vehicle;
    select Status, RecId from vehicle
        where vehicle.RecId == _context.parmRecId();
```

```
    boolean canComplete = false;
    if (vehicle.RecId != 0)
    {
        switch (vehicle.Status)
        {
            case ConVMSVehicleWFApprStatus::Approved:
            case ConVMSVehicleWFApprStatus::Rejected:
                canComplete = true;
                break;
        }
    }
    return canComplete;
}
```

15. The final piece of code to write is the resubmit code. A template was created for us, so open the `ConVMSVehicleAppWFResubmitActionMgr` class.

16. In the `main` method, remove the `TODO` comment and write the following code snippet:

```
public static void main(Args _args)
{
    // The method has not been called correctly.
    if (_args.record().TableId != tableNum(ConVMSVehicleTable)
    || _args.record().RecId == 0)
    {
        throw error(
            Error::missingRecord(
                tableStr(ConVMSVehicleTable)));
    }
    //Resubmit the same workflow, Workflow handles the
    // resubmit action
    WorkflowWorkItemActionManager::main(_args);
    // Set the workflow status to Submitted.
    ConVMSVehicleWFStatusHandler::SetStatus(
        _args.record().RecId,
        ConVMSVehicleWFApprStatus::Waiting);

    _args.caller().updateWorkflowControls();
}
```

17. Finally, open the workflow type and then right-click on the **Supported Elements** node. Select **New Workflow Element Reference** and set the properties as follows:

Field	EDT / Enum	Description
Element Name	ConVMSVehicleApprWF	This is the element's name
Name	ApproveVehicle	This is a short version of the name, prefixed with its type
Type	Approval	This is the workflow element's type

18. Save and close all code editors and designers and build the project. Don't forget to synchronize since we have added a new field.

How it works...

Any workflow approval is set up with outcomes, which are referenced by an event handler class that implements an interface for each outcome it handles. Each outcome is tied, internally, to that interface. When the outcome occurs, it will construct the referenced event handler class using the interface as the type. Then, it calls the appropriate method. This pattern (instantiating a class using the interface as the type) is a common pattern. We used this ourselves in Chapter 6, *Writing for Extensibility*, in the *Defining business actions in data* recipe.

There are some events (Started and Canceled, for example) that are set on the work approval's main property sheet. All this was created for us when we created the workflow approval element.

The class that the code generated for us implements all the required interfaces with TODO statements where we need to write code. The code is usually simple, and, in our case, we are just updating the vehicle's status field. The generated code will always implement all the interfaces that the workflow element can support, so it is common to remove methods and interfaces from the event handler class.

Creating a manual workflow task

A manual task is a task that is assigned to a user in order to perform an action. This action can be any task, such as Inspect vehicle, and the user will then state that the task was complete.

This workflow will be used to instruct the vehicle to be inspected and record whether it was inspected in a new field on the vehicle table.

Getting ready

This recipe is a continuation of the *Creating a workflow type* recipe as we need a workflow document class.

How to do it...

To create the manual workflow task, follow these steps:

1. We need a new Base Enum for the inspection status as this will be used to see whether a vehicle has been inspected and to control the state of the workflow task. Name it `ConVMSVehInspStatus` and create the elements shown in the following table:

Element	Label	Description
NotInspected	Not inspected	This vehicle has not been inspected yet.
Waiting	Waiting	This workflow has been submitted, but has not been allocated to an approver yet.
PendingApproval	Pending approval	This workflow has been allocated to one or more workers to perform the task.
Completed	Completed	This workflow has been completed.

2. Create a new Date EDT for `ConVMSVehInspDate`, setting the properties as follows:

Field	EDT/Enum	Description
Extends	TransDate	This EDT should be used for all dates.
Label	Date inspected	Create a named label for this, such as `@ConWHS:DateInspected`.
Help Text	The date the inspection was carried out	This is generic and not tied to its eventual implementation in order to make the EDT reusable. The help text does not reference the vehicle for this reason.

3. Open the designer for the `ConVMSVehicleTable` table from the **Application explorer** and add the following fields to the vehicle table. Also, set **Allow Edit** and **Allow Edit On Create** to No:

Field	EDT / Enum	Description
InspStatus	ConVMSVehInspStatus	This is the status Base Enum that we created in the previous step.
InspComment	WorkflowComment	This will hold the last note when the task is completed.
InspDate	ConVMSVehInspDate	This is the date that the workflow task was completed on.

We don't have to add the table to our project to edit it as it is in the same package. It is preferable to keep elements in just one project. The only downside is that we will need to build the package using the **Build models** option on the **Dynamics 365** menu. In prior releases of AX, it was common to add the same objects to different projects, but this was usually only due to the fact we were overlaying a lot of standard elements.

4. Create a field group named `Inspection` and set the **Label** property to Inspection. Add the fields to this group and then add the field group to a suitable place in the `ConVMSVehicleTable` form, which is also opened from the **Application Explorer**.

5. Next, let's add a status handler class. Create a new class name, `ConVMSVehicleWFInspStatusHandler`. Create a method to handle the status change and set the `InspComment` and `InspDate` fields from the method's parameters. The code for this is as follows:

```
public static void SetStatus(RefRecId _vehicleRecId,
    ConVMSVehInspStatus _status,
    WorkflowComment _comment = '',
    ConVMSVehInspDate _inspDate = dateNull())
{
    ConVMSVehicleTable vehicle;

    ttsbegin;
    select forupdate vehicle
        where vehicle.RecId == _vehicleRecId;
    if(vehicle.RecId != 0
        && vehicle.InspStatus != _status)
    {
        vehicle.InspStatus = _status;
        // if the inspection is complete set
        // the comment and inspection date fields
        // otherwise clear them, as the workflow
        // may have been canceled.
        switch (_status)
        {
            case ConVMSVehInspStatus::Completed:
                vehicle.InspComment = _comment;
                vehicle.InspDate = _inspDate;
                break;
            default:
                vehicle.InspComment = '';
                vehicle.InspDate = dateNull();
        }
        vehicle.update();
    }
```

```
        ttscommit;
    }
```

6. Against the project, add a new item and choose **Workflow Task** from the **Business process and Workflow** list. Use the `ConVMSVehicleWFInspect` name and click on **Add**.

7. Configure the **Add Task** dialog, as shown in the following screenshot:

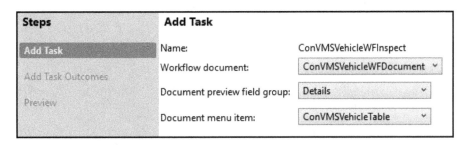

8. Click on **Next**.

9. On the next page, choose **Complete** from the **Type** drop-down list and enter `Complete` in the field before clicking on **Add**.

 You can add further outcomes, which will follow the same pattern when implemented.

10. Click on **Next** and then **Finish**.

11. For each action menu item created by the wizard, complete the **Label** and **Help Text** properties.

 You may have noticed that the code that's generated by this process is very similar to the Workflow approval. We will follow that pattern again by handling the required methods in the `ConVMSVehicleWFInspectEventHandler` class.

12. Since we won't be handling all of the possible outcomes, we should only implement the required interfaces. Also, in order to have access to the `ValidateContext` method, we should extend `ConVMSVehicleWFBase`. The class declaration should read as follows:

```
public final class ConVMSVehicleWFInspectEventHandler
    extends ConVMSVehicleWFBase
    implements WorkflowElementCanceledEventHandler,
```

```
WorkflowElementCompletedEventHandler,
WorkflowElementStartedEventHandler,
WorkflowWorkItemsCreatedEventHandler
```

13. Also, remove methods linked to the interface that we have removed. Change the started method as follows:

```
public void started(WorkflowElementEventArgs
_workflowElementEventArgs)
{
    WorkflowContext context
        = _workflowElementEventArgs.parmWorkflowContext();
    if(this.ValidateContext(context))
    {
        ConVMSVehicleWFStatusHandler::SetStatus(
            context.parmRecId(),
            ConVMSVehicleWFApprStatus::Inspection);

        ConVMSVehicleWFInspStatusHandler::SetStatus(
            context.parmRecId(),
            ConVMSVehInspStatus::PendingApproval);
    }
}
```

This maintains the vehicle status and inspection status fields.

14. The canceled method should reset both status fields back to their initial states:

```
public void canceled(WorkflowElementEventArgs
_workflowElementEventArgs)
{
    WorkflowContext context
        = _workflowElementEventArgs.parmWorkflowContext();
    if(this.ValidateContext(context))
    {
        ConVMSVehicleWFStatusHandler::SetStatus(
            context.parmRecId(),
            ConVMSVehicleWFApprStatus::Draft);

        ConVMSVehicleWFInspStatusHandler::SetStatus(
            context.parmRecId(),
            ConVMSVehInspStatus::NotInspected);
    }
}
```

15. The completed method needs to get the current system date, and also fetch the last comment from the workflow. This is done with the following code:

```
public void completed(WorkflowElementEventArgs
_workflowElementEventArgs)
{
    WorkflowContext context
        = _workflowElementEventArgs.parmWorkflowContext();

    WorkflowCorrelationId correlationId
        = context.parmWorkflowCorrelationId();

    WorkflowTrackingTable trackingTable
        = Workflow::findLastWorkflowTrackingRecord(correlationId);

    WorkflowTrackingCommentTable commentTable
        = trackingTable.commentTable();

    WorkflowComment comment = commentTable.Comment;
    Timezone timezone = DateTimeUtil::getUserPreferredTimeZone();
    if(this.ValidateContext(context))
    {
        ConVMSVehicleWFInspStatusHandler::SetStatus(
            context.parmRecId(),
            ConVMSVehInspStatus::Completed,
            comment,
            DateTimeUtil::getSystemDate(timezone));
    }
}
```

16. Finally, write the `created` method. This is when the task is assigned to one or more users. The code should be written as follows:

```
public void created(WorkflowWorkItemsEventArgs
_workflowWorkItemsEventArgs)
{
    WorkflowElementEventArgs workflowArgs =
     _workflowWorkItemsEventArgs.parmWorkflowElementEventArgs();
    WorkflowContext context = workflowArgs.parmWorkflowContext();
    if(this.ValidateContext(context))
    {
        ConVMSVehicleWFStatusHandler::SetStatus(
            context.parmRecId(),
            ConVMSVehicleWFApprStatus::Inspection);

        ConVMSVehicleWFInspStatusHandler::SetStatus(
            context.parmRecId(),
            ConVMSVehInspStatus::PendingApproval);
```

```
        }
    }
```

17. We should also update the `CanComplete` method on the
    `ConVMSVehicleWFBase` class, but what we do here is dependent on what we
    want to control. We are in danger of hardcoding a business rule, which is
    ironically what workflows are designed to avoid. As a result of this, we just want
    to ensure that the document (vehicle record) is always left in a consistent state
    when the workflow type completes. The following piece of code will only return
    `false` if the approval or task is in progress:

```
public boolean CanCompleteWF(WorkflowContext _context)
{
    ConVMSVehicleTable vehicle;
    select Status, InspStatus, RecId
        from vehicle
        where vehicle.RecId == _context.parmRecId();
    boolean canComplete = true;
    if (vehicle.RecId != 0)
    {
        switch (vehicle.Status )
        {
            case ConVMSVehicleWFApprStatus::Revised:
            case ConVMSVehicleWFApprStatus::Waiting:
            case ConVMSVehicleWFApprStatus::InReview:
            case ConVMSVehicleWFApprStatus::Inspection:
                canComplete = false;
                break;
            default:
                canComplete = true;
        }
        switch (vehicle.InspStatus)
        {
            case ConVMSVehInspStatus::PendingApproval:
            case ConVMSVehInspStatus::Waiting:
                canComplete = false;
                break;
        }
    }
    return canComplete;
}
```

18. Create two labels using the following information and use them to complete the **Label** and **Help Text** properties on the `ConVMSVehicleWFInspect` workflow task:

Label Id	Label Text
InspectionTask	Vehicle inspection.
InspectionTaskHT	Use this task to assign and process a vehicle inspection task.

19. Finally, open the workflow type and then right-click on the **Supported Elements** node. Select **New Workflow Element Reference** and set the properties as follows:

Field	EDT / Enum	Description
Element Name	ConVMSVehicleWFInspect	This is the element's name.
Name	TaskInspect	This is a short version of the name, prefixed with its type.
Type	Task	This is the workflow element's type.

20. Copy and paste the task name into the **Element Name** and **Name** properties.
21. Save and close all designers and code editors and build the project, followed by synchronizing the database with the project.

How it works...

This concept is the same for workflow approval. The workflow task element is a definition that the designer will use when creating a workflow. The code we wrote simply handles events as we need them to be.

The complicated part to understand is the status handling. It seems natural to have a status field for each workflow element (the type, approval, and task), and with this paradigm we're left wondering why there isn't a standard Base Enum we could use. The status of the document can be defined by us – what makes sense to the business, and not what makes sense in code. For the inspection task, we want to know whether a vehicle is waiting for inspection, is in progress, or is complete.

Hooking up a workflow to the user interface

This is the final step in designing our workflow and involves setting a property on the form that's referenced by the document menu item, ConVMSVehicleTable, and adding the option to design workflows to the menu.

Getting ready

For this recipe, all we need is a workflow type.

How to do it...

To be able to design and process workflows, follow these steps:

1. Expand **User interface**, **Menu items**, and **Display** from the **Application Explorer**. Locate WorkflowConfgurationBasic, right-click on it, and choose **Duplicate in project**.

2. Locate the new menu item in the **Solution Explorer** and rename it to ConVMSWorkflowConfiguration.

3. Open the new menu item in the designer, set the **Enum Parameter** property to ConVMS, and then create labels for the **Label** and **Help Text** properties. These labels should be the module name, followed by the word workflows; for example, Vehicle management system workflows.

4. Open the ConVMSVehicleManagement menu from the **Application Explorer** and add this menu item to the Setup submenu in our menu. This should usually be the second option on the list.

5. Open the designer for the ConVMSVehicleTable form from the **Application Explorer**.

6. Select the Design node of the form design and locate the following properties:

Property	Value
Workflow Data Source	ConVMSVehicleTable
Workflow Enabled	Yes
Workflow Type	ConVMSVehicleWF

7. Right-click on the **Methods** node of the form and select **Override |
   canSubmitToWorkflow**. Alter the code so that it reads as follows:

```
public boolean canSubmitToWorkflow()
{
    If (ConVMSVehicleTable.Status ==
        ConVMSVehicleWFApprStatus::Draft)
    {
        return true;
    }
    return false;
}
```

We may need this to be more elaborate in some cases, but the
minimum is that we can't allow a workflow to be submitted that is
already in progress.

8. Save and close all designers and build the project.

How it works...

A workflow configuration is a generic form that builds based on the `ModuleAxapta` Base
Enum. We linked `ConWHS` to the workflow category, which was then linked to the
workflow type. This will allow the workflow designer to create and modify workflows for
this module.

The form changes were simply to link the workflow type to the form and to find out which
data source was the document data source. This is then used to query whether there are
any active workflows for that type, and will show the option to submit the vehicle for
approval if there is an active vehicle workflow design.

Creating a sample workflow design

Let's test the elements we have created. The following workflow design is only intended to
test the workflow we have created and omits many features that we would normally use.
We will also use the same user for submission and approval, and you will see them appear
to be waiting for the workflow engine as we test. This seems like a problem at first glance,
but in real-life scenarios this is fine. In practice, tasks and approvals are performed by
different users and are not done as a series of tasks. They will receive a notification so that
they can perform that action and pass the ball back to the workflow engine.

Getting ready

Before we start, ensure that the package is built and synchronized with the database. To synchronize, it is quicker to open the project that contains the table to synchronize than to perform a full database sync from the **Dynamics 365** menu. If we know the tables we need to synchronize, the following command can be used from a command prompt when you're running as an Administrator:

```
C:\AosService\PackagesLocalDirectory\Bin\SyncEngine.exe -
syncmode="partiallist" -syncList="ConVMSVehicleTable","SalesTable" -
metadatabinaries=C:\AosService\PackagesLocalDirectory -connect="Data
Source=.;Initial Catalog=AxDB;Integrated
Security=true;Enlist=True;Application Name=SyncEngine"
```

The preceding command will synchronize the `ConVMSVehicleTable` and `SalesTable` tables (which will include all the fields we added in all the extensions).

> When performing a full package build, untick the **Build Pre-compiled forms** option on the second tab page of the **Full build** dialog. This means that the PGC process will not run, and is not required. This step is likely to be removed from the development tools in the future.

For this recipe, you should use Internet Explorer on development machines; otherwise, the workflow control may not download.

How to do it...

To create the workflow design, follow these steps:

1. Open the following URL, and from there open **Vehicle management** | **Setup** | **Vehicle management workflows**:

   `https://usnconeboxax1aos.cloud.onebox.dynamics.com/?cmp=usmf`

   > You can navigate directly to the configuration form using the following URL:
   > `https://usnconeboxax1aos.cloud.onebox.dynamics.com/?cmp=usmf&mi=ConVMSWorkflowConfiguration`.

2. Click on **NEW**. You should see the workflow type in the list. It will be listed using the **Label** and **Help Text** properties that we set.

3. Select the workflow type link, as shown in the following screenshot:

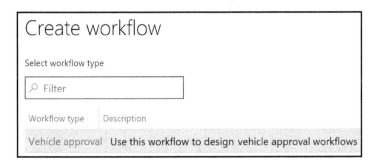

4. You will then be asked to log in, which you should do with the same user you used to log in to SCM. Then, you will be presented with a new window, with the two workflow elements that we wrote and some flow control options in the left-hand pane.

5. Drag the **New vehicle approval workflow** and **Inspect vehicle** elements onto the design surface, as shown in the following screenshot:

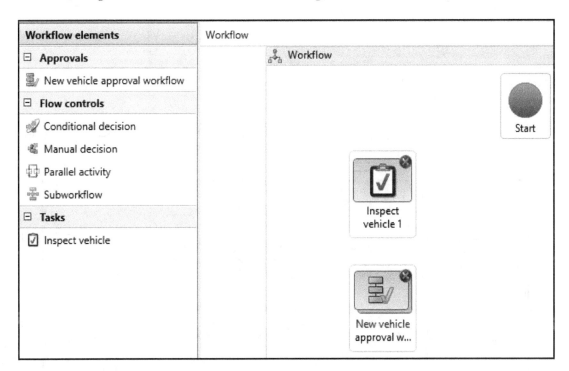

6. As your mouse hovers over the **Start** element, you will see small handles appear – drag one of these handles so that it connects the **Start** element to the **Inspect vehicle 1** element. Connect all elements, as shown in the following screenshot:

7. Select the **Inspect vehicle 1** element and click on **Basic Settings** from the action pane. Configure it as follows:

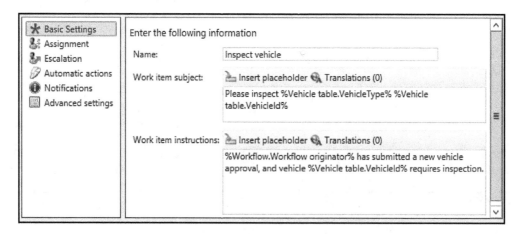

The text within the % symbols was added using the **Insert placeholder** button. If you click on this, you will see that our `parm` method was added and that the `parm` prefix was automatically removed.

8. Click on **Assignment** from the left and choose **User** from the **Assign users to this workflow element** list. Select the **User** tab and manually assign this to `Admin`. This is the default administration user. Since we are simply testing that our code works, we will assign all tasks and approvals to our user.

9. Click on **Close**.

10. Double-click on the **New vehicle approval workflow 1** element and click on **Basic Settings** from the action pane. Change **Name** to `New vehicle approval workflow` and click on **Close**.

 We would normally configure notifications. For example, we would usually notify **Workflow Originator** whether the approval was rejected.

11. Then, select **Step 1**, press **Basic Settings**, and configure it with the following options:

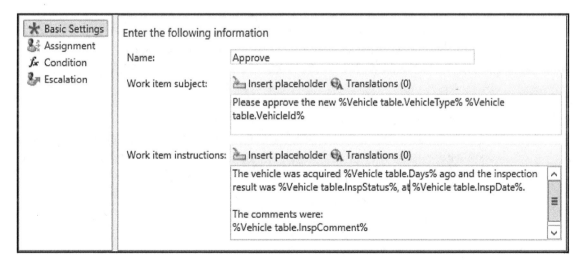

12. Click on **Assignment** and assign this to our user, as we did previously. Press **Close**. There is a breadcrumb at the top of the workflow designer's design surface that shows **Workflow | New vehicle approval**. Click on the word **Workflow** from the breadcrumb.

13. Finally, we must give submission instructions to the person who submitted the vehicle approval. Right-click on an empty area of the workflow designer's design surface and click on **Properties**. Enter suitable instructions in the **Submission instructions** field and click on **Close**.

14. Click on **Save and close**, and then **OK** on the **Save workflow** dialog. Select **Activate the new version** on the **Activate workflow** dialog and click on **OK**.

Now, let's test if the workflow works:

1. Open the vehicle form. You should see the **Workflow** button, as shown in the following screenshot:

2. Click on the button and select **Submit**, which is the label we assigned to the `ConVMSVehicleWFSubmitMenuItem` menu item. Enter a comment and click on **Submit**.

3. The options should change to **Cancel** and **View history**. You can choose **View history** to see the progress of the workflow engine. If the tasks aren't assigned within a minute, check that the `Microsoft Dynamics 365 for Finance & Operations - Batch Management Service` Windows service is running. Also, check that there are batch jobs for `Workflow message processing`, `Workflow due data processing`, and `Workflow line-item notifications`. If not, open **Workflow infrastructure configuration** from **System administration | Workflow** and click on **OK**.

4. After pressing the refresh icon and waiting approximately 2 minutes, you should see the **Complete**, **Delegate**, and **Cancel** options appear under the **Workflow** button. These are the options for the inspection task. Select **Complete**. Enter an inspection comment and click on **Complete**. View the vehicle details and wait for about a minute. Click on the refresh button. You should see information similar to the following:

5. After a further minute, refresh the form, and the options under the **Workflow** button will change to the approval options. Choose **Approve** from the list.

How it works...

Workflow design has many options available to us and is used to tell the workflow engine how approvals and tasks should be processed. When we develop workflows, we do so as generically as possible in order to leave the business logic to the workflow designer. This means that we reduce the need to make changes to the code as the business evolves.

This test was completed to help demonstrate what happens to status fields as a workflow is processed. This should help us in our own workflow development to understand the link between events and status changes.

15
State Machines

State machines are a new concept in SCM and are a very welcome feature. Previously, the control of status fields was handcrafted in code, which could often be hard to read as there was no obvious pattern to follow. Having said that, we will always look at a standard example that's similar to our case and use that idea. This is good practice, as it is good to seek examples in standard code. Using standard code as a pattern often helps other developers understand the code we have written, and, if we can't find a pattern to follow, it might suggest that we rework our technical solution so that we can.

State machines allow us to define how the status transitions from an initial state to its final state through metadata. These rules are then enforced by code that the state machine will generate.

There is a restriction, though: there must be one initial state and one final state. When we are in the final state, there is no going back. If we take the sales order status, we have two final states: **Invoiced** and **Canceled**. There is another reason why we wouldn't use a state machine on this type of status. The sales order status is a reflection of the actual order state; it is system controlled. State machines are designed to enforced status change logic when the state is asserted by a user.

To cover state machine development, we will cover the following recipes:

- Creating a state machine
- Creating a state machine handler class
- Using menu items to control a state machine
- Hooking up the state machine to a workflow

Technical requirements

You can find the code files for this chapter on GitHub at the following links:

- `https://github.com/PacktPublishing/Extending-Microsoft-Dynamics-365-Finance-and-Supply-Chain-Management-Cookbook-Second-Edition/blob/master/Chapter%2015%20-%20main.axpp`

- `https://github.com/PacktPublishing/Extending-Microsoft-Dynamics-365-Finance-and-Supply-Chain-Management-Cookbook-Second-Edition/blob/master/Chapter%2015%20-%20workflow.axpp`

Creating a state machine

This first recipe is all about creating a state machine for vehicle inspection. In `Chapter 14`, *Workflow Development*, we created a workflow task and an inspection status field. In this recipe, we will use a state machine to handle the inspection status change logic.

Getting ready

We need to have a table with a status field with an initial and final status, such as the `InspStatus` field we added to the `ConWHSVehicleTable` table in `Chapter 14`, *Workflow Development*. In this recipe, we will use the main vehicle management project.

How to do it...

To create a state machine, follow these steps:

1. Open `ConVMSVehicleTable` in the designer. Right-click on the **State Machines** node and choose **New State machine**.
2. Rename the new state machine `InspStateMachine` and complete the properties shown in the following table by creating labels for the **Description** and **Label** properties:

Property	Value
Description	Use this to control the inspection status.
Label	Inspection status.
Data Field	InspStatus.

3. Right-click on the new state machine definition and select **New State**.
4. Complete the properties of this state using the following table:

Property	Value
Enum Value	`NotInspected`. Change this to `Waiting`, and then back to the default **Label** property.
Description	The vehicle has not been inspected yet.
Label	Not inspected (this should be the label ID from the `ConVMSVehInspStatus::NotInspected` element label).
State Kind	Initial.

We will create a state for each element in the `ConVMSVehInspStatus` Base Enum, so it is a good idea to create description labels in advance and just paste them in. Use named labels for this, not numeric. I use a suffix of HT, which is short for `Help Text`, for labels that are used for both help text and descriptions of elements.

5. Create the remaining states using the following table as a guide:

Enum Value	Name	State Kind	Description
`Waiting`	Waiting	Intermediate	The vehicle is awaiting inspection.
`PendingApproval`	PendingApproval	Intermediate	The vehicle inspection is pending approval.
`Complete`	Complete	Final	The vehicle inspection is complete.

6. The result should look as follows:

7. Now, we need to tell the state machine the transition rules. We will define these rules as follows:

- `NotInspected` can only transition to `Waiting`.
- `Waiting` can only transition to `InProgress`.
- `InProgress` can transition to both `Waiting` and `Complete`.
- `Complete` is the final state and cannot transition backward.

8. Again, create the labels in advance. The following table explains the type of wording we should use:

Label ID	Label
VehTransWaiting	Add to the waiting list.
VehTransWaitingHT	Add the vehicle to the list of vehicles awaiting inspection.
VehTransPending	Start inspection.
VehTransPendingHT	Start the vehicle inspection process.
VehTransBackWaiting	Revert to waiting.
VehTransBackWaitingHT	Place the vehicle back onto the waiting list.
VehTransComplete	Complete inspection.
VehTransCompleteHT	Complete and finalize the vehicle inspection.

9. Next, right-click on the `NotInspected` state and select **New State transition**. This time, the **Label** and **Description** properties define the action, not the state. Set the properties that will define the transition to the `Waiting` state as follows:

Property	Value
Description	`@ConVMS:VehTransWaitingHT`
Label	`@ConVMS:VehTransWaiting`
Name	`TransitionToWaiting`
Transition To State	`Waiting`

10. Add a new transition state to the `WaitingState` state while using the following table as a guide:

Property	Value
Description	`@ConVMS:VehTransPendingHT`
Label	`@ConVMS:VehTransPending`
Name	`TransitionToInPending`
Transition To State	`PeningApproval`

11. Next, add two transition states to the `PendingApproval` state. The first is to revert back to waiting:

Property	Value
Description	`@ConVMS:VehTransBackWaitingHT`
Label	`@ConVMS:VehTransBackWaiting`
Name	`TransitionToWaiting`
Transition To State	`Waiting`

12. The second state to add to the `PendingApproval` state completes the state machine and should be configured as follows:

Property	Value
Description	`@ConVMS:VehTransCompleteHT`
Label	`@ConVMS:VehTransComplete`
Name	`TransitionToComplete`
Transition To State	`Complete`

13. Save your changes. The result should look as follows:

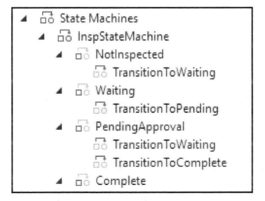

14. The final step is to right-click on the `InspStateMachine` state machine and click on **Generate**. This generates the code that will be used to control the inspection status' progression.

If you get an error stating **Given key does not exist in the dictionary**, this is happening because the name of the state did not match the **Enum Value** property. This may be changed in future releases so that it can be named differently.

15. The generated classes may not be added to your project immediately. To do this manually, locate the classes that start with `ConVMSVehicleTableInspStateMachine` and drag them on to the **Classes** node of your project. Don't modify these classes; these are shown in the following screenshot:

> ▷ 🔧 ConVMSVehicleTableInspStateMachine [Contoso - vehicle management]
>
> ▷ 🔧 ConVMSVehicleTableInspStateMachineEnterEventArgs [Contoso - vehicle management]
>
> ▷ 🔧 ConVMSVehicleTableInspStateMachineExitEventArgs [Contoso - vehicle management]
>
> ▷ 🔧 ConVMSVehicleTableInspStateMachineTransitionEventArgs [Contoso - vehicle management]

How it works...

What this process actually does is generate four classes. The main class is named `ConVMSVehicleTableInspStateMachine`, which is a concatenation of the table's name and the state machine's name. The other three classes are all prefixed with this class and allow typed data to be passed to the delegates that were written into this class.

The fact that we have a state machine does not prevent the user from manually changing the status field's value. It also does not stop us from manually changing the status in code. So, the restriction on the final status being final is only true when using the state machine.

There are two ways in which we can use the state machine:

- Attach it to workflow events.
- Use it with menu items that have been added to a form.

We will explore these options in the following recipes.

Creating a state machine handler class

The state machine provides control over the transition rules, but, sometimes, we want to ensure that other validation rules are obeyed in order to validate whether the transition can be done.

This is done by subscribing to the `Transition` delegate of the `ConVMSVehicleTableInspStateMachine` class that was generated by the state machine.

The code in this recipe will be tied programmatically to the state machine. Should you wish to attach the statement to the workflow directly (which is a great idea), the status will be set by the state machine. Therefore, the event handlers must not set the status. Furthermore, should the validation written in this recipe fail, we must ensure that the workflow's internal status matches the state machine's status. This can be done by canceling the workflow by throwing an error.

Getting ready

This recipe builds on the previous recipe, which created the state machine. This is required in order to complete this recipe.

How to do it...

To create a handler class to add further validation to the state machine, follow these steps:

1. Create a class named `ConVMSVehicleTableInspStatusParameters` and complete it with the following code:

```
class ConVMSVehicleTableInspStatusParameters
{
    public ConVMSVehInspStatus fromStatus;
    public ConVMSVehInspStatus toStatus;
    public ConVMSVehicleTable vehicleTable;
}
```

2. Next, create a class named `ConVMSVehicleInspStatusHandler` and add the following code to it:

```
ConVMSVehInspStatus fromStatus;
ConVMSVehInspStatus toStatus;
ConVMSVehicleTable vehicleTable;

public static ConVMSVehicleTableInspStatusHandler
    NewParameters(ConVMSVehicleTableInspStatusParameters
     _parameters)
{
    ConVMSVehicleTableInspStatusHandler instance
        = new ConVMSVehicleTableInspStatusHandler();
    instance.fromStatus = _parameters.fromStatus;
    instance.toStatus = _parameters.toStatus;
    instance.vehicleTable = _parameters.vehicleTable;
    return instance;
```

```
    }
    public boolean Validate()
    {
        switch (toStatus)
        {
            case ConVMSVehInspStatus::Complete:
                if (vehicleTable.InspComment == '')
                {
                    DictField field = new DictField(
                        tableNum(ConVMSVehicleTable),
                        fieldNum(ConVMSVehicleTable, InspComment));

                    //The field %1 must be filled in"
                    return checkFailed (strFmt("@SYS110217",
                     field.label()));
                }
                break;
        }
        return true;
    }

    public void run()
    {
        if(toStatus == fromStatus)
        {
            return;
        }
        if(this.Validate())
        {
            switch (toStatus)
            {
                case ConVMSVehInspStatus::Complete:
                    Timezone tz =
                     DateTimeUtil::getClientMachineTimeZone();
                    ConWHSVehInspDate inspDate;
                    inspDate = DateTimeUtil::getSystemDate(tz);
                    vehicleTable.InspDate = inspDate;
                    break;
            }
        }
        else
        {
            vehicleTable.InspStatus = fromStatus;
        }
    }
```

> There is nothing new about the preceding code, except that we don't (and must not) call `update` on the record. It is just used to validate the transition; in our case, it will stop the transition if the comment is blank.

3. Create a new class named `ConVMSVehicleTableInspStateMachineHandler` and add the following method. This ties the transition delegate to our handler class:

```
[SubscribesTo(classStr(ConVMSVehicleTableInspStateMachine),
    delegateStr(ConVMSVehicleTableInspStateMachine, Transition))]
public static void
HandleTransition(ConVMSVehicleTableInspStateMachineTransitionEventA
rgs _eventArgs)
{
    ConVMSVehicleTableInspStatusParameters parms = new
     ConVMSVehicleTableInspStatusParameters();
    parms.fromStatus = _eventArgs.ExitState();
    parms.toStatus = _eventArgs.EnterState();
    parms.vehicleTable = _eventArgs.DataEntity();

ConVMSVehicleTableInspStatusHandler::NewParameters(parms).Run();
}
```

How it works...

When the state machine generated the classes, it added a delegate that is called whenever the state changes. This delegate is called before the changes are committed. The table is passed by reference, which means that we can revert the status back without calling `update`. If we did call `update`, we could cause concurrency issues within the standard code.

We used the parameter class pattern as opposed to a contract or simply public variables because it is easier to extend and refactor, and our customers can add parameters using extensibility features. When writing for extensibility, we should consider how we would add a parameter and consume it using extensions. Looking at the code, we should add a delegate that is called in the subscription with the args event and the completed parameter class. This way, another developer could augment the logic with their own business logic.

There's more...

When working with a handler class, be careful with the transaction state. We could update the data in a table, for instance, a manually crafted status history table. We can nicely handle any potential exceptions with a `try...catch` statement within our handler class, but we can't control what happens when control returns to the state machine. For example, if we update a history table but the code fails later on, we could end up with a non-durable transaction if the code handles the exception and continues to commit the transaction.

Using menu items to control a state machine

In this section, we will add the state machine to the form so that we can use it. Using menu items for this is a nice concise way to control the state machine and follows the UI patterns that can be found in other areas, such as the projects module.

Getting ready

The prerequisite for this recipe is that we have a table with a state machine that has been generated.

How to do it...

To create the state machine menu items, follow these steps:

1. Add a new action menu item to the project named `ConVMSVehInspStatusWaiting`. Complete the property sheet as follows, in the order stated in the following table:

Property	Value
State Machine Data Source	ConVMSVehicleTable.
State Machine Transition To	Waiting.
Label	The label you use in the Waiting state's **Label** property.
Help Text	Create a suitable label stating this will move the state to Waiting.
Needs Record	Yes.

2. Create the menu items for the remaining states (`PendingApproval` and `Complete`) by following the same pattern.

3. Open the `ConVMSVehicleTable` form in the designer.

4. Under the form's **Design** node, expand the `FormActionPaneControl` control, `VehicleActions`, and then `VehicleActionButtons`. Right-click on this control and choose **New** | **Menu Button**.

5. Rename the new control `InspStatusMenuButton`. Set the **Text** and **Help Text** properties to the same ones that we used on the state machine, that is, `@ConVMSVehicleWF:InspStatus` and `@ConVMS:InspStateMachineDesc`, respectively.

6. Then, drag the three menu items onto this menu button and set the **Data Source** property to `ConWHSVehicleTable`. This is the table that the state machine operates on.

> If you can't add them directly, drag them onto the `VehicleActionButtons` button group, and then drag them from there to the correct place.

7. Save and close all code editors and design windows and build the project.

How it works...

When we created the menu items, the system defaulted many properties for us. If the table only has one state machine, all we had to do was set the label properties. You may notice that this changed the menu item's properties so that it referenced the state machine class that was generated by the table's state machine.

When we test the buttons, we can see that if we choose a transition that is not valid, we get this error:

 Invalid operation - the state transition from NotInspected state to Complete state is invalid.

We can't change this message as it is controlled by a protected method, and we shouldn't edit the generated classes. With generated code, any changes are lost if the state machine is regenerated.

Hooking up the state machine to a workflow

In this recipe, we will hook up our state machine to the `ConVMSVehWFInsp` workflow task.

Getting ready

We need to have a workflow task and have completed the recipes in this chapter. The changes that will be made here are best made with the workflow project that we created in the previous chapter.

How to do it...

To hook up the state machine to a workflow task, follow these steps:

1. Before we start, the workflow needs to be able to move the state directly to `Complete`. This will cause a fault as our state machine does not have this transition. To continue, open `ConVMSVehicleTable` and add a transition from `Waiting` to `Complete`. Once you've done this, right-click on the state machine and click **Generate**, just like we did when we created the state machine.

 You can copy `TransitionToComplete` from the `PendingApproval` state and paste it onto the `Waiting` state.

2. Open the `ConVMSVehicleWFInspect` workflow task.
3. Set the **Canceled State Machine** property to `InspStateMachine`.
4. Set the **Canceled State Machine Target State** property to `Waiting`; we won't be allowed to use `NotInspected`. Due to this being the state machine's initial state, it will let you set this value, but the state machine will reject the change.
5. Set the **Started State Machine** property to `InspStateMachine` and the **Started State Machine Target State** property to `Waiting`.
6. Select the **Completed** outcome. From here, set the **State Machine** property to `InspStateMachine` and set the **State Machine Target State** property to `Complete`.

7. Since we now have two ways to set the status, we will (as a short-term fix) disable the status update code that sets the status in the `SetStatus` method of the `ConVMSVehicleWFInspStatusHandler` class. Open this class and remove the line that sets the `InspStatus` field in the `SetStatus` method.

 We will usually decide at design time whether or not to use a state machine, so this kind of refactoring won't usually be needed. This is explained further in the *There's more...* section.

8. Upon testing this, we will find that the task sets the comment correctly, but the status doesn't change to complete. The reason for this is that the workflow events fire last, so the state machine's validation rejected the update because the comment was not set. We need to update our validation logic so that it only runs when it's triggered from the form. Alter the `Validate` method of the `ConVMSVehicleInspStatusHandler` class so that it reads as follows:

```
public boolean Validate()
{
    switch (toStatus)
    {
        case ConVMSVehInspStatus::Complete:
            if (vehicleTable.InspComment == ''
                && FormDataUtil::isFormDataSource(vehicle))
            {
                //The field %1 must be filled in"
                DictField field = new DictField(
                    tableNum(ConVMSVehicleTable),
                    fieldNum(ConVMSVehicleTable,
                            InspComment));
                return checkFailed(strFmt(
                        "@SYS110217",
                        field.label()));
            }
            break;
    }
    return true;
}
```

The highlighted code checks if the record buffer is a form data source; if the code was called from within the workflow, the table will not be linked to a form's data source. Also, note that this is the class named `ConVMSVehicleTableInspStatusHandler`, not `ConVMSVehicleWFInspStatusHandler`.

9. Build and test the workflow; all should work correctly.

How it works...

First, we used menu items as our user interface into the inspection status state machine. This is fine and is common as a workflow is not always required. A workflow is sometimes not suitable if the same person will be progressing the state through to completion. This would get in the way and there is always over a minute in delays when handling the workflow event.

To have both code scenarios, we ended up with two classes with a similar name: `ConVMSVehicleTableInspStatusHandler` and `ConVMSVehicleWFInspStatusHandler`. Since we can decide whether to use menu items or a workflow to interface with the state machine, we usually have one class to do this.

The change we have made was to simply tie the events on the workflow task to a state of the state machine. This means that the event handler methods we normally write should not update the status, but that they can perform actions that should happen when the event happens. Due to this, we removed the line to set the status, making the `SetStatus` method only update the date and comment. Had this been designed from the start as a workflow integrated state machine, we would write the state machine in the workflow project and write a method called `SetComment` instead.

The state machine is called by the workflow engine, just before the events are called. This is why we had to remove the validation on the comment – the state was changed before the completed event was called, which means that the comment was empty. There isn't much we can do in this case except allow the workflow to continue. We could use the workflow designer to check for this event and resubmit the task to the user.

There's more...

This seems to greatly simplify workflow development. We don't need all of the event handler methods since most of them only update the record's status. There is some thought required if we consider the following scenario.

The workflow is canceled by the user, which means that the status will go back to Waiting. We chose Waiting when the workflow task was canceled because the state machine will throw an error if we try to set it to the initial state. The problem is that we can't change the status to the same status; we will still get an error. The error is not just a message to the user; it will place the workflow in a failed state, which will require an administrator to cancel, resubmit, or resume it.

 The problem is that we should not have a scenario where a user action can cause a failure that requires an administrator to rescue them; we need to handle this eventuality elegantly within our code.

The first thing we could do is add an internal state to the Base Enum and to the state machine, for example, internal processing. We wouldn't create a menu item for this as it is only for internal use. On the state machine, we would allow any transition from this state; it can transition freely to and from this state.

This is the state we use for the Cancelled event. This means that the workflow can set the status to Waiting after the workflow is canceled.

The next part of the changes we would make would be to remove all calls to ConVMSVehicleWFInspStatusHandler::SetStatus(...). We would write a new method called SetComment, which is called from the Completed event on the workflow task's event handler class.

Other Books You May Enjoy

If you enjoyed this book, you may be interested in these other books by Packt:

Mastering Microsoft Dynamics 365 Business Central

Stefano Demiliani, Duilio Tacconi

ISBN: 978-1-78995-125-7

- Create a sandbox environment with Dynamics 365 Business Central
- Handle source control management when developing solutions
- Explore extension testing, debugging, and deployment
- Create real-world business processes using Business Central and different Azure services
- Integrate Business Central with external applications
- Apply DevOps and CI/CD to development projects
- Move existing solutions to the new extension-based architecture

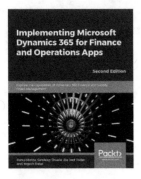

Implementing Microsoft Dynamics 365 for Finance and Operations Apps - Second Edition

Rahul Mohta, Sandeep Shukla, Et al

ISBN: 978-1-78995-084-7

- Understand the technical architecture of Dynamics 365 for Finance and Operations
- Become well-versed with implementing Dynamics to manage finances in your business
- Get up to speed with different methodologies and support cycles of the Microsoft Dynamics architecture
- Explore different best practices to analyze the requirements or scope of your business
- Understand the technique of data migration from legacy systems
- Use the capabilities of Power BI to make informed business decisions
- Manage all your upgrades with the help of One Version service updates

Leave a review - let other readers know what you think

Please share your thoughts on this book with others by leaving a review on the site that you bought it from. If you purchased the book from Amazon, please leave us an honest review on this book's Amazon page. This is vital so that other potential readers can see and use your unbiased opinion to make purchasing decisions, we can understand what our customers think about our products, and our authors can see your feedback on the title that they have worked with Packt to create. It will only take a few minutes of your time, but is valuable to other potential customers, our authors, and Packt. Thank you!

Index

www.ingramcontent.com/pod-product-compliance
Lightning Source LLC
LaVergne TN
LVHW062035060326
832903LV00062B/1412